Supercomputers for Linux SysAdmins

Managing Modern HPC Clusters and Supercomputers from Software to Hardware

Sergey Zhumatiy

Apress®

Supercomputers for Linux SysAdmins: Managing Modern HPC Clusters and Supercomputers from Software to Hardware

Sergey Zhumatiy
Santa Clara, CA, USA

ISBN-13 (pbk): 979-8-8688-1599-7   ISBN-13 (electronic): 979-8-8688-1600-0
https://doi.org/10.1007/979-8-8688-1600-0

Copyright © 2025 by Sergey Zhumatiy

This work is subject to copyright. All rights are reserved by the Publisher, whether the whole or part of the material is concerned, specifically the rights of translation, reprinting, reuse of illustrations, recitation, broadcasting, reproduction on microfilms or in any other physical way, and transmission or information storage and retrieval, electronic adaptation, computer software, or by similar or dissimilar methodology now known or hereafter developed.

Trademarked names, logos, and images may appear in this book. Rather than use a trademark symbol with every occurrence of a trademarked name, logo, or image we use the names, logos, and images only in an editorial fashion and to the benefit of the trademark owner, with no intention of infringement of the trademark.

The use in this publication of trade names, trademarks, service marks, and similar terms, even if they are not identified as such, is not to be taken as an expression of opinion as to whether or not they are subject to proprietary rights.

While the advice and information in this book are believed to be true and accurate at the date of publication, neither the authors nor the editors nor the publisher can accept any legal responsibility for any errors or omissions that may be made. The publisher makes no warranty, express or implied, with respect to the material contained herein.

    Managing Director, Apress Media LLC: Welmoed Spahr
    Acquisitions Editor: James Robinson-Prior
    Coordinating Editor: Gryffin Winkler

Cover image designed by Freepik (www.freepik.com)

Distributed to the book trade worldwide by Springer Science+Business Media New York, 1 New York Plaza, New York, NY 10004. Phone 1-800-SPRINGER, fax (201) 348-4505, e-mail orders-ny@springer-sbm.com, or visit www.springeronline.com. Apress Media, LLC is a Delaware LLC and the sole member (owner) is Springer Science + Business Media Finance Inc (SSBM Finance Inc). SSBM Finance Inc is a **Delaware** corporation.

For information on translations, please e-mail booktranslations@springernature.com; for reprint, paperback, or audio rights, please e-mail bookpermissions@springernature.com.

Apress titles may be purchased in bulk for academic, corporate, or promotional use. eBook versions and licenses are also available for most titles. For more information, reference our Print and eBook Bulk Sales web page at http://www.apress.com/bulk-sales.

Any source code or other supplementary material referenced by the author in this book is available to readers on GitHub. For more detailed information, please visit www.apress.com/gp/services/source-code.

The initial version of this book was originally written in the Russian language and was translated in English with the help of deepl.com. The initial version was updated and edited later.

If disposing of this product, please recycle the paper

Table of Contents

About the Author ....**xv**

About the Technical Reviewer ....**xvii**

Acknowledgments ....**xix**

Glossary of Terms ....**xxi**

Chapter 1: Introduction **1**

Conventions and Notations Adopted in the Book 3

Chapter 2: What Is "Super"? **5**

General Concepts of Parallel Processing and Parallel Programs 5

Types of Clusters 9

    Clusters and Supercomputers – Common and Different 10

What "Super" Means to a Supercomputer Administrator 11

Centralized Management of the Computer Complex 13

Brief Summary 14

Search Keywords 14

Chapter 3: How to Build and Start It? **15**

Anatomy of a Supercomputer 15

Planning 17

Documentation 21

OK, We Got It, What's Next? 22

What Should I Do Later? 24

Short Notes 25

Brief Summary 26

Search Keywords 26

TABLE OF CONTENTS

Chapter 4: Supercomputer Hardware 27
    Control Node 28
    Compute Node 28
    Login Node 29
    Service Nodes 29
    Network Equipment 31
    Data Storage 36
    Hardware Architecture Features 39
    Brief Summary 43
    Search Keywords 43

Chapter 5: InfiniBand 45
    Component Identification and Addressing in InfiniBand Networks 47
    InfiniBand Subnet Management 49
    IP Over InfiniBand (IP Over IB, IPoIB) 50
    Utilities for InfiniBand Network Viewing and Managing 51
    Alternatives 59
    Brief Summary 59
    Search Keywords 59

Chapter 6: How a Supercomputer Does the Job 61
    How a Typical User Session Occurs 62
    Job Life Cycle 62
    What Is Hidden from the User 63
    Brief Summary 64
    Search Keywords 64

Chapter 7: UNIX and Linux – the Basics 65
    Processes 67
    Access Rights 71
    Concept of Service, Key Services 75
    Manuals 77

TABLE OF CONTENTS

File Naming Conventions 78
Extension Agreements 79
Templates 80
Commands for Working with the Directory Tree 81
    Commands for Working with Catalogs 82
Commands for Working with Files 83
Packages 90
Network Commands 93
"Cluster" Commands 104
Brief Summary 105
Search Keywords 106

Chapter 8: UNIX and Linux – Working Techniques 107
The Magic of sysctl 107
udev Subsystem 108
PAM Modules 111
Shell Tricks 114
Tips for Some Often Used Commands 117
Brief Summary 118
Search Keywords 118

Chapter 9: Network File Systems 119
NTP 119
NFS 122
Lustre 126
    Architecture 126
    Creation of Lustre File System 129
    Fault Tolerance in Lustre 132
    Striping and PFL 133
    Quotas 134
PanFS 135

v

TABLE OF CONTENTS

GPFS/IBM Storage Scale 136

Other File Systems 137

Brief Summary 138

Search Keywords 138

Chapter 10: Remote Management 139

ssh and Parallel ssh 139

    Forwarding Environment Variables 142

    Port Forwarding 142

    X Connection Forwarding 143

    File Transfer 143

    SSH Agent 143

    Configuring the ssh Server 144

    Configuring the ssh Client 146

    Host-Based Authentication 150

pdsh 151

Cluster Shell 153

Screen and tmux 155

IPMI 159

Conman 164

iKVM 164

Brief Summary 165

Search Keywords 165

Chapter 11: Users – Accounting Management 167

Account Synchronization 167

Classic Approach 167

NIS/NIS+ 169

LDAP 171

Brief Summary 172

Search Keywords 173

TABLE OF CONTENTS

Chapter 12: Users – Quotas and Access Rights ... 175
File System Quotas ... 175
ulimits ... 179
UNIX Groups, ACLs ... 182
Restrict User Access ... 182
Brief Summary ... 184
Search Keywords ... 184

Chapter 13: Job Management Systems ... 185
Principles of Operation and Capabilities ... 185
Kubernetes, etc. ... 187
Access Problem ... 187
Brief Summary ... 188
Search Keywords ... 188

Chapter 14: OpenPBS and Torque ... 189
Installing Torque ... 189
Setting Up Torque ... 191
Configuring the MOM Server on Compute Nodes ... 196
Customizing the Scheduler ... 198
Using Torque ... 200
Job Control Commands ... 203
Brief Summary ... 204
Search Keywords ... 204

Chapter 15: Slurm ... 205
Slurm Installation ... 206
Accounting ... 207
Accounting Setup ... 209
Basic Setup and Usage ... 210
Partitions ... 212
Nodes ... 214

vii

TABLE OF CONTENTS

- Generic and Trackable Resources 215
- Backfill and Preemption 216
- QoS and Limits 217
- Priorities and FairShare 219
- User Levels 222
- Topology 223
- Reservations 224
- User Experience 225
- Job Life Cycle 230
- scontrol 231
- Accounting and Statistics 233
- Troubleshooting 235
- Advanced Parameters for slurm.conf 236
- Brief Summary 239
- Search Keywords 239

Chapter 16: Containers 241
- Singularity 242
- Apptainer 243
- CharlieCloud 243
- Pyxis + Enroot 243
- Caching 244
- Brief Summary 244
- Search Keywords 244

Chapter 17: Clouds 245
- Brief Summary 246
- Search Keywords 246

Chapter 18: Remote User Access 247

SSH 247

FTP and WWW 248

X-Window 249

Alternatives for X11 254

Brief Summary 255

Search Keywords 255

Chapter 19: Cluster Status Monitoring Systems 257

SNMP 257

Ganglia 264

Nagios 266

Zabbix 267

Modern Approach 268

XDMoD 270

Lm_sensors/Hwmon 271

IPMI 275

APCUPS 275

NUT 279

Healthchecks 282

Security Scans 283

Brief Summary 283

Search Keywords 284

Chapter 20: Backup 285

Tar 285

Bacula 289

Rsync and Others 297

Brief Summary 299

Search Keywords 300

ix

Chapter 21: Compilers and Environments, for Parallel Technologies 301

- gcc/gfortran 304
- Intel and NVIDIA HPC Compilers 306
- PMIx 307
- mpich 308
- OpenMPI 308
- Mvapich/Mvapich2 311
- Proprietary MPI: Spectrum MPI and IntelMPI 311
- SHMEM Library, OpenSHMEM Standard 311
- CUDA 313
- UCX and NCCL 315
- OpenCL 316
- OpenACC 317
- Environment Modules and LMOD 317
- Build Systems 322
- Brief Summary 324
- Search Keywords 324

Chapter 22: Parallel Computing Support Libraries 325

- ScaLAPACK 325
- PETSc 331
- FFT/FFTW 333
- TBB 334
- Debuggers and Profilers 334
- Brief Summary 338
- Search Keywords 338

Chapter 23: Booting and Init 339

- Booting from Hard Disk 339
- INIT in SystemV Style 341
- Systemd 346

Network Booting	351
DHCP	353
TFTP, PXE, and NFS-Root	357
Brief Summary	359
Search Keywords	359

Chapter 24: Node Setup and Software Installation 361

Network and Hardware Drivers	361
Configuring the Control and Compute Nodes	362
Installation and Configuration of the Login Node	363
NFS Server Configuration	364
Configuring the Communication Software	364
Installing Compilers and Libraries	366
Customizing the Job Management System	366
Installation and Configuration of the Cluster Compute Node	367
Brief Summary	371
Search Keywords	371

Chapter 25: Out-of-the-Box Stacks and Deployment Systems 373

ROCKS	373
Parallel Knoppix/PelicanHPC	375
Brief Summary	377
Search Keywords	377

Chapter 26: Cluster Management Systems – xCAT and Others 379

Installation and Initial Setup	380
Architecture and Commands	380
Node Management	384
Loading and Controlling	388
Canonical MaaS	390
Foreman	392
NVIDIA Base Command Manager	393

TABLE OF CONTENTS

Brief Summary 394

Search Keywords 394

Chapter 27: Communicating with Users 395

Correspondence 395

Accounting for Requests from Users 397

Actualization 398

Education 399

Brief Summary 400

Search Keywords 400

Chapter 28: One-Two-Three Instructions 401

NTP 401

Configuring the NFS Server 402

Configuring the NFS Client 402

Installing Lustre (No HA) 402

NIS+ Server Installation 403

Installing the NIS+ Client 404

Installing OpenLDAP (Using RH As an Example) 405

Customizing Xorg 409

APCUPSD 412

xCAT 422

Brief Summary 425

Search Keywords 425

Chapter 29: Shell Scripts – Basics and Common Mistakes 427

Not-a-Mistake 437

Brief Summary 437

Search Keywords 437

Chapter 30: Systemd – A Short Course 439
Units 439
systemctl Commands 448
Journald 449
Network Config, Time Sync, and Hostname Resolving 451
Analyzing 452
Brief Summary 453
Search Keywords 453

Conclusion 455

Index 457

About the Author

Sergey Zhumatiy has been managing supercomputers since 1999, starting out with building and managing HPC clusters at Moscow State University, and holds a PhD in Computer Science. Several supercomputers under his supervision, like Chebyshev, Lomonosov, and Lomonosov-2, achieved top rankings in the top 500 supercomputers list and dominated the Russian top 50 supercomputers list. Now he works as an HPC architect and SysAdmin at NVIDIA.

About the Technical Reviewer

John Roberts spent over a decade as an HPC systems administrator, supporting large-scale scientific computing and advanced research initiatives. He recently transitioned to a new role where he continues to focus on supporting and optimizing HPC environments. John holds a bachelor's degree in computer science and brings a passion for scalable systems, innovation, and advancing scientific discovery.

Acknowledgments

I would like to express my sincere gratitude to the following people:

Vladimir Voevodin for the ideas and criticism

Konstantin Stefanov, Alexander Naumov, Anton Korzh, Ilya Fateev, Ben Evans, and Caio Davi for the provided material and consultations

Hui Li, Paniz Karbasi, Oksana Korzh, and Mark Moe for their patience and valuable advice and ideas

Viktor Datsyuk, Pavel Kostenetsky, Alexei Latsis, and Yuri Khrebtov for important comments

John Roberts, the technical reviewer of this book, for the great work and tons of thoughtful corrections and suggestions

Glossary of Terms

Backup: A copy of data (files, databases) stored on a separate media or a group of media. Data can be restored from the backup copy to the original files, databases, or to other directories, databases.

Cable organizer: A design that allows cables to be stacked within a dedicated space.

Communication network: Used to exchange data by computing tasks.

Compute field: A set of all compute nodes of the complex that are available for user tasks.

DAPL: *Direct Access Programming Library*, a library for using direct access to remote computer memory without having to explicitly describe a particular type of hardware.

D-BUS: *System Message Bus*, a server and protocol that allows any programs to communicate within the same server. A program can register as a service and publish messages (events) and as a client and subscribe to certain events.

DHCP: *Dynamic Host Configuration Protocol*, a protocol that allows a computer to obtain information such as its IP address, network name, etc., from a server at the OS boot stage or later.

File server: A computer that makes part of its file system available to other computers over a network.

File storage: Equipment that provides disk space over a network or locally, such as for a *file server*.

Form factor: Standard dimensions for computer cases, like mini-tower, 1U, 2U, etc.

FPGA: *Field Programmable Gate Array*, a device, which can be programmatically reconfigured into various combinations of "gates" – logical units – and form specialized compute devices.

FTP: *File Transfer Protocol*, a protocol for transferring files over a network.

GPGPU: *General-Purpose GPU*, a *GPU*, which is used for computations.

GLOSSARY OF TERMS

GPU: *Graphics Processing Unit*, device for generating and displaying (via separate display) graphics. Today, any video card.

Host: A no*de* on a network – a server, a computer.

HPC: *High-Performance Computing*, the supercomputing industry.

Interconnect: A jargonism, usually referring to a communications network or just a fast network.

Journaling: Writing messages to a log. Many programs support logging to a file. In UNIX-like systems, there is a standard syslog service, which is used by many programs and services.

KVM: *Keyboard and Video Monitor*, a device that allows you to connect multiple computers to a single monitor and keyboard.

Latency: The time spent when a packet is transmitted through a network regardless of its length.

Linpack: A test for some estimation of real performance of parallel computing complexes. Most often, the High Performance Linpack (HPL) version is used.

Logging: See *journaling*.

LVM: *Logical Volume Manager*, a technology for building logical disks using multiple physical disks and/or RAIDs.

MAC address: The unique address of a network card in the Ethernet standard.

MPI: *Message Passing Interface*, an open library standard intended for message passing inside a parallel application. There are many implementations of this standard (mpich, lam, openmpi, etc.).

NIS: *Network Information System*, a technology that allows user accounts, computer names, and other system information to be stored on a server and retrieved from any computer on the network.

Node (of a cluster): a computer designed for certain tasks in the cluster (computing, controlling, I/O, etc.).

NTP: *Network Time Protocol*, a protocol for synchronizing time over a network.

Rack: See *telecommunication cabinet*.

GLOSSARY OF TERMS

RAID: *Redundant Array of Independent/Inexpensive Disks*, an array of multiple hard disks logically combined for greater fault tolerance, speed, and/or capacity.

RAID-0 (stripe): *RAID*, which disks are combined in such a way that logical blocks of disks alternate: block1 of the first disk, block1 of the second, ... block2 of the first disk, block2 of the second disk, etc.

RAID-1 (mirror): *RAID*, the disks of which are combined into a "mirror" to increase reliability. Information is written simultaneously to all disks in blocks with the same numbers.

RAID-5: A *RAID* whose disks are combined into parity groups. When writing to a logical block, the written data is added by XOR method with other blocks in the group and the resulting information is written to a separate block. When reading, the correctness of the data is checked, and if one of the blocks is corrupted, the information is automatically restored.

RAID controller: A device that combines multiple hard disks into a *RAID*.

RDMA: *Remote Direct Memory Access*, a protocol for direct memory access to a remote computer.

Register: Internal memory of the processor, works very fast, all arithmetic and logical operations are typically performed with registers only.

Samba: A software package that implements the SMB and CIFS protocols used in MS Windows for network disks. It allows accessing Windows network disks from Linux, as well as creating network disks under Linux so that they can be used by Windows clients.

SCI: *Scalable Coherence Interface*, an old standard for high-speed data transmission equipment. It means connecting network cards directly to each other in a ring or torus (two- or three-dimensional).

Service network: Used to monitor and manage the state of compute nodes.

SNMP: *Simple Network Management Protocol*, a protocol designed to monitor and manage equipment on a network.

Software: In addition to the actual set of programs, this includes configuration and other files necessary for its operation.

SSH: *Secure Shell*, a protocol for remote access to computers on a network, involving the use of an encrypted connection.

GLOSSARY OF TERMS

Superuser (a.k.a. *administrator*): A user of the system, with rights that allow performing any regular actions. In UNIX-like operating systems, it is typically a user with UID = 0. Historically, it is named root, although the name itself can be changed.

Switch: A device that allows multiple network adapters to join together to form a network.

System console: A virtual screen and a keyboard connected to it. The system console receives messages from the OS kernel. From the system console, you can control the OS boot process.

Telnet: A protocol for remote access to computers on a network. It uses an unencrypted data channel.

TFTP: *Trivial File Transfer Protocol*, protocol that allows you to retrieve files from a server, such as a boot image.

Telecommunication cabinet: A rack, designed for mounting computers and other equipment that meets certain standards (equipment width, mounting method, etc.). The most common racks are 19 inches wide.

Transport network: Used for network file systems, run commands on nodes, etc.

Tunneling: The forwarding of a network connection through another connection (tunnel). The tunnel itself looks like a local connection or a direct connection to another host.

U: *Unit*, a unit of measurement for the height of rack equipment, equal to 5/4 inches or approximately 4.5 cm. The unit is sometimes referred to as RU – *rack unit*.

UPS: *Uninterruptible Power Supply*.

Glossary of Jargon

Backslash: *"\" symbol*.
Cooler: A fan, cooling the system.
Chiller: A refrigerating machine.
Fiber: Fiber optics.
Folder: The directory of the file system.

GLOSSARY OF TERMS

Gateway: A device or computer, receiving all network packages if they should go out of the local network (and send them forward).
Interconnect: A communication network.
Log: File, containing a journal of some program(s) actions.
Rack: Telecommunication cabinet.
Sharp: "#" symbol.
Slash: *"/" symbol.*
Trap: Exception or a code to catch the exception.

CHAPTER 1

Introduction

Hello, dear reader! Allow me to introduce this book and share with you what it offers.

What it **is about**:

- What is a supercomputer and how it works
- Basics of software you need to know to build and/or manage it
- Which technologies can be useful and when (what you need to learn!)
- Random useful (I hope) stuff

What it is **not about**:

- Detailed info about specific HPC software
- Guides "you have to do it that way"
- Deep info about hardware, protocols, etc.

This book can help you to become a supercomputer administrator, if you already have experience as a Linux one. If you do not have such experience – no problem, you can find some basic info and general principles here. The first chapter is mostly for novice admins; mature guys can just take a quick look. A good approach would be to read books on Linux administration and practice, e.g., on a virtual machine, and review this book again.

Note, "can help," because

- Supercomputing technologies develop so fast, that books become outdated in two to three years.
- There are so many different software and technologies that it is simply not possible to cover everything (but you will read where to look).
- Only real experience can make you a supercomputer admin, sorry (but I hope this book will make this way shorter and easier).

CHAPTER 1 INTRODUCTION

We will consider **only** supercomputers based on Linux, which is the de facto standard at present. By "supercomputer," I mean a computing cluster, and some information in this book can be applied not only to clusters.

In order to have at least a small practical basis, I will give the most important examples directly in the text, and the last three chapters summarize the instructions, techniques, and reference data for the technologies discussed.

A supercomputer is not just a set of servers, switches, disks.... It is a single complex – not only ideologically, but also in essence. All its components are closely connected, and the most significant task of an administrator is to understand and realize these connections, the importance of each component, and its impact on the complex as a whole.

Of course, this cannot be done without knowing how to control all parts of the complex, so one should study the peculiarities (at least the basic ones) of configuring and monitoring all components of a particular cluster. However, don't think that by memorizing the values of all the "ticks" in the administrative interfaces of all the "hardware," you can get full control over the supercomputer.

Since the scale of even a small compute cluster differs significantly from a dozen servers, it is strongly (very strongly) recommended to take the time to learn the capabilities of the command line. If you work with a dozen servers in a graphical mode, it is still possible, although very tedious. But with a hundred – it is simply unrealistic.

How do I find out which servers didn't have the full amount of RAM detected the last time they were powered on? Run "system monitor" on each? Go to the "system" tab and see the amount of RAM? This will take all day. But if you run on each node, e.g., using `pdsh` or `clush`, a command such as

```
grep MemTotal /proc/meminfo | awk '{print $2}'
```

it is possible to get the same amount of RAM in seconds. By adding a couple more shell commands, you can compare the obtained value with the benchmark (even taking into account tolerances) and output the names of nodes that failed the check. Spell-induced magic? In a way – yes, magic, but with clear laws and quite masterable.

It is not uncommon for very complicated actions to be accomplished with a combination of standard commands. Fortunately, this is almost always possible without a lot of work. Labor is required for the initial mastering of these commands, and then – all the Linux magic will be in your hands!

It is highly recommended to study the "Advanced Bash Scripting Guide." This guide allows you to use the huge power of a tool that is always at your fingertips – the `bash` shell (almost everything works for `zsh` as well). By adding a few simple `sed` and `awk` tricks to your arsenal (and if you want absolute magic, then `perl`, and maybe `python` or `ruby`), learning the capabilities of `find`, `ps`, and similar commands, you will increase the efficiency of your work many times over.

This book also provides a basic knowledge of the command line and the basic concepts of Linux to give a good start to those who are not familiar with them at all or have a superficial knowledge of them. Without this knowledge and skills, it is impossible to understand the system as a whole. Experienced Linux administrators can browse through these chapters at a glance: there are not many new things to learn for them. And they are a must for the newbie: you can't be a supercomputer administrator without being a good Linux administrator.

The book touches upon another important topic that at first glance does not seem to be related to system administration – the topic of user support. As you know, supporting users of a supercomputer is very different from supporting users of computers that work in neighboring rooms. I have tried to prepare a novice administrator for the difficulties that await him on this path.

Each chapter provides basic knowledge and concepts on a particular topic. Some of them cover different aspects of the same concept. Each chapter ends with a brief summary of the material and keywords for Internet searches on the topic of the chapter.

Conventions and Notations Adopted in the Book

Script code and text of configuration files are highlighted like this:

```
# This is the text of the script
```

Warnings and important points to keep in mind:

Attention! Do not step on the same rake twice!

Terms or important concepts are given in **bold**.
Short commands are highlighted in the text like this: `ls -la`.

CHAPTER 1 INTRODUCTION

Material for beginners that can be skipped by experienced professionals stands out like this:

To get started, plug the computer into the network.

The book often uses abbreviations and common terms. For many people, they are familiar, but for others, they are not yet. Therefore there is a small glossary at the beginning of the book. Some materials from this book (and beyond) are collected in the git repository `https://github.com/zhum/hpc-book-matherials`.

Please send your feedback and suggestions to `supercomputerbook@gmail.com`.

CHAPTER 2

What Is "Super"?

General Concepts of Parallel Processing and Parallel Programs

All modern supercomputers use parallel data processing. Since the beginning of the computer era, this has been and remains the most important way to achieve high performance. So, let's start from **boring things** and try to understand how parallelism works! Yes, you can skip it if you're sure you know all that stuff.

Nowadays, even the simplest desktop computer, is almost certainly equipped with simultaneous multithreading technology (e.g., Intel's HyperThreading or AMD SMT), which allows two (sometimes more) program threads to run simultaneously. Even cell phones and cameras are becoming parallel and multicore.

The principle of parallel data processing is simple: if two or more operations are **independent** (i.e., the results of their execution do not affect each other's input data), these operations can be performed simultaneously, i.e., in **parallel.** In hardware, there are traditionally two variants of embodiment of this principle – parallelism and pipelining.

Parallelism – Parallel execution of machine instructions by different devices. For example, the commands x=a+b and y=b*c, where a, b, and c are stored in internal processor memory, can be executed independently if the processor has separate addition and multiplication devices (see Figure 2-1). This principle is embodied in most modern processors. GPUs also use this principle – many cores do the same code in parallel.

CHAPTER 2   WHAT IS "SUPER"?

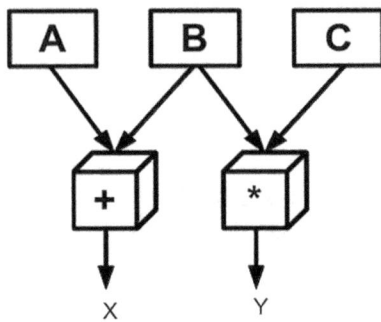

Figure 2-1. *Parallel execution*

Pipelining – Division of commands into stages, each of which is executed quickly by a separate hardware element, and execution of these stages according to the conveyor principle: one after another. Thus, several commands at different stages of the conveyor can be executed simultaneously. This principle is most often used in **vectorization**, i.e., execution of a single-type operation on vectors, i.e., data arrays located in memory on a regular basis (see Figure 2-2). This is used in "vector" processor operations, like AVX.

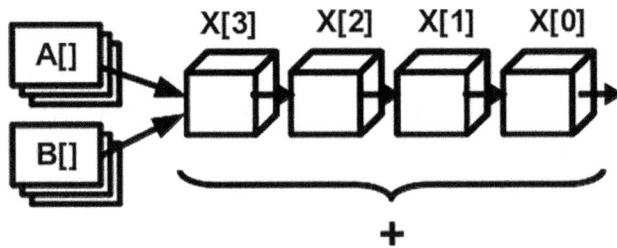

Figure 2-2. *Pipelining and vectorization*

Most frequently, the elements of a vector are arranged one after another. A typical example is the addition of vectors. Since the operation performed on vectors is the same, it is divided into phases – pipeline stages, e.g., loading elements from memory, normalization of mantissas, addition, correction, and writing to memory. After performing the first stage on the first element of the vector, this stage can be immediately performed on the second element without waiting for the completion of the whole operation on the first element.

After each step is completed over one element, you can perform it over the next element. Thus, if the slowest stage of the conveyor is executed in K cycles, and all stages in S cycles, then the vector of N elements will be processed in K*(N-1)+S.

The first element will be processed in the required S clock cycles (this is called "pipeline acceleration time"), and then the device will produce one result per K clock cycle. In modern processors, most often K = 1. However, pipelining does not necessarily imply vectorization and vice versa. For example, if the addition device is pipelined, and there are several regular additions in a row performed, they can perfectly utilize the pipeline.

A system administrator doesn't always need a thorough understanding of the processor, assembly language, and the ability to optimize user programs, but understanding how parallel execution in a processor works is very important.

Many modern processors are multicore, i.e., they contain several full-fledged (or almost full-fledged) processors on one crystal (in one chip). GPUs have hundreds or thousands of cores – small processors, working in parallel. There is also parallelism at the level of memory access, when different memory banks can work independently, and it means that they can give or write data faster. For example, if your motherboard has four memory banks (not slots!), then use of four slots with 8 GB (one for each bank) will work better than one slot with 32 GB. While one data is being written into one bank, the second one can be started to be written into the next.

There is also parallelism at the level of working with devices – you can form a block in memory in advance to write it to a disk or to send it over the network and "command" the controller to write/transmit it. Then the processor can perform other actions, while data from memory will be written to disk or sent over the network.

This is parallelism embedded in "hardware." In order to use it to the maximum, to make calculators (cores, processors, compute nodes...) work in parallel, it is necessary to compose a program in such a way that it uses all these resources. That is, write a **parallel program**. We will not deal with this (at least within the framework of this book), but you probably will deal with parallel programs. You have to deal with parallel programs all the time, and you need to know how they work.

If a parallel program is written, does it mean that it will immediately work faster than a regular (sequential) one? No. Moreover, it may work even slower. The parts of code, that should be executed in parallel may actually conflict with each other. For example, two threads access different memory sections and do not let the processor's cache work efficiently. Or parallel processes constantly have to wait for data from the slowest one. Or...

CHAPTER 2   WHAT IS "SUPER"?

There are many variants of inefficient parallel code, and if you cannot achieve a good acceleration of a program on a supercomputer, it is possible that it uses parallelism inefficiently. It is very difficult to find out the real cause. For this purpose, you should use "debuggers of performance" – parallel profilers, tracers, or at least monitoring of compute nodes by the data of which you can judge what happens while the program is running.

You, as a system administrator, should know all the levels of the parallelism and be able to check them all in case parallel programs work slow. Or advise your users to debug efficiency of parallelism in their programs.

In addition to parallelism on one server hardware level, there is a parallelism of several processes or threads running on one server, coprograms running on accelerators like GPUs or FPGAs, and several servers running in parallel. To utilize these levels of parallelism, special libraries or "parallel programming environments" are used. The most popular are MPI (allows running many processes on one or many servers and pass messages between them), OpenMP (allows run many threads in one process), CUDA (allows run code on NVIDIA GPUs), and OpenACC (allows run code on a wide range of accelerators).

In summary, there can be multiple levels of the parallelism in one cluster, the most frequent are (HW = hardware level, SW = software level)

- [HW] multiple memory banks
- [HW] multiline CPU cache
- [HW] multiple CPUs
- [HW] multiple CPU cores
- [HW] multiple functional devices in one CPU core
- [HW] accelerators, like GPUs and FPGAs
- [HW] network devices, with features like DMA and offloading
- [SW] multiple UNIX processes and thread
- [SW] multiple servers, running one parallel program (maybe many processes each)

System administrators should know all levels of parallelism of the cluster and be able to guess (at least) the root cause of the program slowness. For example, a cluster uses a high-speed communication network (InfiniBand or other) and regular Ethernet for management. The installed MPI environment works, but program performance is poor. Often, the cause is a misconfiguration that results in MPI using a slow control network instead of a fast network.

Types of Clusters

When people say "cluster," they mean a lot of computers combined into something. But there can be several variants of this "something." They differ in purpose and, as a consequence, in implementation.

The first type of clusters is **high availability** clusters. Their task is to provide access to some resource with maximum speed and minimum latency. The resource is usually a website, database, or other service. Today, they typically are used as a part of a set of technologies along with load balancing, A/B or canary testing, continuous deployment, and others.

In such a cluster, if one node fails, the entire resource remains available – clients of the failed node reconnect and access the resource from another node in the cluster. A very similar principle is applied in cloud technologies: you do not know on which node your application or operating system image will run, the cloud itself will select free resources.

Another type of cluster is **high productivity**. This type is similar to the previous one, but in this case, all nodes in the cluster are already working on a single task, broken into parts. If a node fails, its part of the task is sent to another node; if new nodes are added to the cluster, they are allocated parts that have not yet been counted, and the overall count goes faster. Examples include GRID computing, programs like Seti@home and Folding@Home. However, only a narrow class of tasks can be solved with the help of such clusters. And the cluster itself is often unnecessary for such tasks; you can use home computers or servers, connecting them through a local network or the Internet.

The third type is **high performance** (HPC – High-Performance Computing). It is the one we are interested in. Unlike the others, failure of one of the cluster nodes usually leads to emergency termination of a parallel program; only in rare cases, the program execution automatically continues from the previously saved control point. That is why, unlike previous types of HPC clusters, they are less stable in operation, and without proper control and monitoring, they simply cannot be used.

An important difference between this type of cluster and others is the close connectivity of all nodes. They have the fastest networks connecting nodes, high-performance parallel file systems, sometimes additional ways for node synchronization, and other things supporting parallel programs. Applications running on such clusters typically work in the model of message passing between parallel running processes. If you run them on many computers connected by a slow network, they will spend most of their time waiting for information from each other.

The ideal that all cluster manufacturers strive for is to create a virtual computer with a large memory and a huge number of computing cores. Unfortunately, the reality is still far from ideal, and nowadays, any computing cluster is still a lot of separate compute nodes connected by a fast network. The network in such a cluster requires not only speed (throughput) but also low latency or overhead (latency). Most parallel programs exchange messages frequently, which means that the time to initialize sending and receiving a message starts to play a big role. On a network with high latency, some programs may run many times slower than on a network where latency is low.

Clusters and Supercomputers – Common and Different

We just talked about clusters. But does the word "supercomputer" always mean cluster? No, not always. An important feature of a cluster is that it can be built from commercially available components. I mean, you can buy all cluster components in a store and, having sufficient experience, assemble it yourself.

A "supercomputer" in the historical perspective is a product made of unique components produced by a single vendor. For example, let's take IBM's Blue Gene series – the architecture of these machines is similar to a cluster. The same software tools are available on them as on computing clusters, but Blue Gene can be purchased only from IBM or their distributors. It is impossible to build a Blue Gene on your own: key components are not sold separately. And it's not about the brand, it's about the unique technologies. Today, such products are rare, but still exist, e.g., NEC Tsubasa.

The opposite example is "computing farms," i.e., groups of computers working on one task, but usually not even transmitting data to each other, or clusters of the "BeoWulf"[1] class, i.e., assembled practically from improvised means.

---

[1] For more information, see Wikipedia or https://spinoff.nasa.gov/Spinoff2020/it_1.html.

As we can see, the line between the concepts of "cluster" and "noncluster" is quite clear, but which cluster to consider a supercomputer and which not is a blurred question. Often, instead of "cluster," we say more tactfully: "having a cluster architecture."

In this book, I will be looking at technologies that are available to all or most. Therefore, most of them will be related to clusters. But this does not mean that these technologies will not be found in computing systems that we do not formally refer to as clusters.

Most modern supercomputers use the same developments as clusters; moreover, almost all of them are built as clusters with the addition of particularly fast networks, shared memory techniques, synchronization, or other technology, which means all the knowledge about clusters will only help you.

What "Super" Means to a Supercomputer Administrator

At first glance, a large cluster is no different from many office computers connected by a local area network and a few standard servers – disk storage, etc. In fact, there are differences, and very important ones. Let's start with the hardware – the requirements for a cluster are much higher. If in a local network you can temporarily replace a broken switch with a simpler one or even break the network connectivity for a few days (well, you will have to print reports on the second floor, bear with me), in a cluster, it is unacceptable. If we replace an InfiniBand switch (we'll talk about them later) with Gigabit Ethernet or a node with 8 GB of memory with a node with 4 GB of memory, we can easily get a cluster that works really badly and all users will flood us with complaints.

It is strongly recommended that you have an emergency stock of all key equipment components, unless they have a hardware redundancy, and a service agreement to replace the equipment within clearly defined SLAs.

Let's also remember that a cluster, unlike office computers, is packed on several square meters (a large one – on several dozens, rarely – hundreds). Therefore, the cooling requirements for it are much higher; you can't do that with an open window or a household air conditioner. Electricity for a supercomputer is much more than for many office PCs, and household UPS will not be enough here either, and you can't plug it into a household socket or even a dozen of them.

CHAPTER 2   WHAT IS "SUPER"?

In modern clusters, the computing part can occupy less than a quarter of the total installation area; all the rest is taken up by climate and energy equipment. And control and management of this equipment (but not maintenance) also can be a part of the administrator's task. Moreover, unlike in the office, if a computer node, air conditioner, or UPS has failed, you can't find out about it from an employee who came running and "the report is on fire, but nothing works." Worst of all, if you have to learn about it from users whose program stopped working properly or starts two times out of three.

This task is solved by monitoring everything and anything. It is very important to know as much as possible about the state of the cluster. The differences do not end here. One of the most significant is related to the mode of operation. In the office, the load on the computers is not high: they need a few minutes a day to display a large document or play a video clip of a new product advertisement. Ninety-nine percent of the time, these computers are waiting for a mouse click or a keystroke. In a cluster, everything is fundamentally different; its normal mode of operation is 80–100% utilization of each node at all times.

In the office, even the peak load of one or two computers will not be noticeable against the general background. But every experienced administrator knows what it is: "all computers have caught some virus" – the load on the network increases hundreds of times, network storage cannot cope with the flow of requests, everything starts to slow down.... And in a cluster, the situation when all the nodes occupied by one task start exchanging data or writing intermediate data to the network disk is not a virus, but a completely normal situation. A special type of peak load is power-on. In the office, everything happens by itself: in the morning, everyone comes in, some early, some later, turn on computers, connect laptops.... For a supercomputer, the power-on procedure means a sharp increase in power consumption by dozens or even thousands of kilowatts, then all your compute nodes start requesting your storage and service nodes almost at the same time. If you turn on everything at once, the installation will probably just burn down. And even "smooth" switching on of nodes one by one with an interval of a few seconds can lead to network conflicts, overloading of some service with requests.

For example, in large disk arrays (from several racks), shelves and disks are started in a certain sequence not only because of high starting currents, but also in order not to sway the rack from spinning disks, and you have to turn on the array components in a certain sequence; otherwise, array controllers can start thinking that the array is broken and try to rebuild it (or even mark as dead). Another example is that the servers are organized in a corridor – the racks are opposite each other and the servers blow hot air inside the resulting corridor. Then they should be turned on at intervals to avoid overheating the servers that are not yet turned on.

A lot depends on how a particular supercomputer is designed, so study its structure and startup procedure well. Of course, these and other problems apply to large offices as well, but they increase manifold in a cluster. All these issues can be solved with a certain degree of efficiency, but often, the methods of solving them differ from the "office" ones. In many respects, everything depends on the equipment – when planning a supercomputer, it is very important to remember about peak loads. Here, they are a gray everyday occurrence, so from the very beginning, it is necessary to provide solutions that allow you to withstand them.

In addition to purely hardware solutions, software solutions are also significant: if one key service is placed on a superpowerful server, it still may not be able to cope with the load, and it may be necessary to think about duplication or load sharing. If, for some reason, we failed to take everything into account during planning and a cluster with a "bottleneck" ended up under our care, we should be able to find a way to expand or completely eliminate this bottleneck, e.g., by replacing some hardware and/or software, but this is usually not easy.

So, what makes this "super"? In my opinion, it is the overall synchronization – supercomputer is not just a "huge bunch of expensive hardware," it is one complex construction, and all its components have to be aligned and tuned. As in many cases, it is used to solve one huge task, even slight disbalance can significantly drop the performance.

Centralized Management of the Computer Complex

As we will see later, there are many aspects of managing a cluster-scale computing system. These include system deployment, software upgrades, account control, remote access, access and task management, monitoring, backup, and much more. Each of these tasks can be accomplished individually, and this book will show you how. However, the amount of work an administrator has to do when performing bulk operations, such as setting up user groups with specific permissions and changing the settings of network devices or nodes, becomes quite impressive.

This is where knowledge of scripting languages will come to your aid – most of these actions are automated by scripts. But, unfortunately, not all actions can be performed by a set of scripts. In hard everyday life, a system administrator of a large computer complex more and more often thinks about a convenient "console" where you can do everything you need without launching unnecessary programs and scripts and without copying intermediate files and text from the terminal screen. Especially often, such thoughts arise at the sight of products like HP OpenView or Zenoss. "Here it is – the panacea!" — you want to exclaim. Indeed, such products are aimed at solving very similar problems. They inventory equipment themselves, keep records of users and software, do a lot of automated actions.... Moreover, they really can (and if you have the opportunity, you should) adapt them to solve some of your tasks.

Alas, only parts of it. Such products, both commercial and free, are aimed at similar, overlapping with ours, but still different tasks. Getting them to do things which are required, but they don't do, is usually possible, but it requires a huge amount of effort – human, financial, time.... And as soon as the configuration of your supercomputer changes, you will have to do it all over again. According to our personal experience and the experience of many supercomputer administrators we have talked to, there are no universal solutions. Unfortunately, creation of such tools is demanded only by a narrow circle of administrators, and it is expensive in development and support. That is why I want to draw your attention to the importance of a systematic approach to all accounting and organizational actions with the computer complex. However, this does not mean that you should choose as integrated solutions as possible. It does mean that all activities should be well described – not in order not to forget, but to see the big picture and to quickly adapt established processes under changed conditions.

Try to use flexible and extensible tools. And don't forget to learn new things and apply adequate (not only the most fashionable) technologies to solve the whole range of supercomputer administration tasks!

Brief Summary

A supercomputer is very similar to a "many-to-many ordinary server," but at the same time, there are many more peculiarities you should take care of. A lot of server technologies are used here to solve standard tasks, but there are a lot of specific tasks and technologies that are used only in the field of supercomputing.

Search Keywords

HPC, beowulf, supercomputer

CHAPTER 3

How to Build and Start It?

Imagine you need to build a supercomputer cluster. What should you buy? How to connect? What to do first? Let's sort it out.

Anatomy of a Supercomputer

There are four big parts you should think of: compute nodes, compute infrastructure, hardware infrastructure, and software. Let's start with **hardware infrastructure** – it includes power supply, cooling and security systems. Usually, it is not your area, but you should know what you can get for the new supercomputer. How much electricity power is available? How can you connect to it (which types of UPS and PDU do you need)? Include power for cooling and make sure you have 5–10% headroom.

Security systems – Cameras, doors control, etc.; they should be ready or, if not, included into the budget. Think beforehand how your cluster will be connected to the intranet or Internet; maybe you require hardware for this too. A standalone question – where do you plan to install your supercomputer? Do you have enough space? Is it close to the cooling systems and are there people who will connect those things together?

Yes, yes, you are not that person, who should plan and do all that stuff (I hope), but, please, make sure that all of the above was told to **that** person, who will do that, and taken into account (and budget).

Compute nodes – All your compute servers or, sometimes we say, compute fields and compute networks. Before thinking about it, gather the information about the tasks, which this supercomputer is being made for. Ask your potential users, read about the computing packages, what is important for the best performance? Is a low latency interconnect critical or not? Do you need GPUs? What is better – more memory or more CPU/GPU cores? Is the vendor of CPU/GPU significant? How about the storage (we'll talk about it later, but gather info now) – speed, IOPS, latency or size, what matters the most?

After you gather the information, try to write down the optimal configuration of the one compute node and several trade-offs you think are acceptable (see Figure 3-1). Add here compute network requirements and think about the topology (we'll discuss it later). If your topology can be divided into blocks, try to calculate some real configurations – how many could cost one block. Then you can estimate the size and cost of the compute field, depending on the cost of the rest.

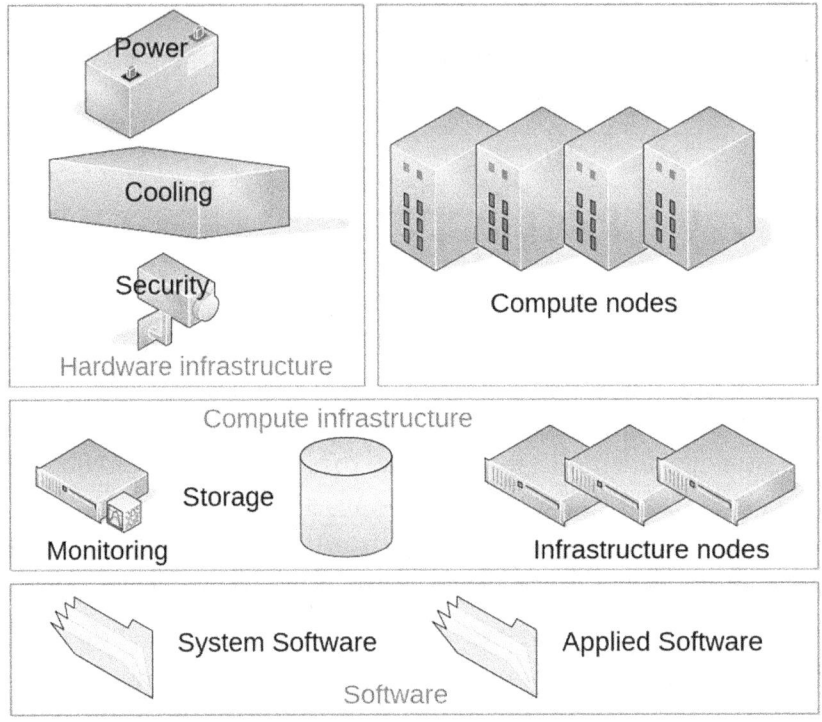

Figure 3-1. Supercomputer anatomy

Compute infrastructure – Your management network, storage, storage network, and infrastructure nodes. We'll discuss infrastructure nodes later, but in short, they are nodes like login server, monitoring server, scheduler server, etc. In the case of a small cluster, all roles can be on a single physical server, or one server can run numerous virtual machines. This also includes shared storage and backups, and you need to take in account not only size, but the speed and scalability of this storage. If a hundred nodes read or write at the same time (which is typical for parallel apps), your expensive shiny server with one big expensive disk will be just swamped by the load, and your compute task probably will fail, because some requests will time out.

Software – You will need computational packages, specific to your users/customers, as system software to control the cluster, tasks, observe the overall status and some other stuff. Plan your software stack beforehand, because it is really painful to change it later, especially system software. Special focus on the planned job run workflow. What job management systems do you plan to use? Are your users ready for it? Is it supported well by the computational stacks you plan to run? Please, do not choose thinking of "Oh, I worked with that stuff, I hope I can apply it here" – it may be a big mistake. Use systems, which are standard in this area.

Deploy and upgrade – How do you plan to make initial software deploy, and how do you plan to manage updates/upgrades? There are many options (and we'll check them out later!); decide wisely and plan carefully.

Planning

Once you collect all requirements and possible implementation options along with your budget, you can start to plan your cluster. Of course, you can ask for quotas of available vendors and get some predefined options, but now you know what you want and which parts and characteristics are more important and have more knowledge for possible trade-offs.

Try to assess your minimum acceptable numbers on **benchmarks and tests**. This is a performance baseline for your cluster. You need to do that at least for computing performance and storage performance, so prepare reliable benchmarks and tests. Other things you can assess – memory throughput and latency, GPU performance (if you have it), network performance….

Take into account the possibility of **upgrading**, which is very likely. How can you expand your compute field in the future? Storage? Do you have any options for space, electricity, cooling capacity? Another critical aspect is integration of your cluster with **existing company services and resources**. Do you want to have centralized authentication, and how do you plan to implement it? How will your users or customers copy data? How will they reach the cluster from the Internet (or they just won't)? What about users **technical support** – who will do this and how? Who will support the hardware – even if you have a supporting contract, you will need to check, diagnose, your hardware, do maintenance, etc.? Special point – support contracts; how your management plans to support this really expensive complex after the contracts expired? This is a big trap, and it requires wise and careful planning beforehand! (If your management says "we have 5 years support, don't worry, and then we'll see," I recommend writing a document and note there that even small break could stop the service; you do not approve work without the service contract.)

Another important question is **capacity planning** – how will your users utilize the cluster resources (CPU, GPU, memory, storage, ...)? How do you plan to divide resources and cluster time between users? How do you plan to control resource usage?

Another significant thing you should mention in a contract and track later is the consistency of all hardware. Memory modules should be the same make and model when possible, especially in compute nodes. Motherboards, firmware, BIOS, network cards, etc., should be the same in similar servers, GPUs should have the same part number, VBIOS, etc., and all that jazz. Don't listen to sales persons, saying "this is the same model, just a bit modern part number, it is even better!" – you probably will have different drivers/applications behavior on different hardware and will waste a lot of your time, fixing that. If it is newer and better – OK, make all that type of hardware have this model!

Here are some things you cannot manage directly, but you can talk to your management beforehand and prevent huge problems. First of such things is **power**. Summarize total servers' power; add network hardware, storage, cooling systems (yes, they consume a lot of power!), UPS, and power systems themselves. You can make a rough estimation, multiply by 1.5 or 2, and ask your manager to have a talk with your power engineers and make a good professional estimation. Do not forget about redundancy and UPS, and check if you need a power generator or not. If power outages are not long, or you can safely stop your hardware and your users are able to restart work later, the generator is probably not needed.

And as a logical continuation, we have questions about the **cooling** and **place** for the hardware. Is it easy to unload and install the hardware? Is there enough space to perform maintenance or upgrade? Do you have space for spare details? Do you consider using water cooling now or in the future, and if yes, is this place ready for such modernization? Is the power and cooling capacity enough, what is reserve? Don't laugh, I have a great example, when a real supercomputer could not be turned on more than 70% because of electricity issues.

If you plan to use remote location, e.g., data center colocation, then how easy can you get access there? How remote engineers can help you to perform tasks? Which tasks can they do, which tasks should do you?

Network aspects – How your users will reach the supercomputer? How about loading data? If they need to upload and download huge amount of data, maybe you require better network channel. Check internal requirements; possibly you need a network switch of better class, than you thought initially to route the data from outside to the data storage. Do not forget about firewall and may be other security features. Even if your supercomputer is entirely in the corporate network, this doesn't mean it should be fully opened. If unsure, talk to network security specialists, maybe simply on special web forums, but a real security consultation will be better. In addition, your external cluster network connection should be capable to transfer user's data in both directions, and if you use NAT (which is typical solution), your switch should be powerful enough.

Special point - High-performance network planning, because the topology is crucial here, you need to minimize the number of hops between nodes, remove possible congestion points, and single points of failure. Again – I recommend having a consultation with an expert and compare different topologies, their strong and weak points in your case, cost (yes, it makes difference!), cabling complexity, and possibilities for the future expansion (compute nodes, storage, …).

We touched the **data and storage**; how do you plan to store the data? What about hot and cold data? Backups? Possibly your users want pre- and postprocessing? How quick will this data be available to compute nodes? Please, take a look to the chapter "Network File Systems" before making the final decision.

Here is a short (please, review and extend it!) checklist – what has to be planned, discussed, and documented:

- **Compute hardware** – Match to tasks, expected performance
- **Infrastructure** – Power, cooling, connectivity
- **Remote access** – Policies, special access, codes, etc.
- **Physical security** – Room access, servers access, cameras, cards policies
- Services and service nodes (we'll talk about them later, but you should have at least a login node and file system server(s))
- High availability and/or load balancing for service nodes and services (Is it needed? How to implement it?)

CHAPTER 3 HOW TO BUILD AND START IT?

- Network topology
- Authentication, sync with existing systems if needed
- Long-term storage, scratch storage, quotas, high availability
- Access from internal/external networks
- **Security policies** – Passwords, two-factor authentication (2FA), ssh keys, local trust zones, regular files check, vulnerabilities scans, security updates policies, firewalls, ...
- Backups/restore policies and hardware
- Cluster management software
- Computing tasks management software
- Jobs policies
- Monitoring
- Baseline benchmarking
- **Cluster resources for users** – access, tracking, revoking
- Capacity planning procedure

Imagine typical situations and think how to act in such cases:

- If you suspect a bad node, what are your steps to prove it is bad and replace it?
- The same, if you suspect network problems?
- If you found that your nodes have different firmware versions and it can affect your application performance?
- What if your management node, running job manager, fails?
- How you will transfer data to the cluster and back, and how much time does it take?
- How to add a user to the cluster? Remove them from the cluster?
- How you plan to do security checks and updates?

Documentation

Yes, this is important. No, don't put it off; you won't be able to do that at the last minute, I promise. And I'm talking not only about those tons of paper, which is going with your hardware. Please, prepare a place and a system where and how to document your supercomputer. There are two types of documentation, and you need both: for SysAdmins and for users. Docs for SysAdmins should include

- Hardware configurations of different types of nodes
- Network topology and hardware
- Software installed, licenses info, special configurations
- System settings, limits, etc.
- Admin and maintenance logins and how to get passwords
- Policies to add accounts, software, etc.
- Backups info (how to backup, restore, schedules, etc.)
- How to add/delete accounts, do the maintenance, and other stuff
- Important contacts (stakeholders, suppliers, engineers, tech support, people, who controls power, cooling, physical access...)
- A journal of incidents and maintenance with detailed info
- Temporary changes (changed quotas for a month? Gave access to external tech support? PLEASE, note it)
- HOWTO
    - Close/open cluster in emergence cases
    - Change quotas
    - Add/delete/update user accounts
    - Quick actions in simple known cases (like how to reboot this damn proprietary license server)
    - Inform users about any problems
    - Run basic tests, etc.
- And many more, of course!

CHAPTER 3   HOW TO BUILD AND START IT?

Please, spend some time choosing the platform (bunch of files on network file storage? Wiki? Corporate portal?...) and creating base documents structure. The next type – user documentation, and it includes

- How to submit a request for access, what is the full process and timing
- How to get password, generate ssh keys, login into the cluster for the first time, first steps
- What is the cluster – hardware, software, file systems, links to user docs
- How to copy data, prepare a task, run, check, cancel a job
- Policies and limits
- How to... here come questions, you didn't imagine, but they were asked

The platform for user docs can differ from admin docs; the most important is its availability and how simple it can be read. Select the platform, where users can collaborate – edit documents, or at least ask questions or leave comments.

OK, We Got It, What's Next?

You, as a SysAdmin, have a lot of things to do. Which skills should you have? Here is a minimum, I recommend:

- Basic network knowledge
- Good/advanced bash scripting (basic awk is a good bonus)
- vim/nano/emacs editor on advanced level
- Screen/tmux basic knowledge
- Basic python and C++ (if you need to support users)
- Ansible, xCAT, or any other technologies you want to use to control and configure your cluster
- Tools like lmod, environment modules, spack, etc.

- How containers work (not docker commands, no, host the technology works)
- All your hardware features, software features, and limitations

What do you need to set up and/or tune after the cluster is built? There are a lot of options, but I recommend paying attention to at least the following:

- DNS server
- NTP sync (internal and external)
- SSH to all nodes (including service)
- Shared file system performance check (on login node, and on compute node)
- Network performance benchmark
- Nodes performance benchmark (each node and all nodes)
- User add/block/unblock/delete check (everything works fine?)
- Partition add/modify/delete
- Compute partition quotas and limits check
- Monitoring check, alerts check
- Test data backup and restore

Now, check your docs, and add all missing parts. Write down all your checks above into runbooks/playbooks and document all numbers you got on the benchmarks. It will really help you later on every maintenance and/or update/upgrade. Plan at least one maintenance per year – firmware upgrade, parts replacements, software upgrade. Plan the checks you want to use for different situations (maybe more often than I recommend):

- Full cluster check (after each maintenance)
- Performance verification (after each maintenance)
- Node performance check (after the node fix or replacement)
- Node readiness check (before/after the job run)
- Node health check (periodically on the nodes)

Some useful benchmarks/tests you can use: HPL (High-Performance Linpack), NCCL-test (GPUs, IB, NVLink), IOR (file system performance), STREAM (memory check and performance), and FIO (file system performance).

What Should I Do Later?

It depends.... In most cases, you are responsible for

- Updating cluster parameters (limits, tunings, etc.)
- User access management
- Applied software installation
- Hardware monitoring, basic fixing, detailed problems reporting to engineers
- Cluster usage monitoring (and usually reporting)
- Technical user support

The list can be longer, or in rare cases shorter. Plan the software and workflows for each point beforehand; test if possible. Get as many people as you can to your team to delegate mentioned responsibilities. No joking.

Some tips for you.

- Try to use standard solutions if there are such; do not multiply complex solutions. For example, if you need to add new software into PATH variable, do not add it into a random bash profile file; think about using modules (see chapter "Compilers and Environments, for Parallel Technologies"). If you use one approach, document it and use everywhere. In our example, you can use modules, global/local bashrc and profile, pam_env module, and some other more sophisticated methods, and in case of problems, it may be really hard to find where PATH was changed.

- In case of issues, try to look to different levels, in one direction, e.g., from top to bottom, from the client to server, etc. For example, slurm client command is not working (see chapter "Job Management Systems"), then you can check if the server is working, if it is listening the network socket (use netstat or ss), if it is available from the client machine (routing, firewall rules), if the client has correct server address. Low-level checks may include running the command under strace and check if DNS address is resolved correctly and the connection is established, or looking into the network traffic using tcpdump.

- Use runbooks for any serious activity like maintenance, software/hardware installation or upgrade, moving data, etc. Runbooks are usually just spreadsheets with columns: phase, action, start, duration, dependency, owner, status, and info (commands to run, links to the docs, etc.). You may add some if you wish, e.g., rollback action description. Always ask someone to review your new runbook, often you can miss something.

Short Notes

Let me give you some additional hints:

- On the compute nodes, try to minimize running services (e.g., ModemManager probably is not required, and postfix should be replaced by simple package like ssmtp or nail, which allows sending emails via smarthost).

- Try to optimize your kernel parameters – don't load not needed modules, disable security fixes (`mitigations=off`), if it is safe, ipv6 if it is not needed, etc.

- Disable cron on the compute nodes; use systemd timers instead.

- Install `molly-guard` (or similar) package to prevent accidental reboot of service nodes; you'll thank you me later.

- Don't use cronjobs, which do ssh on all nodes and do checks/etc.; instead, use local timers, save results to a network file system, database, or message queue, and then process them on a service node.

CHAPTER 3　HOW TO BUILD AND START IT?

- Take care of security, probably install and tune auditd to log critical commands execution, do regular security checks, etc. A good start is to read "High-Performance Computing Security"[1] paper by NIST.

Brief Summary

Know your hardware and software; go into details. Supercomputers have tons of details, so make sure to double-check everything when you plan it. If possible, involve other experts. Their help can be invaluable.

Search Keywords

Data center technologies, runbook/playbook examples, standard operating procedure

---

[1] https://nvlpubs.nist.gov/nistpubs/SpecialPublications/NIST.SP.800-223.pdf

CHAPTER 4

Supercomputer Hardware

We shortly considered the "anatomy" of a computing cluster and know what components it consists of. Depending on the size and architecture of a particular cluster, some logical components may be combined into one physical. In the following, I will often write "node" – it is a synonym for "server," but in HPC, it is the custom.

So, a mandatory part of any cluster is **compute nodes**, or the so-called **compute field**. These are the servers where tasks will be counted. In addition to compute nodes, there should be at least one **control node**; in large systems, additional **service nodes** are added to it; there can be several dozens of them.

Networks are necessary for effective cooperation of compute nodes:

- **Communication network**, through which the data of compute tasks are exchanged

- **Control network,** which is used to remotely access nodes, run tasks, etc.

- One or more **service networks** – for access to the network file system, management via IPMI or iKVM protocols, monitoring, additional synchronization (interruptions, clock frequency, barriers, etc.), and possibly others

A mandatory component of a modern computing cluster is a **network file system**.

For the entire complex to work, it is mandatory to have **infrastructure**: power supply systems and climate systems. For a large installation, they can take up many times more space than compute nodes. As a rule, infrastructure maintenance is not the responsibility of the administrator, but they should, if possible, monitor its condition. If the infrastructure is on planning stage yet, make sure you have enough access to monitor critical infrastructure information.

Control Node

All nodes in any cluster are divided into compute nodes and service nodes. One service node is always present – it is the management node. It is from it that all subsystems are managed (or logged in to manage them), and sometimes it plays role of login node, which users use to access cluster via ssh. In small clusters, it can combine the functions of all service servers, but in general, I recommend having at least two control nodes and one or more user-facing nodes.

Compute Node

The "workhorse" of the cluster is the counting field. As a rule, all nodes here are of the same configuration, but sometimes the field can include nodes of two or more configurations. The more homogeneous the composition of compute nodes, the easier it is to manage them, and the easier to schedule tasks. You should create mixed configurations only when you are sure that **ALL** of them will be actively used by tasks.

The hardware of the compute node is completely determined by the nature of the tasks that will be solved on the cluster, but you should always try to balance the composition of the "hardware" so that there are no bottlenecks, such as many cores with a narrow channel to memory, insufficient width of the channel to the computer network, etc.

Having a hard disk drive has both pros and cons. Minuses are additional space, power consumption, and heat dissipation, as well as a high probability of failure. In addition, they cost a lot of money, especially NVME, and you need to have some valuable count in stock, to be able to replace failed ones, or have a good (priced) support contract. If your nodes are "blade-servers" or use any other high-density architecture, all this is especially relevant. Pros – The possibility to install a local copy of the OS, which greatly simplifies the power-on procedure and speeds up the loading of system libraries (and hence the start of programs), as well as the possibility to add swap space and the local / tmp directory. This greatly improves memory efficiency.

When installing a local copy of the OS, be very careful with software updates and local storage of credentials. To increase efficiency, the software configuration should be kept as light as possible: the fewer unnecessary services, the better.

On the compute node, it is quite possible to do away with such services as **mail** (you can send messages through the head node), **cron** (the most important tasks can be performed via ssh also from the head node), **networkmanager**, **acpid**, etc. Keep only the essentials, and use precreated device files instead of udev if possible – they won't change over time anyway. The most essential services for the compute node are sshd and the network file system client. It is very desirable to set up monitoring of the node.

As a rule, all compute nodes are logically organized into partitions (or queues) within the task management system. If there are nodes of different configurations in the field, it is convenient to create partitions for each configuration separately. Sometimes it is useful to unite several compute nodes into one partition to run small test backlogs (test queue), and it is useful to limit the runtime of such test tasks (e.g., 15–20 minutes).

Login Node

I recommend having dedicated user-facing nodes (login, data preprocessing, visualization, data copying, etc.), and not share them with service nodes. Set strict resource usage limits on those nodes, to prevent incorrect their usage. Simple example – Today (in 2025), many users' workflows are streamlined by IDE plug-ins, like VSCode remote and others. They make remote work with cluster easier, at the first glance. But in fact, many of those plug-ins (VSCode particularly) take a lot of system resources and may paralyze login node.

Service Nodes

All nodes not included in the count field are service nodes. Combining the functions of a compute node and a service node (e.g., an NFS server) is highly discouraged, as it will certainly lead to unbalanced task operation and increased probability of service failure.

There are several roles that service nodes fulfill, but often a single server fulfills several roles, if not all at once. Let's consider typical roles. In large computing complexes, it is not always convenient to load control nodes with user and service system processes. For example, if compute nodes with different versions of operating systems are installed, it is not reasonable to build user programs on the control node; it is more logical to dedicate (or allocate) numerous nodes for compiling programs (**compilation nodes**). If your users need to move a lot of data, it is useful to have dedicated **data copying nodes**.

CHAPTER 4 SUPERCOMPUTER HARDWARE

To protect against unauthorized access to system services and sensitive data (e.g., a database of user passwords), the functions of control nodes are usually divided into two groups: access nodes and control nodes. **Access nodes** are intended for user login and further work in the system, and **control nodes are** intended for operation of the task management system.

Almost any cluster has a **network file system**, which means a server for it, and often a whole farm if the file system is distributed. A fairly common service node is a **license server**, which hosts special services responsible for licensing commercial software and utilities. For example, a FlexLM license server can be used for several commercial packages.

Locating license services on a separate machine is justified both from the point of view of security (protection against theft of license files) and from the point of view of increasing fault tolerance of the complex as a whole. Be sure to make a note of the MAC address of this server; if it is suddenly replaced, it will be enough for most programs to set the old MAC address on the new server. And don't forget to request a license reissue for the new server, of course with its real MAC address.

In modern computing complexes, **input data preparation and output data processing nodes** (so-called pre- and postprocessing nodes) are quite common. Such nodes are characterized by a larger amount of RAM than other nodes (256 GB or more), which is extremely important for preparing large tasks and processing the results of calculations.

So-called **visualization nodes** are often useful. Usually, these are dedicated servers with special graphic cards for processing visual information and outputting the finished picture through the network to a remote user. This can be convenient, in particular, for remote preparation of tasks for calculation (e.g., for visualization of meshes and other input data). Visualization nodes can play the role of pre-/postprocessing nodes.

Storage nodes can be used to organize a distributed data storage. Each such node is connected to its own disk storage, and all storage nodes are united into a single network with common access to the file system from all nodes (more about this in the next section).

There may also be dedicated nodes among the service nodes:

- Backups
- Remote download
- Of software deployment

- Authorization and authentication
- Remote journaling
- Collection and processing of monitoring data
- Collection and display of statistics and equipment status
- Of service databases, etc.

It all depends on what the needs of the users and administrators of the computing complex are.

Network Equipment

Computer networks allow you to organize the interaction of computers with each other. Special equipment is used to build them: network cards and switches. As a rule, clusters have at least two internal networks. One, called a service network, performs the same functions as a regular local computer network; it is used for remote nodes access, monitoring, etc., and includes all the cluster nodes. The other is called compute (or communication) network, has all compute nodes connected to it, and provides data exchange between compute tasks on different nodes. Some clusters may have dedicated storage, remote control, monitoring, or other types of networks, but this is a rare (and usually more expensive) case.

Do not forget about the external network, which is used by users and admins for the cluster access; if users will load a lot of data, it might be a bottleneck. As a rule, compute nodes, storage servers, and most service nodes don't have direct access to the external network; they even don't have public (or corporate) IP addresses. To access the world, NAT or proxy is used, to access internal services (monitoring dashboards, admin ssh, etc.) - port forwarding or reverse proxy. Plan this beforehand, to decide what type of network switch you need for external network, which nodes will have direct access, etc.

The most serious requirements are placed on the communication network. Two basic parameters are used to characterize the capabilities of Networking technologies: throughput and latency.

Throughput characterizes how much information can be transmitted per unit of time (most often a second). Network equipment manufacturers typically specify peak throughput. In real applications, as a rule, the speed is 1.5-2 times lower than the peak speed. The term **latency** (delay) is the net time to transmit a zero-length message. It primarily depends on the time taken by network devices and the system to prepare for transmitting and receiving information.

Throughput and latency provide a measure of how efficiently tasks will be handled on the cluster. If a task requires frequent data exchange between nodes, using network hardware with high latency will result in most of the time spent on preparation rather than data transfer, and the nodes will be idle. With low bandwidth, data exchange between nodes will not keep up with the task count rate, which will also have a negative impact on performance: nodes will spend a lot of time waiting for data over the network.

The latency and throughput of the network are primarily determined by the data transmission technology used. The most widespread network technology is Ethernet, but its parameters meet only the requirements for the organization of the service network of the cluster, for data exchange networks less known, but higher speed networks are used.

Table 4-1 summarizes the most common network technologies in clusters and their typical characteristics. Myrinet is not actively used now; SlingShot is a proprietary network technology by Cray (bought by Hewlett-Packard).

Table 4-1. Some characteristics of networking technologies

Technology	Throughput	Latency (μsec)	MPI latency (μsec)
Gigabit Ethernet	Peak – 1000 Mbit/sec (125 MB/sec), MPI – 60–120 MB/sec	30–100	50
10-Gigabit Ethernet	Peak – 10 Gbit/sec (1.2 GB/sec), MPI – 700–900 MB/sec	9	25–30
100-Gigabit Ethernet	Peak – 100 Gbit/sec (1.2 GB/sec)	0.3–1	1–3
Myrinet 2000, Myrinet-10G	Peak is 2 Gbit/sec (10 Gbit/sec), full duplex. On TCP/IP, speeds on the order of 1.7-1.9 Gbit/sec (9.6 Gbit/sec). On MPI, up to 200 MB/sec (up to 400 MB/sec on duplex operations)	2	10
InfiniBand	10 to 4800 Gbit/sec or higher, implementation dependent	0.1–0.6	1–3
SlingShot	Peak – 200 Gbit/s	0.2–1.2	4–5

Another important issue to consider when designing networks for computing clusters is price. Without going into details, each high-speed network card costs about $1,000, and the price of a communicator can range from $10,000 to $1,000,000 and above. Today, the most popular technology for building clusters for creating data exchange networks is InfiniBand. The reasons for its popularity are related to the perfect performance, a good ratio between the price and capabilities of the equipment, as well as the availability of software. We will consider InfiniBand more precisely in the next chapter.

Some networks can only use one topology (the way network nodes are switched). For example, Gigabit Ethernet only supports star topology, but since it is only used in conjunction with TCP/IP in real-world applications, it is possible to combine multiple stars with links by configuring routing.

InfiniBand allows you to use almost any topology that is supported by the installed subnet manager. Standard subnet manager implementations support star, tree, fat tree, and hypercube topology, but newer implementations are being introduced. Due to the fact that InfiniBand allows multiple routes, the fat tree topology is well suited for medium-sized configurations and makes good use of duplicate links.

Topology is an important factor in network efficiency. Topology bottlenecks can negate high network speeds. For example, two Gigabit Ethernet switches connected to a single link is not a good solution. And if you connect them with multiple links, you need to make sure that they are interconnected at the switch level. Such interconnection is supported by many types of network equipment; there are standard technologies such as EtherChannel, bonding, and trunking. It is significant to make sure in advance that all parties involved in such interconnection use the same standards (e.g., bonding may be implemented differently from one vendor to another).

Let's quickly go through typical types of network topology, available today (2025):

- **Tree (star)** – Typical Ethernet topology. Even if you have several switches, connected in parallel, usually spanning tree algorithm will left running only one and the second will work in standby mode.

CHAPTER 4 SUPERCOMPUTER HARDWARE

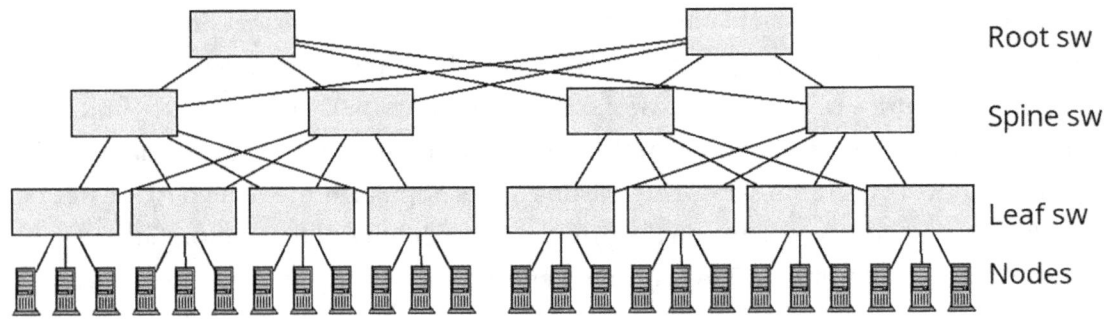

Figure 4-1. *Three-level fat tree network topology example*

- **Fat tree** – There are two options, which may be meant here. First – a regular tree, but on the higher levels, links through output are higher (usually links are aggregated). More interesting option, often used in InfiniBand networks, when higher level switches are "multiplied" (see Figure 4-1). In the simple case, instead of one root switch, we have two or more, and each is connected to each next level switch. This allows traffic distribution and easy recovery if one of the switches fails, except the lowest level, so-called leaf switches, because they are connected to the nodes.

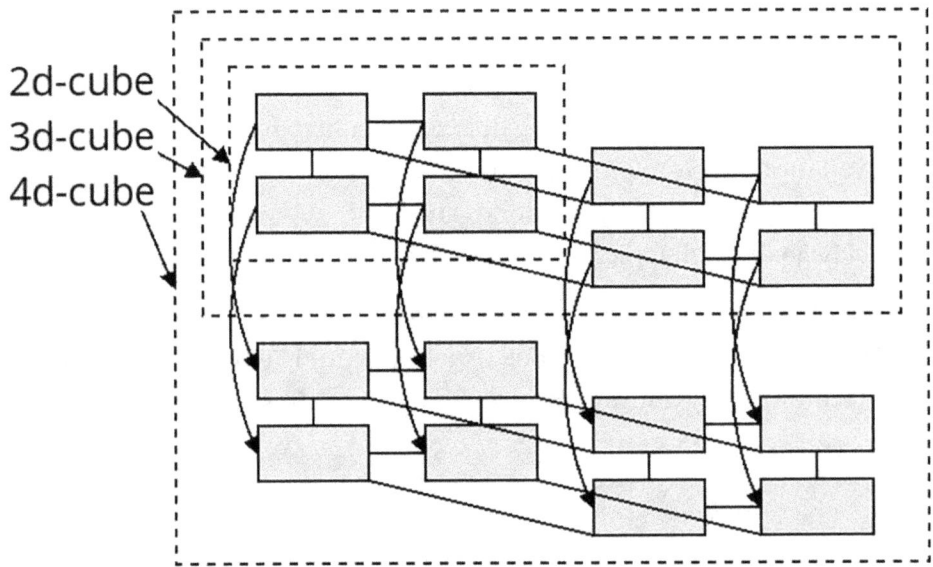

Figure 4-2. *Hypercube topology example*

- **Hypercube** – Rare topology, but is sometimes used as a part of more complex topology (see Figure 4-2). To build N-dimensional hypercube, you take 2 (N-1)-dimensional hypercubes and connect corresponding vertices. In real life, in the vertices, usually you have a leaf switch with some nodes connected. The advantage is that you have no more than N hops between any two vertices. Disadvantage – complicated and expensive cabling.

- **Multidimensional torus** – Similar to hypercube, but in each dimension, you can have multiple vertices, and each dimension is closed into a loop (see Figure 4-3). For example, in case of three-dimensional torus, if we have dimension sizes N, M, and K, we have maximum [N/2]+[M/2]+[K/2] hops between any two vertices ([X] is integer part of X).

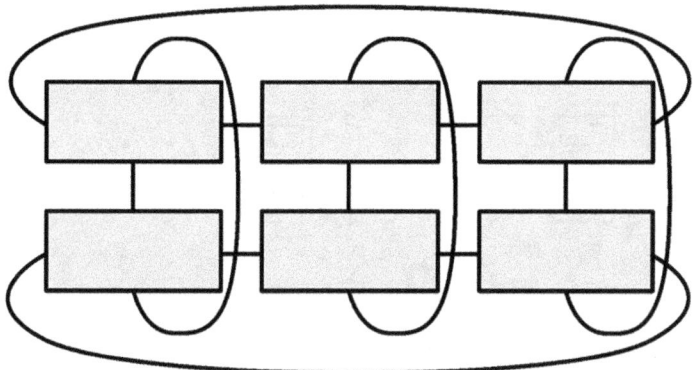

Figure 4-3. 2d torus topology example

- **Dragonfly/Dragonfly+** are the most recently used topology types. In Dragonfly, you have several levels of groups; on the bottom level, the group has a number of switches and each of them is connected to all others in the group. Next level is a group, which consists of previous level groups as members. In basic Dragonfly topology, on each level, group members are connected all-to-all. In Dragonfly+, there may be modifications, e.g., each member of previous level group is connected to a subset of neighbor's group members. This may reduce number of required switch ports (and cables), while the average max number of hops between any two vertices is still low.

CHAPTER 4   SUPERCOMPUTER HARDWARE

Data Storage

Local hard disks can be installed in each node – control, computing, or service nodes. It is also possible to connect external disk subsystems that can be accessed from all nodes simultaneously.

Local hard disks can be used for booting the operating system, as virtual memory (swap space), and for storing temporary data. Of course, compute nodes may not have local disks if the operating system is booted over a network, although even in this case a local disk is useful for swap space and temporary data storage. On a management node, local hard disks are usually installed and network booting is not provided.

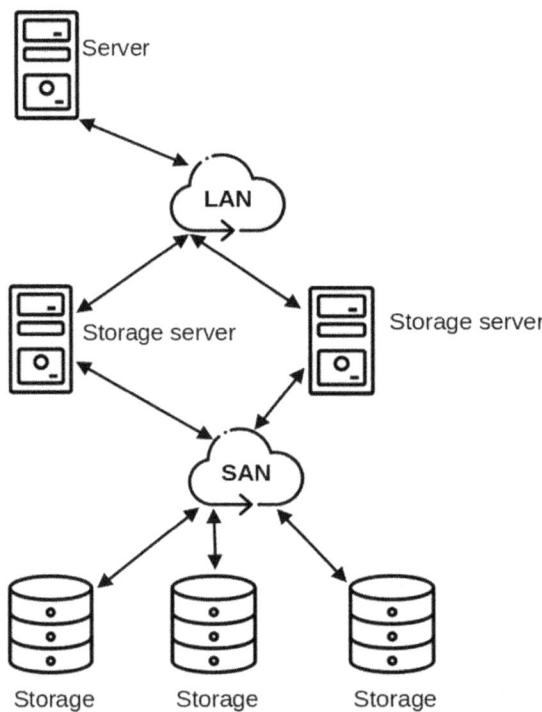

Figure 4-4. *Storage area network (SAN)*

External storage systems (hereinafter referred to as storage) typically host software packages and utilities that need to run on all nodes, as well as user home directories, temporary shared storage (for storing temporary calculation data), and other data that must be accessible from all nodes.

External storage often differs in its internal structure and access method, which determines the level of reliability of data storage and the speed of data access. We will not discuss the internal structure of the storage system here, we will only mention the different access methods.

Storage systems are categorized into at least two types based on their access method:

- Direct attached storage or **DAS**
- Network attached storage or **NAS**

NAS can be connected via servers (or special hardware), connected to physical storage via dedicated storage network – storage area network or **SAN** (see Figure 4-4).

Direct attached storage is connected either to a dedicated storage node or to a management node. Such storage is always visible in the operating system of the node to which it is connected as a locally connected disk device (physical connection – via SATA, SAS, FibreChannel, …). RAID (redundant array of independent disks) technology is often used in storage systems to provide fault tolerance and increase speed. RAID combines several disks of equal capacity into a single logical disk. Combining occurs at the block level (which may not coincide with physical disk blocks). One logical block can be mapped to one or more disk blocks.

There are several "levels" that are accepted as the de facto standard for RAID:

RAID-0 – logical blocks unambiguously correspond to disk blocks, and they alternate: block0 = block0 of the first disk, block1 = block1 of the second disk, and so on.

RAID-1 is a mirrored array, logical block N corresponds to logical blocks N of all disks, and they must have the same contents.

RAID-2 is an array with Hamming code redundancy.

RAID-3 and RAID-4 are disk arrays with striping and a dedicated checksum disk.

RAID-5 is a disk array with striping and an unallocated checksum disk.

RAID-6 is a striped disk array that uses two checksums calculated in two independent ways.

Level 0 provides the highest sequential write speed – blocks are written in parallel to different disks, but does not provide fault tolerance; level 1 provides the highest fault tolerance, as failure of N-1 disk does not lead to data loss.

Levels 2, 3, and 4 are not really used because level 5 provides better speed and reliability with the same degree of redundancy. In these levels, disk blocks are combined into strips, or **stripes**.

In each stripe, one block is allocated for checksum storage (two strips for level 6) and the remaining blocks are allocated for data, with the disk used for the checksum interleaved across successive strips to even out the load on the disks. When writing to any block, the data checksum for the entire stripe is calculated and written to the checksum block. If one of the disks fails to read the logical block that was on it, the entire strike is read and the data of the working blocks and the checksum are used to calculate the block data.

Thus, for RAID-5, it is possible to obtain fault tolerance with less redundancy than for a mirror (RAID-1) – instead of half of disks, only one disk in a stripe (two disks for RAID-6) can be allocated for redundant data. As a rule, the "width" of a stripe is 3–5 disks. The cost of this is the speed of operation – to write a single block, you must first read the entire stripe to calculate a new checksum.

Two-level schemes are often used – RAID arrays themselves are used as disks for other RAID arrays. In this case, the RAID level is indicated by two numbers: first the lower level, then the upper level. The most common are RAID-10 (RAID-0 built from RAID-1 arrays) and RAID-50 and RAID-60 – RAID-0 arrays built from RAID-5 and RAID-6 arrays, respectively. Read more about RAID in the literature and on the Internet.

If distributed data storage is used, e.g., as in Lustre (we will talk about it later), there can be several storage nodes, and the data stored on such storage is distributed across the storage nodes. Storage with LAN access (or network attached storage, NAS) usually provides disk space to nodes using special protocols that can be grouped under the general name of **network file systems**. Examples of such file systems are NFS (network file system), server message block (SMB), or its modern variant – common Internet file system (CIFS).

Strictly speaking, CIFS and SMB are two different names for the same network file system originally developed by IBM and actively used in Microsoft operating systems. Nowadays, CIFS can be used in almost any operating system to provide access to files over a local network, but I don't recommend using it, because of highly possible unexpected problems, related to implementation details. As a rule, besides NFS and CIFS, NAS systems can also provide access to stored data via other protocols such as FTP, HTTP, or iSCSI.

Storage devices connected via dedicated storage area networks (SANs) are usually visible to the operating system as locally attached disk devices. The peculiarity of a SAN is that duplicate switches can be used to form such a network in order to increase reliability. In this case, each node will have several routes for accessing the storage, one of which is designated as the main one, the rest are backup ones. In case of failure of one of the components through which the network passes the primary route, access will be via the backup route.

Switching to a backup route will be instantaneous, and the user will not detect that anything has failed at all. For this to work, the hardware and OS must support multipath. Note that although there are standards for multipath, in reality, there is often "capricious" equipment, which requires nonstandard drivers or system software packages to work correctly with multipath.

Note that SAN exports **block devices**, not a file system, and you should not mount one network device on more than one node at once. There are some exceptions, e.g., for implementing "heartbeat" techniques, or sophisticated databases, but in general this is a bad idea.

Hardware Architecture Features

It is no secret that at the very beginning of the computer era, the terms "processor" and "kernel" (meaning the compute core of the processor) were synonymous. To be more precise, the term "core" did not refer to the processor at all, because there were no multicore processors yet. Each computer usually had a single processor, which could execute only one process at any given time. Modern systems of this type can still be found today, but they are typically designed for special tasks (controllers, embedded systems).

CHAPTER 4   SUPERCOMPUTER HARDWARE

To increase the power of a server or workstation, manufacturers installed multiple "single-core" processors (frequently from two to eight). Such systems still exist today and are called symmetric multiprocessor systems or SMP systems (see Figure 4-5).

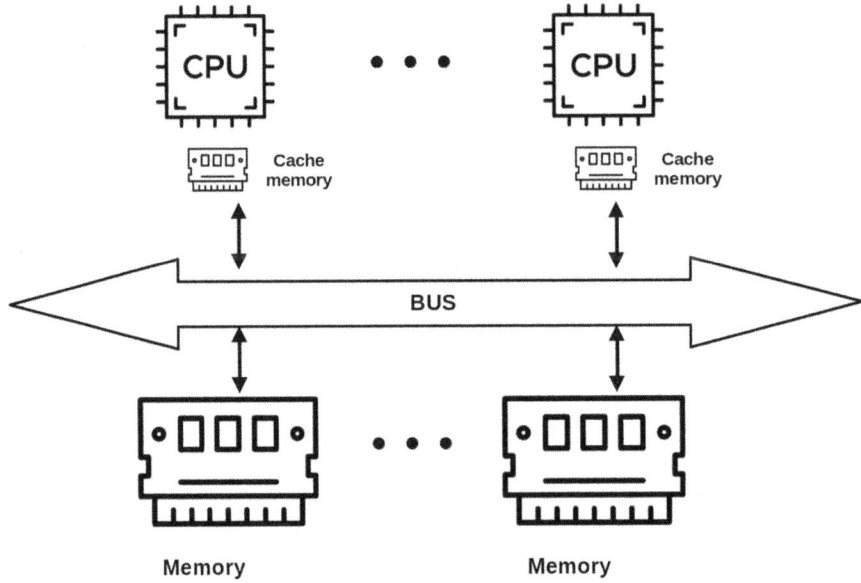

Figure 4-5. *Symmetric multiprocessor system (SMP)*

As you can see from the diagram, each processor, which is a single compute core, is connected to a common system bus. In this configuration, memory access for all processors is the same, so the system is called **symmetric**. More recently, each processor has multiple cores. Each of such cores can be considered as a processor in a specific SMP system. Of course, a multicore system differs from an SMP system, but these differences are almost imperceptible to the user (until they think about subtle optimization of the program).

NUMA technology – nonuniform memory access – is often used to speed up work with memory. In this case, each processor has its own channel to memory, with a part of memory directly connected to it, and the rest – through a common bus. Now the access to "own" memory will be fast and to "others" memory – slower (see Figure 4-6). If this architecture is used correctly in an application, you can get a significant acceleration. The significant problem in both cases is that each processor (or CPU core) uses its own cache, which increases the speed, but makes possible invalid data to be processed. To prevent it, caches should be synchronized (or be coherent), which can lead to performance degradation. If each processor (or core) uses its own memory region, and there is no need to synchronize caches, performance should be good.

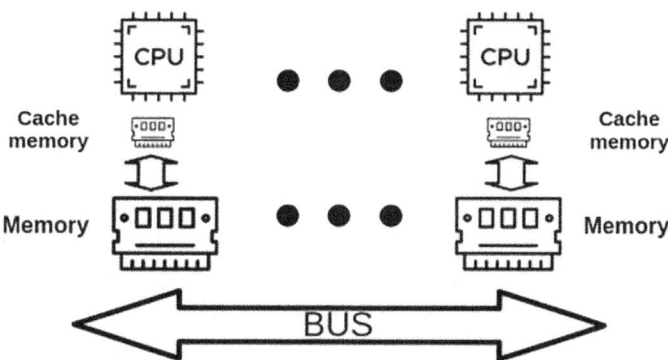

Figure 4-6. *NUMA architecture*

Another "roadblock" in modern multicore systems is the migration of processes between cores. In general, to organize the work of multiple processes, the operating system gives each process a certain period of time (usually about milliseconds), after which the process is switched to passive mode.

The task scheduler, when moving a process out of passive mode, selects a CPU core that is not necessarily the same as the one on which the process was running before. It often happens that a process "walks" on all the cores available in the system. Even in the case of SMP systems, the influence of the speed of program operation at such migration is noticeable, and in NUMA systems, it also leads to large delays at memory access.

In order to get rid of the parasitic influence of process migration between cores, processor affinity (processor pinning) is used. Binding can be performed either to a single core or to several cores or even to one or more NUMA nodes. With pinning, process migration will either occur in a controlled manner or will be eliminated altogether. You can use `numactl` utility to "pin" processes to one or set of CPUs; most implementations of MPI (see later) can set pinning for you.

A similar problem is present in the mechanism of memory allocation to user processes. Suppose a process running on one NUMA node needs to allocate additional memory for its work. In what memory area will the new block be allocated? What if it falls on a rather remote NUMA node, which will sharply reduce the speed of exchange? In order to avoid memory allocation on third-party nodes, there is a mechanism of binding processes to the memory of a certain NUMA node (memory affinity).

In a normal case, each process of a parallel program is bound to certain NUMA node both by core and memory. So the parallel program's speed will not depend on the launch and will be rather stable. When launching parallel programs, such binding is not just desirable but obligatory. This question is considered in more detail in the chapter "System Libraries for Supporting Parallel Computations" where various parallel programming environments are described.

Many modern processors utilize **HyperThreading** technology (or analogs). Thanks to this technology, each compute core is represented in the system as two separate cores, sharing the same computational devices, but having separated code processing modules and registers. Of course, the efficiency of hardware resources utilization in this case highly depends on how the program is written and what libraries and compiler it is built with. In most cases, parallel computing programs are written quite efficiently, so there may be no acceleration from using HyperThreading technology, and even on the contrary, there will be a slowdown from its use, because computational devices are used concurrently.

On supercomputers, this technology can be disabled in the BIOS of each node at all so as not to introduce additional difficulties in the work of parallel programs. As a rule, this technology does not bring acceleration for compute programs. If you use a small set of programs on a supercomputer, test their work with HyperThreading enabled and disabled and choose the best option. I'd recommend that you **enable it**, but tell the task management system **the number of cores as with HT disabled**. This allows you to get additional resources for system services while minimizing the impact on compute tasks. If your task management system detects number of cores automatically, and it cannot be overridden, I strongly recommend to **disable HT**.

Another feature of the architecture concerns not a single node, but several nodes. As it was mentioned earlier, compute nodes in a compute cluster are united by a high-speed communication network. Such a network can provide additional possibilities of data exchange between the processes of parallel programs launched on many compute nodes. Within one node the **Direct Memory Access (DMA)** technology is used, which allows the node devices to communicate with the main memory without the processor's participation. For example, data exchange with a hard disk or network adapter can be organized using **DMA technology**.

The InfiniBand adapter, using DMA technology, provides the ability to access the memory of a remote node without processor participation on the remote node (**Remote Direct Memory Access** or **RDMA** technology). In this case, it will be necessary to synchronize processor caches (we will not consider this aspect in detail). Application of RDMA technology allows solving some problems of scalability and resource utilization efficiency.

CHAPTER 4 SUPERCOMPUTER HARDWARE

In addition to InfiniBand, there is a protocol, called **RoCE** (RDMA over Converged Ethernet), which allows the use many of InfiniBand calls (verbs) to utilize RDMA with Ethernet cards, which support it. It can reduce the price, but please, be aware that overall speed and latency will be still worse than in case of InfiniBand, and you will miss such features as subnet manager, effective topologies, and a lot of included counters.

Brief Summary

Knowledge of hardware, basic principles of your networks, data storage, and other "hardware" components is very important for a supercomputer administrator. Without this knowledge, it is often impossible to solve problems arising in such computing complexes.

Search Keywords

numa, smp, cache, multiprocessor, latency

CHAPTER 5

InfiniBand

Let's separately take a look at InfiniBand network technology. On the one hand, this technology is widespread in the world of high-performance computing, and many administrators of HPC clusters have to deal with this technology in their work. But on the other hand, InfiniBand is quite different from Ethernet, which most network administrators are used to, and there are many difficulties when getting acquainted with it for the first time.

InfiniBand standard is developed by the InfiniBand Trade Association; InfiniBand is an open technology whose standards are published and available, although there are vendor-proprietary extensions. There is also a set of open source software called **OFED** (OpenFabrics Enterprise Distribution), which contains everything needed to work with InfiniBand-based networks (except for adapter drivers, perhaps). InfiniBand equipment manufacturing companies may also release their own versions of the software stack. Most often they include OFED and additional components oriented to work with the equipment of a particular vendor.

A link in an InfiniBand network consists of multiple lanes operating in parallel. Each link works as a serial bidirectional communication channel. The most commonly used links are 4x links (four lanes working in parallel). 12x links are mostly used to connect individual elements, most frequently switch chips, within one large switch, but the latest standards are going to use it for regular links too. The speed of data transmission over the line depends on the generation of the InfiniBand standard. PCB connections, copper wires (for short distances), and optical cables can be used for data transmission, often sold with transmitters. See Table 5-1 for information on data transmission speeds.

InfiniBand networking materials usually specify the "raw" data rate, i.e., the rate at which data is physically transmitted over the transmission medium. In this case, the user data is encoded before transmission to recover from possible line errors. For SDR-QDR generations, the 8 bits of user data are turned into 10 bits to be transmitted, and for

FDR-EDR generations, 64/66 encoding is used, for NDR and higher – 256/257. Therefore, the bandwidth available for user data transmission will be lower than that specified in the specification.

Table 5-1. Performance of InfiniBand networks

	Old standards			
	SDR	DDR	QDR	FDR
Raw data transfer rate, Gbps	2.5	5	10	14.0625
Theoretical effective communication bandwidth 4x, Gbps	8	16	32	54.4
12x communication bandwidth, Gbps	24	48	96	163.2
Coding method	8/10	8/10	8/10	64/66
	Modern standards			
	HDR	NDR	XDR	GDR
Raw data transfer rate, Gbps	53.125	106.25	200	400
Theoretical effective communication bandwidth 4x, Gbps	200	400	800	1600
12x communication bandwidth, Gbps	600	1200	2400	4800
Coding method	64/66	256/257	Not known yet	Not known yet

An InfiniBand Host Channel Adapter (**HCA**) is installed in each device connected to the InfiniBand network (a cluster node, typically referred to in InfiniBand literature as a Processor Node, Storage Server, etc.). The standard provides a simplified version of the HCA, called TCA (Target Channel Adapter), which was intended to be used for connecting storage systems, but this type of adapter has not become widespread.

An adapter can have several ports to connect to the network. An InfiniBand network (also called InfiniBand Fabric) consists of adapters that are connected by switches and routers. Switches and routers always have more than one port. Each switch has a dedicated virtual port 0, through which the switch can be managed.

The ports to which packets can be directed are called end ports. A set of adapters connected by switches make up a subnet. Subnets have a limit on the number of devices it can contain – no more than $2^{15} + 2^{14} - 1 = 49,151$ end ports and switches. Subnets are connected using routers, allowing the creation of InfiniBand fabrics of virtually unlimited size.

Component Identification and Addressing in InfiniBand Networks

InfiniBand network components have identifiers called GUIDs (globally unique ID), which are 64 bits long. Depending on the type of device, there may be more than one of these identifiers. GUIDs are assigned by the device manufacturer, although there may be means to change them. Each adapter has a NodeGUID and one PortGUID for each port of the adapter. One of the PortGUIDs can be the same as the adapter's NodeGUID. The switch also has a NodeGUID and a PortGUID, but all PortGUIDs must be the same for all switch ports.

There is also an identifier called SystemImage GUID. Its purpose is to allow you to determine which components make up a single system (are under the control of a single software instance). For multichip switches, e.g., this parameter is the same for all elementary switches that make up one large composite switch. For adapters installed in a single server, this parameter will be different because each adapter has an independent management program (what is called firmware). SystemImage GUID can be equal to the NodeGUID of one of the components that make up a single system, or null if the component is not part of any system (or the vendor does not want to allow the components of their system to be identified).

GUIDs are used to identify the components of an InfiniBand network, i.e., to distinguish one component from another. They are not used as addresses for data transmission. LIDs (local ID) are used as addresses for data transmission within a subnetwork. GIDs (global ID) are used as addresses when transferring data between subnets. GIDs can also be used for data transmission within the same subnet, but addressing with GIDs requires an additional GRH (Global Routing Header) in the data packet, which increases the size of the service information in the data packet.

The local ID – **LID** – is 16 bits long. LID = 0 is reserved and cannot be used; LIDs from 1 to 0xBFFF are regular LIDs used for point-to-point (unicast) transmission; LIDs from 0xC000 to 0xFFFE are for multicast; LID = 0xFFFF is a so-called permissive LID, a packet addressed to such an LID will be processed by the first port to receive it. Each end port and each switch (the LID is assigned to the switch as a whole, not to its individual ports) in the subnet is assigned at least one LID during its initialization, and LIDs should be unique within the same subnet.

The available number of LIDs results in a limit on the number of devices in the subnet. The LID of the packet recipient is used by switches to determine which port to forward the received packet to: entries in the forwarding table of switches use the LID as the key. To simplify the processing of subnets, where there are many possible alternative routes between given pairs of points, a port or switch can be assigned several LIDs. In this case, a Base LID and an LMC (LID Mask Control) are assigned. The LMC is a number between 0 and 128.

The lower LMC bits of the Base LID must be zero, and it is considered that the port is assigned 2LMC of consecutive LID values, i.e., the values from `Base LID` to `Base LID + 2LMC - 1`. If only one LID is assigned to a port, then LMC = 0. Typically, no more than two LMC values are used per subnet: one for assigning LIDs to adapter ports and one (most often zero) for assigning LIDs to switches.

The global ID – **GID** – is 128 bits long. It is assigned to each end port. In fact, a GID is an IPv6 address in which the lower 64 bits are the GUID of the port to which the GID is assigned. The higher 64 bits of the GID (GID Prefix) default to `0xFE80::/64` (see RFC2373 for details on the textual representation of IPv6 addresses and prefixes). The scope of this prefix is the subnet (link-local scope). Data packets with a destination GID with this prefix will not be transmitted by routers between subnets, i.e., GIDs with this prefix can only be used to transmit data within a subnet. One (or none) GID prefix other than the default prefix can be assigned during subnet initialization. The GID with the default prefix should still work as the port GID.

Prefix `0xFEC0::/64` is a site-local scope prefix. Data packets destined for such addresses can be transmitted by routers from subnet to subnet, but must not leave the site-local scope.

A global scope prefix can also be assigned, and should be chosen according to the rules established for IPv6 addresses.

In addition to unicast GIDs, there are also GIDs designed for multicast data transmission. The prefix of multicast GIDs has the high byte `0xFF`; the meaning of the other prefix bits can be found in RFC2373 and RFC2375.

In addition to LID and GID addressing, there is another addressing method, directed route addressing. This method can only be used for sending subnet management packets (SMP). It is mainly used during initial subnet initialization, when ports are not yet assigned LIDs and switch forwarding tables are not set, or after rebooting an adapter or switch, when access to them using LIDs is not yet possible. In directed route addressing mode, the packet lists the switch ports through which the data packet must pass (initial path). The packet also contains a hop count that indicates the number of elements in the port list, a pointer to the current element in the port list (hop pointer), a D direction pointer (direction, 0 – the packet is forwarded from the source to the destination of the request, 1 – the packet contains a response and is forwarded toward the source of the original request), and a reverse path.

Upon receiving a packet with field D = 0, the switch uses the pointer to the current hop pointer element to determine the port to which the received packet should be routed, writes the port number through which the packet was received to the reverse path field to store the reverse route, and increments the hop pointer field by one. If the list runs out, the receiver processes the packet, generates a reply, changes the direction pointer to reverse path (sets the D field to 1), and sends the reply. When receiving a packet in which the direction pointer is set to reverse, the switches use the reverse route to determine the port to forward, and accordingly do not write a new reverse route, and decrease the hop pointer value by one at each step.

In addition to a pure directed route, it is also possible to specify the LID of the switch to which the packet should be forwarded using normal addressing (by LID) and the LID of the destination to which the packet should be forwarded after the path defined by the directed route has been traveled. Obviously, the parts of the fabric before and after the path defined by the directed route must already be initialized and support LID-based forwarding.

InfiniBand Subnet Management

As it was mentioned above, for normal operation, the InfiniBand subnet must be configured: LIDs are assigned to adapter and switch ports, and switch forwarding tables are configured (unlike Ethernet networks, in InfiniBand networks, switches do not form their own forwarding tables; it must be configured externally).

The component that is responsible for configuring and then maintaining the subnet is the **subnet manager** (SM). A subnet manager is a program that can run on a computer with an InfiniBand adapter or on the switch (not all InfiniBand switches support running SM). For reliability, several managers can be launched in a subnet, in which case one of them is the master and the others are standby. In case the master manager stops working, one of the standby managers takes over its functions. The master manager can also explicitly delegate the role of master to one of the standby managers, e.g., during a normal shutdown.

Once started, the subnet manager uses subnet management packets transmitted via directed routes to find out the structure of the subnet: which adapters, switches, routers, and which links there are between them. If after determining the subnet structure it turns out that there are no other higher priority SM in this subnet, this manager becomes active and configures the subnet, i.e., assigns LIDs to all end ports, tells each end port the LID of the port on which the SM is working, sets up switch forwarding tables, and makes some other settings. After that, the subnet is ready for operation. While the subnet is running, the SM receives notifications about changes to the network structure and reconfigures the subnet accordingly. The SM also periodically collects information about the topology of the subnet from scratch, like when the subnet initialization occurs, not relying on the reliability of topology changes notifications. This process is called **Sweeping**.

The spare managers poll the master from time to time, and if the master stops responding, one of the spare managers becomes the master and reconfigures the subnet by pointing it to the location of the new SM.

Note that bad ports in the network (node hangs, bad cable, etc.) slow down the collection, and SM sweep time, which can lead to the overall network failures, such as nodes network loss, shared file system break, etc. The same can happen if the spare SM takeover takes too long.

In the modern IB networks, you can see **Uniform Fabric Manager** (UFM), which also has the role of SM. UFM usually has more features than a regular SM, like WebUI, regular network check and sending reports, etc. It is required if you need support for NVIDIA Scalable Hierarchical Aggregation and Reduction Protocol (SHARP). This technology allows performing many collective operations, like barriers, summation, etc., directly on the switches, and UFM is required to configure them accordingly.

IP Over InfiniBand (IP Over IB, IPoIB)

The operation of the TCP/IP protocol stack over InfiniBand is not part of the InfiniBand specification; it is defined in the relevant RFC documents. InfiniBand operation is quite possible without IPoIB. However, some programs and libraries, although designed to work over InfiniBand, also require working IP over InfiniBand. Most often IPoIB is used to determine InfiniBand identifiers (LIDs, GIDs) of processes running on other compute nodes, and once determined, further communications are performed without the TCP/IP stack.

Configuring IP over InfiniBand is basically the same as configuring IP over Ethernet. There are only a few things to pay attention to.

The IPoIB interfaces in the system usually are called ib0, ib1, etc. (one interface per InfiniBand port). It is better to assign addresses statically by writing them in the configuration files of servers and compute nodes. DHCP protocol over IPoIB is possible, but for reliability, it is not recommended to use it.

The link layer address, which in Ethernet networks are called MAC address or hardware address for IPoIB, has a length of 20 bytes. That is why some utilities, in particular, the widely used ifconfig utility, in which the length of Ethernet MAC address is fixed at 6 bytes, cannot work correctly, and display link layer addresses for IPoIB. The ip utility, which is recommended to replace ifconfig, does not have this disadvantage. The link layer address contains the GID of the port, the Queue Pair Number (QPN, analogous to the TCP port number for InfiniBand), and flags indicating which InfiniBand transport layer protocols can be used for IP transmission.

Utilities for InfiniBand Network Viewing and Managing

In this section, a number of examples of output is given from some utilities in the OFED kit with explanations of the output information. This information will help you to understand what is happening in the InfiniBand network and diagnose some errors in its operation.

The ibstat command shows the status of all ports on all InfiniBand adapters installed on the host where it is running.

```
CA 'mlx5_0'
    CA type: MT4113
    Number of ports: 2
    Firmware version: 10.12.1100
    Hardware version: 0
    Node GUID: 0x00123456000073f0
    System image GUID: 0x00123456000073f0
    Port 1:
            State: Active
            Physical state: LinkUp
```

```
              Rate: 56
              Base lid: 913
              LMC: 0
              SM lid: 43
              Capability mask: 0x26516848
              Port GUID: 0x00123456000073f0
              Link layer: InfiniBand
    Port 2:
              State: Active
              Physical state: LinkUp
              Rate: 56
              Base lid: 1361
              LMC: 0
              SM lid: 698
              Capability mask: 0x26516848
              Port GUID: 0x002658020000073f8
              Link layer: InfiniBand
```

First, the adapter information is displayed: its name (`mlx5_0`), adapter type (model name), number of ports, firmware and hardware versions, as well as Node GUID and System Image GUID.

For each port, the `Link layer` line displays the connection type: InfiniBand or Ethernet. Some InfiniBand adapters allow both InfiniBand and Ethernet connections. The connection type is determined by the transceiver installed, and the adapter should be set up accordingly. The `Port GUID` line shows the GUID of the port. `Base lid` is the first LID assigned to the port. There are a total of two consecutive LIDs assigned to the port, as mentioned above. `SM lid` – The LID of the port on which this subnet manager is running. Rate – The baud rate at which the port is operating (56 in this case is 4x FDR mode).

`Physical state` – The state of the physical layer of data transmission. The normal state is `LinkUp`. It can also be `Disabled`, `Polling` (the port enters this state after powering on), `Configuration` (coordination of operating modes with the other side of the link), and `Recovery` (recovery after a link failure). There are other states, but their appearance means a serious failure in the operation of the equipment, and I will not describe them here.

`State` – State of the data transmission link layer. `Active` – States of normal operation, any type of data transmission is possible. `Down` – Data transmission is impossible (the physical layer has not yet entered the `LinkUp` state). `Initialize` – The state to which the link layer passes immediately after the physical layer has passed to the `LinkUp` state. In this state, only SMP (subnet management packets) can be received and transmitted. In this state, the subnet manager must configure the port (set the LID and other parameters) and put the port in the `Active state`. There are other states, but ports should not be in them for a long time, so I will skip their descriptions.

`Capability mask` – A set of flags describing the modes of operation (speeds, etc.) supported by the port.

The `ibstatus` command also outputs information about all ports, but in a slightly different format, and produces a partially different set of data:

```
InfiniBand device 'mlx5_0' port 1 status:
    default gid: fe90:0000:0000:0000:0000:0026:5802:0000:73f0
    base lid: 0x391
    sm lid: 0x2b
    state: 4: ACTIVE
    phys state: 5: LinkUp
    rate: 56 Gb/sec (4X FDR)
    link_layer: InfiniBand

InfiniBand device 'mlx5_0' port 2 status:
    default gid: fea0:0000:0000:0000:0000:0012:3456:0000:73f8
    base lid: 0x551
    sm lid: 0x2ba
    state: 4: ACTIVE
    phys state: 5: LinkUp
    rate: 56 Gb/sec (4X FDR)
    link_layer: InfiniBand
```

Note that the base LID and subnet manager LID information is given in hexadecimal. More detailed information about the speed at which the port operates is given. Also added the `default gid` line, which specifies the GID for the port.

CHAPTER 5   INFINIBAND

Really useful command is `ibdev2netdev`; it shows you IB interfaces and corresponding network interfaces with network status. Here is an example:

```
mlx5_0 port 1 ==> eth0 (Up)
mlx5_1 port 1 ==> ib0 (Up)
```

Note that the first interface is Ethernet, most probably RoCE, which means that IB utilities can interact with it.

Extremely important command is `perfquery`; it reads performance counters from **any point** of the IB network. That means you can check how many packets were dropped by the remote compute node being on a management node, connected to the IB network, e.g., `perfquery -a 123` – read all basic counters from device with LID 123. If you want to specify GUID, add `-G` switch in the front of all options. If you want to get extended counters, use `-x` option instead of `-a`. For different series of IB devices, list of the supported counters can vary. To collect most significant errors from the network, you can use `ibqueryerrors` command. For RoCE network, this may not work; in this case, you should use `ethtool -S device_name`, e.g., `ethtool -S eth0`.

If you need a deeper look, and you have Mellanox (NVIDIA) adapters, you can use `mlxlink` command to get more details about the adapter and cables. Here is an example of how to get counters from the device (`-c`):

```
# mlxlink -d mlx5_1 -c

Operational Info
----------------
State                         : Active
Physical state                : LinkUp
Speed                         : IB-EDR
Width                         : 4x
FEC                           : No FEC
Loopback Mode                 : No Loopback
Auto Negotiation              : ON

Supported Info
--------------
Enabled Link Speed            : 0x0000003f (EDR,FDR,FDR10,QDR,DDR,SDR)
Supported Cable Speed         : 0x0000003f (EDR,FDR,FDR10,QDR,DDR,SDR)
```

```
Troubleshooting Info
--------------------
Status Opcode                      : 0
Group Opcode                       : N/A
Recommendation                     : No issue was observed.

Physical Counters and BER Info
------------------------------
Time Since Last Clear [Min]        : 12824.8
Effective Physical Errors          : 0
Effective Physical BER             : 15E-255
Raw Physical BER                   : 15E-255
Raw Physical Errors Per Lane       : 0,0,0,0
Link Down Counter                  : 0
Link Error Recovery Counter        : 0
```

Here BER is for "**Bit error rate**," which is low-level counter and may indicate problems, which are not shown by perfquery yet. In this example, this rate is low.

To get detailed info about the device itself, you can specify -m switch:

```
# mlxlink -d mlx5_1 -m

Operational Info
----------------
State                              : Active
Physical state                     : LinkUp
Speed                              : IB-EDR
Width                              : 4x
FEC                                : No FEC
Loopback Mode                      : No Loopback
Auto Negotiation                   : ON

Supported Info
--------------
Enabled Link Speed                 : 0x0000003f (EDR,FDR,FDR10,QDR,DDR,SDR)
Supported Cable Speed              : 0x0000003f (EDR,FDR,FDR10,QDR,DDR,SDR)
```

CHAPTER 5   INFINIBAND

```
Troubleshooting Info
--------------------
Status Opcode                     : 0
Group Opcode                      : N/A
Recommendation                    : No issue was observed.

Module Info
-----------
Identifier                        : QSFP+
Compliance                        : N/A
Cable Technology                  : 850 nm VCSEL
Cable Type                        : Active cable (active copper / optics)
OUI                               : Mellanox
Vendor Name                       : Mellanox
Vendor Part Number                : MFXXXXX-EXXX
Vendor Serial Number              : MT2135FT12345
Rev                               : B2
Attenuation (5g,7g,12g) [dB]      : N/A
FW Version                        : XX.XX.XXX
Wavelength [nm]                   : 850
Transfer Distance [m]             : 10
Digital Diagnostic Monitoring     : Yes
Power Class                       : 2.5 W max
CDR RX                            : ON,ON,ON,ON
CDR TX                            : ON,ON,ON,ON
LOS Alarm                         : N/A
Temperature [C]                   : 38 [-10..80]
Voltage [mV]                      : 3255.2 [3100..3500]
Bias Current [mA]                 : 6.750,6.750,6.750,6.750 [5.492..8.5]
Rx Power Current [dBm]            : 0,0,0,0 [-14..6]
Tx Power Current [dBm]            : 0,0,0,0 [-12..6]
```

   --json switch can be used to get the output in JSON format and use it in your scripts! There is much more information you can get, but usually it is needed only in rare cases.

In case you want to check the connectivity between two ports, you can use `ibping`. In the contrast to regular `ping`, you have to start server process on the other side first: `ibping -S`, then you can ping it as `ibping 123` (here we are pinging LID 123).

Sometimes it is necessary to find out which machine a particular LID is assigned to. The `smpquery` utility can be used for this purpose. In general, this utility is designed to send SMP (subnet management packet) and provide answers in a human-understandable form. In our case, we need a request for a node description. Here is an example of issuing the `smpquery nodedesc 914` command (request for node description with LID 914):

```
Node Description:...................n51001 HCA-1
```

The node responded that LID 914 is assigned to the HCA-1 adapter of the compute node named n51001.

With `smpquery`, information about the node to which the query is addressed is available. At the same time, the subnet manager has information about all nodes in the subnet. You can request information from the subnet manager using the `saquery` utility. Information about a subnet node with LID 914 can be requested with the `saquery 914` command. Here is an example of how to issue such a command:

```
NodeRecord dump:
          lid.....................914
          reserved................0x0
          base_version............0x1
          class_version...........0x1
          node_type...............Channel Adapter
          num_ports...............2
          sys_guid................0x0012345600003740
          node_guid...............0x0012345600003740
          port_guid...............0x0012345600003740
          partition_cap...........0x80
          device_id...............0x1011
          revision................0x0
          port_num................1
          vendor_id...............0x2C9
          NodeDescription.........n51001 HCA-1
```

CHAPTER 5   INFINIBAND

The last line provides a description of the node, including the hostname. Additional information is also provided. Once again, please note that the smpdump command allows you to request information about a node in the InfiniBand network from the node itself, while the saquery command allows you to request information about the node from the subnet manager. If the results of these queries are different, or if the saquery command gives an error, it is an indication that there is a problem with the subnet manager.

Two more useful utilities for troubleshooting InfiniBand networks are ibnetdiscover and ibdiagnet. The ibnetdiscover tries to find all subnet components, end nodes, switches, routers, and links between them, and displays information about all found components. The ibdiagnet utility also tries to find all subnet components, but it also tries to find subnet configuration errors, such as matching GUIDs, port speeds, etc. I should also note ibswitches, and ibnodes, which are a quick way to get the network inventory.

I'm not going to give examples of these utilities because they are quite large, and for ibdiagnet, the output also consists of several files. I mention these utilities to have an idea of what tools can be used to diagnose issues with the InfiniBand network.

Utilities that send information to the network have options to select the adapter and port to work with (remember that the same LID can refer to different devices in different subnets). The -C key is used to specify the adapter (e.g., mlx4_0 in the examples above), and the -P key is used to specify the port number of the specified adapter (ports are numbered starting from 1).

ofed_info – Useful command if you need to get information about your OFED version and other details.

In the end of this subchapter - some information, which can help you debug user's applications errors. Most communications via RDMA are made using so-called "queue pairs," or QP. QP can be created in two modes – connected mode (dedicated QP) or datagram mode. In the first case, QP can be used only for one dedicated connection between two peers, while in the datagram mode, data can be sent to many destinations and received from many sources. There are two types of connections – "reliable" and "unreliable". In case of "reliable connection" every time the data is sent, it is required to get a confirmation, that the data was received. If no confirmation was gotten, the data is re-sent. In case of "Unreliable connection" there is no control if data was received or dropped.

Alternatives

Today, real alternatives to InfiniBand are **RoCE** and **SlingShot**. RoCE may be cheaper but usually lacks advanced routing and still had higher real latency. In addition, you miss the network observability. SlingShot is very similar to InfiniBand; it has FabricManager, similar to SubnetManager in IB, supports wide range of topologies, has convenient network management tools, and has low latency and high speed and Ethernet compatibility. The key disadvantages of SlingShot in my opinion are limited community and in fact computational software support via libfabric.[1] Libfabric is an open source and well-supported initiative, which allows using almost any network for the communication with low overhead. But still the libfabric itself is the overhead and gives slightly lower performance than raw IB verbs.

Brief Summary

InfiniBand and RoCE are bare-bones of the modern HPC, so fine-tuning and diagnostics of these networks significantly impacts the overall supercomputer performance.

Search Keywords

InfiniBand, OFED, rdma, hpc interconnect, latency, performance counters

---

[1] https://ofiwg.github.io/libfabric/

CHAPTER 6

How a Supercomputer Does the Job

Which software stack is necessary to make a supercomputer alive? Let's try to look at this stack:

- Operating system
- The system software, which is required for hardware operation – drivers, etc., as well as software for the network file system
- Overall system control software (boot, images, etc.), remote access software, monitoring
- Task control system (queuing system, batch system)
- Applied software – software required for parallel programs, like parallel packages and libraries, e.g., MPI, CUDA, etc.

An optional, but frequently required, component is compilers and additional libraries often required for compute programs, such as BLAS, FFT, etc. If your users are developers, or you plan to use applications, which require compilation (e.g., VASP, NAMD, etc.), this is really needed, because compilation on the target architecture usually turns on all needed optimizations, which maximizes performance, and makes the installation easier.

For complete management of the supercomputer, you will also need software for backup, alerting, statistics, and visualization of the supercomputer state.

How a Typical User Session Occurs

There are many options for organizing work with specific compute packages that provide their own interface for working with a supercomputer. Let's consider the "general" variant.

So, a user is working on their computer – workstation, laptop, tablet, etc. To start a session, they start an ssh client (putty, openssh, IDE ssh plug-in, etc.), enter an address, login, specify a password or a private key file (or use a profile where all this is already specified), and open a connection to the supercomputer. Depending on the organization requirements, additional access procedures may be used, 2FA, key certificates, etc. Once at the access node, the user can access local files, edit and compile their own parallel programs, scripts, copy input data via sftp protocol, etc.

To start a program, the user executes a special command that queues his job. The job queue (or often "partition") is implemented by a **job management system**, and users talk to it using special commands. In the command, they specify the number of required parallel processes, possibly the number of nodes and other preferences, like memory, GPUs, licenses, etc., as well as the program and its arguments. The user can check the status of their job and see the list of job in the queue. If it turns up that there is an error in the program, the user can cancel it or remove it from the queue if it has not yet started.

If necessary, the user can submit to the queue several jobs (e.g., if they need to process several sets of input data). Once a job is queued, its I/O will be redirected to the files, so user can safely end the session and check the job status or view/download the results later in another session. Most job management systems allow you to run a job interactively as well, linking its I/O to the user's terminal. In this case, you will have to leave the session open till the job is finished.

All work is done at the command line, so the user must know the minimum set of Linux commands (usually this is not a problem). An elementary Linux self-study book or even a page on a website with a description of the necessary commands is sufficient in general. For file management, many users use the Midnight Commander (mc) program, which makes the job even easier.

Job Life Cycle

A typical job on a supercomputer goes through several phases. The first phase is queuing the job. In this phase, the user specifies the path to the executable program, its arguments, and startup parameters, such as the number of MPI processes, number of nodes, node requirements, etc. Explicitly or implicitly, the user also specifies how the job should be started – via the `mpirun` or `mpiexec` command (for MPI applications), as a regular application, etc.

The job management system regularly checks whether a new job can be started by reviewing the queue. As soon as our job reaches the beginning of the queue or is otherwise suitable for launching, the management system (or rather, its scheduler) will select a set of nodes on which to launch, notify them, possibly execute an initialization script (the so-called prologue), and proceed to launch the job.

The startup phase may vary from system to system, but the general idea is the same: a startup process, such as `mpirun`, is started on a compute or management node and is passed a list of nodes and other parameters. This process starts job workflows on the compute nodes, either by itself (via ssh) or with the help of the job management system. From this point on, the job management system considers the job to be running. It can monitor the state of the workflows on the nodes, if supported, or it can monitor only the state of the start process. As soon as the start process terminates or the job is forcibly canceled (either by the user or by the job management system itself), the job enters the termination phase.

In this phase, the control system tries to terminate the job correctly – to make sure that all its processes have finished, there are no unnecessary files left in temporary directories, etc. A separate script, the so-called epilogue, is often used for this purpose. At the end of the termination phase, the job is considered completed. For some time, information about it may be stored in the management system, but usually, the data about it can now only be found in logs. In the described cycle, there can be nonstandard actions, e.g., changing the priority of a job that changes the speed of its passing in the queue, blocking that temporarily prohibits the start of the job, suspending the job, and some others.

What Is Hidden from the User

All that was described above is what is visible to the average user. However, there is also something that remains "behind the scenes" for the user, but plays an important role for the administrator. These are the services that ensure correct operation of the supercomputer: account management, distributed file system, quota management, remote node monitoring, statistics collection and journaling, equipment and infrastructure monitoring, emergency notification and shutdown, and backup. All these services work invisibly for the user, but their importance can hardly be overestimated.

CHAPTER 6   HOW A SUPERCOMPUTER DOES THE JOB

Brief Summary

You can build the simplest computing cluster "on the knee": take two laptops, connect them to a common network, set up passwordless access via ssh, run an NFS server on one of them, and mount an NFS file system on the other, and – done, you can run MPI programs. But the performance of such a cluster is very low, and when you try to connect 20 laptops instead of 2, problems arise: the network cannot cope with the load, NFS slows down, one laptop hangs, and it takes us half an hour to figure out what happened, and much more.

If the cluster is not a "toy" cluster, but is intended for real jobs, then its planning and operation must be taken seriously. We have briefly outlined the main components of the supercomputer software "stack"; further, we will try to consider them in detail.

Search Keywords

MPI, session, ssh client, NFS

CHAPTER 7

UNIX and Linux – the Basics

If you already use Linux and have a good idea of its administration, you can safely **skip this chapter**. If the information in this chapter is completely new to you, it is advisable to read additional literature and practice writing scripts in bash for further reading.

In any case, I recommend checking out the books on the list below; they have a wealth of information useful even to seasoned professionals:

> Evi Nemeth, Garth Snyder, Trent Hayne, Ben Whaley.
>
> *Unix and Linux: A System Administrator's Guide*

This is a classic textbook on Unix and Linux. It often refers to ancient systems such as VAX and PDP-11, but it still captures the essence of UNIX perfectly and is still relevant today.

> Thomas Limoncelli, Christina Hogan, Strata Chaylap.
>
> *System and Network Administration. Practical Guide*

An updated Linux tutorial contains tons of useful examples.

> Brian Kernighan, Rob Pike
>
> *Unix – Software Environment*

This book is more about programming both in the bash shell and with other tools. Even if you don't have to do this regularly, I strongly suggest reading this book, as it will reveal to you the principles that govern how to work in UNIX; you will become more familiar with many of the processes that occur within the OS.

> Thomas Limoncelli
>
> *Time Management for System Administrators*

CHAPTER 7   UNIX AND LINUX – THE BASICS

The title speaks for itself. The book contains many situations in which any system administrator finds himself and practical advice on how to get out of them with minimal losses.

This chapter does not pretend to be a textbook on UNIX, but I have tried to collect in it all the basic concepts that you will need to know later on. The vast majority of supercomputers today use a UNIX-like operating system. I say "UNIX-like" because the legendary UNIX OS in its pure form is not developed and practically not used nowadays.

Brief historical background. After the breakup of AT&T, which developed the operating system, the UNIX trademark and the rights to the original source code changed hands several times, most notably for a long time they belonged to Novell. In 1993, Novell transferred the rights to the trademark and to certify the software for compliance with this mark to the X/Open consortium, which then merged with the Open Software Foundation and is now called "The Open Group." This consortium develops open standards for operating systems, such as POSIX (now renamed the Single UNIX Specification).

According to The Open Group, only systems certified to the Single UNIX Specification can bear the name "UNIX." Currently, numerous operating systems have passed different versions of this certification, e.g., Solaris, AIX.

Even those operating systems that have not passed UNIX certification (e.g., Linux) try to comply with these standards. This is why the architecture of applications on these OSes is very similar, and porting an application from one OS to another is easy, especially if only standard libraries and functions were used to write the program.

It is these qualities and the immense popularity of UNIX in the past, as well as its well-established successors – Solaris, OpenBSD, FreeBSD, AIX, and, of course, Linux – that have given UNIX-like OSes leadership on servers around the world.

Computing clusters and supercomputers are no exception. The de facto standard here is Linux. It is this operating system that we will focus on. Although there are many installations on other operating systems, such as Windows, FreeBSD, Solaris, and others, we will not dwell on their peculiarities in the HPC class in this book.

Processes

The basic concept in any OS is a process. It is something like a container (actually – a description in OS tables) containing a unique identifier (PID), rights (owner, group, and some others), program code, data area, stack, set of memory pages, table of open files, and other attributes. For the OS, a process is a unit of processor time scheduling; each process can be executed as follows: processor, pending execution, system call state (pass a request to the OS and wait for a response), stopped, and or terminated. They are denoted as **R** (running), **S** (sleeping), **D** (uninterruptible sleep), **T** (stopped), and **Z** (zombie).

For example, if you run 10 π calculation programs on a computer with two cores, then only two will be able to count simultaneously. But the OS will pause the active process with a high frequency (e.g., 100 times per second), put it in the queue and send the next process from the queue (very roughly, but the essence is exactly the same). For the process, it looks like it monopolizes the processor; it's just that the speed of this processor is five times slower than it could be.

The average number of processes in the queue is referred to as "**Load Average.**" If it is higher than the number of cores, it usually means that not all tasks "get" the processor and work slower. It should be taken into account that the queue also includes processes in **D** state, i.e., a high LA can cause processes that, e.g., read a lot from disk or write (and constantly wait for read or write calls). So high LA is a signal that something is potentially wrong, but it is good to check it.

A process is stopped only if another process has sent it a STOP signal. In this case, it "freezes" and stops executing until it receives the CONT signal (or is terminated). If the process is in state **D,** the signal is ignored, and in most cases, you cannot do anything to clear it. In principle, the process can ignore the STOP signal, but this is rarely done.

The zombie state occurs when a process has terminated, but its parent has not "acknowledged" it (has not called the wait system call). This is done so that the parent process can get data about how the process terminated. That is, processes in the zombie state do not consume any resources, neither processor and memory. For the same reason, they cannot be forced to terminate – they are already terminated.

Every process in the system has a parent process (PPID); if the parent process has terminated, it becomes a process with PID 1 (usually a special init process in the system, we will talk about it below), which performs a wait for all such processes.

CHAPTER 7   UNIX AND LINUX – THE BASICS

You can view the list of processes and their status using the ps command. It has had a difficult fate, as it has historically had many, including conflicting, options in different versions of popular operating systems (UNIX, BSD, Solaris). As a result, Linux uses a GNU variant that tries to combine them. In particular, there are options that must necessarily be specified with a minus in front and others that must be specified with only no minus. Below are the most useful ones from our point of view:

```
ps fax    # all processes grouped into a tree,
          # you can see who's descended from whom
          # add 'u' flag to see processes owners too
ps aux    # all processes with most useful fields
ps -eLf   # show processes and threads
ps -eo pid,ppid,user,vsize,pmem,pcpu,stat,wchan:32,comm
          # explicitly specify the output format
          # (-e = all processes)
```

You can add w to most combinations, then the process name field (typically a program with arguments) will be wider. If you add it twice, it will be even wider, and if you add it three times, there will be no width restrictions at all.

It can be convenient to track the activity of processes in real time. This is where the top command and the newer htop command can help. They show processes in the form of a table sorted by one field and update it every five seconds (you can change the interval). In this case, only those processes that fit on the screen are shown, plus some general data about the system – CPU load, memory load, average load, and number of processes in different states.

You can switch display and sorting modes. There are several hotkeys for top; their list can be obtained by pressing 'h'. The most convenient sorting options and commands:

<Shift>+<P> – Sort processes by CPU usage

<Shift>+<M> – Sort processes by memory usage

1 – Show the load of each core or total

k – Send a signal to the process

r – Change the process priority

u – Filter by user

q – Quit

htop has a friendlier interface, uses color output where possible, displays CPU and memory load in the form of text progress bars, and can organize processes into trees (and collapse them into a single line, which is sometimes very convenient). Control keys are displayed in the bottom line in the style of Norton Commander (Midnight Commander/FAR manager).

Other useful features of htop: Space key tags/untags processes (so you can kill or do anything else with many processes if you want), s key allows to trace syscalls, made by process, l key shows opened files (using lsof, it should be installed), w key shows full command line is a separate window, and x key shows all locks. See full list of hotkeys on the man page.

I have already mentioned signals many times – they are a simple way for processes to communicate, any process can send a signal to another if it belongs to the same user (root user can send to everyone). A signal is an integer, so it doesn't convey much information, but its function is to ask a process to perform some action. All signals except STOP and KILL can be intercepted and processed; if the process does not process the signal, the OS performs a predefined action for it.

There are standard values for most signals and actions; below are the most commonly used (See Table 7-1).

Table 7-1. Some signals in Linux

Number	Designation	Action
9	KILL	Terminate immediately.
15	TERM	"Politely" end the process.
3	QUIT	Keyboard completion signal (if the Ctrl-C combination is pressed).
19	STOP	Stop execution.
18	CONT	Continue implementation.
4	ILL	Is sent to the OS if a process has attempted to execute an invalid processor instruction. By default, the process is terminated.
11	SEGV	Is sent to the OS if the process has accessed a nonexistent address in memory. By default, the process is terminated.
8	FPE	Is sent to the OS if a floating-point operation exception occurred. By default, the process is terminated.
10	USR1	Custom signal, ignored by default

The "default" actions can be changed by the process (except for the STOP and KILL signals). They can be handled or ignored. If the process terminates correctly, the process memory can be written to a so-called core file so that the cause of the error can be investigated by a debugger afterward. Whether a core file is created is determined by the OS settings and limits (see chapter on quotas).

You can send a signal from the command line with the `kill` command. For example, `kill -9 1234` will forcibly terminate the process with PID 1234, and `kill -STOP 2345` will stop the process with PID 2345. As you can see, you can use either the signal number or the signal designation. `kill -l` will show a list of all signals.

Sometimes it is necessary to send a signal not to one process, but to many, e.g., to all processes of a user. Then the `pkill` program comes to the rescue: `pkill -u foo -TERM` will send the TERM signal to all processes of the user `foo`.

It was mentioned above, the processes that are to be executed are put into a queue. They are not always executed in a row; each of them has a priority and a `nice` parameter affecting it. The higher the priority, the faster the process moves to the beginning of the queue. You cannot set the priority explicitly, but you can change the politeness (often it is also called priority for simplicity, but it is not quite true). This is done with the `nice` or `renice` command, the first one starts a program with the specified priority, and the second one changes the priority of the already started program. The higher the politeness, the lower the priority; the program will more frequently "pass" others ahead. Historically, politeness varies from -20 to +19, and a normal user cannot specify it less than 0, e.g.,

```
nice -n 15 ./my_program # start a program with low priority
renice -n -10 -p 3322 # prioritize process 3322
```

Here we change the politeness from 0 to 15 (priority down) or to -10 (priority up).

In addition to the queue for CPU resources, there is a queue for hard disk resources, several processes can read-write simultaneously and their requests will compete. This queue also has a priority; it is controlled by the `ionice` command. There are three priority classes – `idle` (execute the request if there is no one else in the queue), `best effort` (normal queue), and `real time` (the request must be executed in a given time). Within the classes, besides `idle`, there are own priorities, but in our tasks, we can limit ourselves to assigning the idle class to a process that takes a lot of time on disk operations but is not a priority:

```
ionice -c 3 -p 89 # set idle class to process with PID 89
```

The concept of a process is a basic concept in any OS. Processes and threads should not be confused; it is important to know what is real and virtual memory of a process, how shared objects (so) and dynamic linker (ld.so) work. Look for documentation on these topics in your OS distribution or in the extensive documentation on the Internet.

Access Rights

UNIX-like operating systems were originally designed as multiuser systems, which means that user data and processes need to be protected from unwanted encroachment by other users. I already mentioned "process rights", e.g. that your process cannot send a signal to a process of another user, unless you have special rights to do that. The same principle is applied to the division of rights to other objects in the OS.

The basic mechanism for separating rights in UNIX-like systems is based on the concepts of **UID** or **user ID** and **GID** or **group ID**. UIDs and GIDs are numbers, but it is common to associate text names with them. Each process has a "real" UID and GID (ruid/rgid) that does not change over time, as well as a list of additional groups to which it belongs. In addition to the real ones, a process has "effective" UIDs and GIDs (euid/egid), which define its current capabilities (i.e., they are used to determine its rights), and "saved" UIDs and GIDs (suid/sgid) – the effective UIDs/GIDs are copied into them when the UID/GID is changed. UID/GID can be changed if a process has such permission (capability) or its EUID or SUID is 0.

A user with UID = 0 usually has the text name 'root' and has almost unlimited permissions, so they are often referred to as 'superuser'.

Most typically, we have to deal with rights on the file system. Here each object (file, link, directory, device, socket, channel, hereinafter we will write "file" for brevity) has an owner and group, as well as associated rights – read, write, and execute. Typically, the octal notation or the format of the ls command is used to write them. For example, permissions with the octal code 750 (in ls output rwxr-x---) mean that the owner is allowed to read, write, and execute (rwx / 7), the group is allowed to read and execute (r-x / 5), and the rest are allowed nothing (--- / 0).

The rights are checked in this order – if the owner of the file matches the EUID, the owner's rights are taken. Otherwise, if the group or one of the additional groups coincides with the group of the file, the rights of the group are taken and otherwise the rights of "others" are taken.

For a directory, the "execute" permission means that you can enter the directory. However, you are not guaranteed to see the list of files in the directory – you need to read permission for that. Write permission means the ability to create and delete files in the directory.

Only the owner of a file (or other object) can change permissions for it. If you need to change permissions for a group, the owner must be a member of that group. And, of course, a superuser can change any rights, as well as the owner and group of any file.

As it was already mentioned, the right to write to a directory allows you to create and delete files in it, including other people's files. In order to ensure the comfort of working with shared directories, such as /tmp, and not to allow deleting other people's files, the following was invented with an additional "sticky" flag. If a directory has this flag, then only those who own the file and have write permission to the directory (and root, of course) are allowed to delete files.

Speaking of the file system, two more flags should be mentioned – suid and sgid. If a file has the suid flag, the EUID of the process will change to the owner of the file when it is started. For sgid, it is similar, but for a group. It is most often put on files whose execution is required with superuser rights, such as passwd. For scripts, they do not work. If the sgid flag is set on a directory, the files and directories created in it automatically inherit the group. The suid flag on directories is ignored.

Note that sgid flag on the directory is really useful for your users, working on the same project. Make sure that all project members have umask like 0002, i.e., new files will allow group to write by default, give a project group to the project directory and sgid bit, then all new files and directories will inherit the group and will be available for all group members to read and write.

As mentioned above, you can view permissions with the ls command. In the rights line, the first character shows the file type ('-' = file, 'd' = directory, 'l' = link, 's' = socket, etc.), then three groups of rights for owner, group, and others with three characters each 'r/-', 'w/-' 'x/-' for read, write, and execute, respectively ('-' means no rights). The sticky flag is indicated by a 't' instead of an 'x' in the 'others' group. suid/sgid flags are indicated by an 's' instead of an 'x' in the 'owner' or 'group' group, respectively. If this line is followed by a '+' character, it means that acl is installed on this file (see below).

You can change file permissions with the chmod command. Change the owner of a file with the chown command, and change the group with the chgrp command. In order to change file permissions, the chmod command needs to specify the new permissions in octal or character form. The latter option allows you to add or remove separate permissions for the owner, group, or others, e.g.,

```
chmod 660 myfile # read and write for owner and group
chmod g-w myfile # remove write acces for the group
```

In character form, chmod specifies one or more 'u/g/o/a' characters (owner, group, others, all three groups together), followed by a '+' or '-' character to set or reset permissions, and then one or more 'r/w/x' characters to indicate which permissions are affected. For example, chmod go+rx myfile would add read and execute permissions for group and others to myfile.

The system described above covers many needs, but not all. To improve it, various extensions implemented in Linux file systems have been created. One of them is **extended file attributes**. These are enabled by default and can be viewed and modified with the lsattr and chattr commands. The most important ones for us are presented in Table 7-2.

Table 7-2. Some extended attributes

Attribute	Char	Meaning
Append only	a	You can't "erase" a file; you can only overwrite the information
Compressed	c	Use compression (if supported)
Immutable	i	File cannot be modified
Secure deletion	s	File data is overwritten when deleted
Undeletable	u	File cannot be deleted
No time updates	A	Do not update the "last access time" field

If an extended attribute prohibits some action (such as deletion), this applies even to the superuser (unlike regular attributes). But the superuser can easily unset or set any of them. Another extension, usually requiring activation on the file system, is **ACL** (Access Control List). These can be viewed and modified with the getfacl and setfacl commands. They work similarly to the traditional access rights discussed above, but read/write/execute permissions can now be set for individual users and/or groups, as well as restricted by a mask. A mask is a set of "maximum" permissions from acl rules (traditional permissions do not apply) that will work. For example, let's allow user foo to read and write to the test.txt file:

```
setfacl -m u:foo:rw test.txt
getfacl test.txt
# file: test.txt
# owner: root
# group: root
user::rwx
user:foo:rw-
group::r--
mask::rwx
other::---
```

Here, the '-m' key specifies to modify acl rules. By specifying the '--set' key, you can replace rules, i.e., remove old rules and replace with new ones (multiple rules can be specified in setfacl at the same time). With the key '-x', rules can be deleted. The string 'u:foo;rw' indicates that the rule refers to a user (u = user, g = group, o = others), its name is foo, and read and write permissions are set.

Now let's set a mask - allow user foo (and others with access via acl rules) "no more than" reading:

```
setfacl -m m:r test.txt
getfacl test.txt
# file: test.txt
# owner: root
# group: root
user::rwx
user:foo:rw- #effective:r--
group::r--
mask::r--
other::---
```

As you can see, the rule remains, but write privileges are restricted by the mask.

Another useful property of ACL is rule inheritance. You can set ACL "default" on a directory, they may not be the same as ACL on the directory itself, and they will be automatically applied to all files and directories created.

I suggest you read more about Linux permissions and the options of the above commands; we have touched on them only a bit here.

Concept of Service, Key Services

I have used the terms "service" and "daemon" many times above. They all mean the same thing: a process or a group of processes that run continuously or are automatically started on demand. Their task is to serve certain requests from users, other processes, and other computers on the network. For example, the `apache` web server is a service that serves requests using the http protocol. SMTP-server is responsible for requests to transfer mail messages, etc. Let's consider the services often used in supercomputers.

Some services are launched via the "super daemon" `inetd` or its newer implementation, `xinetd`. In this case, the `inetd/xinetd` configuration file describes the required services: the start command, on which port to listen, on behalf of which user to start, etc. After launching, `inetd/xinetd` starts listening on the specified ports and upon receiving a request launches the corresponding command, which directs the established network connection to the standard input stream. This principle makes it easier to write the service and also allows for more flexible access policy customization. For example, `xinetd` allows you to specify the range of addresses from which access is allowed, the maximum number of simultaneous requests to the service, etc.

To find out if a particular service is running, you can check if the corresponding process is running (except for services started via `inetd/xinetd`), if any process is listening to the required port (if the service is bound to a port) with the `ss -lepn` command (socket stats).

Basic (but not all) services for the cluster are presented in Table 7-3.

Table 7-3. Some standard services and their ports

Service	Port	Description
sshd	22	Encrypted remote console access
nfsd	2049/...	Network file system. The actual set of ports is determined by the portmap service
portmap	111	RPC service management
smtp	25/587	Email reception
dns	53	Domain name server. A bind (named) or dnsmasq implementation is often used
bootps	63	Information for initial BOOTP booting as well as DHCP
tftp	69	Trivial File Transfer Protocol – protocol for downloading initial files over the network
http	80/443	World Wide Web protocol – WWW
ntp	123	Time synchronization
snmp	161	Protocol for managing and monitoring network devices
idap, ldaps	389, 636	Lightweight protocol for accessing catalogs (databases)
syslog	514	Remote log
rsync	873	Server side of the rsync command
nfs	2049	NFS master server
nut	3493	UPS control
x11	6000..6000+N	X server
x font server	7100	Font server for X server
bacula	9101..9103	Bacula backup
zabbix	10050/10051	Zabbix monitoring server

A more complete list can be found in the /etc/services file – it contains the correspondence of the port number to the traditionally used service. Some services are not represented in it because they are not very widespread, and, of course, nothing prevents you from running any service on a nonstandard port, don't forget about it. Via super-daemon, inetd/xinetd often runs services such as tftp, echo, ftp.

Manuals

There are several thousand commands in the UNIX system, but a few dozen commands are enough for a user to know well in normal work. In this manual, we will briefly review a small set of the most common commands. First, we will need commands for working with directories and files. As before, we will specify optional parameters in square brackets.

The most important command you will need is man. Its name comes not at all from man, but from manual. It is the main source of reference information on commands, packages, and much more in UNIX and Linux. All information in man is divided into sections, historically numbered (see Table 7-4).

Table 7-4. Sections of the man help

Number	Section
1	User commands
2	System calls
3	C standard library functions
4	Devices and special files
5	File formats and format conventions
6	Games, etc.
7	Miscellaneous
8	System administration and daemons

As a rule, to get help on a command, just type man command_name. Man command will find the first page with the given name and display it. Since there may be pages with the same name in different sections, sometimes it is necessary to specify the section number explicitly. For example, the man crontab command will display information on the crontab command from section 1. To display help on the format of the crontab file, you should type man 5 crontab, to display the list of files in which the required word is mentioned – man -k word. And of course, don't forget to execute man man.

In addition to man, there is also the info command, which was intended to replace man, but despite a lot of new features, it has not become popular. But many aspects of standard programs and services are described in info in much more detail than in man.

File Naming Conventions

One of the most common tools for UNIX is the shell. In shell, some characters have a special value (which can be overridden) – this makes it easier to work with files. Any characters except '/' and '\0' can be used in file and directory names, including those, which are used **as special in shell**. In the Table 7-5 you can see the list of shell special characters.

Table 7-5. *Shell wildcards*

Special symbol	Meaning
Backslash	Special character value escape character
Ampersand (&)	Symbol of command execution in the background
Parentheses '(', ')'	Tells the shell to run commands in a new instance of the shell
Angle braces (< and >)	Output/input redirection characters
Space ' '	Command argument delimiter
Question mark (?)	Means any character in the pattern
Dollar sign ($)	Means substituting the value of the variable
Square braces ([])	Define a range of characters
Curly braces ({ })	Define a list of values in bash
Asterisk (*)	Any (including 0) number of any characters
Vertical bar (l)	Conveyor operator
Colon (:)	In many programs separates the name of a remote server from the path to a file on that server, does not have special meaning in shell
Semicolon(;)	Character to indicate the end of a shell command
Newline (\n)	Line feed also means the end of the command in shell
Single and double quote (' ")	Used to make strings

UNIX does not prohibit the use of these characters in file names, but you must escape their special purpose with the '\' character or enclose them in single quotes '...'.

Extension Agreements

The file extension is the part of the file name after the last dot; e.g., the file 'text.cc' has the extension '.cc'. For most programs, the extension is not essential, but its presence makes it easier to understand the purpose of the file. The most common extensions are presented in Table 7-6.

Table 7-6. Common file extensions

Extension	Common usage
.c	C program file
.cc .cpp	C++ program file
.h .hpp	Include-file of C/C++ program
.f .for	Fortran program file
.o	Object file
.a	Static library
.so	Dynamic library
.html	HTML document
.tar .cpio	Archive file
.gz .bz2 .7z .zip	Compressed file

It is important to understand that the file extension is not crucial for the OS and most programs. Changing the file extension to '.exe' or '.sh' will not make the file executable. But a script named 'do_it_now' can be made executable by executing 'chmod a+x do_it_now'. Extensions just make it easier to see what the file is, so you know what it is.

Names starting with a dot (.) are supposed to be hidden and often assigned to service files and directories. These files and directories are usually ignored by programs and file managers by default, but are visible if explicitly asked. For example, the ls command does not show them unless you specify the '-a' switch.

Many commands allow the use of lists of file names as arguments. These lists can be conveniently generated using shell templates. Let's consider them below.

Templates

The standard **shell** in UNIX is a very powerful tool and, in addition to running commands, has a lot of features that simplify work in the console. The simplest tool is file name templates. For example, writing the command 'ls *.c' will list all files with the extension '.c' in the current directory.

It is important to realize that '*.c' is not a single argument, the shell itself will substitute the desired list instead. If there are only two files in the directory, 1.c and 2.c, the command 'ls 1.c 2.c'. If there is no file with a name matching the template, the template itself will be substituted (i.e., the command 'ls *.c' will be expanded to 'ls 1.c 2.c.').

Table 7-7. Templates in shell

Template	Meaning
*	Matches any string (except '.' at the beginning of the name)
?	Matches any character (except '.' at the beginning of the name)
[c1- c2]	Any character from the range c1..c2
[!c1-c2]	Any character other than the specified range (bash/zsh only)
{a,b,c}	Exact list of words, comma separated (only in bash/zsh)
{10..20}	Sequence of numbers from 10 to 20 inclusive

All templates except '{}' apply to the actual list of files and select only those that fall under the template. Using '{}' brackets, you can construct more complex templates (see Table 7-7).

For example, 'ls *.{cxx,h,la}' will turn into ls *.cxx *.h *.la. A more interesting trick is 'cp config{,.bak}', which will turn into cp config config.bak. The second file does not exist; the template explicitly sets it.

If a template is specified by '*', '?', or '[]', but no file falls under it, the template itself will be passed to the command. For example, if a directory is empty, and we execute the 'ls *.abc' command in it, the command 'ls *.abc' will be executed, i.e., the template text will be given to the command as an argument. Be careful with accidentally or deliberately created files starting with dashes, as their names may be taken by the command as the name of the command's control key after the template is expanded!

To undo a wildcard, just precede it with a backslash '\' or enclose the entire argument in single quotes. For example, if we want to delete a file named "-rf *.?", we can use the command

`rm -- -rf\ \*.\?`

or

`rm -- '-rf *.?'`

Note the first argument '--' – this is often used in Linux commands and means "no more keys here, just file names." It is not necessary in this case, but, e.g., if you want to delete a file named '-f', the command 'rm -f' will not work because '-f' is the key of the rm command. The command 'rm -- -f' will work.

Commands for Working with the Directory Tree

`pwd` – Print the full name of the current directory.

`cd [ dirname ]` – Go to the specified directory (home directory if `dirname` is not specified); `dirname` here is the name of the directory, which may consist of the name itself and the path to it. The path can be absolute if it starts with / and relative if it starts with any other character.

Examples of moving through the directory tree:

- `cd /export/home/user1` – Move to the home directory of user1
- `cd /` – Move to the root directory of the file system
- `cd prog/cc` – Move from the current directory to the cc directory located in the prog directory
- `cd ../foo/bin` – Go back one step and move to the bin directory of user foo
- `cd` – Go to your home directory

Special catalog names:

. (dot) is the current directory.

.. (two dots) – Parent directory in relation to the current directory.

In bash or zsh, you can use wildcards that shell converts to directory names:

~ (tilde) – Home directory

~name is the home directory of username

- (dash) – Return to the previous directory (feature of the built-in `cd` command)

Please read about shell expansions; there are special hotkeys, allowing you to expand paths, usernames, variables, and more directly in your command line.

Commands for Working with Catalogs

`mkdir [options] directory_name ...` – Create new directories.
Options:

-m mode – Set access rights.

-p – Create parent directories if necessary

`rmdir directory_name ...` – Delete directories (directories must be empty).

`ls [options/names]` – Outputs the contents of a directory or file attributes. `names` are the names of directories or files. If no names are specified, the contents of the current directory are displayed.

The most commonly used options are

-a – Output all files (even if the names start with a dot).

-l – Display detailed information about files and folders (access rights, owner and group name, size in blocks by 512 bytes, last modification time, file or directory name).

-t – File names are sorted not alphabetically, but by the time of last modification.

-R – Recursively go through all subdirectories, outputting information on them.

Commands for Working with Files

`touch [options] file_name` – Create the file if it did not exist or change the time of the last modification of the file.

`rm [options] file_name ...` – File deletion.

Options:

    `-i` – Interactive delete (with confirmation required)

    `-f` – Without issuing messages

    `-r` – Recursively delete directories along with their components

Examples:

```
rm file1 file2     # delete files file1 and file2
rm data            # delete empty directory
rm -r data         # delete non-empty directory
rm /tmp/file1      # delete file by full name
```

Templates can be used to specify the list of files, but they should be used with extreme caution. Command:

`rm test*` – Will delete all files with names beginning with `test`

`rm test *` (with a space after test) – Deletes all files in the directory (except those starting with a dot)

`mv [options] source destination` is to move files and directories.

Options:

    `-i` – Interactive move (with confirmation required)

    `-f` – Without issuing messages

The `mv` command performs many functions depending on the type of arguments.

1) **Renames** files and directories if both arguments are either files or directories:

    `mv file1 file2` – `file1` will be named `file2` in the working directory.

    `mv dir1 dir2` – If `dir2` did not exist in the working directory, the `dir1` directory will be named `dir2`; if `dir2` did exist, the `dir1` directory will be moved to it.

2) **Moves a** file or directory to another directory with the same name or a different name:

`mv file1 dir2` - Moves `file1` from the working directory to the directory `dir2` with the same name

`mv file1 dir2/file2` - Moves `file1` from the working directory to the `dir2` directory named `file2`

If the source is a list of files and the destination is a directory, you can use templates:

`mv file* ../dir2` - Moves all files whose names begin with the string `file` to the directory of the same level as the working directory

In all operations, objects acting as source disappear: change name or location.
`cp [options] source destination` is to copy files and directories.
Options:

- `-i` – Interactive copying (requiring confirmation if the `destination` object already exists)
- `-f` – Without asking for confirmation
- `-r` – Recursively copies directories along with their contents
- `-p` – Copying with preserving file attributes (access rights, modification time)

Examples:
`cp file1 file2` - A copy of `file1` will be created in a file named `file2`.

`cp file1 dir2` - A copy of `file1` will be created in the `dir2` directory (i.e., named `dir2/file1`).

`cp -r dir1 dir2` - A copy of directory `dir1` will be created in directory `dir2`.

`cp file1 file2 file3 /tmp` - Copies files named `file1`, `file2`, and `file3` to the `tmp` subdirectory of the root directory. This can be done with the command:

cp file* /tmp
cat [options][file][file][file]...

The `cat` command merges files and outputs them to a standard output stream. If there is no `file` argument, the `cat` command will accept input from a standard input (keyboard) file. Since the command works with a standard output file (terminal), it is most often used to view the contents of a file on the screen. It is not recommended to output binary files to the screen.

> `cat ls.txt` – Outputs the contents of a file named `ls.txt` to the terminal.

> `cat ls1.txt ls2.txt ls3.txt` – Outputs the contents of files `ls1.txt`, `ls2.txt`, and `ls3.txt` to the terminal in turn.

> `cat ls1.txt ls2.txt ls3.txt > lsall.txt` – Merges three files into one. The old files are preserved. If the file `lsall.txt` already existed, it will be overwritten by the new content. It can be added to the end of the file if you use the `>>` sign (two "more" signs) for redirection.

The `cat` command can be used to create a file:

> `cat > ls.txt` – Everything typed on the keyboard will be written to the file `ls.txt`. You can stop typing by pressing `Ctrl-D`.

The `cat` command displays the entire contents on the screen. If the file is large, you will only see the last lines on the screen.

You can directly use commands to view text files in chunks:

- `more file.txt`
- `less file.txt`

The `less` command contains a large set of internal commands for navigating through a file, finding context, and even editing (see Table 7-8).

Table 7-8. *Some keyboard commands for* `less`

Command	Meaning
d / Ctrl-d	Move forward half screen
SPACE	Move forward one screen
b / Ctrl-b	Move back one screen
Return	One line forward
b	One line backward
g	Jump to the beginning of the file
G	Jump to the end of file
F	Switch to "follow" mode – go to the end and show new lines in real time. Press Ctrl-C to exit the mode
/string	Search for a string further down in the file
?string	Search for a string in the file backwards (upwards)
n	Search for the next occurrence of a previously entered string
h	List of available commands
q	Quit

`tail [options] file` – View the end of the file. By default, the last ten lines are displayed. Using options, you can start viewing from any position.

Options:

    `-n number` – How many lines to output

    `-r number` – Display in reverse order

    `-f` – Continuous output of the file as it fills up

Interrupt the interactive output with the `Ctrl-C` combination.

`grep [options] string [file][file]...` – Search for the context "string" in the specified files.

Options:

-i – Case-insensitive search

-n – Display line numbers containing the context

-v – Display context-free strings

find dir [options] [expression] – Recursively search for files in the specified directory by various attributes, such as name, size, modification time, and permissions.

Expressions:

-name filename – Search for a file named filename. It is possible to use templates, but then it is necessary to put them in quotes 'test*' or to escape characters of the template test*.

-size [+|-]number – Search for files with specified size, exceeding it (+), or smaller (-). The size is specified in blocks of 512 bytes.

-atime number – Search for files that were accessed a number of days ago.

-mtime number – Search for files that were modified number of days ago.

-exec command \{\} \; – exec command over the list of files found by the find command. Here the expression "{}" will be replaced by the name of the found file, and ';' means the end of the command. Since these characters are processed by the shell, they should be escaped, for example.

find . -name 'core.*' -ls -l \{\} \; – Recursively search for coredump files starting from the current directory and print their information using long ls format.

-delete – Delete files matching the conditions.

It should be noted that many of the actions listed above and related to manipulations with directories and files can be performed with the help of a special program – **Midnight Commander** file manager. It does not require a graphical shell and is called in a terminal window with the command:

mc

CHAPTER 7   UNIX AND LINUX – THE BASICS

With this program, you can navigate the directory tree, view the contents of directories and files, create directories (but not files), delete, copy, move directories and files, and search for files. For many users, the Midnight Commander text editor is a very good choice. It can be invoked separately with the `mcedit` command.

Editing files is an important topic. There are numerous editors that work in both text and graphical modes. As administrators, we will foremost be interested in an editor that can work in the most difficult conditions – without a graphical interface, possibly over a network, when function keys are not available or do not work properly. There are several such editors, e.g., `nano` and `emacs`. But, in our opinion, the most guaranteed to work, which is installed on 99% of Linux systems, is the `vim` editor; it is installed almost everywhere.

Its interface at first glance is not at all friendly and logical, but in fact, most of its commands are well-thought-out and logical. Its main advantage is the ability to work in almost any environment and quick execution of mass operations (search, replace, etc.). It has two modes of operation – command mode and insert mode. Initially, the file is opened in command mode. Use the cursor keys to move through the text; if they don't work, use the 'h,j,k,l' keys (look at the keyboard and you'll understand why it's such a strange set). The w and b keys move forward and backward per word.

The main terms in `vim` are

- **Buffer** – Place where you view or edit the text; `vim` can run several buffers at the same time.

- **Window** – A view port to the buffer; you can have several windows on your screen, showing the same or different buffers (files).

- **Register** – A place you can use to store some text (like a clipboard, but `vim` has many of them!).

- **Mode** – How your input will be interpreted.

There are also macros, bookmarks, tabs, and many more, but this is not a book about `vim`… Anyway, the most nonintuitive thing at first in vim is mode. By default, after starting vim, you are in **normal mode**. You can move around the text, search, delete and replace it, copy to the registers, and paste from the registers. But if you want to type something new, then switch to the **insert mode**. Here you just type new text. There are several hotkeys, which allow you to paste from the register quickly (`Ctrl-r x`, where x is a register name) or indent the line (`Ctrl-t`) and even run a normal mode command quickly (`Ctrl-o CMD`), but usually if you don't add new text, you use a different mode.

Visual mode is used to select text and then use the selection for some action. Useful commands in the normal mode are presented in Table 7-9.

Table 7-9. Some vi keyboard commands.

Command	Meaning
x	Delete the character under the cursor (and copy it to the register)
dd	Delete a line (and copy it to the register)
yy	Put the current line into the register
p/P	Paste text from the buffer before/after the current line
r	Replace the character under the cursor
R	Scribble on top of old text
cw/dw	Replace/delete the word (read below for more options)
i/a	Switch to insert mode at/behind the current position
o/O	Add a new line after/before the current line
/	Search by regular expression (? – search backwards)
n	Repeat the search
.	Repeat the last command
u	Cancel previous command (undo)
NN<cmd>	Repeat the <cmd> command NN times
:	Extended command

And of course, the 'most important' command is exit with save: ':wq' or simply 'ZZ' (in capital letters). Exit without saving can be done with the command ':q!'. Insert mode allows you to insert text in the desired position. It can be exited with the <ESC> key. You can type a number before any command, then the command will be repeated that number of times. For example, '10dd' will delete 10 lines (and put them together in the buffer, then you can insert them elsewhere with the 'p' command). Repeating an insert or replace command will also repeat the input. For example, typing 'cwNEW_WORD<ESC>' will replace the word after the cursor with 'NEW_WORD', and if you then move the cursor to the beginning of another word and press '.', it will also be replaced with 'NEW_WORD'.

Instead of 'w' in the previous command, you can use any "navigation" sequence, e.g., 'c$' – till the end of line, or 'c/qwe' – till the first occurrence of 'qwe' (but not including it). The same works for d (deletion) and y (yanking).

Of the extended commands, the 's' mass-substitution command is particularly convenient. Its syntax is taken from the sed command. The command can be preceded by a comma to indicate the range of lines on which it will act. '.' denotes the current line, '$' denotes the last line, and the '+N' indicates that the number is relative to the current line.

For example, you can replace the address '**old-cluster**' with '**new-supercomputer**' in ten lines after the current line inclusive by typing:

:.,+10s/old-cluster/new-supercomputer/g<Enter>

Then you can use v to switch mode to **visual mode** and start visual selection of text. After selecting, use any command like c, d, y, s, etc., and the selection will be used as a range by default. Using V, you can select whole lines of text.

Very uncommon, but very effective. I strongly recommend reading the vim tutorial and try using it for editing. Features such as fast word/regexp/anything replacement, easy macros record and use, instant navigation, and support for huge file sizes make it extremely effective for editing configuration files, logs, and more, comparing to nano, pico, mcedit, and others.

Yes, I know about Emacs, if you're the fan and it is installed on all your servers – sure, use it, it is also rocket-fast!

Packages

All Linux distributions have an excellent (in our opinion) system – packing software into so-called "packages." There are many variants of package systems; the most popular are rpm (RedHat, Fedora, CentOS, SuSE and others), deb (Debian, Ubuntu, Mint, and others), ports (Arch Linux and derivatives), ebuild (Gentoo and derivatives), and pkg (Slackware and derivatives).

They all offer to store the tree of all files of some software, such as a web server, or a part of it, such as an encryption module, in a single file (usually a compressed archive). In addition to files, a package stores metadata such as package name, description, and other data. The set of metadata varies from package system to package system, so the capabilities vary.

The most important features of package metadata in our opinion:

- Dependencies – Specifies other packages that are required or desired to be installed. A function (e.g., smtp-server) may be specified instead of packages, if it can be obtained from the metadata.
- Checksums of the files.
- Specifying which files are configuration files.

Dependencies make software installation much easier, and you can quickly figure out which additional packages need to be installed. Often "package managers" such as `yum` or `dnf` (RedHat), `apt` or `aptitude` (Debian), `pacman` (Arch Linux), etc., take care of calculating and installing all additional packages.

In `deb` format, dependencies can be specified flexibly from "required" to "desirable" (typically documentation and examples) to "optional," so an interactive package manager like `aptitude` can choose just the right set of optional packages. In the world of rpm format frequently along with a package automatically a dozen more unnecessary packages are installed, that possibly be required with it.

Having checksums of all files in a package, you can check the integrity of the system to see if any important files have changed (of course, only those included in packages); most package systems have separate commands for this.

Knowing the configuration files allows you not to overwrite them when upgrading – the new version is copied "next to" the original one, so you can check the difference. And in the interactive `aptitude` mode, you can see the difference at a glance and select whether to use the old or the updated version. Similarly, when you uninstall a package, as a rule, its configuration files remain and are not overwritten during a new installation. It is usually possible to uninstall a package with its configuration files by specifying an additional key when uninstalling it.

Information about packages installed on your computer is stored in a database, and if it gets corrupted, it is very hard to restore it. Therefore, I do not recommend uninstalling or installing packages on a file system that is 100% occupied, as this may result in loss of the database.

Package files themselves can be simply downloaded or copied from somewhere, but most often **repositories** are used – indexed directories of packages, often available from the Internet. On the CD/DVD with the OS distribution disk, the package repository takes up almost all the space, and after installation, it will be specified in the settings. In addition to it, the main network repository of the OS (or several) will almost certainly be specified.

Besides the main repository, you may need additional or even third-party repositories. For example, the standard RedHat repository does not contain many packages, and it is frequently necessary to plug in proven third-party packages like EPEL. Some software projects create their own mini-repositories just for their software, e.g., OFED. Sometimes it makes sense to create your own local repositories, e.g., for computers without Internet access.

The most important `yum` and `dnf` commands and useful keys are presented in Table 7-10.

Table 7-10. Important commands and keys of the yum command

Command	Meaning
install pkg1 pkg2 ...	Install packages and their dependencies
remove	Uninstall packages
update	Update all packages on the system, if there are new versions
check-update	check for updates to installed packages
reinstall pkg1 pkg2....	Reinstall the packages
--enablerepo/ disablerepo=REPO	Temporarily activate/deactivate the repository
--nogpgcheck	Disable signature verification (caution!)
--skip-broken	Skip dependency checking, use only if you are 100% sure it is needed
--downloadonly	No installation, just download
--downloaddir=DIR	Package download directory

When you have to work with a particular package or rpm file, the `rpm` command comes to the rescue. The list of most important rpm key are presented in Table 7-11.

Table 7-11. Some keys of the rpm command

Key	Meaning
Modes	
-q	Search mode – get information about the package
-i	Package installation mode
-U	Package update mode
-e	Packet removal mode
Keys of choice	
-a	Select all packages
-f path	Find the package that owns this file/directory
-p file	Package by rpm file
Setup/test/uninstall keys	
--nodeps	Disable dependency checking
--force	Overwrite files if they conflict with files of other packages, allowing them to install an earlier version of a package

Network Commands

Since computing clusters are inherently networked structures, networking commands play an important role for cluster administrators. Let's consider the most essential of them.

The ping command is a command for checking the connection between two computers in networks based on the TCP/IP protocol stack. The command sends Echo-Request requests to the other computer via ICMP protocol and receives incoming responses. By timing the time between sending a request and receiving a response, the program determines the delay in packet transmission along the route and the frequency of packet loss, allowing you to assess the quality of the network connection between two nodes.

CHAPTER 7   UNIX AND LINUX – THE BASICS

Command syntax:

```
ping [options] the host name or its IP address
```

Example:

```
ping host1.mynet
PING host1.mynet (10.0.1.2) 56(84) bytes of data.
64 bytes from host1.mynet (10.0.1.2): icmp_seq=1 ttl=64 time=4.69 ms
64 bytes from host1.mynet (10.0.1.2): icmp_seq=2 ttl=64 time=0.169 ms
64 bytes from host1.mynet (10.0.1.2): icmp_seq=3 ttl=64 time=0.120 ms
--- host1.mynet ping statistics ---
3 packets transmitted, 3 received, 0% packet loss, time 2002ms
rtt min/avg/max/mdev = 0.120/1.661/4.694/2.144 ms
```

When run without a special option, the ping command in UNIX-like systems runs indefinitely, sending requests to the specified host. Each sent request has its own number, by which the program determines whether it reached the target computer or not. In the command output, the number of the request is shown in the `icmp_seq` field, the `ttl` – Time To Live – field defines the lifetime of the response packet, specified in the number of nodes. This is exactly how many nodes the packet can pass through while traveling along the route to the destination node.

Each node through which the packet passes decreases the `ttl` value by one; if the counter value becomes zero, the packet will be destroyed as "lost" and will not be sent further along the route. The last field shows the message exchange time between the two nodes.

You can terminate the `ping` command from the terminal by pressing the Ctrl-C key combination, after which the `ping` command will display the work statistics: how many packets were sent, how many were received, the percentage of lost packets, and the total running time in milliseconds. In addition, the minimum, average, and maximum packet transit times are displayed.

The main options of the `ping` command:

- `-c count` limits the number of packets sent to the count value.
- `-n` cancel conversion of the IP address of the responding host to its DNS name. This mode can speed up the program and eliminate problems with DNS settings during network diagnostics.

- `-i interval` sets the time to wait before sending the next packet.
- `-l size` sets the packet size.

This command can also be used to test the InfiniBand network if the IPoIB (IP over InfiniBand) protocol is raised on the InfiniBand interfaces. If you realize that a remote host or network is unreachable, you can find out where the link is down. To do this, use `traceroute`. In most distros by default, more modern command `tracepath` is installed, but you still can install `traceroute` or more advanced command `mtr`. The command takes the address of a host as an argument.

It sends **ICMP ECHO** packets (like `ping` command) to this node with a ttl value of 1, then 2, and so on. The output of the program shows which nodes along the path of the packet processed the fact that the ttl was zeroed and reported it. Thus, we can trace the path of the packet.

Please note that some networks can block ICMP packets and ping, traceroute and similar programs won't work, but other types of traffic may be still available.

An example of how the `traceroute` command works:

```
traceroute 8.8.8.8
traceroute to 8.8.8.8 (8.8.8.8), 30 hops max, 60 byte packets
 1  333.444.9.161  0.233 ms  0.223 ms  0.226 ms
 2  333.444.9.1  1.262 ms  1.660 ms  2.143 ms
 3  333.444.1.8  0.651 ms  0.652 ms  0.959 ms
 4  333.444.0.190  0.933 ms  0.935 ms  0.943 ms
 5  193.232.246.232  0.915 ms  1.187 ms  1.176 ms
 6  72.14.236.220  8.712 ms  9.226 ms  9.221 ms
 7  209.85.243.135  51.475 ms.
 8  209.85.249.79  23.483 ms  24.171 ms
 9  72.14.233.168  23.33 ms  12.3 ms  24.5 ms
10  * * *
11  8.8.8.8  12.678 ms  12.509 ms  23.694 ms
```

You can see that the 10th node has not responded; this means that it simply ignores the packet without notifying the sender.

Useful options for the `traceroute` command:

- `-n` don't resolve DNS hostnames.
- `-f N` start with TTL with the specified number.
- `-m N` limit TTL to the specified number (default is 30).
- `-w N` response timeout (default is five sec.).
- `-t` use terminal output.
- `-g` use graphical (gtk) output.
- `-T/-u` use TCP/UDP protocols instead of ICMP.
- `-P PORT` use specified port, if -T or -u option was used.

`mtr` output is updating in real time and looks like this:

```
mtr -t destination.server.org
Keys:  Help  Display mode  Restart statistics  Order of fields  quit
                           Packets                Pings
Host                       Loss% Snt   Last   Avg  Best  Wrst StDev
1. _gateway                 0.0%  39    4.4  11.2   2.7  91.1  22.9
2. 10.11.12.13              0.0%  39   16.6  18.0  10.6  96.1  14.6
3. super.server.net         0.0%  39   12.2  18.0  10.6  91.0  14.7
4. destination.server.org   0.0%  38   13.0  17.0   9.7  89.3  13.7
```

Here you can see how many ping packets were sent and overall stats. You can change the view using the 'd' key and see the graphical presentation of the stats.

In the modern Linux kernels, viewing and managing network-related stuff mostly is done by `ip` command from the `iproute2` package.

The format of the `ip` command is simple:

```
ip [options] command object
```

"**Object**" can be one of more than ten subsystems; here we will briefly review only a few. "**Command**" is the action we want to perform. With optional options, it is possible, e.g., to restrict the command action to ipv4 networks only, or to request more detailed output.

CHAPTER 7 UNIX AND LINUX – THE BASICS

The link object reflects physical devices. For example, you can view the status of physical interfaces with the following command:

```
# ip link show
1: lo: <LOOPBACK,UP,LOWER_UP> mtu 65536 qdisc noqueue
   state UNKNOWN mode DEFAULT
   link/loopback 00:00:00:00:00:00 brd 00:00:00:00:00:00
2: eth0: <BROADCAST,MULTICAST,UP,LOWER_UP> mtu 1500 qdisc pfifo_fast
   state UP mode DEFAULT qlen 1000
   link/ether 00:10:20:30:40:5F brd ff:ff:ff:ff:ff:ff:ff:ff.
3: eth1: <BROADCAST,MULTICAST,UP,LOWER_UP> mtu 1500 qdisc pfifo_fast
   state UP mode DEFAULT qlen 1000
   link/ether 00:10:20:30:40:5E brd ff:ff:ff:ff:ff:ff:ff:ff.
```

Interface IP address data can be obtained and managed through the address object:

```
# ip addr sh
1: lo: <LOOPBACK,UP,LOWER_UP> mtu 65536 qdisc noqueue state UNKNOWN
   link/loopback 00:00:00:00:00:00 brd 00:00:00:00:00:00
   inet 127.0.0.1.1/8 scope host lo
   inet6 ::1/128 scope host
   valid_lft forever preferred_lft forever
2: eth0: <BROADCAST,MULTICAST,UP,LOWER_UP> mtu 1500 qdisc pfifo_fast state UP qlen 1000
   inet 10.0.0.2/24 brd 10.0.0.255 scope global eth0
   inet 192.168.222.1/24 brd 192.168.222.255 scope global eth0
   inet6 fe80::52e5:49ff:fe31:dd60/64 scope link
   valid_lft forever preferred_lft forever
2: eth1: <BROADCAST,MULTICAST,UP,LOWER_UP> mtu 1500 qdisc pfifo_fast state UP qlen 1000
   inet 9.10.11.12/24 brd 9.10.11.255 scope global eth1
   inet6 fe80::52e5:49ff:fe31:dd60/64 scope link
   valid_lft forever preferred_lft forever
```

CHAPTER 7   UNIX AND LINUX – THE BASICS

By the way, here we did not write the object and command names in full – instead of `address show`, we wrote `addr sh`. The `ip` command allows such abbreviations down to one letter, but only in the names of objects and commands. Be careful: some objects and commands start the same way. In many cases, you may want to see only essential data, use `--brief` or `-br` option before object, e.g., `ip -br a`.

Note that the interface eth0 in this example has two IPv4 addresses, and there may be even more.

Static routing table is managed by the `route` object:

```
# ip route sh
9.10.11.0/24 dev eth1 proto kernel scope link src 9.10.11.12
10.0.0.0/8 dev eth0 proto kernel scope link src 10.0.0.2
default via 9.10.11.1 dev eth1
```

Along with classic route table, there is special set of rules (policy routing tables and rules), allowing route the traffic using flexible conditions, like the source address or interface, IP protocol, and many others. For this, use `rule` object. It may be useful when you have several interfaces and want to control the traffic to minimize hops and some other cases. This approach creates a set of routing tables and list of rules when to use them. Read about it in the manual.

Another useful object is the `neighbor`. This is a table of IP addresses matching MAC addresses, which is supported by the kernel (ARP-table). It can be used, e.g., to make the kernel "memorize" MAC addresses of nodes forever and not allow them to be refined again using ARP requests. Here only the `show` command was demonstrated, but for each object, of course, a large set of other commands is supported – add, delete, modify, etc. For example, adding the IP address `172.16.0.1` for interface eth0 would look like this:

```
ip addr add dev eth0 local 172.16.0.1/24 scope link
# or just
ip addr add 172.16.0.1/24 dev eth0
```

Here `dev`, `local`, and `scope` are keywords with arguments. Their order is not important.

Adding a route:

```
ip route add to 172.0.0.0/8 dev eth0 via 172.16.0.2
```

The keyword to indicates the destination address or network, and via indicates the router for it.

All `ip` commands can be abbreviated to a single-digit prefix, i.e., instead of `ip addr show`, you can write `ip a s` (or even `ip a` since `show` is the default action). Frequently used:

```
ip a  = ip address
ip r  = ip route
ip l  = ip link
ip ru = ip rule
```

I already mentioned VLAN (Virtual Local Area Network). This is a general name for a whole family of technologies and protocols, but the essence is the same – to unite several devices in one or more connected physical networks into one virtual network, as if they were connected to one switch. We are interested in two cases – combining various switches into one virtual switch and splitting a common physical network into two or more logically separated ones.

The first case can be implemented in different ways, not only with VLAN (e.g., stacking and others), but it all depends on the models of switches used. And even with the help of VLAN, such aggregation is done differently for different switches and manufacturers. If you need to do this kind of aggregation, call an experienced network engineer.

The second case also requires configuring the switch (and supporting such technology in it, of course), which varies from vendor to vendor, but it is much easier to handle. There are two ways to create VLANs in one physical network: untagged and tagged.

An untagged VLAN is created by specifying the switch port(s) that will be included in it. Once configured, all traffic, even broadcast traffic, from these ports will be visible only within the created VLAN.

What if there are several devices on the same port? That's when a tagged VLAN comes to the rescue. It's an open IEEE 802.1Q standard, so it is widely supported, but requires configuration on the endpoint side (connected server). In Linux, this requires creating a new interface specifying a tagged VLAN:

```
ip l add link eth0 name vlan101 type vlan id 101
```

Here eth0 is the physical interface, `vlan101` is the name of the new interface through which traffic will flow to the VLAN, and 101 is the VLAN identifier. Accordingly, a VLAN with ID 101 must be created and configured on the switch.

To have this interface automatically created at startup, on RedHat-like systems, create the file /etc/sysconfig/network-scripts/ifcfg-vlan101 and write a text similar to the one below:

```
VLAN=yes
VLAN_NAME_TYPE=VLAN_PLUS_VID_NO_PAD
DEVICE=vlan101
PHYSDEV=eth0
BOOTPROTO=static
ONBOOT=yes
TYPE=Ethernet
IPADDR=10.10.101.0
NETMASK=255.255.255.0
```

Please note that in modern Linux, distributives may be newer network manager systems, e.g., **NetworkManager** (please don't use it on compute nodes and servers…), or **netplan**.

I strongly recommend that you study the documentation for the `ip` command and use it.

It is not necessary (although desirable) to know how to configure switches in detail; often you can invite a specialist to configure them only once. I'm not a big expert in switches, but I want to mention several Ethernet technologies you should take care of or be aware of, as an HPC admin: spanning tree protocol and links aggregation groups (LAG).

Spanning tree protocol (STP) is described in the IEEE 802.1D standard, but there are some variations. This protocol is aimed to eliminate any loops in the Ethernet network. If this protocol detects a loop, one of the ports, included into the loop, is disabled and entire network (subnet) becomes a tree. Because of that in most cases in an Ethernet network there is exactly one central (top) switch, which becomes a single point of failure. There are some strategies on how to eliminate this, but they highly depend on switch models and supported protocols.

As we can create virtual networks (vlans), most switches use STP for each vlan and the non-vlan network. If we need to pass more data, than one link allows, we can make several parallel links, but all of them except one will be disabled by STP. To fix that, switches allow declaring virtual links, combining many parallel physical links – links aggregation. There are various standards, e.g., IEEE 802.1AX, LACP, and others, so not all switches, even made by one producer, can "understand" each other.

"If it is so restrictive, maybe I can just disable it?" – you may think. Sometimes it is not so bad idea, but only in cases, when your subnet is simple, and you have strong control on it. But if you don't use Ethernet network as a compute network, I'd recommend keep it enabled.

Short resume – Find a good network expert and take a consultation.

In legacy Linux systems and old scripts, you can see old-style network managing commands; most common are `route`, `ifconfig`, and `arp`. I want to slightly cover first two, but you can safely skip this part.

The `route` command shows the current routing table, which is the rules by which a node determines where to send a packet. This is old version of `ip route`. Typical output of the command:

```
# route -n
Kernel IP routing table
Destination     Gateway         Genmask         Flags Metric Ref    Use Iface
0.0.0.0         192.168.0.1     0.0.0.0         UG    600    0        0 eth0
169.254.0.0     0.0.0.0         255.255.0.0     U     1000   0        0 eth1
192.168.0.0     0.0.0.0         255.255.255.0   U     600    0        0 eth0
```

Column values:

- `Destination` – The destination address of the packet
- `Gateway` – The address of the host (router) to which the packet will be sent
- `Genmask` – Address(destination) mask
- `Flags, Metric, Ref, Use` – Service information
- `Iface` – Name of the interface to which the packet will be transmitted

If it is necessary to send a packet over the network to the address x.y.z.q, the kernel will sequentially check this address against the table: a mask (genmask) will be applied to the address and the destination field, and if the results match, the packet will be forwarded to the gateway via the network interface. Masking is done by a bitwise AND operation, i.e., all zero bits in the mask will also be zero in the result, and the bits set to 1 in the mask will result in the same as the original address.

It follows that the 0.0.0.0 mask specifies a route that will always work, since the result of its application will always be 0.0.0.0. Such a route is often referred to as the default. In our example, network 9.10.11.* is accessible through eth1, network 10.*.*.* is accessible through interface eth0 (this is the internal network), and all other packets are routed to router 9.10.11.1, which is accessible through interface eth1.

You can also add and delete routes with the route command. To add a route to a network, use

```
route add -net 1.2.3.0 netmask 255.255.255.255 gw 1.2.3.1 dev eth0
```

Here we added a route for network 1.2.3.* on interface eth0:

```
route add default gw 1.2.3.4
```

This command is a shortened version of the command

```
route add -net 0.0.0.0 netmask 0.0.0.0 gw 1.2.3.4
```

The interface is determined automatically if the router (gw) is accessible through other rules. If we replace 'add' with 'del' in the previous commands, we get the command to delete a route. Note that when deleting, you must also specify all parameters: netmask, gw, dev, etc., even if they are obvious; otherwise, the command may not work.

The ifconfig command controls the operation of a network interface. Without arguments, it shows the status of active interfaces:

```
eth0  Link encap:Ethernet HWaddr 00:10:21:37:37:40:5F
      inet addr:10.0.0.2 Bcast:10.255.255.255 Mask:255.0.0.0
      UP BROADCAST RUNNING MULTICAST MTU:1500 Metric:1
      RX packets:25400911846 errors:0 dropped:5419 overruns:0 frame:0
      TX packets:22217149338 errors:0 dropped:0 overruns:0 carrier:0
      collisions:0 txqueuelen:1000
      RX bytes:13736261041 (12.4 GiB) TX bytes:10704560149 (9.7 GiB)
      Memory:d8900000-d8920000
```

```
eth1 Link encap:Ethernet HWaddr 00:10:21:37:40:5E
    inet addr:9.10.11.12 Bcast:9.10.11.255 Mask:255.255.255.0
    UP BROADCAST RUNNING MULTICAST MTU:1500 Metric:1
    RX packets:3419282263 errors:0 dropped:0 overruns:0 frame:0
    TX packets:5796890559 errors:0 dropped:0 overruns:0 carrier:0
    collisions:0 txqueuelen:1000
    RX bytes:1111996013 (1.0 GiB) TX bytes:7592797386 (6.9 GiB)
    Memory:d8920000-d8940000

lo Link encap:Local Loopback
    inet addr:127.0.0.1 Mask:255.0.0.0
    UP LOOPBACK RUNNING MTU:16436 Metric:1
    RX packets:27777839 errors:0 dropped:0 overruns:0 frame:0
    TX packets:27777839 errors:0 dropped:0 overruns:0 carrier:0
    collisions:0 txqueuelen:0
    RX bytes:10171240527 (9.4 GiB) TX bytes:10171240527 (9.4 GiB)
```

Here, we can see MAC addresses of the cards (`HWaddr`), IP addresses of the interfaces (`inet addr`), network broadcast address and mask (`Bcast`, `Mask`), as well as statistics:

> `RX/TX packets` – Packets transmitted/received.

> `RX/TX bytes` – Bytes transmitted/received.

> `UP BROADCAST RUNNING MULTICAST` – Interface status.

> `MTU` is the Ethernet frame size.

> `txqueuelen` – Packet queue limit.

> `errors` – Number of errors.

> `dropped` – Number of dropped packets.

> `overruns` – Number of buffer overflows.

> `frame` – Number of errors when accepting a frame.

> `carrier` is the number of communication loss.

> `collisions` – Number of collisions during transmission.

To see data about all interfaces, not just the running interfaces, run `ifconfig` with the `-a` switch. With root privileges, the `ifconfig` command can be used to control interface parameters. You can quickly disable the `eth0` interface with `ifconfig eth0 down` and enable it again with `ifconfig eth0 up`. Example of quick interface configuration and its address:

`ifconfig eth0 192.168.0.1 netmask 255.255.255.0`

This command will set the eth0 interface to `192.168.0.1` and mask `255.255.255.0`. After that, the interface must be enabled (up) with the `ifconfig eth0 up` command. In most implementations, the `ifconfig` command automatically creates a routing rule. In contrast to `ip addr` command, ifconfig cannot manage and even display multiple ip addresses, assigned to an interface. In old kernel versions, this issue was addressed, using "interface aliases," when one interface could be represented by various virtual devices, e.g., eth0, eth0:1, eth0:2, etc. This technology still is supported, but highly not recommended (because routing and firewall rules turn to hell).

"Cluster" Commands

Cluster commands are commands that perform operations on all nodes or on some set of nodes. As such, **there are no** standard commands for clusters, but cluster administrators with shell programming skills can create their own scripts to organize the execution of commands on cluster nodes.

In real practice, I advise using commands like `pdsh` or `clush`, but here I show a few variants of "cluster" scripts that can be taken as the basis of scripts for nonstandard cases.

Let's take a look at an example of a command to copy a file to all nodes in the cluster:

```sh
#!/bin/sh
for host in `grep -v ^\# /etc/nodes` ; do
  for file in "$*"; do
    scp -r "$file" "$host:$file"
  done
done
```

It is understood that the /etc/nodes file stores a list of all nodes in the cluster and the command for all nodes in this list copies all files or directories specified as arguments from the management computer to each node, preserving its name. If you add '&' to the end of the 'scp...' line and add 'wait' to the last line, the copying will run in parallel. However, the output of all scp commands will be mixed up, and in case of a large number of nodes, the head node may be significantly overloaded.

As you can see, the script is very simple, but it makes the administrator's task of managing the cluster much easier. Pay attention to the grep command: with its help, we do not get the entire list of nodes, but only those whose names are not "commented out," i.e., there is no "#" in front of them. Thus, if a node fails, its name is not removed from /etc/nodes, but simply "commented out" for the time being.

An even simpler form is a script to execute an arbitrary command on all nodes in the cluster:

```sh
#!/bin/sh
for host in $(grep -v ^\# /etc/nodes) ; do
   echo "$host =================" && ssh $host "$*"
done
```

Here, the script is passed the name of the command with arguments to be executed on all nodes in the cluster.

It is important that passwordless access to nodes is configured (see below).

Brief Summary

Knowing how the OS works, how the file system works, and how to manage services, network, memory, and processor is an essential necessity for any administrator, especially for a supercomputer administrator. Here is not even a young fighter course, but a microintroduction to Linux for those who already want to read more, but have not read a good Linux book yet.

But it is absolutely necessary to read such a book, and preferably more than one. And not only to read it, but also to apply the acquired knowledge in practice, at least in a virtual machine.

CHAPTER 7   UNIX AND LINUX – THE BASICS

Search Keywords

Bootloader, dhcp, bootp, pxe, grub, lilo, loadlin, sysv init, bsd init, runlevel, systemd, Advanced Bash Scripting Guide, bash, iproute2, iptables, static routing, awk, sed, ssh, procutils, netutils, chattr, facl, suid, sticky bit

CHAPTER 8

UNIX and Linux – Working Techniques

For those who are already familiar with Linux and bash, here are a few tricks that can save time, nerves, and effort. We will also look at a few Linux-specific subsystems that allow you to fine-tune your system.

The Magic of sysctl

The Linux kernel allows you to change some parameters of its operation on the fly and to keep track of internal information. For this purpose, a special virtual file system proc is used, usually mounted in the /proc directory. Its subdirectories with numeric names reflect data about processes with corresponding PIDs (this is where ps, top, etc., commands get their data from). Other files and directories reflect various information about the system, but we will be interested in the sys subdirectory. It contains global settings, which are organized according to the principle of one file – one value. It is very similar to the registry in Windows.

To read a value, it is enough to output the contents of the corresponding file, e.g., with the cat command. To change the value, write the desired number or string to the file, e.g., with the echo command, and redirect the output:

```
$ echo 1 > /proc/sys/net/ipv4/ip_forward
$ cat /proc/sys/net/ipv4/ip_forward
1
```

To "ennoble" actions with these settings, the sysctl command was created. In its arguments, the parameter name is specified relative to the /proc/sys directory and dots are written instead of the directory separator. For example, the previous commands can be executed as follows:

```
$ sysctl -w net.ipv4.ip_forward=1
$ sysctl net.ipv4.ip_forward
net.ipv4.ip_forward = 1
```

If you specify the `-a` switch or a partition (directory) name, `sysctl` will show all settings values or all values from the specified subdirectory, respectively. This can be very handy for finding the right setting. Many distributions have a `/etc/sysctl.conf` file that contains the settings that are enabled at system startup. You can read more about the settings on the Internet and in the `Documentation/proc.txt` file of the Linux kernel source code.

udev Subsystem

Almost every device in Linux has a special "**device** file." In reality, there is nothing in this file, the most important thing is the **minor** and **major** numbers, which are properties of the file. By these numbers (not by name!), the kernel knows which device you want to access. Usually, the major number defines the device class, and the minor number defines the number of the device in the class. For example, a hard disk would have a minor number of 0, its first partition would be 1, its second partition would be 2, etc. Another disk will have a different major number, and its partitions will have corresponding minor numbers.

Here is a sample output of the '`ls -l /dev/sda`' command. Note the first letter of the output: '**b**' stands for block device. The digits **8** and **0** are the major and minor numbers, respectively:

```
brw-rw---- 1 root disk 8, 0 Jun 27 17:27 /dev/sda
```

Some devices have historically assigned numbers, but many get them dynamically. Take a look at file `/proc/devices` – there is a correspondence of major device numbers to the current drivers for this computer.

In older versions of Linux, there was a MAKEDEVICES script that created the necessary device files, but with the kernel's support for a huge number of devices, it became impossible to cram them all into the script. At the moment (when this book was written), the kernel has a separate `/sys` file system containing information about all devices. You can "subscribe" to changes that occur in it and learn about connecting, disconnecting, and changing the state of devices.

This is what a special udev service does. It filters events in /sys and creates or deletes device files according to a set of rules. In addition, it can do other operations, but it is better not to get carried away with such tricks. The udev rules can be located in different places, usually /lib/udev/rules.d/. Do not change the rules located there, but create your own in /etc/udev/rules.d.

Each rule consists of a sequence of "matches" and "assignments," all listed comma-separated on a single line. At least one match and assignment must be specified. The matches specify the condition that the event must satisfy. If more than one match is specified, all listed matches must match. An assignment always looks like assigning a value to a variable, but in reality, it can also specify an action. For example:

KERNEL=="loop*", NAME="loop/%n", SYMLINK+="%k"

This rule will work when a device named 'loop0', 'loop1', etc., appears. It will create a /dev/loop/N device and a /dev/loopN reference to it.

The match must be of the form NAME == VAL orNAME != VAL, where NAME is one of the options from Table 8-1.

Table 8-1. Some names for match rules in udev

Name	Meaning
ACTION	Event name – add or remove
KERNEL	Kernel device name
SUBSYSTEM	Subsystem name
DRIVER	Driver name
TEST{file}	Permissions on file {file}
ATTR{name}	File "name" in the appropriate **/sys** branch
ENV{name}	Device name property
PROGRAM	Run the program
RESULT	Execution result

Other names are also possible – see the documentation for details. In the right part of comparisons, you can specify shell-style substitutions: *, ?, and [ ].

Assignments have the same form, but instead of '==' and '!=', '=', '+=', and ':=' are used. The '=' sign means assigning a value to a variable, the old value (action) is canceled. The '+=' sign means adding a value, the old value is not lost. For example, you can create several symbolic links – by label, name, and UUID. The sign ':=' means assignment and prohibition of new assignments – other rules will work, but no assignments will be made to this variable. Table 8-2 presents a shortened list of possible variables.

Table 8-2. *Some udev rule variables*

Name	Meaning
NAME	Set the name of the network device
SYMLINK	Create a link
OWNER, GROUP, MODE	Change owner, group, rights
ATTR{name}	Assign a value to an attribute in **sysfs**
ENV{name}	Assign a value to the devices property
RUN	Run the program
LABEL name	Tag a **GOTO**
GOTO name	Jump to the line 'LABEL=name'; the line should be further down in the text of the rule

See the documentation for additional variables.

You can use special variables like **$name** or **%X** in the right part of the assignments. Their full list is available in the documentation; Table 8-3 presents the most useful ones in my opinion:

Table 8-3. Some special variables in udev

Name	Meaning
$kernel, %k	Kernel name
$number, %n	Core number
$devpath, %p	Path
$driver	Driver name
$attr{file},%s	sysfs attribute
$env{key}, %E	Environment variable
$major, %M	Major device number
$minor, %m	Minor device number
$result, %c	Output of the start of the matching program PROGRAM
$parent, %P	Parent device name
$name	Current device name
$sys, %S	Mount point in sysfs
$$	'$' sign
%%	'%' sign

The only but powerful udev management command is udevadm. With this command, you can debug rules and see the current state of the system. For example, the following command will give all information about the sda device from the udev point of view:

```
udevadm info -a -p /sys/block/sda
```

PAM Modules

Later, I will often refer to the PAM modules, so let me tell you what it is. PAM stands for "pluggable authentication modules," and it is a library, which is widely used in many programs, that requires authentication. The library gives a standard API and loads modules – shared libraries, implementing authentication methods and some other stuff and loaded when they are needed. Note, it is a library, not a service!

Functions, implementing by modules, are divided into four groups:

- **Auth** – Authentication/credential acquisition
- **Account** – Account management
- **Password** – Authentication token (e.g., password) updating
- **Session** – Session management

Auth identifies the user and sets the credentials (UID/GID) and also can update some information, like last login time, set limits, etc. **Account** checks if this account is available/enabled, **password** allows changing password (or other auth token), and **session** makes any action when user session is about to start or is finished. One module can implement any subset of those groups. Each service using PAM has its own list of modules, groups involved, and their options.

PAM configuration file may be in "BSD-style" – one big file for all services, where the first word in every line is a service name, or a set of files named as the services. In Linux, the second approach is used mostly, and I'll refer to it. The format of the line in the PAM config file is "`group flag module [options]`" where **group** is `auth`, `account`, `password`, or `session`; **flag** is required, requisite, sufficient, optional, or a list of conditions; **module** is the modules name; and **options** is the module options. The lines are scanned one by one in the same group, so the order is important.

For each line, the mentioned module is called, and depending on the result (OK or FAIL) and flag, an action is taken:

Flag	Action
Required	OK=continue, FAIL=continue to process, but deny request in the end
Requisite	OK=continue, FAIL=stop processing, and deny the request
Sufficient	OK=stop processing and accept the request, FAIL=continue processing
Optional	Ignore the result

Flag also can be a list in format "`[value=action, ...]`", where value is the value, returned by the module call, and action is what to do. Possible values are the following:

Value	Meaning
Success	Module says it's happy = OK
Ignore	Module signals it wants its return value to be ignored
Abort	Module says stop now
Default	"All return values not explicitly mentioned in this set," often used to catch all errors/failures (because there's a bunch of those) having this often forces you to mention ignore=ignore (and sometimes other things = some obvious thing), or they would fall under the default action
Errors/failures	FAIL – all values from the list: open_err, symbol_err, service_err, system_err, buf_err, auth_err, session_err, cred_err, conv_err, authtok_err, authtok_recover_err, user_unknown, perm_denied, cred_insufficient, authinfo_unavail, new_authtok_reqd, authtok_lock_busy, authtok_disable_aging, authtok_expired, acct_expired, maxtries, cred_unavail, cred_expired, try_again, module_unknown, bad_item, conv_again, incomplete, no_module_data

The actions can be

- **ok** – This module's return code should be considered (...if there are no errors).
- **bad** – Flag ourselves as having failed (doesn't terminate).
- **die** – Bad + terminate.
- **done** – OK and termination.
- **ignore** – Module's return status will not contribute to the stack's return code.
- **n (an integer >0)** – OK and skip the next n rules.
- **reset** – Clear stack module state.

In this "list notation," we can define regular flags as follows:

```
required   = [success=ok new_authtok_reqd=ok ignore=ignore default=bad]
requisite  = [success=ok new_authtok_reqd=ok ignore=ignore default=die]
sufficient = [success=done new_authtok_reqd=done default=ignore]
optional   = [success=ok new_authtok_reqd=ok default=ignore]
```

Here is an example of a simple authentication description, using unix, permit, and deny modules. unix module checks password via /etc/passwd and /etc/shadow, permit allows the access, and deny denies the access:

```
auth    [success=1 default=ignore]    pam_unix.so nullok_secure
auth    requisite                     pam_deny.so
auth    required                      pam_permit.so
```

For debugging the chains of rules, the debug module is really useful; it returns values, specified in the arguments, e.g.:

```
auth optional pam_debug.so. auth=perm_denied cred=perm_denied
auth sufficient pam_debug.so auth=success cred=success
```

Special instruction in the config file is @include, which allows including the text from another file – often used for common parts. Lines starting with '#' are comments. There are a lot of different modules, but I'd recommend reading at least about pam_limits, pam_exec, pam_env, pam_warn, pam_listfile, and pam_access.

Shell Tricks

The command line has been and remains the administrator's primary tool. The reason is its versatility. To know how to work in the shell means to be able to quickly solve administration tasks. These techniques become especially relevant when you need to execute dozens or even hundreds of commands simultaneously (or, even worse, sequentially).

For example, rebooting at least ten nodes via IPMI in the command line is no more than one minute. But it takes much longer to open a browser window with the desired address ten times, select the desired menu with the mouse, and press the "reboot" button with the mouse. The person performing these actions will curse everything already on the fifth window. And if you need to reboot 100 or 1000 nodes?

Let's share some techniques for working in bash (or zsh) that improve efficiency. Many will work in the "standard" sh interpreter (e.g., dsh), but not all.

The curly brackets specify an enumeration, for each element of which, including the empty one, a different argument will be created. Let's use it!

```
$ cp file{,.bak}        # equivalent to cp file file.bak
```

Or even so:

```
$ for i in node-{1,2,3,4}-{1,2,3,4}; do ... ; done
  # use a list of 16 nodes
```

You can also use them to generate ranges:

```
$ echo {1..15}
1 2 3 4 5 6 7 8 9 10 11 12 13 14 15
```

But, as you can see, leading zeros are missing. If this is necessary, you need to call the `seq` command for help. It can generate sequences of numbers according to specified rules. For example, you can quickly check the "liveliness" of nodes named node-001 ... node-100 in the following way:

```
$ for i in $(seq -w 1 100); do ssh node-$i true; done
```

Note that the true command is executed on the node, which produces nothing. Thus, we will only see error messages from failed nodes on the console.

Many people know about the history of commands and even often refer to it by clicking the "up" button and editing the previous command. Very often, we need either the whole previous command or only its last argument. And we can access them through special sequences '!!' and '!$', respectively:

```
$ chown user1 my_special_file
$ chmod 600 !$          # change permissions on the same file
$ tail /var/log/syslog
Permission denied
$ sudo !!               # repeat the command under sudo
```

To find a command in the history, just press **Ctrl-R** and type any substring of the command. Bash will find and display the last command with this substring. The next occurrence can be found by pressing **Ctrl-R** again, and if you have missed what you need, you need to search forward instead of backward – **Ctrl-F**. If you don't want to search interactively, use the `history` command. It will show all history commands:

```
$ history | grep sudo
```

Note the numbers in front of the lines – any command can be addressed by number!

```
$ !123 # call command number 123
```

Sometimes you need to perform a simple (or not so simple) calculation. Running a graphical calculator is long and inconvenient, but bash has one ready! The expression in double brackets after the '$' sign will be calculated according to the rules of integer arithmetic:

```
$ echo $((123*55+18))
6783
```

You can substitute variables there too, but without the '$' sign in front of the name:

```
$ offset=18
$ echo $((123*55+offset))
6783
```

This is especially useful for scripts. If you want something more complicated, such as real arithmetic, call the bc command for help; you may have to install the appropriate package first.

You probably know that sh commands on the same line are separated by semicolons. But this is not the only separator – the '&' sign not only sends the command to the background, but also separates it from the next one:

```
$ abc & xyz & wait
```

This code will run the abc and xyz commands in the background and wait for them to complete.

Other valid delimiters are '&&' and '||'. They differ from the others in that they specify conditional execution: the second command will be executed only if the first command succeeds for '&&' or fails for '||'. Sample code to output the contents of a file, only if it exists:

```
$ [ -f 'testfile' ] && cat testfile
```

Note that here '[' is a command, and in the old UNIX tradition, it is a reference to the test command.

Sometimes you may want to process only the error stream and ignore the standard output stream or write it to a file. But the '|' operation works only with the standard output, what can we do? This trick of creating a dummy file descriptor can help; it swaps the output and error streams:

```
$ my_command 3>&1 1>&2 2>&3
```

If you need to have the raw output of a command in a file and process it somehow, e.g., to look for a line occurrence, use the tee command. It writes its input to the file and to the standard output:

```
$ my_command | tee out.log | grep warning
```

By the way, giving it a '-' as the file name will double each line in the output.

You can use the tar command to quickly copy a directory with subdirectories to another host:

```
tar cf - mydata/ | ssh remotehost 'cd place/to/go; tar xf -'
```

For more details, see the chapter on backups.

And lastly, important built-in variables that can help in scripts:

$? – Return code for the last command executed

$$ – PID of the current bash process

$! – PID of the last command run in the background

Tips for Some Often Used Commands

less is often used when you need to look at a long output or big file. Here are some useful command-line options:

f – Open binary files

r – Print special symbols (colors!)

F – Quit if file fits screen

n – No line numbers

less -fFnr /tmp/dd

grep – I bet, you use it a lot…. Did you know that if you use '-E' option, grep will use "extended regexp" syntax, and instead of searching for 'a\+bc\|xy\?z\(qwe\)\{1,4\}', you can use just 'a+bc|xy?z(qwe){1,4}'?

sort – Did you use sort file | uniq? You can use just sort -u file.

CHAPTER 8   UNIX AND LINUX – WORKING TECHNIQUES

Brief Summary

Knowledge is power. In Linux, knowing the basic commands and their features is a great way to solve administrator tasks and save time.

Search Keywords

ABS guide, tar, bash tricks

CHAPTER 9

Network File Systems

Starting with this chapter, we will not only talk about the technologies used in supercomputers, but also give practical recommendations or brief instructions on how to install and configure them. Let's start with network file systems and consider only the most common ones at the time of writing. In reality, there are many more, but not all of them are suitable for HPC.

In a compute cluster, all nodes must have write access to the user's directory. This imposes very serious limitations on the implementation, in particular, technologies like iSCSI, ATA-over-Ethernet, Network Block Device, etc., immediately disappear, as they do not provide synchronization of data on nodes during writing.

Another important limitation is the speed of data access. If there are several dozens of nodes in a cluster, the bandwidth of a single server is simply not enough for all of them. Already on two dozen nodes, a single task can easily create a load that completely blocks the NFS server, creating large time-sensitive files. This leads to the need to use distributed file systems that can balance the load between multiple servers, as well as distribute the load to disk subsystems, increasing their throughput.

NTP

NTP (Network Time Protocol) is not a network file system, as the name suggests, but a protocol for time synchronization. I have intentionally included its description here because time synchronization is of paramount importance for almost all network file systems (and for cluster operation).

I will not go into the details of the protocol; I will note one thing: the closer the server is to the client on the network, the better and faster the synchronization. Therefore, I recommend installing NTP server on at least one of the service servers, configure it to work with the local network and to synchronize with one of the external NTP servers. There are several implementations of NTP servers; we will shortly consider openntpd and `chrony`, as most popular. The server is installed from the package on all nodes, including client nodes. The configuration file is usually found in /etc/ntpd.conf. Example settings:

```
server 1.ru.pool.ntp.org
server 2.centos.pool.ntp.org
listen on 10.1.2.251
restrict default kod nomodify notrap nopeer noquery
```

This specifies the two ntp servers ours will synchronize with, as well as the IP address of the interface from which clients can connect. For the client, the `listen` string is simply not specified.

The last line specifies restrictions for the clients:

- kod – "Kiss-of-death," special packet, sent to the client to reduce unwanted queries.

- nomodify restricts remote configuration updates.

- notrap turns off protocol traps support.

- nopeer prevents a peer association being formed (peers are clients and servers for each other).

- noquery option prevents ntpq and ntpdc queries, but allows time queries.

If you server IPv6 interfaces, copy "restrict line" and add a -6 option. If you want to limit the IP addresses, allowed to request, you can replace "default" keyword by, e.g., `192.168.2.0 mask 255.255.255.0`.

`chrony` is a modern ntp client and server, available in many popular Linux distributives. For the client part, the most important setting in the config file (/etc/chrony.conf by default) is `server` or `pool`, following the remote server name and optional parameters. `pool` assumes that the specified name resolves into multiple IP addresses, and crony will try to connect to all of them. The common parameter is `iburst`, which means "send requests with higher frequency in the beginning." This allows to sync time quicker on the server start.

To enable ntp server feature, just specify `allow` option with IP subnet, e.g., `allow 10.20.30.0/24`. If subnet is missing, or you specified `all`, then any client is allowed. Crony has a lot of possible options; take a look into official documentation and guides.

An important feature of most ntp servers is their default policy of not changing the time too quickly. For us, this means that if the time on the client is different from the server, e.g., by an hour, then synchronization may take many minutes. And during these minutes, some file systems that require precise synchronization may not be mounted, or other troubles may occur.

Of course, sudden time jumps can also bring them, but they typically do not occur at system startup, but a long "pulling" to a single time can bring a lot of problems. That's why I recommend running forced synchronization before starting the ntp service on the client node with the command:

ntpdate server_ntp_server_address

In many distributions, the ntpdate package also provides a "service" of the same name, which quickly synchronizes the time with the server specified in /etc/ntpd.conf. Note that the ntpd command cannot be executed while ntpd is running.

In many modern systems, ntpd is replaced by systemd component timesyncd. Note that this service cannot run as a server; it can only synchronize the local time with remote servers. If you want to use it (or it is already enabled), check if it is installed, then check the configuration files; this service reads these configs:

- /etc/systemd/timesyncd.conf
- /etc/systemd/timesyncd.conf.d/*.conf
- /run/systemd/timesyncd.conf.d/*.conf
- /usr/lib/systemd/timesyncd.conf.d/*.conf

Format is following systemd standards; there is one section 'Time':

```
[Time]
NTP=0.ubuntu.pool.ntp.org 2.ubuntu.pool.ntp.org
FallbackNTP=0.pool.ntp.org 1.pool.ntp.org
```

Here we specify default and fallback NTP servers list. Now we can start the service:

systemctl enable --now systemd-timesyncd

To verify your configuration and status, run

```
$ timedatectl show-timesync --all
LinkNTPServers=
```

CHAPTER 9   NETWORK FILE SYSTEMS

```
SystemNTPServers=
FallbackNTPServers=0.pool.ntp.org 1.pool.ntp.org
ServerName=0.ubuntu.pool.ntp.org
ServerAddress=50.218.103.254
RootDistanceMaxUSec=5s
PollIntervalMinUSec=32s
PollIntervalMaxUSec=34min 8s
PollIntervalUSec=1min 4s
```

NFS

NFS (Network File System) is one of the first network file systems. It was developed by SUN in 1984 and allows you to work with a part of the file system of a remote server over the network. The client does not even know what file system is used on the server – all file operations are completely abstracted, and for the client, this file system looks like a local one.

NFS implementation is based on the **RPC** protocol – Remote Procedure Call. This protocol allows the implementation of remote subroutine calls and is used in many other programs and protocols besides NFS. For RPC to work, it is necessary to install and run the `portmap` (Port Mapper) service. This service is something like DNS for RPC. By the name of an RPC service, it gives its "coordinates" on the server – the port on which it works. Therefore, an NFS server may not have a fixed port, although in practice it is usually port 2049.

There are two most common NFS protocol versions – v3 and v4.1 (usually specified as v4). NFSv4 has a lot of new features, comparing to v3, like encryption, parallel NFS (pNFS), and smarter files lock support. In reality, there are a lot of "peculiarities" in implementations as for the server and as for the client side. If everything is highly compatible and well implemented, v4 may give you great performance boost, but in many cases, it gives performance drop, instability, and even data loss. Be careful and test any NFSv4 feature before you enable it in the production.

If you don't plan to use NFS as main network file system, I would recommend to use NFSv3. Most common case today is using NFS for home users directories, and Lustre or other parallel file system for "scratch" directories, where users store data, used for compute jobs. "Scratch" file system is not supposed to be a long-term storage, but provides high performance. Here I will speak **only about NFSv3**. For v4 features, please refer to your storage supplier, check for available features, decide if you want to use them, and test them, not only for performance, but under long load too!

Depending on the settings, NFS can work via UDP or TCP. In modern versions, TCP is used by default, as it is more reliable and adapts to network traffic. UDP requires slightly less overhead, but when using it, NFS is worse at detecting communication errors. Package and service names may vary from distribution to distribution, but to successfully start an NFS server, it is sufficient to run `portmap`, followed by `nfsd` and `mountd`. The latter is often started together with `nfsd`, i.e., the command `systemctl start nfs`[1] often starts both services.

NFS server (`nfsd`), as mentioned above, allows clients to work with a part of their local system, or rather with a separate directory (as they say, "exports a directory"). In order to provide some kind of directory for clients, you need to specify it in the `/etc/exports` file. Startup options, `nfsd` typically has no startup options, or accepts the number of server threads to be started. The number of these threads is equal to the number of concurrent operations, so it makes sense to run as many as there are clients planned.

The `/etc/exports` file consists of lines, each of which describes an export rule for a directory. One directory can be specified several times with different rules:

`/export/dir host1,host2,host3(rw,root_squash)`

Here, `/export/dir` is the directory to be exported, followed by a list of nodes to which access is granted, and options in brackets. The list of hosts is comma separated and can include both DNS names and IP addresses and subnets in the format `1.2.3.4/8` or `2.3.4.5/255.0.0.0`. In the names of hosts, you can specify * and ?, denoting any string or any character, e.g., `*.local.net` or `host??.my.org`. If you specify * or `0.0.0.0/0` as a list, any client will be granted access.

The options may vary depending on the server implementation, but most are standard:

- `ro` – Read-only access.

- `rw` – Read-write access.

- `root_squash` (default) – The client root user will have nobody rights (see below) on the server.

- `no_root_squash` – The client root user will have root privileges on the server.

---

[1] or `/etc/init.d/nfsd start` on older systems

Table 9-1 presents some additional options.

Table 9-1. Some NFS exports options

Option	Meaning
all_squash	All client users will have nobody rights (see below) on the server
anonuid	User, whose rights will be given to clients during root_squash or all_squash operations (by default – nobody)
anonguid	Similar to anonuid, but for the group
no_subtree_check	Do not check user rights in directories above the mount point
async	Allow the server to confirm operations before they are actually executed
sync	Confirm operations only after they have been performed

A more complete set of options can be obtained by running the man exports command. Note that the sync option does not mean that the server will confirm the write operation only when the data gets to the disk. The confirmation will be given after the 'write' system call is completed on the server, and the data may remain in the OS file cache.

After modifying the exports file, the exportfs -r command should be run to have the nfs server reread the configuration. The exportfs command also allows you to manually add or remove an export rule, but I do not recommend this, as the changes are not written to /etc/exports and will not be saved when the nfs server is restarted.

Another command that allows you to view nfs server statistics is showmount. It shows the list of clients using the nfs server resources. Since the client and server do not have to be connected all the time, the list may include clients that are no longer on the network.

The -d option shows a list of directories used by at least one of the clients, -a shows a list of host:directory pairs, and -e shows the contents of the /etc/exports file. NFS clients are computers that mount the directories exported by the server into their file system. Therefore, all options for clients are contained in the /etc/fstab file or in the value of the -o switch of the mount command. The most typical options, supported by Linux are presented in the Table 9-2. There are many more in specific implementations, but as a rule, they have almost no impact on performance.

Table 9-2. Some NFS mount options

Option	Meaning
soft/hard	Algorithm for behavior after a server connection timeout; hard (default) forces the client to repeat the request until a response is received; soft stops sending after retrans (see below) sends and returns an error to the calling program. This prevents program hangs, but can lead to data corruption
retrans=n	Number of request resends to the server before an operation error is generated (if the soft option is used)
rsize/wsize=n	Maximum packet size for read/write operations in bytes; must be a multiple of 1024 and greater than zero. For modern clients, this is of little relevance, since the maximum packet size is determined dynamically when mounting the file system
ac/noac	Client can/can't cache file attributes
proto=udp/tcp	Which protocol to use for connection – tcp or udp
intr/nointr	You can/can't interrupt file operations by signal (Ctrl-C, etc.). If intr is used, if a signal is received during an operation, it is terminated and the program returns an EINTR error
acl/noacl	Use/not use the NFSACL auxiliary protocol to add access control lists to files
nfsvers=N	Use the specified version of NFS. The default is the maximum version supported by both the client and the server
sync/async	Whether or not to send data to the server before exiting the system call
lock/nolock	Enable/disable the use of an additional protocol that allows flock calls to be made for files on NFS. Using lock requires running an additional lock manager (usually lockd or nfslockd) on the server. In addition, using lock increases the overhead of file operations

NFS is not a secure file system unless additional features are used, such as encryption and Kerberos authentication (available in NFSv4). This means that if someone can gain access to the network over which NFS data is transmitted, they can gain access to all of that data or connect with the highest possible privileges.

Encryption alleviates this problem, but catastrophically reduces performance. So when using NFS, make sure that only trusted computers are on the network. For large systems, NFS is, alas, a poor fit. Its bottlenecks are the inability to scale (multiple NFS servers cannot be made to work together, sharing the load) and the need to synchronize clients when writing to a file.

Lustre

The Lustre file system architecture allows you to use multiple devices and storage nodes to serve many clients at the same time. Unlike NFS, there is no single server bottleneck – data is accessed by many servers simultaneously. And it is open source! And you can get commercial support – please check which company does it today, they are changing so rapidly.

Compared to NFS, the advantage of this file system is that it is designed to support not only concurrency in the storage part of a compute cluster, but also to support concurrent data access by clients (i.e., compute nodes in the cluster). To the user, Lustre looks like a typical POSIX-compliant file system. Note that only Linux clients and servers are supported; for any other clients, you will need to reexport mounted Lustre file system as NFS or SMB, which zeroes its benefits.

An undeniable advantage of this architecture is its easy scalability: at any time, a new server can be added to a running file system, increasing both speed and storage capacity. Lustre supports both traditional TCP/IP networks and fast networks such as InfiniBand. Note that the overall architecture is similar to other distributed file systems.

Architecture

Let's take a closer look at the Lustre architecture (see Figure 9-1). It includes the following components:

- **Management server (MGS)** – Stores configuration information for the whole Lustre file system (or even multiple fs), like all OSTs locations, MDTs, OSSes, MDSes, etc. It is recommended to dedicate a separate disk to store MGS data, but it is allowed to combine it with MDT (see below) and usually it is the case.

- **Metadata servers (MDS)** – Their purpose is to store metadata of all objects on the file system, like files names, permissions, and where are they stored (which OST). You can have multiple MDSes in one file system.

- **Object storage servers (OSS)** – Provide file system objects, like file chunks, directories, etc.

- **Metadata target (MDT)** – A metadata repository, such as a hard disk, DAS, or NAS. An MDT can be accessed by multiple MDSs, but only one of them is capable of using it. This helps to provide fault tolerance for the MDS.

- **Object storage target (OST)** – Object storage (chunks of user files). Like MDT, it can be either a hard disk or a network storage.

- **Lustre clients** – Compute and other nodes with Lustre software installed that allows them to mount the Lustre file system.

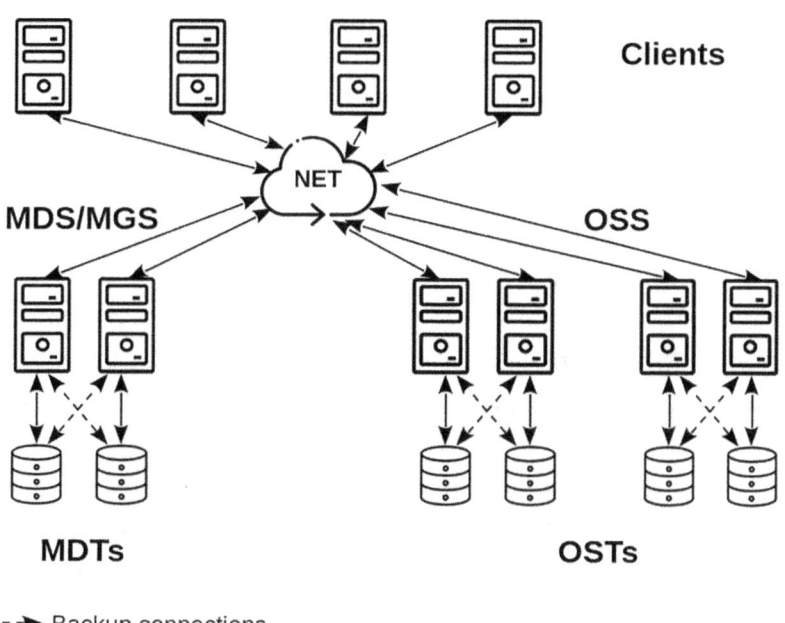

Figure 9-1. Simple Lustre architecture

CHAPTER 9   NETWORK FILE SYSTEMS

Each OSS can mount several OST (and this is typical) and also can be configured to be able to mount OSTs of one of its neighbors. This allows to survive if one OSS is down – its partner can mount volumes and continue to manage them. We'll return to this later.

The Lustre **client software** consists of the Metadata Client (MDC), Object Storage Client (OSC), and Management Client (MGC). Each client provides interaction with the corresponding component of the Lustre server side. The OSC group forms one LOV – Logical Object Volume.

In the Lustre architecture, component communication over the network takes place through the **LNET** interface – **Lustre Networking**. LNET allows the use of different networks using Lustre Network Drivers (LNDs). LNET supports message passing for RPC request and RDMA for bulk data movement and allows Lustre to work across InfiniBand, TCP/IP, Quadrics Elan, Myrinet (MX and GM), and Cray. At the LNET level, recovery capability is supported when any connection fails.

Each network interface in the LNET network has a unique **NID** – Lnet Network Identifier, which has the format `<address>@<LND protocol><lnd#>`. For address part, IPv4 address is used. Even in IB networks, where no IP is used as the transport layer, the NID will take ip-over-ib address to identify the interface. For example, `10.20.30.40@o2ib1` may be a typical NID for and IB interface and `192.168.2.3@tcp2` – for TCP/IP. Each "protocol+index" represents an isolated network from the LNET perspective, so `1.2.3.4@tcp0` never can talk to `2.3.4.5@tcp1`. Note that on IP level, LNET module uses port 988, do not block it by firewall.

When storing files, Lustre automatically divides them into blocks, and each block can be stored on an OST, and the blocks can be accessed in parallel. It is important to remember that Lustre **does not provide redundancy** when storing data. Consistency can be provided on OST and MDT level by using RAID. MDT should use RAID-10 due to small I/O size, while OSTs should use RAID-6 due to larger I/O size, usually 1 MB or larger.

When planning a farm for Lustre, remember that MDT data is the most critical – its loss or corruption is equivalent to the loss of all other data. Read current recommendations from the official Lustre documentation to choose chunk size, raid levels, and check your servers' memory size. Please refer to the latest Lustre recommendations; they may change pretty fast!

CHAPTER 9   NETWORK FILE SYSTEMS

Creation of Lustre File System

Lustre has no user-space services, clients and servers are kernel modules. In some cases, it is possible to build Lustre kernel modules for vanilla kernel, but the recommended way is to download precompiled kernel module from official Lustre website[2] and matching Lustre packages.

To deploy Lustre, you need to install the appropriate software on all components (both servers and clients), configure LNET networks, format the MDT and OST partitions, mount them on the appropriate MDS and OSS, and then mount the resulting file system on the clients. Here is an example for a simple configuration.

Create (or edit, if exists) file /etc/modprobe.d/lustre.conf, which contains LNET configuration. There are two options to defile an LNET network – networks and ip2nets. The first option is highly recommended. The second one gives you more flexibility, but in most cases is redundant because of complexity. To specify networks LNET configuration, put into the lustre.conf file a line in format "<lnd><#>(<dev>) [,…]", e.g.,

options lnet networks="o2ib0(ib0),tcp0(eth2)"

To check if everything is OK, you can load lnet kernel module and run lnetctl command (in this example, networks="tcp0(eth1)" was used):

```
# modprobe lnet
# lnetctl net show
net:
    - net: lo
      nid: 0@lo
      status: up
    - net: tcp
      nid: 192.168.2.3@tcp1
      status: up
      interfaces:
          0: eth1
```

---
[2] https://Lustre.org as for 2025.

129

lo interface is shown always by default. Next step – Format MGS and MDT volume(s)! Let's run this command on the MDS:

```
mkfs.lustre --mdt --mgs --index=0 \
  --servicenode 192.168.2.3@tcp0 \
  --servicenode 192.168.2.4@tcp0 \
  --fsname=large-fs /dev/sdX
mount -t lustre /dev/sdX /mnt/mdt
```

Here we use one volume for both MGS and MDT. In this example, we use two nodes, which can manage this target and specified their NIDs. Only one node can mount this volume at the same moment. /dev/sdX is the device name and large-fs is the file system name. The file system name is limited to eight characters. Index is used for MDTs and OSTs only. If you use more than one MDT, increase the index when you create the next one. Created volume can be mounted immediately.

Note that MGS and MDTs are recommended to be mounted first; all OST volumes are safe to be mounted later. Remember that if you shut down the Lustre and then need to power it up.

We then perform initialization on all OSSs:

```
mkfs.lustre --ost --index=0 --fsname=large-fs \
  --mgsnode=192.168.2.3@tcp0 --mgsnode=192.168.2.4@tcp0 \
  /dev/sdZ
mount -t lustre /dev/sdZ /mnt/ost1
```

Here /dev/sdZ is the device name, fsname is the system name, we used in MGS/MDS creation, and mgsnode is our MGS node(s) NID(s). You also can use --servicenode to allow several nodes to manage this volume; this is useful for the Lustre redundancy – if one node goes down, you can mount the volume on the other.

After all MGS, MDTs, and OSTs are mounted, the Lustre is ready to run; you can mount the file system on the clients with the command

```
mount -t lustre 192.168.2.3@tcp0,192.168.2.4@tcp0:/large-fs /mnt/lustre
```

Specify all MGS NIDs via comma. If you forgot your MGS NID, access it via ssh or console and run the command

`lctl list_nids`

Remember that Lustre does not route its traffic between the different networks, so both the client and MDS must be on the same network, and it is important to specify the correct NID list if you are using multiple networks.

Lustre is quite demanding on RAM size, especially on OSS. For each OST, the default is 400 MB for logging and about 600 MB for metadata caching. In addition, 1.5 MB for each service thread (the number of threads can be roughly estimated as the number of clients divided by the number of connected OSTs). For MDS, the calculation formula can be found on the official website, and I'd recommend having more memory, than it gives.

The buffers of the operating system and network devices should also not be forgotten. For normal OSS operation, it is recommended to have 2 GB of RAM plus 1 GB for each OST. Additional memory is not a bad thing; it will be used for additional caching. Fine-tuning the Lustre settings is done with the `lctl` and `tunefs.lustre` commands.

The `lctl set_param` command performs on-the-fly configuration. The parameters can be changed either temporarily (by default) or permanently and will be saved after a reboot (add -P option). The `lctl get_param` command gives a list of currently valid parameters. `lctl ping` can be used to test if an OSS or MDS is available via the `lnet` transport. These commands affect the internal logic of Lustre, so don't use them unless you really need to. Be sure to study the documentation carefully, as the wrong combination or order of commands can cause the file system to malfunction.

The `tunefs.lustre` command is used in rare cases, like changing OST/MDT NIDs, and is only executed on OSS or MDS when the server is stopped!

If an OST has failed in the process of creation, the best recommendation is to reformat it. If it has failed while the file system has data, you should unmount all clients, then unmount all OSTs, then MDTs and MGS, and try to recover the OST. Usually it is done by mounting the OST as a `ldiskfs` file system if ext4 was used as a carrier file system and then checking using a special patched version of `e2fsck`. Please refer to the documentation of the exact version of Lustre you are using, the instructions may differ, and you can easily ruin your OST data. You're warned.

If you want to retire the OST, e.g., you see the hardware issues, you can disable it using `lctl --device N deactivate`, where N is the "device number" of desired OST. You can get it using `lctl dl` command, which lists all "devices" visible on the client. After that, Lustre will stop to allocate new objects on this OST and you can migrate the data to others OSTs using `lfs_migrate` command. Removing and replacing of OSTs is in active development in 2025; check your Lustre version instructions, if they are supported.

Fault Tolerance in Lustre

Lustre **does not support data duplication or redundancy**,[3] i.e., if data on OST or MDT is physically lost, it is impossible to recover it using Lustre tools. In the case of MDTs, this usually equates to losing the entire file system. That is why RAID is recommended, although it does not guarantee data safety. You can try to recover the (some) data, using officially recommended methods for your Lustre version.

To make the situation a bit better, and at least minimize the risk of failing a server, but not a data volume, we use multiple service nodes in the volumes definitions. If one node fails, the "partner" can mount its volumes and continue to serve them. The problem is that Lustre cannot do this on its own. As a rule, for this purpose, **Corosyc+Pacemaker** or similar software is used. Here we will not consider their configuration, but there is nothing complicated in it. Please pay attention to the order of the installation and configuration; it does matter. In order for this mapping to work, the OSTs must be physically connected to two (or more) OSSs – service nodes. Common case is when two OSSs share the same OST set, but first mounts the first half of them, and the second – the rest.

Network redundancy means that the OSS can be accessed via multiple addresses, e.g., via InfiniBand and via Ethernet. Both routes are used at the same time, but if one of them stops working, communication will only continue via the second route. The addresses (and LNET drivers) must be prescribed in the file system settings in advance.

> If multiple interfaces on the same subnet are used, traffic will always go through the first one. This is a limitation of the Linux kernel, use bonding for such configurations.

---

[3] In the beginning of 2025

Striping and PFL

It was mentioned before that when storing a file, Lustre splits it into blocks. It is known as "**striping**" in Lustre. You can manage stripe size and number of OSTs, between which file stripes will be distributed. Here is an example how to apply new striping settings to a directory:

```
lfs setstripe -S 4M -c 8 /lustre/testdir
```

Here we set stripe count to 8 and size to 4 megabytes. Each **new** file, created in this directory, will get such stripe parameters. You cannot change stripe parameters for any existing file; the only method to change them is to copy the file into the directory with desired parameters set. To check the current file configuration and placement, you can use this command (-y gives you yaml-formatted output):

```
lfs getstripe -y /lustre/testdir/testfile
lmm_stripe_count:   8
lmm_stripe_size:    4194304
lmm_pattern:        raid0
lmm_layout_gen:     0
lmm_stripe_offset:  2
lmm_objects:
    - l_ost_idx: 2
      l_fid:      0x100020000:0x2:0x0
    - l_ost_idx: 3
      l_fid:      0x100030000:0x2:0x0
...
```

Lustre 2.10+ supports "**Progressive File Layouts**" (PFL), which allows having different stripe counts and sizes for different file regions (components in terms of Lustre). Let's modify our directory:

```
lfs setstripe -E 1M -S 512K -c 1 \
              -E 256M        -c 4 \
              -E -1 -S 1M    -c 8 /lustre/testdir
```

-E option sets the end of the component, and the options followed it – striping parameters. In this example, the first megabyte of the file will be placed in 2 stripes by 512K on the same OST, the next 255 megabytes on 4 OSTs using the same stripe size, and the rest of the file (after 256 megabytes) on 8 OSTs using stripes of 1 megabyte size. See Figure 9-2 for the graphical representation of this layout. Note that OST's indexes here are just for the illustration; they are chosen randomly and can repeat in different components. For example, if we have only 8 OSTs in our file system, the last component will take OSTs from 1 to 8.

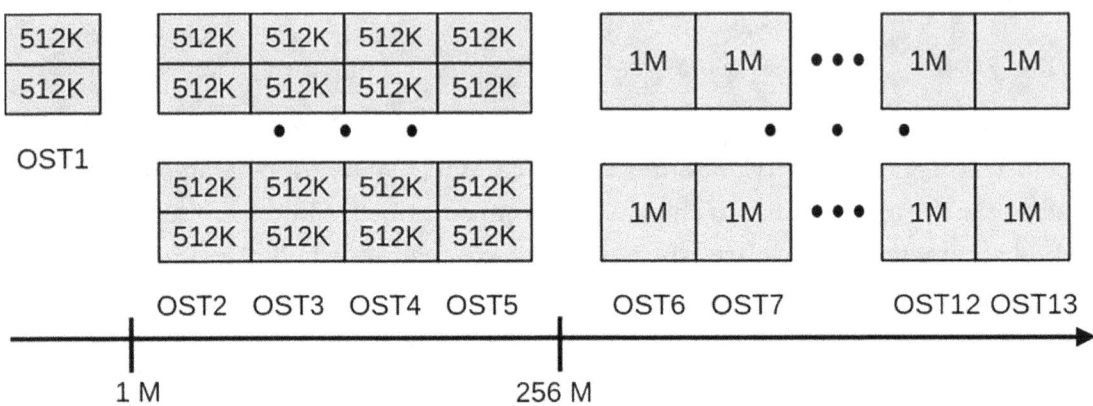

Figure 9-2. PFL example

Quotas

Lustre supports user, group, and project quotas. Soft and hard quotas are supported. Hard quota cannot be exceeded, but soft quota can for a grace time period. Here are some examples:

```
lfs setquota -u foo -b 200G -B 300G -i 2M -I 3M /lustre
lfs setquota -g bar -b 200G -B 300G -i 2M -I 3M /lustre
lfs project -r /lustre/testdir
lfs setquota -p 1 -b 200G -B 300G -i 2M -I 3M /lustre
```

Here we set the same limits for user foo, group bar, and project 1 (projects have only numbers): maximum 3 million inodes and 300 gigabytes. Soft quota is lower – 2 million inodes and 200 gigabytes. For the project 1, we marked all files under /lustre/testdir. Default grace time is one week; it is global for each type – user inodes, user block, group inodes, group block, project inodes, and project block. To change it, use this command:

```
lfs setquota -t -u -i 1d8h -b 2d /lustre
```

Here we set grace times for users inodes and block quotas as one day, eight hours, and two days, respectively. Default quota is also supported; to set it, use -U, -G, or -P to set user, group, or project default quota. If you set some quota to a user, e.g., and want to reset it to default, use this command:

```
lfs setquota -u foo --default /lustre
```

This works for groups and projects too, of course. To remove any quotas to user/group/project, specify 0 as value when you use setquota.

Lustre is a good choice for a distributed file system used during computations to store temporary as well as input and output data (so-called **scratch file system**). However, for permanent storage of user data, I recommend using a more robust file system. You're warned.

PanFS

The PanFS file system is another representative of the parallel file system. Solutions based on this file system are a hardware-software complex produced by Panasas (now VDURA), consisting of one or more ActiveStor storage systems and file system drivers for installation on clients.

At the time of writing, file system drivers are available for Linux only. File system access is also possible via CIFS and NFS protocols, but in this case, the modules that provide file system reexport would be a potential bottleneck for the system. Nevertheless, in this way, it is possible to provide, e.g., access to the network root file system for diskless nodes.

Note that file system drivers for clients (unlike, e.g., GPFS) are not licensed additionally by the number of clients. The PanFS driver does not use the DKMS mechanism, so the set of compatible distributions and kernel versions is very limited. A driver for a specific kernel can be obtained from VDURA on a separate request. The VDURA storage system includes metadata and management nodes (**Directors**) and object data storage nodes. The data network may be only Ethernet (1, 10, or 25 GB), but VDURA provides an InfiniBand router server, which allows using this product in IB networks (but may be a bottleneck).

VDURA storage management software runs on the metadata and management nodes. The following configuration mechanisms are available to the cluster administrator: https access, console access via ssh, or serial port. Note that even with multiple VDURA systems (with different volumes and access levels), it is possible to configure all systems from a single point.

Data fault tolerance is provided by storing object data with RAID-1 level redundancy for small files or RAID-5 for large and medium files (these settings can be changed). RAID redundancy is provided on the file system level, and different stripes are stored on different nodes, which means, that if a node is down, the file system is still alive.

Fault tolerance for metadata is provided by mirroring it from the metadata node, which is the primary node for this volume, to the standby node. If there are three or more metadata and management nodes in the system, you can enable the fault-tolerant cluster mode. In case of failure of the primary metadata node, the standby node will start to perform the functions of the metadata controller transparently for the user.

A distinctive feature of the system is the transfer of part of the file system work to the client driver (i.e., to the cluster nodes), in particular, RAID checksum calculation is performed by the client part driver. If possible, the client part also caches data, so a lot of RAM on the client can be occupied by system buffers.

PanFS storage systems are highly scalable. To increase data transfer speed and capacity, one or more storage systems can be added, and system expansion can be performed on-the-fly without stopping running applications.

VDURA has a user-friendly administration and configuration system that makes it easy to manage the system for personnel who do not have in-depth knowledge of parallel file systems. Metadata nodes, object data nodes, and file system clients must have well-synchronized time for the file system to function properly. I strongly recommend that all nodes be configured to synchronize with the NTP server on the PanFS management node and that it in turn be synchronized with a public NTP server. This allows you to remain operational in case of temporary problems with the external network.

GPFS/IBM Storage Scale

General Parallel File System (GPFS) was developed by IBM in 1998 and has been available for Linux since 2001. It is a proprietary distributed file system that supports a wide range of Linux distributions. According to IBM's 2013 information, this file system can scale to 9300 nodes and 16386 clients, with the largest installation having 5000 nodes. GPFS supports RDMA technology for InfiniBand.

Metadata in GPFS is distributed, there is no dedicated metadata servers, and it supports indexing of directory entries for very large directories. It includes special heartbeat and quorum protocols, which allows keeping working in degraded mode even if a network fail divided the file system servers into two isolated subnets. Data is duplicated, and if one server goes down, the whole file system is still alive.

The maintenance can be performed online; if you add new disks, do a bad disk replacement, or rebalance the data, the file system is up and going. You can install GPFS on any host, and depending on how you configure it, it will be either a GPFS server or a GPFS client. Both server and client must be licensed. There is a large amount of documentation on GPFS, both official and accumulated by the community, including on wikis and forums. It is recommended to study the documentation and recommendations well before installation, as many parameters cannot be changed once the file system has been created.

Unfortunately, I have no serious experience in using GPFS, and cannot give sound advice about it. Nevertheless, this file system is used on many HPC clusters, which indicates its suitability in our domain. If you decide to purchase GPFS, pay attention to the OS and RAM requirements and of course plan your licenses and support (it will take remarkable part of you budget), not only for current needs, but for possible extension.

Other File Systems

Among other distributed proprietary file systems, I can also note Weka. I didn't use it, but have good feedback from my friends. It has a lot of features, like POSIX, NFS, SMB, S3 and GPUDirect storage support, storage tiering, namespaces, encryption, and snapshots. It protects data on the file level, and in case of failure, actively used files are recovered first, which reduces the time of recovery and recovery overhead. If you deploy Weka cluster in cloud, it supports auto expand and auto shrink. I have no information about the pricing plans or real performance tests and cannot compare it with GPFS or Panasas, but it seems like a real competitor.

The list of distributed file systems supported by Linux is certainly longer than the one discussed above. For example, I can name **Gluster**, **Coda**, **CEPH, Hadoop HDFS, BeeGFS, MooseFS**, **zFS** (not to be confused with ZFS), and others. So far I can't say anything positive about them as applied to HPC. Most of them are not POSIX-complaint which breaks a lot of applications, some have problems with file sharing, others with reliability, others with performance under heavy load, some are still under development and not yet ready for serious production use.

This does not mean that the list of solutions is strictly limited – file systems evolve and improve, new ones appear. I just want to warn you against making hasty decisions, the file system is always one of the most "bottlenecks" of a supercomputer.

CHAPTER 9   NETWORK FILE SYSTEMS

I should note that not always you need high-performance parallel file system; in some cases, you may use NFS, or, e.g. CernVM-FS.[4] They may be useful for read-only access, delivery of local container images, or static data; NFS is often used for home user directories (in this case, I recommend mounting it in read-only mode on compute nodes). You can combine different types of file systems depending on requirements.

If you use LDAP or NIS, it might be beneficial to use autofs for automatic mounting of user home directories or other shared resources. I would not recommend using it on compute nodes, but on the login and data copying nodes, it might help. Make sure that your server software support it.

Before installing an advertised distributed file system, try to test it. You should be interested in the degree of scalability, work under load of a large number of clients (e.g., virtual clients), fault tolerance, and the ability to recover from failures that do occur.

Brief Summary

Network file system is one of the key elements of a supercomputer. A mistake with its choice can be very expensive – catastrophic performance losses, difficulty of installation and diagnostics, support costs, etc. Take a responsible attitude to its choice and try to test the selected system in advance on a test site or with your colleagues.

Search Keywords

NTP, NFSv4.1, NFSv4, NFSv3, mount, RPC, Lustre fs, parallel fs, pNFS, LustreFS, Panasas, GPFS, Ceph, Corosync, Pacemaker

---

[4] https://cvmfs.readthedocs.io/en/stable/index.html

CHAPTER 10

Remote Management

For the simplest organization of remote access, it is enough to run `sshd` server on the nodes. This is the basic means of access to compute (and not only) nodes. But what to do if there is a problem with a node and `sshd` does not start? How do you find out the cause of the issue? IPMI or iKVM/KVM-over-IP can help. In order to use remote access via IPMI, you need to activate it beforehand; by default, only local access works, and network access is disabled. There are other similar technologies, e.g., Redfish and DCMI, but IPMI specification still is most common.

IPMI remote access can be activated via BIOS, if it allows it, or by booting as root and configuring IPMI network settings with the `ipmitool` command (see IPMI chapter below). Ensure that IPMI network is enabled by vendor, and getting IP via DHCP is enabled (and you have MAC address list); otherwise, you'll have to set up IPMI manually for all your nodes, which may take weeks. Access via iKVM usually needs to be preconfigured as well. In many implementations, it is combined with IPMI. Don't forget to change the default password!

ssh and Parallel ssh

SSH is a secure shell; this protocol replaced the telnet and remote shell protocols, which were previously widely used for remote access, but were absolutely insecure. The same still applies to the FTP.

In 1995, Finnish computer scientist Tatu Ylönen designed SSH – open secure protocol for remote access and file transfer. Now the most common implementation of client and server is OpenSSH, evolved by OpenBSD developers, but there are alternatives. By default, SSH server uses 22 port. Below we will use the abbreviation SSH for the protocol and ssh for the name of the client command of the same name.

SSH is based on two types of encryption: symmetric and asymmetric (public key). Symmetric encryption uses the same key for both the encryption and decryption, i.e., both parties must have the same key to exchange data.

Asymmetric encryption algorithms use a pair of keys: one of them can encrypt the data and the other can decrypt it. But with only one key, you cannot perform both operations or recover the second key.[1]

Thus, we can generate a pair of keys, one of which will be "**public**." It can be transmitted through open channels to everyone with whom we need to communicate, published on the Internet (there are even special key servers). The second key is called the **private key**; it should remain a big secret. Now, for secure communication between two parties, they need to exchange public keys and start encrypted data exchange: everything that one of them encrypts with its private key, the other can decrypt with the received public key. Moreover, it is often enough to have one key pair, since the second respondent can send data to the first one by encrypting it with the public key received, while the first one decrypts it with the private key!

The SSH protocol uses keys to identify not only clients but also servers. Each SSH server has its own so-called host key. When connecting to a server for the first time, the client will ask the server for the public part of the key and ask the user to confirm that this is the right server by showing the key fingerprint. If the user knows the correct fingerprint beforehand, the user can compare it to the reference and refuse the connection if they differ. If the user has confirmed the connection, the client stores the match between the host key and the server address (usually in the ~/.known_hosts file). In case the next connection shows that the host key has changed, ssh will reject the connection.

This is done to make it impossible to replace the remote server with your own and intercept the transmission of information while acting as a transmitter. This type of attack is called a man-in-the-middle attack.

In the SSH protocol, a typical session occurs like this:

- The client connects to the server and establishes an encrypted connection with a symmetric key using the Diffie-Hellman algorithm, then all communication is encrypted with this key.

---

[1] In some algorithms, the private key can be used to recover the public key, but not vice versa. In openssh, the public key is also stored in the private key file.

- If the client has the server's public host key, it generates a random string, encrypts it with this key, and passes it to the server (if the key is not available, the client requests it from the server and asks the user to authenticate).

- The server decrypts the string with the private host key and sends it to the client.

- If the string matches the initial string, the client sends the server the username under which access is requested.

- The client tries possible key pairs for connection, and each attempt starts with sending the public part of the key to the server.

- The server checks if the public key is in the list of allowed keys (in the ~USER/.ssh/authorized_keys file).

- If there is no key, the client tries the next key pair.

- If the key exists, the server encrypts a random string with it and sends it to the client.

- The client decrypts the string with a private key and sends it to the server.

- If decryption is successful, the server acknowledges the session and starts the required command or console session.

Symmetric encryption is used because it is less resource intensive and to reduce the amount of data that can be intercepted and attempt to recover the private key. The symmetric key is periodically changed during an ssh connection. SSH servers typically support nonpublic key authentication, such as password or Kerberos. In this case, all data is also encrypted with symmetric keys.

I strongly recommend that you do not use password authentication. Passwords are not very resistant to brute force, i.e., an attacker can simply pick the right password and no encryption will save them. That's why "secure" versions of telnet and ftp over SSL/TLS encrypted connections are also considered insecure. It is almost impossible to find a private key. There is a possibility that the key itself will be stolen, but even in this case, there is an additional guarantee: SSH private keys can (and should!) be password protected.

Let's consider the most popular ssh server and cldient for Linux – `openssh`. In most distributions, the server and client are installed as separate packages. When installing the server, a host key is automatically generated. If you reinstall the ssh server, take care to save and restore the host keys!

In addition to providing console access, the openssh server provides several other features. The most important ones are present in Table 10-1.

Forwarding Environment Variables

SSH allows us to set some environment variables (e.g., `LANG`) in a remote session to be the same as on the work computer running the `ssh` client. The list of variables that the client passes is set in its configuration or on the command line, and the list of variables that the server can "cast" is set in the server configuration.

The variable must be enabled for both client and server to be able to proxy. Some variables, such as `LD_PRELOAD`, are not allowed to be thrown unless specific server options are specified (see below).

Port Forwarding

A very flexible tool that allows you to create a small proxy server for a single connection. There are two options for port forwarding – on the client and on the server. Port forwarding on the client means that on your work computer, a connection on a given port will be automatically tunneled to the ssh server.

For example, you need to access an internal web server with the address `192.168.0.10`, which is available only on the internal network. When running `ssh`, we will specify that we need to forward port 8080 to `192.168.0.10:80`. After that, the connection to local port 8080 will be automatically tunneled to port 80 on the server. For the web server, this connection will look like a connection from the computer where the ssh server is installed.

This is easily done by the command

```
ssh -L 8080:192.168.0.10:80 your.server.address
```

Similarly, it is possible to forward connections in the opposite direction (a port on the server is forwarded to the client): assign a port on the server to which a connection will be established through a secure channel to a host accessible from the machine where the client is running. In this case, `-R` is used instead of the `-L` switch.

X Connection Forwarding

Similar to port forwarding, you can forward connection to the X server. Remember, the X server is your local server; it handles your graphical display, mouse, and keyboard. If you use Windows, you may run a Windows implementation of X server, like Cygnus, Xming, or its fork VcXsrv. When you run an ssh client locally and connect to the remote computer with X connection forwarded, you may run an X application, e.g., xterm on the remote computer, and it will show you the window on your local X server managed display. You cannot run your local browser, e.g., on the remote computer.

You must have xauth program installed on both computers and be careful running remote sudo – you will need to pass your XAUTHORITY variable through it (remote variable, which ssh set after you logged in).

File Transfer

SSH has two built-in protocols for file transfer: **SCP** and **SFTP**. In addition to the not very convenient console clients of the same name, there are many client implementations, such as sshfs for Linux/MacOS, built-in support in Nautilus/Dolphin for Gnome/KDE shells, FileZilla, WinSCP for Windows, and many others.

SSH Agent

This is an ssh built-in tool for storing keys. At the beginning, the agent loads ssh keys from files and asks for passwords to decrypt them, then stores them in memory. When new ssh/sftp connections are established, any data can be encrypted or decrypted with these keys via the agent. This is useful for loading keys not from the ~/.ssh directory or with nonstandard names. Access to the agent can also be forwarded, which means that on the remote computer, you will have access to all keys from the local computer, but indirectly, only be able to crypt/decrypt the data.

In case of all forwards, data is transmitted in a single encrypted channel, and no additional connections to the ssh server are made. This means that the ability to connect to the server on port 22 (or other port if the ssh server configuration is nonstandard) is sufficient for operation.

CHAPTER 10   REMOTE MANAGEMENT

Configuring the ssh Server

The openssh server settings are usually stored in the /etc/ssh/sshd_config file. The most important ones are present in Table 10-1.

Table 10-1. *Some configuration options for the openssh server*

Option	Meaning
AcceptEnv	Specifies a space-separated list of environment variables that the server can set to the same value as on the client. Variable names can include '?' and '*' similar to shell.
AllowAgentForwarding	(yes/no) enable agent forwarding.
AllowGroups	If this parameter is set, only users belonging to the specified groups will be allowed to log in. It is convenient to use it during preventive maintenance by restricting access to the administrators group. Only group names are allowed, not numbers.
AllowTcpForwarding	(yes/no) enable port forwarding.
AllowUsers	Similar to AllowGroups, but specifies a list of users. It is allowed to specify the name in the format user@host[/mask]; in this case, access will be allowed only from the specified address or range of addresses.
Banner	Path to the file whose contents will be output immediately after connection to the server (before authentication).
DenyGroups	Similar to AllowGroup, but lists the groups whose members are denied access.
DenyUsers	Similar to AllowUsers, but lists the users for whom access is denied.
ListenAddress	Sets the addresses and ports on which the SSH server will run. The defaults are 0.0.0.0:22 (for ipv4) and :::22 (for ipv6).
ForceCommand	No matter what command the client requests to execute, only this command will be executed. This parameter is conveniently set in the Match block (see below). To restrict access using sftp, you can specify "internal-sftp" in this parameter.

(continued)

Table 10-1. (*continued*)

Option	Meaning
LogLevel	One of the following values: QUIET, FATAL, ERROR, INFO, VERBOSE, DEBUG, DEBUG1, DEBUG2, DEBUG3. The default is INFO. Sets the logging level. Convenient when analyzing problems with the input.
Match	Sets the conditional block (see description below).
PasswordAuthentication	(yes/no) enables password authentication.
PermitEmptyPasswords	(yes/no) allows the use of blank passwords.
PermitRootLogin	(yes/without-password/forced-commands-only/no) allows superuser login. If the parameter value is without-password, then login is allowed only by key, and if forced-commands-only, then only by key for which command forcing is specified.
PermitUserEnvironment	(yes/no) allows a list of environment variables to be set in ~/.ssh/environment. Setting this list explicitly allows you to bypass restrictions on scrolling variables such as LD_PRELOAD.
Port	Specifies the port on which the ssh server is running. The default is 22. You can specify multiple ports by specifying different strings with the Port parameter.
PrintMotd	(yes/no) specifies to output the contents of the /etc/motd file after login (message of the day).
PubkeyAuthentication	(yes/no) enables key authentication.
StrictModes	(yes/no) specifies to check the permissions and owner of the user's home directory and ssh-critical files.
UseDNS	(yes/no) specifies to use DNS name resolving when logging.
UseLogin	(yes/no) specifies to use the standard login program when logging in. If this option is enabled, X connection forwarding will not work.
X11Forwarding	(yes/no) enables X connection forwarding.
XauthLocation	Path to the xauth command. Used to forward the X connection if the path is different from /usr/X11R6/bin/xauth.

Only one of the parameters `AllowUsers`, `DenyUsers`, `AllowGroup`, and `DenyGroups` can be specified. Any of them can be specified more than once if a large list is to be specified.

The `Match` block specifies a set of options that will be applied only if the specified condition is met. The condition can be `User`, `Group`, `Host`, `LocalAddress`, `LocalPort`, or `Address` followed by a comma-separated list of arguments, e.g.,

`Match User admin,superuser,lab*`

For `User` and `Group`, you specify the lists of users and groups respectively, and for `Host`, `Address`, `LocalAddress`, and `LocalPort`, you specify the remote hostname, remote host address, local address, and local port, respectively.

When specifying user, group, and hostnames, you can use '?' and '*', and when specifying a remote address, you can use masks, e.g., `1.2.3.4/8`. The `Match` line is followed by an option block. `AcceptEnv`, `AllowAgentForwarding`, `AllowGroups`, `AllowTcpForwarding`, `AllowUsers`, `Banner`, `DenyGroups`, `DenyUsers`, `ForceCommand`, `PasswordAuthentication`, `PermitEmptyPasswords`, `PermitRootLogin`, `PubkeyAuthentication`, `X11Forwarding`, and some others are allowed in this block. See the documentation for more details.

Configuring the ssh Client

The openssh client also has a set of settings. Most of them do not need to be changed, and they are located in the `/etc/ssh/ssh_config` file. If a user needs to change something, it is enough to create a file `~/.ssh/config` and make the necessary settings in it. The `~/.ssh` directory contains public and private keys, as well as the file `authorized_keys` (sometimes `authorized_keys2`), which contains all the public keys that can be used to authenticate to a given user, and the `known_hosts` file, which contains the public keys of those computers that have been connected to in the past.

Let's consider the process of configuring remote login from client computer to server computer under `foo` user. On the client, run the command `ssh-keygen -t rsa` (if we have not done it before).

The `-t rsa` key instructs you to create a key pair in **RSA** format. You can also use **ecdsa, ecdsa-sk, ed25519, ed25519-sk,** or a newer format if available. You can add `-b NNN` key, to specify key length in bits; the more bits, the stronger is the key. For RSA, default length is 3072, and for ec-/ed-keys (elliptic curves), only 256, 384, and 521 values are available. The `ssh-keygen` program will ask where and with what name to form the private key, offering a standard option. It is better not to change it. Then the program will ask what password (passphrase) to protect the key and ask you to confirm the password and generate a pair of keys. The public key will have the same name as the private key, but with a `.pub` extension. For example, for a standard RSA key, we will get the files `~/.ssh/id_rsa` and `~/.ssh/id_rsa.pub`.

Next, copy the `id_rsa.pub` file to the `~foo` directory on the server computer. On the server, add the contents of `id_rsa.pub` to the list of allowed keys: `cat ~/id_rsa.pub >> ~/.ssh/authorized_keys`. Make sure that the `.ssh` directory and the `~/.ssh/authorized_keys` file belong to the user `foo` and are not allowed to be written to by anyone except `foo`.

Now from the client computer, it is enough to execute the `ssh` command `foo@my_server`, confirm the addition of the public host key to `known_hosts`, and enter the private key password. To allow a user to log on to a host without a password, it is sufficient to generate a key pair by specifying an empty password. If the user's directory is on a network drive, after that it is enough to add the public key to the same user's `authorized_keys`.

To ensure that the first time a user logs in, they are not asked for confirmation of being added to `known_hosts`, you can log in to all nodes in a loop using the command `ssh -o StrictHostKeyChecking=no HOSTNAME true`. This command will automatically put the node `HOSTNAME` key into `known_hosts`. The "true" at the end is the command to be executed on node name. You can specify any command, e.g., `date`, `uname`, and `yes`, but `true` is executed instantly and without display. If no command is specified at the end, the normal login to the remote system will be performed and the interactive shell will run.

In the process, `ssh` intercepts a special control key combination – "Enter ~". After pressing this sequence, you can enter a control character command. The list of commands is displayed by pressing "?". The most convenient commands are

- '~' – Pass the '~' symbol itself
- '.' – Terminate the session immediately
- 'Z' – Suspend and take the ssh process to the background
  (it can be resumed with the fg shell command)

Let's take a closer look at the set of ssh commands and their options. The ssh client itself has an extensive set of keys. The most important ones for us are presented in Table 10-2.

Table 10-2. Some keys of the ssh command

Key	Meaning
-A	Forward agent
-a	Don't forward agent
-i path	Specify the path to the private key
-R [bind_address:]port:host:hostport	Forward the server port port to the hostport port of the locally available host
-L [bind_address:]port:host:hostport	Forward the local port port to the hostport port of the remote host
-l username	Username on the remote host
-N	Not to execute a remote command. Convenient for port forwarding
-o option	Set an option for a specific connection (see below)
-p port	Specify the port on the remote machine if it is different from 22
-q	Suppress informational messages (useful when using ssh in scripts)
-t	Force the allocation of a pseudo-terminal. May be necessary when using ssh in scripts for commands that require a terminal, such as sudo
-v	Output more debugging information. You can specify several times in a row – the more options, the more detailed the output. Specifying -vvvv is often enough to diagnose input problems
-X / -Y	Enable X connection forwarding (using slightly different strategies)
-M	Try to reuse existing connection, see the ControlMaster option below.

In addition to command-line keys, ssh supports many options that can be set in the ~/.ssh/config file or via the -o switch. More details can be found in the documentation. The most useful ones are listed in Table 10-3.

Table 10-3. Some ssh client options

Option	Meaning
ConnectTimeout	Connection timeout time
EscapeChar	Change the control character from '~' to the specified character
ForwardAgent	Forward ssh agent
ForwardX11	Forward an X connection
IdentityFile	Specify the path to the private key
PasswordAuthentication	Force password authentication
SendEnv	Forward the listed environment variables
XauthLocation	Specify where the `xauth` command is located
StrictHostKeyChecking	(yes/no/ask) action if remote server host key is not in ~/.ssh/known_hosts file: yes = terminate session; ask = ask what to do; no = add key to file
ControlMaster auto ControlPath ~/.ssh/ssh_mux_%h_%p_%r	Enables ssh connection re-using, if there is existing ssh connection to a host, and you run `ssh -M host`, then the existing connection will be reused (but new ssh session will be started)

In addition to the general parameters in the ~/.ssh/config file, it is possible to specify sets for individual nodes. This is done with the keyword 'Host', followed by a list of hostname templates. The templates can include '?' and '*' signs, in particular a single asterisk matches any name. After this line, all parameters up to the next line 'Host' refer only to nodes matching the template.

This syntax, in particular, allows you to greatly reduce the string length in ssh commands, since you can specify such in the parameters. Table 10-4 presents some useful options for 'Host' section.

Table 10-4. Some options in the host section

Option	Meaning
HostName	Remote server name
IdentityFile	Path to the private key file
Port	Remote server port
User	Username on the remote server
ForwardX11	(yes/no) forward X11 connection
ForwardAgent	(yes/no) agent forwarding

The name specified in the template does not have to be the server name at all, because if the HostName parameter is specified, its value will be used. Here is a simple example of how to use this feature:

```
Host home
    HostName home.my.provider.com
    User foo
    Port 2222
    IdentityFile ~/.ssh/home_key
```

Such a fragment in the ~/.ssh/config file allows you to log on to your home computer with the ssh home command instead of ssh -p 2222 -i ~/.ssh/home_key foo@home.my.provider.com.

ssh is undoubtedly one of the main tools for managing a computer system. The main difficulty of its use arises in cases when it is necessary to perform one operation on many nodes, e.g., to perform a forced remounting of a network file system, to clear a temporary directory, to check the presence of processes of a particular user, etc.

Host-Based Authentication

Enabling passwordless authentication on dozens/hundreds/thousands of nodes may be painful. Good, if you have your ssh keys on the shared file system, or baked into the installed image. In other case, you may use much less secure, but efficient "trusted" host-based authentication. In this case, server checks if the client is allowed to use this authentication method, if the host key matches saved one, and if the user is allowed to use it.

To enable it, put configuration block like this into sshd_config file on server side:

```
Match Address 10.20.30.0/24 User admin
    HostbasedAuthentication yes
```

In this example, we enable this method for local subnet and for admin user only. You can enable it globally, without Match restriction. Now we need to add our trusted nodes into /etc/shosts.equiv file, one address per line, no netmasks allowed. Make sure that this file is not allowed for reading and writing to group and others. The next step is to collect client host keys. For each client node, run

```
ssh-keyscan CLIENT-IP-ADDRESS >> /etc/ssh/ssh_known_hosts
```

Now we need to enable it on clients. On each client node, run the ssh-keyscan command like above, but set server address, then add config block like this into /etc/ssh/ssh_config file:

```
Host server.my.cluster
    HostbasedAuthentication yes
    EnableSSHKeysign yes
```

Last line enables special helper; it is required in the modern ssh implementations. There may be some peculiarities in the configuration; please check man pages for your openssh version. Please note that this method is much less secure, than public key authentications.

pdsh

Let's take a look on the script from "Cluster" Commands subchapter of "UNIX and Linux – The Basics" chapter. It **should** work well, but disadvantages of this approach are

- The output of all commands will be messed up, and it is hard to "mark" output by its source.
- If at least one ssh commands hangs, the script also hangs. If the script is interrupted with Ctrl-C, the console will sometimes receive error messages from hung ssh commands.
- If the number of nodes is large, several hundred concurrently running ssh-es will cause significant impact to the server performance.

Of course, the script can be improved and even rewritten in a more convenient language. But this has already been done for us, e.g., by the authors of the `pdsh` program, which can run any commands on specified nodes in parallel, annotate the output, and limit the number of simultaneously running programs.

The simplest example of using `pdsh`:

```
pdsh -w node-[01-10] 'w| grep loadaverage'
```

This command will execute on nodes node-01 ... node-10 shell with the given command line. Due to the fact that the string is executed in the shell, we can run not just one command, but several, as in the example. Each output string will have a prefix – the name of the node from which it is received.

`pdsh` supports various transports other than `ssh`, so it can work in many exotic environments. Its most useful options are presented in Table 10-5.

Table 10-5. pdsh basic keys

Key	Meaning
-a	Run the command on all machines listed in the `hostfile` (see below)
-w	Execute the command on the listed nodes. The list is specified using commas (no spaces); ranges of numbers can be used, e.g., node-[10-20].[2] If '-' is specified as the list, the list is read from standard input
-x	Exclude the listed nodes
-g	Run the command on the nodes of the listed groups; the list of groups is specified using commas
-N	Do not output the node name before each line of output
-f	Specify the number of parallel execution threads
-u	Set the timeout in seconds of command execution on the node (by default there is no timeout)
-l	Execute the command as the specified user (similar to `ssh`)
-b	Terminate execution by pressing `Ctrl-C` (by default, pressing `Ctrl-C` gives the current execution status, and the second press terminates execution)

---

[2] Note that the standard shell may interpret square brackets, so specify the node list in quotes.

It is very inconvenient to specify node lists manually each time, so you can save the list of nodes in the /etc/pdsh/machines file, one per line. You can then run the command on all nodes using the -a switch. Since nodes may be of different types, it can be useful to use node groups in addition to a single file with a complete list of nodes. These can be specified in /etc/dsh/group/ (note that it is dsh, not pdsh) or ~/.dsh/group/. Each group is specified in a separate file with a list of nodes; the group name will be the same as the file name.

In addition to keys, you can use environment variables:

PDSH_SSH_ARGS_APPEND – Keys to be added to the ssh command. For example, some commands require a terminal to work even in noninteractive mode; for them, you need to specify the '-t' key to the ssh command. WCOLL – Name of the file with the list of all nodes.

In addition to pdsh, the package includes a parallel version of file copying, pdcp, which requires pdsh to be installed on nodes as well.

Cluster Shell

Another package, able to run commands in parallel on many nodes and copy files, is cluster shell. It is written in python and often is available as a system package, but can be installed as a python module:

```
pip install --user ClusterShell
```

The command to run something on many nodes is clush. Here is an example:

```
clush -w node-[01-10] uname -a
```

-w specifies the list of nodes, and after all switches and options, the remote command comes, so -a in this case won't be treated as a clush switch. You can put the remote command in quotes if needed, e.g., in this case, we want grep to be executed on the remote nodes:

```
clush -w node-[01-10] 'ps aux | grep foo'
```

CHAPTER 10   REMOTE MANAGEMENT

Some important options of clush:

Key	Meaning
-w NODES	Nodes where to run the command
-x NODES	Exclude nodes from the node list
-g GROUP,--group=GROUP	Run command on a group of nodes
-X GROUP	Exclude nodes from this group
--hostfile=FILE,--machinefile=FILE	Path to file containing a list of target hosts
-q, --quiet	Be quiet, print essential output only
-v, --verbose	Be verbose, print informative messages
-d, --debug	Output more messages for debugging purpose
-N	Disable labeling of command line
-P, --progress	Show progress during command execution
-b, --dshbak	Gather nodes with same output
-B	Like -b but including standard error
--diff	Show diff between gathered outputs
--outdir=OUTDIR	Output directory for stdout files
--errdir=ERRDIR	Output directory for stderr files
-f FANOUT,--fanout=FANOUT	Run no more than FANOUT parallel commands at once
-l USER,--user=USER	Execute remote command as user
-o OPTIONS,--options=OPTIONS	Pass the OPTIONS to ssh command (e.g., use a jumphost or different port)
-t TMOUT,--connect_timeout=TMOUT	Limit time to **connect** to a node
-u TMOUT,--command_timeout=TMOUT	Limit time for **command to run** on the node

Note -b option - it is really useful when you do come check on the nodes and expect the same results. --outdir is useful when you want to inspect the output of each node, as it stores each node's output in a separate file. As the pdsh, clush can be used for copying files, to do that specify -c switch (or --copy). All names after this switch will be treated as files and directories to be copied.

By default, they are copied in the same paths on the remote hosts. To change that, use `--dest PATH` option **after** the files list. To copy files from the remote hosts, use `--rcopy` switch instead of `--copy`.

The groups support is more flexible in cluster shell, than in pdsh, but a bit more complicated. The big advantage is that there is ability to integrate with external programs, e.g., SLURM (we'll talk about it in the "Job Management Systems" chapter). To enable it, just rename a file:

```
mv /etc/clustershell/groups.conf.d/slurm.conf{.example,}
```

The exact path may depend on the way you installed the package. After doing that, you can run a command on all nodes of specified partition or in specified state:

```
clush -w @sp:main uptime    # nodes of the partition 'main'
clush -w @st:idle           # all idle nodes
```

Check the docs if you want to make your custom integration. Note that lists of nodes are cached for 60 minutes by default (for slurm – 1 minute), so sometimes lists can be inaccurate.

Except the `clush` command, the package includes `cluset` command, which allows you to manipulate with host lists – convert a list to "folded" format and back, count nodes, join, intersect lists, etc. Here are some examples:

```
# cluset -e node-[01-03,11-13]     # expand the list
node-01 node-02 node-03 node-11 node-12 node-13
# echo node-01 node-02 node-03 | cluset -f # fold the list
node-[01-03]
# cluset -c node-[01-03,11-13]                 # count nodes
6
```

Read more in the docs; there are also tree mode for large clusters, special execution modes, etc.

Screen and tmux

There are at least two packages I want to mention, which are not remote access tools, but they make it much less stressful. Both tmux and GNU screen make two important things – make possible to have many terminals opened on a remote host via single connection (ssh, or any other) and keep your remote session if the connection was dropped. It is critical, e.g., if you started a long operation and your network connection was interrupted, if you were in an ssh session, you have to start everything over and may lose or, even worse, break some data. If you worked in a tmux or screen session, then after reconnection you just join back to your session and continue to work, from the perspective of any programs you started in this session nothing happened.

Let's take a look on the most common options of GNU screen first:

Option	Meaning
-x	Join the latest session in "shared" mode – if there is another connection to this session it won't break (and you can share your actions with someone else, e.g.)
-d / -D	Detach the existing connection to the session. If there was no active connection, -d will fail, -D won't
-r / -R / -RR	Reattach to the existing session. -R – if there is no session, create it. -RR = "Attach here and now. Whatever that means, just do it." (Taken from the official docs)
-S [name]	Create a new session, optionally giving it a name
-list	List current sessions and their states

Usually, a good idea is to run screen with options -xRR or -DRR. After you started a screen session, you get a new(!) virtual terminal, which starts your login shell. Being attached to the screen session, you can send commands to screen, pressing a hotkey, then a command key. By default, the hotkey is `Ctrl-a`, but you can redefine it in the configuration file `~/.screenrc`. Useful keys (there are much more, of course):

Key	Meaning
c	Create new window – a new virtual terminal
k	Kill current window
n	Go to the next window
p	Go to the previous window
"	List all the windows

(continued)

Key	Meaning
d	Detach from the screen session
a	Send Ctrl-a to the window
0..9	Go to the window with number 0..9
ESC	Copy mode – move cursor through the window history. You can press space to start selection, press it again to end selection, then '>' to save the selection into a file
h / H	Put the current window history into a file, or start saving the window history into a file
t	Show current time, hostname, and load average
Ctrl-x	Lock the screen, to unlock it you have to enter your password (be careful if you use passwordless ssh!!!)
F	Fit the window to the actual terminal size (e.g., when you reattached to the session from another computer)
|	Split the current window vertically into two regions, each region is a window (new region goes empty, just run Ctrl-a 0 to show the first window in it, or start a new with Ctrl-a c)
S	Like the previous one, but split horizontally
TAB	Change the focus to the next region
Q	Leave the only current region, kill the others (regions, not the windows they show)
X	Kill the current region
Z	Suspend the screen
?	Show the key bindings
:	Enter a command mode – you can type a command, which is not bind to a key, e.g., "resize +20%" – increase current region size by 20%

See more info and commands in the docs. New key bindings can be made in the configuration file. Also, I recommend adding some useful commands into it:

```
# Enable scrolling back for 1000 lines in copy mode
defscrollback 1000
```

```
# Enable search in screen commands with Ctrl-a {
history
```

CHAPTER 10   REMOTE MANAGEMENT

```
# Enable mouse support (switch between regions and some more)
defmousetrack on

# Reset terminal settings
termcapinfo xterm* ti@:te@

# Enable a status line - STR is a format string
hardstatus alwayslastline STR

# Sample of the STR:
%{+b rk}%c%{gk}|%t [%n] %{y.}%l%{wk}
# it gives you the status like
#10:23|root@server2:~/bin [2] 0.17 1.27 1.21
```

TMUX is another project, similar to screen, but it gives you more flexibility. The most valuable feature is a command, starting new window with a given command, running inside. Tmux also uses a hotkey, but instead of Ctrl-A in screen, here default is Ctrl-B, and you can reassign it in the config file `.tmux.conf`. To imitate the screen -xRR options, you can use either `tmux attach || tmux new` command or `tmux new -A -s 0`.

Keys 0-9, c, d, x, p, and n are the same, as for screen. Here are other useful keys for tmux:

Key	Meaning
l	Switch to the last used window
,	Rename a window
'	Show windows list and select a window you want to switch to
%	Split window vertically
"	Split window horizontally
w	Quick all windows check
→←↑↓	Navigate between opened panels (regions)
Ctrl/Alt+→←↑↓	Change the current panel (region) size: with Ctrl – by one character, with Alt – by 5
z	Show the current panel only in full window (zoom), pressing it again restores it back

There is no useful scroll mode, as with screen, so if you want to look back in the history, press hotkey (Ctrl-b), then '[', which activates copy mode. Use arrow keys or PgUp/PgDn to navigate and `Ctrl-c` to exit from the copy mode. To copy text in the copy mode, use `Shift-SPACE` to start copying, then `Ctrl-w` to copy it. After exiting copy mode, you can press hotkey, then ']' to paste copied text. If you use mouse, I recommend enabling it in the `~/.tmux.conf`, adding the line `set -g mouse on`; this allows to copy text without copy mode, resize panes, and switch windows clicking on status line. The status line is enabled by default and highly customizable. Read the official docs to now about all tmux features.

For both tmux and screen, I highly recommend not to use any commands, executed for the status line update – in case of any issues, when this command hangs, you just lose access to your windows.

IPMI

Intelligent Platform Management Interface is a standard for remote server management. The standard assumes the presence of a special component in the server hardware – management controller (**MC**). In fact, it is a small independent server that monitors the performance of the main server by various sensors (e.g., **I2C**, **SMB** buses). It is able to manage the power of the main server and often emulates a serial port for the main server, giving a remote user access to it. The latter allows console access to the main server through the MC, if the OS is configured correctly. MC can (must!) be configured for access to it over the network, which allows remote access to information about the state of the server, even if it is hung, as well as to reboot it or simply shut it down.

Since IPMI is an open standard, there are several implementations of its client part. For Linux, the most popular are `ipmitool` and `openipmi`. We will take a look at `ipmitool` and give the most common scenarios of its use. The `ipmitool` package is available in all popular distributions, install it through the package manager, including on compute nodes.

Most often network access to MC is disabled by default, and you need to enable it from the BIOS (which is not always implemented in the BIOS itself) or from the OS on the node. The second method always works, so let's consider it. First, you need to load the kernel modules that are responsible for communication with MC, if these modules are not already loaded or statically connected to the kernel:

CHAPTER 10 REMOTE MANAGEMENT

```
modprobe ipmi_devintf
modprobe ipmi_si
modprobe ipmi_msghandler
```

Now the `ipmitool` command can work with the local MC, and we can configure it, e.g., for network access. If network access is already configured, you can do something on the remote MC with the command:

```
ipmitool -I lan/lanplus -H host -U user -P password COMMAND
```

The `-I` option specifies the protocol version: `lan` for 1.5 and `lanplus` for 2.0 and higher. These versions are not compatible with each other, and backward compatibility is typically not ensured, so you must explicitly specify the protocol version. For local MC, the command is specified directly after `ipmitool`. Table 10-6 presents the main commands, or rather classes of commands, since almost every command has many subcommands.

Table 10-6. *The main ipmitool subcommands*

Subcommand	Meaning
Lan	Network configuration
Power	Power management
Mc	Controller management
Sensor	Sensor value printing
Sol	Serial over LAN – remote console
User	MC user management
Channel	MC channel setup
Session	Session information
Shell	Input commands interactively

Use the `ipmitool lan print` command to view the current MC network settings. Here is the typical output of this command:

```
Set in Progress     : Set Complete
Auth Type Support   : NONE MD2 MD5 PASSWORD
Auth Type Enable    : Callback : NONE MD5 PASSWORD
                    ...
```

```
                         : OEM : NONE MD5 PASSWORD
IP Address Source        : Static Address
IP Address               : 10.0.1.2
Subnet Mask              : 255.255.255.0
MAC Address              : 00:11:22:33:44:55
Default Gateway IP       : 0.0.0.0
Default Gateway MAC      : 00:00:00:00:00:00
Backup Gateway IP        : 0.0.0.0
Backup Gateway MAC       : 00:00:00:00:00:00
802.1q VLAN ID           : Disabled
802.1q VLAN Priority:    0
```

The command is used to set the parameters:

`ipmitool lan set <channel> <command> [option]`

Here, channel is the channel number (usually 1), and command is an indication of what and how to configure. Table 10-7 presents the list of the main subcommands.

Table 10-7. Main ipmitool channel subcommands

Subcommand	Meaning
ipaddr <x.x.x.x>	IP address
netmask <x.x.x.x>	Set the IP address mask
defgw ipaddr <x.x.x.x>	Set the default route IP address
password <password>	Set a password for access

The `ipmitool` power command allows you to control the server's power supply. Its subcommands are presented in Table 10-8.

Table 10-8. ipmitool power subcommands

Subcommand	Meaning
on	Power up
off	Power off
cycle	Turn the power off and on (not always reliable, it is better to explicitly use two off/on calls with a pause)
reset	Perform actions similar to pressing the "reset" button
status	Output the current power status

As of IPMI version 2.0, the sol (serial over LAN) command is supported, which allows you to connect remotely to a virtual or real serial port. This means that if we run a getty or similar program (mgetty, mingetty, etc.) on this port on the server, we can access it via IPMI. To test this, run the /sbin/mgetty /dev/ttyS0 command on the server (if IPMI is configured for the first serial port).

Example of running a sol session in ipmitool:

```
ipmitool sol activate
```

To exit a sol session, type "~.". Be careful if the same keyboard shortcut is used in ssh to end the ssh session. A complete list of available MC sensors, along with their values and other parameters, can be obtained with the sensor command or (in a slightly different form) sdr. To get the value and details of a sensor named NAME, use the command:

```
ipmitool sensor get <NAME>
```

To set up remote command execution, we need to create (or use an existing) user, give it a password and a network interface. Below is the command sequence that allows us to do this:

```
ipmitool user set name 3 adminuser
ipmitool user set password 3 MYPASSWORD
ipmitool user priv 3 4 1
```

Here in the first line, we give user number 3 the name `adminuser`. Then for this user, we set the password `MYPASSWORD`, and in the last line, we give him (number 3) administrator rights (level 4) and the ability to log in from the first channel (1). The user number, password, and channel number can of course be different, look at your current settings.

Now we need to configure the channel:

```
ipmitool lan set 1 access on
ipmitool lan set 1 auth admin md5
ipmitool channel setaccess 1 3 privilege=4
ipmitool sol payload enable 1 3
ipmitool sol set enabled true
```

First line allows access on the first channel; second line allows password authentication on it for `admin` level (this is not the username!). In the next line, for the first channel and user number 3, we allow access with level 4 (`admin`). The next two lines enable SOL payload for the channel 1 and user 3. In some cases, one of them or both are not needed, but better to run them to be sure.

As you can see, the settings are partially duplicated, and in reality, only the `user` settings may suffice, but this depends on the specific BMC IPMI model.

Now you can control the BMC remotely. You can enter a command from another server:

```
ipmitool -I lan -U admin -P MYPASSWORD -H 10.0.1.2 sdr list all
```

It will connect to the BMC at `10.0.1.2` and show the list of sensors. If the remote BMC is running IPMI 2.0 protocol, but instead of `-I lan` you should write `-I lanplus`. To avoid writing the password directly in the command line, which is unsafe, it is better to write it to a file and specify it with the `-f pass_file` key instead of `-P`.

IPMI network is not really secure, and good practice is to separate it into dedicated physical network (yes, cheap Ethernet switches, miles of cables...), or, if it is possible, set up a dedicated VLAN and enable it only on management (not user-facing!) nodes. VLAN option is supported by most BMC makers, but, please, double-check that before planning your management network. Also, setting up VLAN on all compute nodes manually would be painful, so ask your supplier to set it up automatically if possible.

163

CHAPTER 10 REMOTE MANAGEMENT

Conman

Using a remote console connection via IPMI is really helpful in many cases, but sometimes raw `ipmitool` is not convenient, especially when you need to monitor consoles on several remote servers. In this case, you can use helper programs, like `conman`. It is a "console manager," which can keep the connection to a remote (or local) console open, so you can see the current status. In the case of conman, you can even automate some operations. There are some alternatives, e.g., xCAT includes `rcons` utility, which has similar functions. Conman does not support power management, but for this goal, I recommend using powerman[3] project, which supports IPMI and wide range of remotely controlled PDU models.

I highly recommend using such console managers, as they significantly improve your efficiency in remote debugging.

iKVM

KVM is an abbreviation for Keyboard+Video+Mouse. This is a system that allows you to connect a single console set (monitor, keyboard, and possibly a mouse) to multiple system units. These were originally physical signal switches and can still be found on the market today. Many rack-mounted consoles provide this capability.

iKVM (or KVM-over-IP) is a device that allows you to get a picture from the screen and emulate the work of a keyboard and possibly a mouse connected to a computer via a network. There is no single standard for implementing this technology, so different manufacturers provide completely different features and interfaces.

Most of them use a browser with Flash, Java, or a special plug-in installed as a client. The iKVM support itself can be either built into the server or implemented by an external device. In the latter case, you will have to connect video and keyboard cables from the required servers to it. External iKVM devices cannot always provide power management of the connected servers unlike built-in ones, so I advise you to choose in favor of built-in iKVM support.

---

[3] https://github.com/chaos/powerman

As it was said, there is no standard for the iKVM protocol, which means that you probably can't automate iKVM for mass administration tasks, such as changing a parameter in the BIOS for all nodes. If there is a protocol description for the iKVM implementation you are using, that would be a big plus for you. Either way, iKVM will be a great complement to `ssh` and IPMI. Unlike them, iKVM allows you to see the output of a hung node, which makes diagnosing problems much easier.

Brief Summary

Because the number of nodes in a cluster is usually large, remote command execution for administration and monitoring becomes critical. Use all the options you have available for effective remote management – ssh, pdsh, IMPI, ILO, iKVM, SNMP, and other services.

Take into account the peculiarities of these programs and services: they can poorly tolerate intensive load, as well as not very sparing to your network, and, running in parallel a thousand copies of the file via scp, you can create difficulties connecting the head machine with the rest of the nodes.

Search Keywords

SSH, pdsh, parallel shell, remote server control, connman, connection manager, ipmi, ikvm, ILO, redfish, gnu screen, tmux

CHAPTER 11

Users – Accounting Management

Account Synchronization

Account management becomes a challenge in a supercomputer environment. One of the most important issues here is to ensure account synchronization between all nodes. This can be achieved in different ways: by using single data source over the network, like LDAP or NIS+, and by running periodic (or event-driven) synchronization of static information.

In most cases, it is sufficient to keep basic information (uid, gid, home dir, ...) synchronized, but don't forget about things like quotas, access limitations, etc. Information about them may be stored separately from the basic credentials, and their synchronization should be organized separately. Moreover, it is not always necessary to synchronize it, and in some cases, it should even be different on different service nodes. For example, the CPU time quota on the compute node should not be limited, but on the main machine, rather the opposite is true.

User access to service nodes (e.g., backup server) is generally undesirable, but information about them is necessary. Do not forget about such moments and think about the synchronization scheme in such cases in advance.

Classic Approach

Historically, Linux systems have stored user account information in /etc/passwd, /etc/shadow, and /etc/groups. The disadvantage of this approach for clusters is obvious – it is necessary to maintain a consistent state of these files for all nodes in the cluster.

CHAPTER 11   USERS – ACCOUNTING MANAGEMENT

The simplest solution is to use the widely used LDAP or NIS+ technologies, but they have significant scalability limitations. How to get around them?

We can use the classical variant and store data in the `passwd` file and synchronize its content with the master on all nodes. Let's consider the pros and cons of this approach and try to take them into account in the implementation.

Pros:

- Absence of network requests "storm" when a user logs on to a lot of compute nodes (starts a large task)
- Low time to obtain accounting information
- Removing the point of failure as a network authentication service

Cons:

- In case of synchronization failure or node replacement, we get a hard-to-diagnose error (missing or incorrect user data).
- Possible high load on the network when updating data.
- When adding/removing multiple users, there is a lot of unnecessary data copying.
- Low flexibility of the solution.

So, the "bottlenecks" of our solution are potential data desynchronization and shock loads on the network. To eliminate the first threat, I suggest using the following synchronization scheme: data copying is started not on the master node, where the master files are stored, but on the destination node. Copying can be organized via `scp` or `rsync`, and it is better to put it in a separate script. This script should be automatically started at node startup; if necessary, it can also be started remotely from the master node.

Here is an example of such a script; let's call it /usr/sbin/master-sync:

```
#!/usr/bin/env bash
SYNC="rsync -e 'ssh -i /root/secret_key'"
SRC_ADDR=root@master.cluster

$SYNC $SRC_ADDR:/etc/passwd /etc/passwd
$SYNC $SRC_ADDR:/etc/shadow /etc/shadow
$SYNC $SRC_ADDR:/etc/group /etc/group
```

Thus, if a node is replaced or temporarily disconnected, the data will still be updated when the node is started. To reduce the load on the network, it is necessary to organize synchronization properly: do not start many copying processes at once and monitor their execution.

In order to avoid multiple repetitions of data copying during mass additions or deletions of users, it makes sense to create a separate command that starts synchronization and execute it manually only when the administrator finishes changing the credentials. The workflow should be organized to run synchronization to remote nodes with some delay or pools so that the network is not overloaded. You can use running commands at 0.1- to 0.5-second intervals or use the pdsh/clush program, which is better.

An example of such a script is as follows:

```bash
#!/usr/bin/env bash
TIMEOUT=600
CT=3
# exit the script after getting ALRM signal
trap 'exit' ALRM
# schedule ALRM signal to self
(sleep $TIMEOUT && kill -ALRM "$$") &
# do the sync!
for i in $(grep -v \# /etc/nodes); do
  ssh -o connecttimeout=$CT $i /usr/sbin/master-sync
  echo -n .
  sleep 0.1
done
echo
```

NIS/NIS+

NIS (Network Information System) was created by Sun in 1985. Initially, it was called Yellow Pages, but the owners of the trademark of the same name sued and Sun changed the name, although the names of all services and programs retained the prefix '**yp**'.

CHAPTER 11   USERS – ACCOUNTING MANAGEMENT

The purpose of NIS is to distribute information over the network that must be identical across multiple clients, such as account data and passwords, /etc/hosts files, and so on. The first version of the system had fundamental security problems, so it was replaced by a new version, NIS+ (NIS plus). Note that despite the identical program names and many configuration files, NIS and NIS+ are not compatible and the client from one system will not work with the server of the other. Hopefully, there should be no NIS packages available, only NIS+.

The NIS+ server is rarely used for user authentication on clusters. This is due to two circumstances: first, even NIS+ is not sufficiently secure; second, there are reliability and performance issues with handling multiple RPC requests. If the number of clients is more than 30–40, it is likely that a single NIS server will struggle to cope with the load.

On the other hand, the NIS+ subsystem has obvious attractive features such as simplicity and ease of administration, server redundancy, and hierarchy, so it is sometimes still used on some small-scale cluster systems.

Current administration consists of modifying (by any means, such as manual editing) source files to be translated over the network, such as passwd, shadow, and group, and executing the make command to modify the network databases. Connecting a new node or even an entire cluster is a matter of configuring it to a running NIS+ server. The initial configuration of the NIS+ server is usually performed with the help of special utilities, which may differ from one Linux distribution to another, but the actions performed by these utilities are quite standard:

1) Configure NIS server components to start during the OS boot process. There are three server processes running in NIS:

    - ypserv is the main NIS+ server.

    - yppasswdd is a server that monitors password modifications by users.

    - ypxfrd is a server that performs database synchronization on secondary NIS+ servers.

2) Open the necessary services in firewall (rpcbind, portmap, ypserv, yppasswdd, ypxfrd).

3) Create a NIS+ domain (which has nothing to do with DNS domain) - specify its name in a ypserv config file or start options; on the clients, put this name into the /etc/defaultdomain file.

4) Create server configuration files `/etc/ypserv.conf` and `/etc/sysconfig/ypserv`; specify there the directory for source files for building network databases (usually `/var/yp`) and rules for the clients subnets.

5) Create a `Makefile` in the directory with network databases for operative updating of network databases and a file `securenets`, in which the segments of IP networks from which access to the NIS+ server is allowed are specified.

6) On clients, the `/etc/defaultdomain` and `/etc/yp.conf` files specify the NIS+ domain and a list of servers.

7) `ypbind` service is started.

8) Add `nis+` to the necessary lines in the `/etc/nsswitch.conf` file, to change the order of data search.

If the choice of authentication system is NIS+, the management computer must also be configured as a NIS+ client. After configuration, the data on users, groups, and hosts will be available to the clients via the NIS server. After updating the local data on the server (adding users, changing passwords, etc.), you must go to the `/var/yp` directory and perform the update with the `make` command. The procedures may differ slightly in different distributions; pay attention to the documentation. For large clusters, I recommend having several slave servers and distribute the load.

LDAP

The purpose of LDAP (Lightweight Directory Access Protocol) is to provide a universal way to access structured data.

The protocol defines so-called **schemes** that specify what kind of data, with what structure and of what type, can be stored and received by the user, e.g., data about an organization (its name, address, etc.), a user (his login, password, password validity time, etc.), a computer, and much more. Most of the schemes are standard, so different client programs can retrieve the information without problems.

There are many LDAP server implementations, both commercial and free. The well-known Microsoft Active Directory product is actually an LDAP server with a set of extensions. As you can see from the description, the idea is very similar to NIS+, but in this case, the functionality is wider: the information is not strings from text files (like `passwd`, `group`, `hosts`, etc.), but full-fledged database records, which can include links to other records, binary information (a picture, for example), you can search by a wide range of parameters and much more.

A very important feature of LDAP is a complete system of access separation and authentication, i.e., a user can access only those records to which his rights allow. Approximately, as in a file system. LDAP is actively used to store user data and often successfully replaces passwd and NIS+. Therefore, it is tempting to use it to manage supercomputer users and many other things as well.

Unfortunately, this idea works only with small clusters. The point is that a computing cluster is characterized not by uniform access to LDAP server, but by "explosive" access – at the moment of launching a task, all nodes on which it is launched simultaneously access LDAP server for information about the user. This mode of operation is not acceptable for LDAP server, and with large number of simultaneous requests, it simply discards the "unnecessary" ones, which leads to the impossibility of launching tasks.

This problem can be solved by configuring a hierarchy of caching LDAP servers, but in practice, I have not yet encountered such solutions for clusters, so it is difficult to say anything about their effectiveness. Besides purely technical concerns, such a solution requires additional physical servers and careful implementation of the network, which entails, among other things, lower reliability and more complicated support. Nevertheless, for small clusters, such a solution can be very convenient, as it allows storing in LDAP-based advanced user data and integrating with various applications and web services.

Configuring an LDAP server is not easy and is described in detail in the literature and on the Internet. Note that configuration on the client in RedHat-like distributions can be done with the interactive `authconfig` program. After installing and configuring LDAP server, you can install programs for its administration. There are many such programs, such as phpLDAPadmin or LDAP Account Manager. Besides OpenLDAP, there are other free implementations, such as Fedora Directory Server, Apache Directory Project, and Mandriva Directory Server. Some of them include administration tools as well.

Brief Summary

The organization of account management seems very simple because it is built into the OS. But this is only the technical part, and how to use it is not always clear either.

CHAPTER 11   USERS – ACCOUNTING MANAGEMENT

To effectively manage records, you need to make an informed decision about what technology to use to do so, how to keep records, what to include and what not to include, and very clear descriptions of all procedures, both in-house and not so in-house.

Search Keywords

LDAP, openldap, NIS+, PAM, passwd, rsync

CHAPTER 12

Users – Quotas and Access Rights

No matter how good our users are, there is always a need for restrictions on various resources both within the supercomputer as a whole and within an access node. This task breaks down into two: a rigid "can/can't" restriction and a flexible "can do no more than" restriction. The first restriction, as a rule, is realized by means of user and/or group rights to certain files and devices. The second one is realized with the help of quota mechanisms that are built into some subsystems.

File System Quotas

Quotas and limits have been and still are one of the most effective methods of optimizing resource usage and keeping order on any computing system. Quotas, as a rule, refer to file systems, where they have existed for quite a long time. However, some other resources can be quoted as well.

So how do disk quotas work? Most standard file systems in Linux have quota support by default, but to activate it, you often need to specify special mount options – `usrquota` and `grpquota`. Sometimes both options can be replaced by a single option – `quota`. To work with disk quotas, you need to install a separate package, usually called `quota`. Please note that some file systems, like zfs, btrfs, and lustre, have special commands for managing quotas and have advanced quoting features. For such file systems, commands, listed below, won't work, but the general idea is the same.

After mounting the file system with the required options, you need to run the command from the superuser:

```
quotacheck /path/to/fs
```

or

```
quotacheck -a
```

These commands will correct or create data on the current usage of the file system by users and groups. You cannot run the command while users are working, because the data obtained will be incorrect. To avoid this situation, it is better to run the command with the `-M` switch, then it will set the file system to read-only mode before checking. It is recommended to reboot into single-user mode with the command `systemctl isolate rescue`,[1] to stop all running services.

Linux supports so-called soft and hard quotas. When a user or a group reaches a hard quota, disk space allocation is stopped and the corresponding system calls (write, seek, etc.) are terminated with an error in the user's applications. When a soft quota is reached, the user is allowed to continue using the resource for some fixed time (of course, if the hard quota is not exceeded). After the specified time, if the soft quota continues to be exceeded, disk space allocation stops.

Once the quota data has been created, the `quotaon`, `quotaoff`, `setquota`, `repquota`, and `edquota` commands can be used. The `quotaon` and `quotaoff` commands turn quota counting on and off, respectively. As an argument, they take the path to the mounted file system or the `-a` switch, which means all file systems for which the quota option is specified in the `/etc/fstab` file.

`setquota` sets a quota for a specific user or group. Command format:

```
setquota username block-soft block-hard \
   inode-soft inode-hard filesystems
```

Here:

- `username` or UID of the user
- `filesystems` list of file systems or the `-a` key, meaning all file systems for which the quota is enabled
- `block-soft` number of blocks (soft quota)
- `block-hard` number of blocks (hard quota)
- `inode-soft` number of files (soft quota)
- `inode-hard` number of files (hard quota)

---

[1] On systems with systemV-style init – `init 1`

Quota is set for each specified file system; quotas on different file systems are not summarized. If some quota does not need to be specified (e.g., a soft quota on the number of files), then 0 is specified in the corresponding field. If you specify the -g switch, username will be the name of the group and the group quota will be set. The user quota is set by default; you can specify it explicitly with the -u switch.

If you specify the -b switch instead of username and quota fields, setquota will expect these values on the standard input stream – one line per user or group. The fields must be specified in the same order as on the command line.

The size of disk space is specified in blocks, not (kilo)bytes.

The time after which a soft quota exceedance becomes a blocking quota is also specified by the setquota command using the -t (default for all) or -T (for an individual user or group) switch. Either time in seconds or the string 'unset' is specified if time is not limited. Command format:

```
setquota -t [-u | -g] block-grace inode-grace -a | filesystems
setquota -T [-u | g] name block-grace inode-grace -a | filesystems
```

Another way to change quotas is the edquota command. Unlike setquota, it starts an editor (set in the EDITOR environment variable), which is passed a text file in a special format. You can view a report on current quotas and occupied space with the repquota command. Its format is similar to edquota and setquota: the -u (default) and -g keys specify the type of quota (user or group), -t and -T specify the times for soft quota, the name of the user or group, and the list of file systems (or the -a key). If no user (group) name is specified, statistics for all users (groups) are given.

Typical output of the repquota command with -s switch to show information in human-readable format:

```
# repquota -m /
*** Report for user quotas on device /dev/sda
Block grace time: 7days; Inode grace time: 7days
                        Space limits              File limits
User            used    soft    hard   grace   used   soft  hard  grace
--------------------------------------------------------------------
root        --  52806M    OK      OK           803k    0     0
...
```

177

CHAPTER 12   USERS – QUOTAS AND ACCESS RIGHTS

As you can see, the header lists the default soft quota grace times for the size and inodes count, and then there is a table by user that lists all the quota settings and current usage statistics. Note that for different file systems, quota parameters may vary, like there can be default quota (like for Lustre), projects quota support, etc.

A brief set of steps required to enable quota on an individual file system:

1. Edit the /etc/fstab file. Add usrquota key to the file system mount options (in this example – /dev/sda6 mounted on /export):

   /dev/sda6 /export ext3 acl,user_xattr,**usrquota** 1 2

2. Set the file system to read only or unmount:

   mount -o remount,ro /dev/sda6

   or

   umount /export

3. Create a quota database:

   quotacheck -vugc /dev/sda6

4. Remount the file system with the new options:

   umount /dev/sda6
   mount /dev/sda6

5. Enable quota on the file system:

   quotaon -va

   This is usually done automatically in startup scripts.

6. Set quotas for users:

   edquota username

You can use any existing user or group as a reference to set quota for other users/groups – use -p option. In this example, we copy quotas on all file systems from user foo to user bar:

setquota -p foo -u bar -a

Quoting is also supported for the NFS file system; it is typically sufficient to install the quota package on the NFS server and enable quota support on the partition being exported. Do not forget to restart the NFS service. If quota is not enabled (repquota on the network disk does not work), make sure that the rpc.rquotad service is started on the server.

Note that some file systems, e.g., zfs and btrfs, can have their own quota utilities and may slightly differ from "traditional," but the overall principle would be the same. Lustre quotas are similar and were described in the "Lustre" subchapter.

ulimits

In addition to disk space quota, Linux provides quota, or rather, limitation of some other resources using the ulimit tool. Let's run the ulimit -a command and see what is available for limiting:

```
# ulimit -a
core file size          (blocks, -c) 0
data seg size           (kbytes, -d) unlimited
scheduling priority             (-e) 0
file size               (blocks, -f) unlimited
pending signals                 (-i) 63616
max locked memory       (kbytes, -l) 64
max memory size         (kbytes, -m) unlimited
open files                      (-n) 1024
pipe size            (512 bytes, -p) 8
POSIX message queues     (bytes, -q) 819200
real-time priority              (-r) 0
stack size              (kbytes, -s) 8192
cpu time               (seconds, -t) unlimited
max user processes              (-u) 63616
virtual memory          (kbytes, -v) unlimited
file locks                      (-x) unlimited
```

The resource name is given at the beginning of the line, followed by the units in parentheses and the ulimit command key that specifies this parameter.

Let's take a closer look at what these are. Limits that are not displayed by `ulimit -a` command, but are available for modification, are presented in the Table 12-1 (the limits that are important for us are highlighted in bold).

Table 12-1. Main limits set via ulimit

Limit	Meaning
core file size	Size of core file to which the memory dump of the crashed process is written
data size	Process memory size for data
scheduling priority	Minimum priority, which can be specified in the nice or renice command
file size	Maximum size of the file to be created
pending signals	Maximum number of pending signals
max locked memory	The maximum amount that a process can lock in RAM, preventing it from being unloaded into swap
max memory size	The maximum amount of memory that the process can allocate
open files	Maximum number of simultaneously opened file descriptors
pipe size	Maximum pipe size
POSIX message queues	Maximum number of queues created
real-time priority	Maximum real-time priority
stack size	Maximum stack size
cpu time	CPU time limit
max user processes	Limit of simultaneously running processes
virtual memory	The maximum amount of virtual memory that the process can allocate
file locks	Number of simultaneous file locks
maxlogins	Number of simultaneous user logins
maxsyslogins	Total number of simultaneous inputs

To avoid a **fork-bomb** attack,[2] I strongly recommend limiting the number of simultaneously running processes on control nodes for ordinary users. Fifty to one hundred processes per user are usually more than enough for comfortable work. It is also worth limiting the processor time, e.g., to 100 seconds. This is not an astronomical process running time, but exactly the time the processor spent on it. This will help to limit random and nonrandom runs of calculations on the head machine.

A CPU time limit that is too small will cause large file transfers via sftp/scp to the host machine to crash.

All ulimits can be also set via cgroups, e.g., in the user slice in systemd. Note that some limits may have global limitation via kernel parameters, e.g., maximum number of opened file descriptors can be limited via sysctl parameter `fs.file-max`, and in this case, if you set ulimit higher, it actually will be limited by sysctl value.

Some limits, especially on compute nodes, should be increased. First, it is open files, because when starting many processes via ssh, a socket is created for each connection, which is also a file in UNIX ideology. Second – max locked memory, because memory for RDMA system buffers should be locked. On the user-facing nodes, e.g., login nodes, I recommend restricting system resources usage, like CPU, memory, and number of processes, to prevent accidental user misbehavior.

In many cases, you should change the stack size limit, because it is actively used by OpenMP applications to store local variables. But don't make it too big; otherwise, it will take up a lot of memory by default, even if it is not required. All these limits are specified in /etc/security/limits.conf and set by the PAM module pam_limits.

If you use systemd (most probably yes), then you can use limits per service. Check the chapter "Systemd – a Short Course" for details.

---

[2] A program or even a script (for example, "./_ & ./_ &" written to a file named "_") that runs itself many times. The consequences of not setting a limit on the number of processes are fatal – the computer stops responding after a few seconds, and it is impossible to bring it back to life.

UNIX Groups, ACLs

Access to resources is rarely equal for all users. Not even because "everyone is equal, but some are more equal than others." Different types of tasks often require different amounts of disk space, time for counting, and, in rare cases, higher priority for a short time, etc.

To control access to disk space, the UNIX rights sharing system is traditionally used. For example, to organize joint work on a project, it is convenient to create UNIX groups and a common directory with a "sticky" bit per group. Sometimes more flexible control of access to files and directories is required. In this case, an extension of the traditional rights system – access control lists (ACLs) – can help.

Not all file systems support them, especially network file systems. The principle of ACL is simple: in addition to the usual rights, lists of users with their own rights are added. This allows you not to create a group for each case, but to set an explicit list of users with the necessary rights. For example, it is possible to allow users `user1`, `user2`, and `user3` to read and write in the `mydir` directory; users `reader1`, `reader2`, and `reader3` to read only; and all others to deny access completely by commands:

```
setfacl -m u:user1:rw, u:user2:rw, u:user3:rw mydir
setfacl -m u:reader1:r, u:reader2:r, u:reader3:r mydir
chmod o-rwx mydir
```

If ACLs are set for a directory or file, the `ls` command will add a '+' sign to the list of permissions. You can view ACLs with the `getfacl` command. For more information, see the documentation, e.g., `man acl`.

Restrict User Access

Blocking is an extreme measure prohibiting the use of an individual resource (as a rule, direct access to compute nodes) or the supercomputer as a whole (login prohibition). Such means should be used cautiously, only in cases when it is seriously justified – the rules of operation are grossly violated or the user's actions violate the operation mode of the complex.

Now let's look at ways to block a user if necessary. There are different locking options available: blocking login; blocking login except for file access; and blocking access to computing resources. Access to computing resources is controlled by the task management system, so it depends heavily on which system you are using. Access to the system can be restricted in several ways: in the `sshd` configuration, through the `pam_access` module, by changing the shell. There are other options, but these are the most common.

To block with `sshd`, insert a line of the form in the `sshd_config` configuration file

```
DenyUsers user1,user2
```

and restart `sshd` (running sessions will still work). After that, `user1` and `user2` will not be able to log in. This option can also be used in the `Match` section if you want to limit its effect by some condition. Instead of `DenyUsers`, you can use `AllowUsers` if you want to deny access to all but a few users (e.g., during maintenance work).

You cannot mix `AllowUsers` and `DenyUsers` options – only one of them will work.

An alternative to this method is to use the `pam_access` module. First, you need to include it in the PAM chain for `sshd` (`/etc/pam.d/sshd`) or for all kinds of authorization (`/etc/pam.d/system-auth`). Open the file in an editor and insert a line at the beginning:

```
account required pam_access.so
```

Now edit the `/etc/security/access.conf` file by adding a line to the end:

```
+:ALL:ALL
```

The file format is simple: each line has three fields separated by a colon. The first field is a plus sign to allow access or a minus sign to deny access. The second field is a list of user and/or group names, separated by a space. The third field is a list of addresses to which the rule applies.

To specify a user group, add an '@' sign to the beginning of its name, e.g., '@wheel'. The `ALL` keyword means all users. It is allowed to use the `EXCEPT` keyword, which indicates to exclude from the listed users or groups (e.g., 'ALL EXCEPT (@wheel)'). You can specify the `ALL` keyword in the address list, as well as the IP or DNS address or network (e.g., `10.0.0.0/8`), terminal name (e.g., `tty1`, `:0`), or the `LOCAL` keyword (to log in from the console or on behalf of a local service).

I would recommend you to immediately write "permission" for administrators to log in and do not delete this line. In the last line, I propose you to forbid all access:

```
+:@admins:ALL
# ... other access rules
-:ALL:ALL
```

Since the rules are executed sequentially, nothing else will be processed after this line.

The last method is to change the shell. As you know, when a user logs in successfully, a shell process is started for the user to execute commands. Even if the user executes a separate command (e.g., `ssh remotehost uptime`), it is still executed through the shell. So if you change the default shell to a command like `/bin/false`, the user will not be able to execute any program. To change the shell, use the `chsh` command:

```
chsh -s /bin/false user1
```

For the command to work, you must first put the `/bin/false` command in the `/etc/shells` file. In some cases, this method can be bypassed, be careful.

Sometimes you want to restrict user logins, but still be able to access files via `scp/sftp`. This can be done through the `Match` settings in the `sshd` configuration, which is usually very cumbersome. You can use the `scponly` package, which is available in most distributions and provides a special shell that allows only executing commands for sftp/scp. After installing the package, just change the user shell to `/usr/bin/scponly`.

Blocking a user from logging in via `ssh` with `usermod` may not work if `pam` is not enabled in `openssh` settings. In addition, it will be difficult to get a current list of blocked users, so this method is not very good.

Brief Summary

Restriction systems serve not so much to prohibit as much as possible, but to protect the users themselves from making silly mistakes and, of course, deliberately (or not so deliberately) causing harm. Use them wisely and you can avoid a lot of trouble.

Search Keywords

chmod, chown, setfacl, ulimit, setquota, sshd_config

CHAPTER 13

Job Management Systems

Principles of Operation and Capabilities

The most optimal mode of supercomputer utilization is continuous launching of tasks occupying the entire counting field. However, in reality, such a mode is practically uncommon, except for cases when the supercomputer is actually built to solve a single task. This is due to various reasons: limitations on the scalability of tasks, conditions on the number of processes (e.g., power of two), etc. Even if all the tasks can occupy the entire counting field, it is necessary to start a new task immediately after the previous one is finished. It is not easy to track this manually.

What if you need to provide resources to more than one user? To solve this problem, there are **batch systems,** or **batch managers,** a.k.a. **resource managers**. Originally, batch managers were used to manage the resources of large machines for the needs of composite tasks. Hence, the combination "batch processing" – in old large machines, a task consisted of several steps that required different resources (disks, tapes, teletypes, processor, etc.), and the task of a batch manager was to plan the use of all resources as efficiently as possible.

Modern supercomputers rarely have tasks described in this way; as a rule, only one type of resource (processors, GPUs) and its quantity are specified. Sometimes some additional requirements (attributes) are given: memory size, availability of licenses, etc. But the way of launching tasks and tracking their work has changed a lot. This has led to difficulties in using old control systems in the new realities.

As a rule, the task management system itself is a software complex of three or more components: queue manager itself, scheduler, and agents on compute nodes. The resource manager allows you to put a task in the **queue**, view the status of queues and tasks, and change the statuses of nodes, queues, and tasks. It is also responsible for launching a task and tracking its status during the task. **Agents** on compute nodes help to start a task and track its status. If a task has crashed or has been forcibly withdrawn from the account, agents must terminate the running processes of the task.

Scheduler is a component that determines when and on which resources a task should be started. Many systems support replacing a simple built-in scheduler with a third-party one. The efficiency of supercomputer utilization depends on the quality of task scheduling. The usual "first-come, first-served" algorithm often leads to the idle time of numerous processors when many tasks are waiting for a large task to run. The scheduler can also use predefined priorities, allowed time intervals, and other rules set by the administrator to make more efficient use of the supercomputer.

It is very important to choose a scheduler that works efficiently with your task flow. The scheduler may require significant resources for its operation – complex logic, large amounts of resources, and large number of tasks may result in scheduling times of tens of minutes, which is unlikely to be acceptable in a real-world environment. In some systems, the scheduler may be described by the administrator himself; some may use an external service such as MAUI (http://www.adaptivecomputing.com), e.g., Torque. Today, there are many task management systems available, both commercial (Moab, LSF) and freely distributed (Torque, Slurm, SGE, Condor, OpenLava).

For many clusters, it makes sense to divide the compute field into separate **partitions**. For example, if there are compute nodes with and without accelerators, two corresponding partitions can be created. The same problem is solved by describing the resources of nodes and explicitly specifying the list of resources when a task is queued. But in this case, the task of planning becomes more complex, and the description of priorities and quotas becomes less transparent. As practice shows, it is easier for users to specify the name of a partition than to write lists of additional resources.

For clusters in general, a small partition for testing is very useful. In such partition, you should set a strict time limit (10–15 minutes) and the number of tasks in the queue from one user (3–5), which will allow you to quickly (within 1–2 hours) guarantee to run the task on several nodes with minimal data and make sure it works.

Here I want to note the most important concepts of any HPC resource manager – **partitions** (usually they are the same as "**queue**"), **jobs priorities**, **users**, **agents**, and **schedulers**. Another essential thing is **batch scripts** – almost all systems run a script, not a single command line. Even if they allow this, they just wrap it into a temporary script. The batch script is executed on the first allocated node, when the job is started, and has full information about the allocated resources. Many MPI implementations have support for resource managers, and commands like `mpirun` typically can be executed without specifying the full nodes list. There is a special standard `PMIx`, which unifies the interface as for resource managers, as for parallel libraries, like MPI. Using this interface, parallel program can start its processes using resource manager's agents, which makes the program start fast and controllable.

Kubernetes, etc.

Why cannot we use modern managers like Kubernetes, Swarm, or something like this? We can! And actually sometimes, it is a good solution, but... You should clearly understand what do you do and what are your goals. Kubernetes is good for managing scaling services; this is its initial (and current) goal. It is not intended to be good at network topology support, job priorities, and even job queuing; the common user's workflow is "submit it to the K8s and forget," and it works, because it is supposed that you have more resources than you request.

In HPC world in most cases, it is different. The resources demand is usually much higher, than you have, and you should be able to organize your jobs queue in the optimal way. Yes, it is possible in the K8s world too, if you install and/or write a lot of plug-ins, sidecars, operators, etc. But is it worth it? Why should you tune a tractor for the Formula-1 races, when you have special race cars?

There are still some cases when it is reasonable, but please, think twice before using such instruments for managing your cluster resources.

Access Problem

Resource management systems usually only allocate resources between tasks but do not always set strict restrictions on access to these resources. So user can sometimes run a task "directly" – bypassing the system by simply explicitly specifying a list of nodes to the mpirun command or by ssh-ing to the desired node and running his program there.

There are several ways to solve this problem. In our experience, the best way is to use PAM modules that either integrate with the task management system themselves or the management system itself sets the necessary rights in the prologue and epilogue[1] of the task, e.g., via the `pam_listfile` module. Some systems, e.g., SLURM, provide special PAM module, which controls user access.

Brief Summary

The job management system is one of the most important parts of your HPC cluster. Choose it wisely, know it well, and use it smart. How the task management system is configured directly affects whole cluster efficiency. Different scheduler settings can change the average waiting time of tasks in the queue and node idle time by times. Don't forget about statistics: only with its help will you be able to understand how efficiently your supercomputer works, what the real demand for it is, and whether there is a need for expansion or modernization.

Search Keywords

batch system, resource management systems, SLURM, PBS, LSF, Moab, Grid Engine Scheduler

---

[1] Prologue and epilogue are usually the names of the scripts called by the resource management system before and after the task is started, respectively.

CHAPTER 14

OpenPBS and Torque

PBS (Portable Batch System) and its clones have gained great popularity. The system started to be developed in 1991 by NASA order. Most of the developers involved in its creation were employees of MRJ Technology Solutions. MRJ was absorbed by Veridian, from which Altair Engineering acquired the rights to PBS. Transfer of PBS technologies to Altair Engineering and discontinuation of support for the open source version of OpenPBS led to the fact that there are now three implementations of distributed computing management systems based on PBS:

1. The original "open source" OpenPBS project, developed in 1998 by MRJ (not supported since 2004).

2. Torque (Terascale Open-Source Resource and QUEueue Manager) is a project based on OpenPBS and maintained by Adaptive Computing Enterprises, Inc.

3. PBS Professional (PBS Pro) is a commercial implementation offered by Altair Engineering.

Installing Torque

The Torque package consists of four main components:

1. A set of commands that includes system administrator commands to configure the system and control its operation and user commands to run and manage tasks.

2. `pbs_server`, which is the central PBS server. The central server accepts tasks from users, deletes tasks, changes their status, logs completed tasks, and so on.

3. pbs_mom is a "machine oriented mini-server" (agent) that must be run on each compute node and that monitors the state of the compute node and the program running on it; starting with torque 4.0, the trqauthd authentication server must run with it.

4. pbs_sched is a scheduler that manages task queuing and running tasks for execution.

Note that Torque allows the use of third-party schedulers, and often Maui scheduler is used in conjunction with Torque, which has more functionality than the standard scheduler. Depending on what functional tasks are assigned to the computer included in the compute cluster, either all or some components of the system can be installed on it.

The Torque system is most fully installed on the cluster management computer. Since tasks are not started on the management computer, there is no need to run the pbs_mom server on it. As a rule, it is started to be able to monitor the status and load of the control server. Torque does not require all of the above components to run on a single computer. For large clusters, individual Torque components can be spread across different computers; for small clusters, the management computer can easily handle all services.

Torque is installed from distribution packages or from source code, which can be obtained from https://github.com/adaptivecomputing/torque. Installation from source is done in the standard Linux way in three steps: ./configure; make; make install # or make packages.

Torque services communicate with each other via fixed network port numbers. Port numbers for Torque are defined in the /etc/services file, which links port numbers and network service names:

```
pbs         15001/tcp   # pbs server
pbs_mom     15002/tcp   # mom to/from server
pbs_resmom  15003/tcp   # request mom to manage resources
pbs_sched   15004/tcp   # scheduler
```

Make sure that these ports are not blocked by a firewall. For compute nodes, the only required component of the Torque system is the pbs_mom server.

Setting Up Torque

It is advisable to start Torque configuration with the configuration of the control node. The main configuration file of the main Torque server is $PBS_HOME/server_priv/nodes. The location of the file depends on the directory that was specified during system installation.

The nodes file contains a list of compute nodes served by the server. This file contains a description for each node managed by the server, one line per node:

node_name[:ts] [property ...] [np=NUMBER]

node_name – Node name described in the /etc/hosts file; if :ts is after the node name, this node belongs to the timeshared type. The state of nodes of this type is polled by the server and their status is shown by information commands, but no tasks are sent to them by the server. These nodes can be used to directly run interactive programs.

property – A set of any characters. Usually this attribute is used to associate a node with a particular task queue.

parameter np = NUMBER defines the number of cores on the node.

The busy sign is set as soon as a task appears on a node, but any number of processes can be started on a node within that task.

Example nodes file:

ib02 MYCLUSTER
ib03 MYCLUSTER
ib04 MYCLUSTER
ib05 MYCLUSTER

The list of nodes and their properties can be changed dynamically using the qmgr administrator command, after which the system enters the waiting mode for input of internal subcommands.

Add nodes:

qmgr: create node node_name [attributes=values]

The values that the attributes parameter can take are listed in the Table 14-1.
Example:

qmgr: create node ib01 np=1,ntype=cluster,properties="MYCLUSTER"

CHAPTER 14 OPENPBS AND TORQUE

You can change the properties of a node with the command:

qmgr: set node node_name [attributes[+|-]=values]

Table 14-1. qmgr command attribute values

Name	Meaning	Possible values
state	Node state. In addition to these states, there is an additional excl state, which is set by pbs_mom when a task is started on the node	free, offline, down
properties	Value similar to the nodes file	any
ntype	Node type	cluster, time-shared
np	Number of processors on the node	any number

The qmgr command is the main command of the PBS administrator. In particular, it is used to create and configure task queues.

Creating a queue:

qmgr: create queue MYCLUSTER

The created queue is also configured using the qmgr command. First, define the queue type:

set queue MYCLUSTER queue_type = Execution

The possible queue types are either execution or routing. The routing queue is created for passing tasks to other queues. For attributes with numeric values, it is possible to set three values: maximum, minimum, and default:

set queue MYCLUSTER resources_max.ncpus = 20
set queue MYCLUSTER resources_min.ncpus = 1
set queue MYCLUSTER resources_default.ncpus = 1

For example, to specify the number of cores that can be used in a given queue, you can do this:

set queue MYCLUSTER resources_max.nodect = 20

The command below sets the maximum possible calculation time for this queue:

```
set queue MYCLUSTER resources_max.walltime = 336:00:00
```

If more time is ordered in the task, it will not be put in this queue.

This is how you can set the number of cores and nodes to default, meaning that these values will be used if the user has not explicitly set them:

```
set queue MYCLUSTER resources_default.ncpus = 1
set queue MYCLUSTER resources_default.nodect = 1
```

The default task counting time is set in the same way:

```
set queue MYCLUSTER resources_default.walltime = 01:00:00
```

If the user has not specified the required time for the task, their task will run for one hour. After this time, the task will be terminated forcibly.

An important parameter is the maximum number of nodes a user can simultaneously occupy in a given queue with a single task or any number of them:

```
set queue MYCLUSTER resources_max.nodect = 12
```

The maximum number of user tasks is set as follows:

```
set queue MYCLUSTER max_user_run = 12
```

Start or stop the queue operation:

```
set queue MYCLUSTER enabled = True # allow receiving tasks
set queue MYCLUSTER started = True # allow tasks to start
```

To disallow receiving tasks or launching them for execution, set the corresponding command to `False`. Since the qmgr command accepts commands from the input stream, it is easiest to prepare a text file with a set of commands for a given queue and send its contents to the qmgr command input. For example, such as this one:

```
create queue MYCLUSTER
set queue MYCLUSTER queue_type = Execution
set queue MYCLUSTER resources_max.ncpus = 20
set queue MYCLUSTER resources_max.nodect = 20
set queue MYCLUSTER resources_max.walltime = 336:00:00
set queue MYCLUSTER resources_default.ncpus = 1
```

```
set queue MYCLUSTER resources_default.nodect = 1
set queue MYCLUSTER resources_default.walltime = 01:00:00

set queue MYCLUSTER max_user_run = 12
set queue MYCLUSTER enabled = True
set queue MYCLUSTER started = True
```

and then execute the command:

```
qmgr < MYCLUSTER.txt
```

From some existing queue, you can retrieve such a file with all descriptions using the command:

```
qmgr -c "print server" > MYCLUSTER.txt
```

The -c option indicates a one-time, noninteractive execution of the command contained in the quotation marks.

The first startup of the head server is performed with a special option:

```
{sbindir}/pbs_server -t create
```

This creates special PBS files to store the system databases. Previously, it was recommended that the first startup be done manually. Now the standard startup script of the head server contains a check if it is the first startup, and if it is confirmed, it is started with the appropriate parameters. This defines the minimum required set of server parameters. More fine-tuning of the server parameters is also done with the qmgr command.

Starts server interaction with the scheduler:

```
set server scheduling = True
```

If this parameter is not set to True, the server does not communicate with the scheduler and tasks are not executed except those started manually with the qrun command.

Allow access to the Torque server from the computers listed in the acl_hosts parameter:

```
set server acl_host_enable = True
set server acl_hosts = *.mycluster.com
```

Add a computer from which you can work with Torque:

`set server acl_hosts += server.mycluster.com`

Specify a user on the specified computer who acts as Torque administrator:

`set server managers = root@server.mycluster.com`

Specify the queue in which tasks will be placed by default:

`set server default_queue = MYCLUSTER`

Define which events the server will display in the log file:

`set server log_events = 511`

To the right is the bit sum, which in this case indicates to display all events. The bit decoding can be found in the Torque manual.

Command

`set server mail_from = root`

determines on behalf of which user Torque will send mail.

Allow viewing tasks in the queue, even those for which it is not the owner:

`set server query_other_tasks = True`

The time in seconds between server attempts to start the task for execution:

`set server scheduler_iteration = 600`

The time interval, in seconds, at which the server checks the status of nodes:

`set server node_ping_rate = 300`

The time interval after which the server, having received no response from the node, will put it into the down state:

`set server node_check_rate = 600`

Timeout time for TCP socket when pbs_server connects to pbs_mom:

`set server tcp_timeout = 6`

The frequency at which the server will check the status of MOM processes:

```
set server task_stat_rate = 30
```

The name of the server to which Torque will send mail messages:

```
set server mail_to = mail.mycluster.com
```

After setting up the server, I recommend saving its configuration for quick recovery in case of failure.

It's done by this command:

```
qmgr -c "print server" > /tmp/server.conf
```

All server and queue settings will be saved in the /tmp/server.conf file. To restore the configuration, it is enough to execute the command:

```
qmgr < /tmp/server.conf
```

Configuring the MOM Server on Compute Nodes

Configuring Torque on compute nodes involves configuring the pbs_mom server to start during the operating system boot process, creating a $PBS_HOME/server_name file specifying the name of the computer running the head pbs_server, and creating a configuration file /var/spool/PBS/mom_priv/config for the pbs_mom server. This file is read when pbs_mom starts. Example file:

```
$logevent 255
$pbsserver rsufs
$cputmult 1.0
$ideal_load 1.0
$max_load 2.0
```

Here:

$logevent is a bit string indicating which events will be logged in the log files.

$pbsserver is the name of the computer running pbs_server.

$cputmult is a multiplier that scales the performance of the node.

$ideal\_load$ is the normal load level of the node.

max_load is the level of maximum node load.

All configuration files are identical on all compute nodes, so they can be created once and copied to all nodes.

For most batch systems, including Torque, this problem is typical: when executing a parallel program, the head process terminates for some reason, while processes on other nodes continue executing, often actively consuming resources. At the same time, the status "free" is set for these nodes, and they are considered ready to receive the next task. In Torque, this can be dealt with using the so-called "epilogue": when any task on the head node is finished, the pbs_mom server automatically launches the epilogue executable file located in the mom server working directory /var/spool/PBS/mom_priv.

By default, this script simply does not exist, and no clear sample is offered either. Below is an example of a working epilogue script that kills the remaining application processes and cleans the file system:

```
#!/usr/bin/env bash
JOBID=$1
USER=$2
######### Get the list of task nodes ###########
if test -r "/var/spool/PBS/aux/$1"; then
   PBS_NODEFILE="/var/spool/PBS/aux/$1"

# Perform cleanup on each node of the task
  for node in $PBS_NODEFILE; do
  ssh -o ConnectTimeout=5 $node \
    'pkill -KILL -u $USER; \
      find /tmp -user $USER -exec rm -r \{\} \; >& /dev/null'
  done
fi
```

The script is designed so that only one user task is executed on one node. Otherwise, when one task is finished, other tasks will be deleted as well.

CHAPTER 14   OPENPBS AND TORQUE

Customizing the Scheduler

In Torque, a separate process, the scheduler, is responsible for selecting the next task to launch it for execution. This allows the implementation of a more flexible policy of task execution organization on the computer system. The scheduler evaluates each task according to its strategy and decides which one to run. The strategy can take into account many factors such as time of day, system load, task size, queuing time, etc. When the `scheduling` attribute is set to `True`, the server, responding to events, calls the scheduler to select the next task to run. Events in Torque can be

- Adding a task to the queue
- Completion of the assignment

Torque comes with several schedulers with different strategies for advancing tasks in the queue. A third-party scheduler can be used if the proposed algorithms are not suitable. Scheduler selection is done at the Torque installation stage when executing the `configure` command using the `--set-sched` and `--set-sched-code` options.

For example:

```
configure --set-sched=cc --set-sched-code=sgi_origin
```

By default, a FIFO scheduler is installed during installation, which implements the "First In First Out" strategy. The task that was first placed in the queue will be the first to be executed if there are enough free resources for it.

In addition to the basic FIFO scheduling strategy, a number of additional strategies can be configured using the scheduler configuration file, which is located in `/var/spool/PBS/sched_priv/sched_config`. The format of the entries in the file is

```
name:value [prime | non_prime | all]
```

Parameter `round_robin` – If `true`, tasks will be executed one by one from each queue cyclically; if `false`, tasks will be executed from one queue until they reach any of the limits (`resources_max`, `max_running`, `max_user_run`) set on the server, and only then the system will switch to processing tasks from another queue.

`by_queue` – If `true`, the scheduler will work with queues; if `false`, all tasks on the server will be interpreted as one big queue.

strict_fifo – If the value is true, the FIFO strategy will work strictly. This will cause that if a task cannot be executed for some reason (no resources available), other tasks will not be executed. If strict_fifo is not set, this can lead to longer queue times for large tasks. Smaller tasks will go first, and there will be constantly insufficient resources to run the larger tasks.

fair_share – If set to true, the fair share algorithm is enabled.

load_balancing – If set to true, tasks will be distributed only on time share nodes.

help_starving_jobs – If set to true, a special strategy for "suffering" tasks is enabled. A task is considered to be suffering if it has been waiting to start for more time than specified by the max_starve parameter. Other tasks will not be started until the suffering task is started.

sort_by – Enables sorting of tasks. Possible values are presented in the Table 14-2.

Table 14-2. *Sorts of the built torque scheduler*

Sorting	Meaning
no_sort	Don't sort tasks
shortest_task_first	In ascending order by cput attribute
longest_task_first	Descending by cput attribute
smallest_memory_first	Ascending by mem attribute
largest_memory_first	Descending by mem attribute
high_priority_first	In descending order by task_priority attribute
low_priority_first	In ascending order by task_priority attribute
large_walltime_first	Descending by task_walltime attribute
short_walltime_first	In ascending order by task_walltime attribute

multi_sort – Sorting by a set of keys

For example:

```
sort_by: multi_sort
key: sortest_task_first
key: smallest_memory_first
key: high_priority_first
```

- `log_filter` – Specifies the list of events that should not be displayed in the log

- `max_starve` – The time a task is in the queue, after which it is considered to be suffering

- `half_life` – Half the term of use of `fair share`

- `sync_time` – Time interval between writes to disk of data on `fair share` usage

Documentation on the official website is incomplete and doesn't include scheduler options, so I recommend to look into the source code for the comprehensive options list.

Using Torque

Running a program through Torque is done with the `qsub` command with the script name as an argument, which specifies the resources required by the task (node architecture, number of processors, and solution time). The command has the following form:

```
qsub -q QUEUE -l ncpus=CORES script_name
```

Where

- QUEUE is the name of the queue in which the task is placed.
- CORES is the number of cores.
- script_name is the name of the running script, which can be created by any text editor.

The `qsub` command actually has many options, but almost all of them can be placed inside the running script, including the `-q` option.

Then the launch command is even more simplified:

```
qsub script_name
```

To run a single-processor program on a MYCLUSTER cluster, you can generate a file (e.g., named `myprog.batch`) with the following contents:

```
#!/usr/bin/env bash
#PBS -l nodes=1:ppn=4
```

```
#PBS -q MYCLUSTER
cd $PBS_O_WORKDIR
./progname
```

In this case, a task, requesting one node and four processes per node, will be generated to run on the MYCLUSTER cluster with a program named `progname` and a default time order of one hour. The "#PBS" special comments are recognized by the `qsub` command and set the limits for the task.

The `cd` command specifies the path to the working directory of the executable program. It is assumed here that the task is started from the working directory where the executable program named `progname` is located. The `progname` program should be started with the command:

```
qsub myprog.batch
```

A simple multithreaded program is run on a single node, and its startup is no different from the startup of a regular single-processor program, neither in terms of the startup script nor in terms of the startup command. By default, an OpenMP program spawns as many threads as there are cores on the node. If you want to control the number of threads spawned, the `OMP_NUM_THREADS` line is added to the script:

```
#!/usr/bin/env bash
#PBS -l nodes=1
#PBS -q MYCLUSTER
#PBS -v OMP_NUM_THREADS=2
cd $PBS_O_WORKDIR
./progname
```

In this task, two threads will be spawned that engage two cores.

Torque often defaults to a maximum time for a task to run. For tasks that require more time, you need to explicitly specify the task runtime:

```
#!/usr/bin/env bash
#PBS -l walltime=300:20:00
#PBS -q MYCLUSTER
#PBS -v OMP_NUM_THREADS=2
cd $PBS_O_WORKDIR
./progname
```

Here 300 hours and 20 min are ordered for solving the task. When the ordered time expires, the task will be forcibly terminated. The administrator has the ability to set limit values for any limits (solution time, maximum number of nodes, maximum number of running tasks).

To run a parallel MPI program on four nodes of the MYCLUSTER cluster, the same command format is used, but the contents of the script must be different:

```
#!/usr/bin/env bash
#PBS -l walltime=30:00:00
#PBS -l nodes=4:MYCLUSTER
cd $PBS_O_WORKDIR
mpirun -np 4 ./progname
```

When the program is started via the `qsub` command, a unique number is assigned to the task. This number can be used to track the progress of the task, to withdraw it from the account or to remove from the queue, move in the queue relative to your other tasks.

Everything that is output to the standard output and error streams while the task is running will be written to a file and copied to the directory from which the task was started at the end of the count. The names of these files are automatically generated as follows:

> `<script_name>.o<task_number>` – Standard output
>
> `<script_name>.e<task_number>` – Error stream

These names can be changed using the `qsub` options. If you want to view the results as the task progresses, you can use the output redirection mechanism in the program start command. Moreover, Torque internal variables can be used to make each output file have a unique name.

For example:

```
#!/bin/sh
cd $PBS_O_WORKDIR
mpirun -np 4 progname > $PBS_JOBID
```

In this case, the results will be written to a file whose name will be formed from the task ID. This file can be viewed during program execution using the `cat`, `less`, or `tail -f` command.

If the program is interactive, i.e., contains keyboard input, the script must use the input redirection mechanism.

```
mpirun -np 4 progname < input_file > $PBS_JOBID
```

If the system has trouble finding the path where the output files should be written, they remain in the system directory `/var/spool/PBS/undelivered/` on the cluster node where the task was read, and a mail message is sent to the user about it.

Job Control Commands

In addition to the `qsub` command described briefly, there is a set of commands for task management. Their detailed description can be seen with the help of the man command:

- `qdel` – Delete the task
- `qhold` – Prohibit execution of the task
- `qmove` – Move the task
- `qmsg` – Send a message to the task
- `qrls` – Remove the execution ban set by the `qhold` command
- `qselect` – Task selection
- `qsig` – Sending a signal (in UNIX OS sense) to the task
- `qstat` – Output queue status (the most useful commands are `qstat -a` and `qstat -q`)
- `qsub` – Puts the task in the queue
- `pestat` – Output the state of all compute nodes (the command is built separately)

CHAPTER 14   OPENPBS AND TORQUE

- `xpbs` – Graphical interface for working with Torque (X-server required)
- `xpbsmon` – A graphical program for outputting the state of compute resources

Brief Summary

Torque is still widely used and may be a good option for you.

Search Keywords

PBS, Torque

CHAPTER 15

Slurm

Slurm Workload Manager, formerly called "Simple Linux Utility for Resource Management," is a freely distributed resource manager for supercomputers. It is written in C and was built entirely from scratch by a coalition of Lawrence Livermore National Laboratory, SchedMD, Linux NetworX, Hewlett-Packard, and Groupe Bull. SchedMD is currently providing primary development and commercial support for this project.

Slurm is designed to be extensible and modular. In practice, there are very few additional (not included in the distribution) modules, primarily because the interfaces of modules are not always well-thought-out. That's why you often have to use internal Slurm functions and structures to implement a module that extends functionality. Many standard modules do exactly that. This approach makes modules intolerable between versions, because internal data formats and functions frequently change from version to version. Nevertheless, Slurm has a lot of plug-ins available by default or which you can compile/install in addition. They give you a lot of flexibility, but remember to turn on needed and off not needed ones.

I'd specially note SPANK plug-ins, which have fixed API, so are portable between Slurm versions. Also job_submit plug-ins have fixed API and reach functionality. Moreover, there is a possibility to use LUA for writing such plug-ins, which makes some tasks much easier to implement. I won't stop on them here, but the official doc is really good. Also, you can check the git repository https://github.com/zhum/hpc-book-matherials for some useful scripts (and contribute yours!).

The basic Slurm modules give good flexibility and wide capabilities, so they are sufficient for most cases. Most Linux distributions include ready-made packages for Slurm.

The manager architecture is similar to Torque. The main process slurmctld runs on one or more servers (this provides fault tolerance). This daemon controls compute nodes, task accounting, resource scheduling. Optionally, the slurmdbd process can be run, which writes task, user, etc., credentials to a database and can analyze resource usage. The same database stores an extended set of restrictions for users, which are not available without slurmdbd.

The `slurmd` agent runs on compute nodes, and `slurmctld` determines the state of the node based on its operability. The same agent is used to launch applications, but the `slurmstepd` process is started beforehand, which launches and further controls the application.

Launching an application in Slurm happens in stages. First, on the nodes allocated by the scheduler, agents execute "prologue" scripts that can prepare a node for launching. Then, on the first of these nodes, the script that the user queued is run. The script can get a list of all the allocated nodes and, e.g., run something on them with the `ssh` command. But it is more correct to execute the `srun` command, which will run what it was asked to run on all the nodes allocated to the task, with the `slurmstepd` process controlling the running processes. After the task is finished, the agents run the "epilogue" scripts and the task is finished. As noted above, only scripts can be queued, and Slurm will generate an error if you try to queue a binary file.

Unlike Torque, Slurm configuration is stored in a file. If a database is used, Slurm stores statistics and additional settings in it, such as the number of simultaneously running tasks of one user, the number of tasks in the queue of one user, etc. The runtime data, which should be saved between Slurm controller restarts, is stored in a set of files, located in the directory specified by `StateSaveLocation` option in the config file.

Important additional service required for Slurm is `munge` – it "confirms" which user sent the request to the controller and agents. `munge` servers on all nodes (compute, controller, submit, etc.) should share the same certificate, and all nodes should have synchronized time.

Slurm Installation

Before installation, make sure that the compute and control nodes have synchronized credentials (`passwd`/`ldap`), time (`ntp`), and the `munge` package installed and running. The latter is available in the repositories of almost all distributions and serves for authentication of remote requests; without it, Slurm will not work. I also recommend creating a Slurm user on the control node to prevent the main daemon from running as a superuser.

Most distributions have Slurm packages, but they are often pretty old and not updated for a long time. But you can install them if you want. On compute nodes and Slurm control nodes, we put packages: `slurm` and `slurm-munge`; if desired, we add `slurm-perlapi` and `slurm-torque` (for compatibility with torque-scripts). On the controller node, we have to install `slurm-slurmctld` and `slurm-plugins` packages, optionally (but recommended) `slurm-plugins`, and on compute nodes `slurm-slurmd`. On the node with database (if used), we install MySQL/MariaDB and packages `slurm`, `slurm-munge`, `slurm-slurmdbd`, `slurm-sql`, and if desired `slurm-plugins`. Of course, the actual names may vary in different distributions.

In the Slurm versions starting from 23.11, there is a `slurm-sackd` package, containing internal plug-in for authentication as an alternative to munge; see the documentation if you want to use it.

If you need a fresh Slurm version, you can compile it from source code and even build packages, which is pretty convenient. To do this, download the latest version from schedmd.com or from https://github.com/SchedMD/slurm repository. Then unpack the archive, navigate to the created directory, checkout the desired version by tag, e.g. slurm-24-11-5-1, and execute the commands:

```
./configure --prefix=/opt/slurm
make
make install
```

You can do it even easier – build rpm- or deb-packages by yourself; just run

```
rpmbuild -ta slurm-XX.YY.Z.tar.bz2
```

or

```
mk-build-deps -i debian/control
debuild -b -uc -us
```

Don't forget the devel packages for mysql/mariadb if you plan to use accounting and all prerequisite devel packages. If you don't have any preinstalled slurm config file, you can generate a simple one at https://slurm.schedmd.com/sched_config.html.

Accounting

All (almost) information about the user jobs, like submit time, start and end time, requested and actual resources, user login, etc., may be stored in the database and used for traditional accounting and for dynamic priority changing. Also without accounting, many things won't work, like QOS, multifactor priority, FairShare, and some others.

If you use accounting, each user should be a member of at least one "account" – a group of users. Accounts can be nested and intersected, and each account can be associated with its own parameters and limits.

Slurm has two main commands for working with accounts: `sacct` for viewing statistics and `sacctmgr` for managing accounts and associations. An association is a relationship of four parameters user, cluster, partition, and account, where user is the user login, cluster is the cluster name, partition is the cluster partition, and account is the account name. First, you need to create a cluster with the `sacctmgr create cluster mycluster` command.

You can create an account with the command:

```
sacctmgr create account name=first
```

You can create an association with the command:

```
sacctmgr create user name=user1 cluster=mycluster \
  account=first partition=def maxtasks=2 maxwall=60:00
```

Here, for login `user1`, we have created an association with cluster `mycluster`, partition `def`, and account `first`. Within this association, the user will be able to run no more than two tasks at a time, and the maximum time a task can run is limited to one hour. A user can log in to multiple accounts through different associations, in which case you can explicitly specify the account with the `-A` switch of the `sbatch` or `srun` commands.

You can change the association like this:

```
sacctmgr modify user where name=user1 partition=def set \
  MaxSubmit=10
```

Here we set records with the `where` parameter (all records that fall under the condition will be changed) and changes with the `set` parameter. As a result, the maximum number of tasks in the queue for `user1` in all accounts and on all clusters in the `def` partition will be limited to 10.

To view the current associations, you can command:

```
sacctmgr list assoc
```

or

```
sacctmgr list assoc user=user1
```

In the second case, only the associations for user1 will be shown. Here is an example, showing account hierarchy and formatted in a friendly way:

```
# sacctmgr -P list account withassoc \
   format=account,parentname,user,share,qos | column -ts \|
Account         ParentName    User              Share         QOS
foo             root                            1             normal
foo                           foo1              1             normal
foo                           foo2              1             normal
foo                           foo3              1             normal
bar             root                            1             normal
bar                           bar1              1             normal
bar                           bar2              1             normal
bar                           bar3              1             normal
...
```

Accounting Setup

To set up the accounting, you have to compile SLURM with mysql (or mariadb) support or have a prebuilt package (most of them have this support compiled it). If building, make sure that the configure script finds the mysql_config program or specify the path to it explicitly. After installation on the account node, prepare the database: log in to the mysql console and run

```
mysql> create user 'slurm'@'localhost' identified by 'pas';
mysql> grant all on slurm_acct_db.* TO 'slurm'@'localhost';
mysql> create database slurm_acct_db;
```

Here 'pas' is the password to access the database; change it to your own. After that, check and edit the /etc/slurm/slurmdbd.conf file. Its main options are

> AuthType – Authentication type; 'auth/munge' is recommended.
>
> DbdHost – The name of the host on which slurmdbd is running.
>
> SlurmUser – The username on behalf of which slurmctld runs (recommended 'slurm').

> `DebugLevel` – Level of logging granularity; 'error' is recommended.
>
> `PrivateData` – Types of data stored in the database. Recommended 'accounts,users,usage,reservations,tasks'.
>
> `StorageType` – The method of data storage. In our case, it is 'accounting_storage/mysql'.
>
> `StorageHost` – The address of the node with the database.
>
> `StoragePort` – Optional – the port on which the database is running.
>
> `StorageUser` – Database user; 'slurm' is recommended.
>
> `StoragePass` – Database password in plaintext.
>
> `StorageLoc` – Name of the base in the database. Recommended 'slurmdb'.

In the configuration file /etc/slurm/slurm.conf, change/add lines:

```
AccountingStorageType=accounting_storage/slurmdbd
AccountingStorageHost=ADDRESS_slurmdbd
AccountingStoragePass=secret-password-here
```

Now you can run `slurmdbd` and check from the log that table creation and initialization was successful.

Basic Setup and Usage

At https://slurm.schedmd.com/configurator.easy.html, there is a configuration file generator, but it may not be suitable for your version, be careful. Typically, the configuration file is located in /etc/slurm/slurm.conf and already contains most of the default settings, so a good option is to make a backup of a file and edit it the way you want. Below are the main parameters to pay attention to:

```
ControlMachine=slurm_master
ControlAddr=10.0.2.3.
SlurmctldPidFile=/var/run/slurmctld.pid
SlurmdPidFile=/var/run/slurmd.pid
```

```
SlurmdSpoolDir=/var/spool/slurmd
SlurmUser=slurm
StateSaveLocation=/var/spool/slurmctld
SwitchType=switch/none
TaskPlugin=task/none
#
# TIMERS
#KillWait=30
#MinJobAge=300
#SlurmctldTimeout=120
#SlurmdTimeout=300
#
# SCHEDULING
FastSchedule=1
SchedulerType=sched/backfill
SelectType=select/linear
#
# LOGGING AND ACCOUNTING
AccountingStorageType=accounting_storage/filetext
JobCompType=taskcomp/filetxt
ClusterName=mycluster
JobAcctGatherType=taskacct_gather/none
#SlurmctldDebug=3
SlurmctldLogFile=/var/log/slurmctld.log
#SlurmdDebug=3
SlurmdLogFile=/var/log/slurmd.log
#
# COMPUTE NODES
NodeName=node[1-10] State=UNKNOWN
PartitionName=def Nodes=node[1-10] Default=YES\
  MaxTime=2-00:00:00 State=UP
```

ControlMachine specifies the name of the Slurm control node; `slurmctld` should run on it. SchedulerType specifies the scheduler; I recommend `sched/backfill`. SelectType specifies the node selection algorithm – `select/linear` will select free nodes sequentially by name.

AccountingStorageType and JobCompType specify how to store the accounting data. In this example, the task data will simply be written to a file. Commands to process this data, such as sacct, will not work.

The NodeName and PartitionName can be repeated, i.e., you can enter a different NodeName string for each node or group of nodes, and if you need multiple partitions, each is described by its own string. Note the node name range entry, Slurm uses it wherever it can. You can use square brackets in the multiple node entry to specify: a numeric range (e.g., [15-33]) or a list that can include ranges ([1-4,6,8]). Slurm does not include any tools to convert "brackets" notation to plain lists and vice versa, but there are some external tools for that, e.g., cluset from ClusterShell package.

Partitions

Slurm uses several concepts in addition to those mentioned before, and here you can find the most useful of them. You already know about partitions if you read the subchapter above; if not, it is a set of compute nodes, possibly with some limits. Partitions can be nested, share the same nodes, or even intersect. Each partition in Slurm can have some important attributes, which you can specify in the partition definition in the configuration file and change temporarily via scontrol:

Name	Meaning
Nodes	The list of nodes belongs to this partition
AllowAccounts, AllowGroups	List of accounts or groups, allowed to use this partition; Deny-based options also are here
Default	If "yes," all commands without explicit partition name specified will use this partition
DefaultTime	If no time limit is specified in sbatch/srun, this value will be used
MaxTime	Maximal time limit, which can be specified
Hidden	If "yes," the partition won't be shown by default in any commands for nonadmin users; if the name is given explicitly, it will be shown
MaxCPUsPerNode	Force number CPUs per node, useful, e.g., if you don't want to use hyperthread CPU cores

(continued)

Name	Meaning
MaxNodes	Maximum nodes, the job can requested
OverSubscribe	yes[:N] = one node can run multiple jobs all resources except GRES can be shared and oversubscribed explicitly (no more than N times)no = one node can run only one jobforce[:N] = like yes, but oversubscription works by default (user don't have to specify --oversubscribe option in srun/sbatch)exclusive = like no, but with different behavior in preemption. See the docs, for more info
PriorityJobFactor	Factor for calculating job priority (partition factor)
PriorityTier	Any job in the partition with higher priority tier will be planned before the jobs in partitions with lower PriorityTier
QOS	QOS associated with this partition, only one QOS can be specified
TRESBillingWeights	See below in "Priorities and FairShare"

Partition configuration can be changed on the fly, like this:

```
scontrol update partitionname=main nodes=node[1-29] \
  MaxNodes=5 MaxTime=24:00:00 DefaultTime=12:00:00
```

Here we explicitly specify the list of partition nodes; you can add or remove nodes using "+=" and "-=". Note `PartitionName` instead of `Partition` – such a change is normal for Slurm control programs.

Partitions in Slurm may have four states, and you can change them using `scontrol`. They are

- `Up` – New jobs can be submitted and started.

- `Down` – New jobs can be submitted, but no jobs can be started (already started won't stop).

- `Drain` – No new jobs can be submitted, but queued jobs will start.

- `Inactive` – No jobs can be submitted or started.

Create a new partition:

```
scontrol create partition name=new nodes=node[30-32] \
  allowaccounts=acc1,acc3
```

Note that here you should use `partition` and `name=....` separately. Only accounts `acc1` and `acc3` will be able to submit jobs to the new partition.

Nodes

In `slurm.conf` file, nodes are declared via `NodeName=...` lines. You can use several lines to specify several sets of nodes or even declare each node in its own line (don't do that, please). After the equal sign, the list of nodes follows, and after space, you can specify nodes attributes. If you specify special name `DEFAULT`, then the attributes in this line will be applied to all following `NodeName` line, till the next `DEFAULT` line if any. Explicit values in the attributes list override default values.

Some important attributes for nodes:

Name	Meaning
NodeHostname	If the real node hostname differs from NodeName, specify it here
NodeAddr	Node IP address (optional)
Boards, CPUs, Sockets, SocketsPerBoard, CoresPerSocket, ThreadsPerCore, RealMemory	Motherboards, CPU cores, CPU sockets, and memory on the node. Detected by default, but may be overridden
Features	List of any node feature strings, see below
Gres	List of generic resources, see below
Weight	If you really want some nodes to be more often used for jobs, set higher weight for them

Node features are generic node markers. For example, some nodes have access to additional file system, then you can just mark them using Feature attribute. Users can require node with exact features when they submit a job. Features are Boolean – node either has a feature, either not.

Generic resources are measurable resources the node has, e.g., GPUs, fast network access, etc. Their names should be defined in `GresType` config parameters before the use. Format is `<name>[:<type>][:no_consume]:<number>[K|M|G]`. Type is optional and may be used to distinguish resource subtypes. `:no_consume` means that Slurm won't count it if a job requires this resource. Here is an example:

```
GresType=gpu,fastfs
Gres=gpu:volta:8,fastfs:lustre:no_consume:100G
```

Some generic resources, e.g., GPUs can be autodetected by Slurm. Add `gres.conf` configuration file in the same location as other config files. In this file, you can specify the autodetect method and specifications for specific nodes. Here is an example:

```
AutoDetect=nvml
NodeName=nv4-[1-8] AutoDetect=off Name=gpu \
  File=/dev/nvidia[0-3]
NodeName=amd-[1-4] AutoDetect=rsmi
```

Here for all nodes by default, autodetect NVIDIA GPUs are enabled. For nodes nv4-[1-8], we force having four GPUs and specify their devices. If any device is missing, Slurm will mark the node as **invalid**. For nodes amd-[1-4], we enable AMD GPUs autodetect.

Please refer to the docs for current supported autodetect methods and additional options.

You can use `NodeSet` to shorten your nodes lists in partition definitions:

```
NodeSet=Set1 Nodes=n[10-20],n[55,66,77]
```

Generic and Trackable Resources

Slurm supports tracking and limiting nodes resources, some of them are predefined (trackable resources), and some you can declare by yourself (generic resources, see above). List of supported trackable resources, which are tracked by default:

- Billing
- CPU
- Energy

- Mem (memory)
- Node
- Pages
- VMem (virtual memory/size)
- FS (file system – only **disk** and **lustre** are valid)

You can enable additional trackable resources, to enable limiting them:

- BB (burst buffers)
- GRES
- IC (interconnect – only **ofed** is valid)
- License

To enable such resources, use the line like this:

AccountingStorageTRES=gres/gpu,license/cad,ic/ofed

In addition, make sure that you enabled SelectType=select/cons_tres in the config file. Also, refer to the docs about SelectTypeParameters, because it defines which resources are consumable and are taking in account in scheduling at first. For example, you can track CPUs or CPU cores.

Backfill and Preemption

Pretty common situation is when the next job in the queue has not enough free resources and cannot be started, but there are some free resources. To reduce the resource waste in such situation, there is a **backfill** algorithm. It scans the queue back and looks for small jobs, which can be started right now, and the estimated start time of the first job in the queue won't increase (or increase not so much).

To enable this algorithm, set SchedulerType=sched/backfill in the config file. Some parameters of the algorithm can be tuned via SchedulerParameters; they usually have bf_ prefix. See most important options in the "Advanced Parameters for slurm.conf" subchapter below.

In Slurm, jobs can be **preempted** by other jobs in several ways. The preempted job can be stopped, canceled, requeued, or started to share time slots with the other job with a low priority ("gang scheduling" – I don't recommend using it in HPC and will not stop on this option). Preemption happens, e.g., if you have two partitions sharing the same nodes, but one of them has PriorityTier higher than other. Then if all nodes are occupied by jobs, and new job comes from the high-priority partition, it can preempt a running job, belonging to the low-priority partition.

To use or not use preemption in Slurm, you need to specify some parameters in the slurm.conf: PreemptType – plug-in name, which chooses the jobs, which should be preempted. It can be preempt/none – to disable preemption, preempt/partition_prio – to use PriorityTier, like in the example above, and preempt/qos – use QoS in addition to PriorityTier. Also, you have to specify PreemptMode, to set how the jobs will be preempted. Possible values are

- **OFF** – Disable job preemption and gang scheduling (default). PreemptType should be preempt/none.
- **CANCEL** – The preempted job will be canceled.
- **GANG** – Enable gang scheduling.
- **REQUEUE** – Cancel the job and requeue it, --requeue sbatch option was set or if JobRequeue parameter in slurm.conf was set to 1.
- **SUSPEND** – The job will be stopped and then resumed after the high-priority job finishes, requires gang scheduling to be turned on.

Preemption is a tricky option; I recommend using it only for partitions, where job interruption is not critical, if you have such. Your users should be well-informed of this behavior to exclude any surprises.

QoS and Limits

QoS or quality of service is the most inappropriate title in Slurm. Actually, it is a named limit, which can be associated with user, partition, or account, and can be attached to a job automatically or manually. Except of limits, QoS can specify priority or preemption. If QoS is associated with a partition, it will override others by default, but if you create a QoS with Flags=OverPartQOS, it will override partition QoS.

CHAPTER 15   SLURM

As QoS can set some limits, there is the order, to determine which limit definition will be enforced:

1. Partition QOS limit (if OverPartQOS is set, goes after Job QoS)
2. Job QOS limit
3. User association
4. Account association(s), ascending the hierarchy
5. Root/cluster association
6. Partition limit

There are a lot of different limits, please check them in the docs,[1] here I will describe some most useful:

- `GrpJobs` – Max jobs, allowed to run at the same time and **sharing this QoS**, e.g., if you associate it with two accounts, they could run **in sum** no more jobs than this limit.
- `GrpSubmitJobs` – The same as above, but for jobs in queue (including running jobs).
- `GrpWall` – The same as above, but for summary jobs work time.
- `MaxJobsPerUser` – Max running jobs from one user.
- `MaxSubmitJobsPerAccount` – Max jobs in the queue (including running) from an account, including subaccounts.
- `MaxSubmitJobsPerUser` – The same as above, but for user.
- `MaxTRESPerAccount` – Max TRES, which all running jobs from an account can use at the same time.
- `MaxTRESPerJob`, `MaxTRESPerNode`, `MaxTRESPerUser` – Same as above, but relates to one job, each node, and one user, respectively.

---

[1] https://slurm.schedmd.com/resource_limits.html

Note – Limits with prefix Grp summarize the resource usage between all jobs, having this QoS, limits with Max prefix – only between jobs, sharing specified attribute (username, account, …). To specify TRES limits, you can use a list, e.g., GrpTRES=cpu=20,gres/gpu:tesla=10, which will set limit of 20 CPUs and 10 GPUs.

User associations are set by using sacctmgr command. With the sacctmgr command, you can set not only associations, but also additional constraints on each association. Below are the most useful ones:

Name	Meaning
MaxJobs	Total number of counting tasks
MaxNodes	Number of nodes per task
MaxSubmitJobs	Total number of tasks in the queue
MaxWall	Task time limit

The time limit cannot exceed the limit set in the partition settings, be careful. Here are some examples:

```
sacctmgr add account name=acc1 [parent=acct0]
sacctmgr add user name=user1,user2 account=acc1
sacctmgr add assoc user=user1 account=acc1 maxsubmit=5
sacctmgr modify assoc where user=user1 account=acc1 \
        set maxjobs=2
```

To delete a limit, just set its value to -1. An important feature of the limits set via sacctmgr is that there is no way to set default limits – only per individual association.

Priorities and FairShare

Each job in Slurm has a priority. It can be set directly by admin using command like scontrol update jobid=123 priority=1000000, or, by default, a formula calculates it. In most cases, a "multifactor priority plug-in" is used, which calculates each job priority summing several "factors," multiplied by a coefficient; each factor is in the range from 0 to 1. All coefficients are tunable, so you can decide which factor impacts the priority the most. The list of factors is as follows:

Name	Meaning
Age	How long the job was waiting in the queue
Assoc	Each association can have this factor value, so you can give boosts to groups of users, e.g., in different partitions
FairShare	See below
JobSize	The number of nodes or CPUs a job is allocated
Nice	Users can use it to change their job priorities (usually to lower it); it always has the coefficient = -1
Partition	Each partition can have a priority, not a `PriorityTier`!
QOS	Each quality of service can have its own priority factor
Site	Slurm can manage several clusters (sites), and they can have different priorities; its coefficient is always = 1
TRES	Each TRES can have its own factor too

For each factor, except `Nice` and `Site`, you can set the coefficient by `PriorityWeight[FACTOR]=number` line in the config. `PriorityFavorSmall` parameter says if `JobSize` factor prioritizes small jobs or large jobs. `PriorityMaxAge` specifies which job wait time in the queue makes this factor max, by default it is seven days.

FairShare is an algorithm, which distributes resources according to number of "shares" it has. The idea is to give each account some shares, like this:

`sacctmgr modify account foo set fairshare=100`

Then, if any job of this account is running, it consumes given shares, proportionally to allocated resource, and its FairShare factor becomes lower. By default, the resource is number of allocated_cpus*seconds. You can change it, adding any TRES resources with weight using configuration file option `TRESBillingWeights`, e.g.,

`TRESBillingWeights=GPU=1.0,CPU=0.001,Mem=0.01G`

In this example, if the job requires 2 GPUs, 16 CPUs, and 1024 G memory, the number of shares will be calculated as 2*1.0 + 16*0.001 + 1024*0.01. There is another method, when instead of sum, the maximum value of each weighted TRES is taken. It may be turned on by the option `PriorityFlags=MAX_TRES` in the config file. It is a list; you can have different flags together.

By default, Slurm uses more complicated `FairTree` algorithm, which calculates shares hierarchically; you can read more about it on the `slurm.schedmd.com` website. If you don't want to use it and want to use simple FairShare algorithm, add to `PriorityFlags` value `NO_FAIR_TREE`.

As resources are consumed, you have either to give new shares to the accounts sometimes, either consumed resources should be reset somehow for all accounts. In Slurm, it is implemented by two options. First is a half-decay – period of time when the historical usage lowers its impact into FairShare value. Here is an example:

`PriorityDecayHalfLife=3-6:30`

Here we set the half-decay period to 3 days, 6 hours, and 30 minutes. If we set it to 0, then the second option goes in play – reset period:

`PriorityUsageResetPeriod=WEEKLY`

In this example, every Sunday at 00:00, FairShare usage is reset. Unfortunately, there is only fixed list of periods: `DAILY, WEEKLY, MONTHLY, QUARTERLY, YEARLY` – do reset at the midnight of the first day of the period, and special ones: `NONE` (default) and `NOW` – on the Slurm controller restart.

There are `sshare` utility, which shows the current FairShare values. Here are some hints on how to "decode" its output. `NormShares` is a number of given shares, divided by total shares given to all, i.e., normalized shares; it is always in range from 0 to 1. `RawUsage` – how many normalized shares are used. `EffectvUsage` – if it is under 0.5, then account used more shares, than it has, and its priority will be lowered a lot; if it is in the range 0.5-1, then its priority will be increased by the FairShare factor, the closer to 1, the higher. Here is an example:

```
$ sshare
Account          RawShares   NormShares      RawUsage   EffectvUsage    FairShare
root                          1.000000     694362950       1.000000     0.500000
 abc                 2000     0.011481            28       0.000000     0.999998
 foo                 3000     0.017221      45166247       0.065072     0.072870
 bar                  100     0.000574             0       0.000000     1.000000
 baz                  300     0.001722         19770       0.000028     0.988597
 ...
```

Here `foo` account consumed a lot of resources (`RawUsage`) and has low FairShare factor, which will decrease the priority; other account will have higher priority (if you made the FairShare factor significant in the priority formula of course).

The overall checking, if one job has higher priority than the other or should preempt the other, follows this order:

- **Reservation** – Jobs with a reservation are higher priority than other jobs.

- **Partition priority tier** – Jobs in a partition with higher tier has higher priority.

- **Job priority** – In case of multifactor priority plug-in use, calculated priority is used.

- **Job ID** – Jobs, submitted earlier (with lower job id), have higher priority.

User Levels

Slurm allows executing privileged commands to non-root users, if they are allowed to. There are several levels of privileged users in Slurm:

> **Administrator** – Can do any commands, by default `root` and user specified in `SlurmUser` have these rights.
>
> **Operator** – Can add, modify, and remove any database object (user, account, etc), and add other operators. On a SlurmDBD served cluster, these users can view information that is blocked to regular uses by a PrivateData flag and manage reservations.
>
> **Coordinator** – Trusted users, who can change limits on account and user associations, as well as cancel, requeue, or reassign accounts of jobs in their accounts. Also, they can add new users and subaccounts in their accounts. They cannot increase job limits above the parent account allows.

To give or revoke a user privilege, use the command:

```
sacctmgr update user name=USERNAME set \
  adminlevel=[admin/operator/coordinator/none]
```

Topology

Optional description of the network topology. I recommend using it if you have InfiniBand network or similar, do minimize number of network hops, and as a result latency and neighbor noise. To enable it, specify `TopologyPlugin=topology/TOPO_NAME`, where TOPO_NAME is one of:

Name	Meaning
default	One-dimensional topology
block	Block topology, see below
3d-torus	3d-torus topology
tree	Hierarchical topology, like tree, fat-tree, dragonfly

Block topology describes a simple network with several leaf switches (blocks) and one top switch. Topology configuration is specified in the `topology.conf` file. Here is an example for the block topology:

```
# topology/block
BlockName=block1 Nodes=n[1-32]
BlockName=block2 Nodes=n[33-64]
```

And here – for the tree topology:

```
# topology/tree
SwitchName=s0 Nodes=n[0,2,4,6]
SwitchName=s1 Nodes=n[1,3,5,7]
SwitchName=top Switches=s[0-1]
```

Note that in the second example, nodes are in the mixed order. If you have similar situation, this may cause communication problems in the apps, if they allocate nodes from several leaf switches, because by default neighbor ranks will communicate via top switch. To prevent it, use `TopologyParam=SwitchAsNodeRank` parameter in the `slurm.conf`. It will sort ranks (nodes list actually) by switches first, then by node names.

Be careful – if you add new nodes, update the topology file; otherwise, those nodes will never be selected for jobs!

CHAPTER 15 SLURM

Reservations

Reservation is a way in Slurm to request some number of nodes or specific nodes for individual users for a time in the future. Other users' assignments to these nodes will not be allocated, even if the nodes are free. This is useful as for dedicated calculations, as for the maintenance, because admins can run test jobs on the nodes and keep user jobs in queue.

In a reservation, you should specify the number or exact list of reserved nodes, start time, end time, or duration. You also can specify a list of allowed users or accounts, reservation name, and special flags. Let's look at an example:

```
scontrol create reservation name=important \
  StartTime=2100-06-01T08:00:00 Duration=5:00:00 \
  Users=user1,user2 NodeCnt=100 Flags=IGNORE_JOBS
```

Here we have created a 100 node reserve for users user1 and user2, which will be available to them from 8am on 2100-06-01 for five hours. The IGNORE_JOBS flag means "if the required number of nodes have not been released by this time, ignore it," and in this case, there may be fewer nodes than requested at the start of the reserve. To use the reservation, user must specify a key to the sbatch/srun command:

```
sbatch --reservation=important -N100 ./my_task
```

Other useful (but not all) flags are

- OVERLAP – Allow the list of nodes to overlap other existing reservation(s).

- NO_HOLD_JOBS_AFTER – By default if the reservation ends, any tasks submitted to it will be held. This flag allows such tasks to just remain in pending state. This flag cannot be removed using '-='.

- DAILY, HOURLY, WEEKLY – Repeat the reservation every day, hour, or week.

- WEEKDAY, WEEKEND – Like DAILY, but on weekdays or weekends.

- STATIC_ALLOC – By default if you ask to reserve a number of nodes and any node, selected for the reservation, goes down, then a new node is added to the reservation (if possible). This option prevents this.

- MAINT – Like OVERLAP and STATIC_ALLOC together.

If you want to modify the reservation, use the command shown below. Note "reservationname" without space and "+=" operator in flags. You can use it in users/accounts lists too, and "-=" operator, if you want to delete flags or names.

```
scontrol update reservationname=important \
  duration=14-00:00:00 flags+=STATIC_ALLOC
```

User Experience

For users, the basic Slurm commands are

- `sbatch` – Put the task in the queue.
- `srun` – Run the program interactively (it is queued as in `sbatch`, but control is not given to the shell until the program terminates).
- `salloc` – Allocate nodes for a task, but do not run anything on them, the user must do it himself. It is necessary, e.g., for some interactive programs.
- `squeue` – List of tasks in the queue.
- `sinfo` – Information about the partition.
- `sacct`, `sshare`, `sprio` – Information for advanced users about priority, resource usage, and FairShare.

A job is a script, like in PBS. And in the similar way, the script can include special comments, starting with '#SBATCH ' and following any `sbatch` options, which will be applied by default. They can be overridden by the environment variables or explicit `sbatch` options. This script is executed on the first allocated node and has set of environment variables, specific to the job. Unlike PBS, you can run 'srun something' inside the batch script and `something` will be executed on all allocated resources, e.g., if we run the script like this:

```
#/usr/bin/env bash
#SBATCH --nodes 2
#SBATCH --ntasks-per-node 2
echo Start
srun hostname
echo End
```

We can expect the output like:

```
Start
n10
n11
n11
n10
End
```

Note the random order of hostname outputs. Batch script can include several srun executions; they are called **steps** in Slurm. Step 0 is always the script run itself. If it is needed, several srun runs can be executed in parallel, e.g., if four CPUs were requested, first srun can be executed with option '-n 1', requesting only one CPU and the parallel one – with option '-n 3', requesting the rest CPUs. Such cases are rare, but possible.

Slurm supports work with containers directly, but requires some additional software to be installed. But I would recommend to use enroot software and pyxis Slurm plug-in – they are open source, well-supported, lightweight, and pretty customizable.

Each command has a lot of possible keys; the main ones for sbatch/srun are listed in the Table 15-1.

Table 15-1. sbatch/srun primary keys

Key	Meaning
-p partition	Partition name
-n NUMBER	Number of processes (cores) for a task
-N NUMBER	Number of nodes to specify
--ntasks-per-node N	Combined with -n/-N specifies the number of processes on the node
-A account	Explicitly account
--gres=...	Require some GRES in format NAME:NUMBER[,...], e.g., --gres=gpu:8
-C/--constraint=...	Require a list of features for nodes
-d condition	Specify dependencies on other tasks, e.g., start this task only after another task has been successfully completed
-i/-o/-e file	Specify the name of the I/O/errors file. The name can include the name of the node/user/task, etc. Default slurm-%j.out (%j = task name)

(*continued*)

Table 15-1. (*continued*)

Key	Meaning
-J name	Set the task name, by default – its ID
--[no-]requeue	Queue tasks again on failure [not]
-t/--time=TIME	Maximum time of task operation, after expiration of this time the task is forcibly terminated
-w nodelist	Require specific nodes
-x nodelist	Ask to not select specified nodes
--qos=NAME	Use QoS with name NAME

The -p, -A, and -J keys also work for sinfo/squeue, and you can specify a list of partitions/accounts/tasks. The -u key for squeue restricts the list to tasks of specific users, and -w restricts the list to specified nodes. Option --me shows only jobs of the current user and --start adds a column with estimated job start time. The -o/-O keys can be used to specify the output format in short or long format, respectively. The basic format characters in both formats for squeue are shown in the Table 15-2.

Table 15-2. *Formats for squeue*

Short	Long	Meaning
%a	account	Account
%C	numcpus	Number of cores requested or allocated (for a running task)
%D	numnodes	Number of nodes requested or allocated (for a running task)
%e	endtime	Task completion time
%i	taskid	Task ID
%j	name	Task name
%l	timelimit	Time limit in the format [[[DDD-]HH:]MM:]SS, either "NOT_SET" or "UNLIMITED"
%L	timeleft	Remaining operating time in the format [[[DDD-]HH:]MM:]SS
%M	eligiletime	Task runtime in the format [[[DDD-]HH:]MM:]SS

(*continued*)

Table 15-2. (*continued*)

Short	Long	Meaning
%N	nodes	List of task nodes, for a task in COMPLETING state – list of nodes that have not yet been released
%o	command	Launch command
%P	partition	Partition
%r	reason	Reason for the current task status
%t	statecompact	Task status in compact form: PD(pending), R(running), CA(canceled), CF(configuring), CG(completing), CD(completed), F(failed), TO(timeout), NF(node failure), and SE (special exit state)
%T	state	Task status in expanded form: PENDING, RUNNING, SUSPENDED, CANCELED, COMPLETING, COMPLETED, CONFIGURING, FAILED, TIMEOUT, PREEMPTED, NODE_FAIL or SPECIAL_EXIT
%u	username	Username
%U	userid	User ID
%v	reservation	Reserve name
%V	submittime	Queueing time

You can specify the size and alignment of the field: for short format, "%[.[size]NAME", and for long format, "NAME[:[.]size]", e.g., "%.18i" or "userid:.8". A dot in the format means right-alignment; the default is left-alignment.

Default format:

"%.18i %.9P %.8j %.8u %.2t %.10M %.6D %R"

Most notable keys for sinfo are presented in the Table 15-3.

Table 15-3. sinfo primary keys

Key	Meaning
-T reservation	Only what is relevant to the specified reservation
-t STATES	Only nodes in the specified states (list of states: ALLOC, ALLOCATED, COMP, COMPLETING, DOWN, DRAIN, DRAINED, DRAINING, ERR, ERROR, FAIL, FUTURE, FUTR, IDLE, MAINT, MIX, MIXED, NO_RESPOND, NPC, PERFCTRS, POWER_DOWN, POWER_UP, RESV, RESERVED, UNK, and UNKNOWN
-n NODES	Only on the specified nodes
-R	Show reasons
--json / --yaml	Output the data in JSON / YAML formatted
-s	Show only partitions summary
-h	Don't print the header (useful for scripts)

The -o option also works in the case of sinfo. Table 15-4 presents the short list of format characters.

Table 15-4. Basic sinfo formats

Symbol	Meaning
%a	Partition status
%A	Number of nodes in the "busy/free" format
%C	Number of processors in the format "busy/free/other/total"
%D	Number of nodes
%E	Node lockout
%F	Number of nodes in "busy/free/other/total" format
%P	Partition name, "*" is added for the default partition
%S	Whether tasks are allowed to run
%t	Node condition, short form
%T	Node condition, long form

Width and alignment control: %[.][number]character. Number specifies width; dot specifies right-alignment. The given lists of options and format symbols are by no means complete; see the documentation for more details.

Sometimes you can see that the node state is "duplicated," but a symbol is appended to it. Slurm does it to show additional information:

> * The node is not responding.
>
> $ The node is in the maintenance mode.
>
> ~ The node is presently in powered off.
>
> # The node is presently being powered up or configured.
>
> ! The node is pending power down.
>
> % The node is presently being powered down.
>
> @ The node is pending reboot.
>
> ^ The node reboot was issued.

Job Life Cycle

There are a lot of different steps happening during the job life in Slurm. I'll skip some, which are rarely used, but I recommend you to look in the docs about prologues/epilogues types and plug-ins invocation types. Here are the most common steps:

- **Submit the job (sbatch/srun/salloc)** – Here Slurm makes some checks, if this job is allowed to be queued, and also invokes SPANK plug-ins, which are registered for this step. Such plug-ins can add options and flags to sbatch and srun, like pyxis does. Special type of plug-ins, also invoked on this step, are job_submit plug-ins, where you can make special checks or actions.

- **Job start** – Before it happens, several types of prologue scripts and plug-in hooks are executed. Most common and interesting is the script (or a set of scripts) specified in the Prolog line in the config file. It is executed on all allocated nodes from the root user, and I highly recommend using it for making additional checks, if all hardware is ready, if all resources are clean (shared memory, semaphores, temporary directories, etc.). Note the prologue script time is limited!

- **Creating the job step** – The slurmstepd is starting, running any plug-ins hooks, if needed, then it starts the job script. By default, the cgroup plug-in is used, so it creates a special namespace and sets some limits before the step starts.

- **Job is running, new steps start and end via srun** – Also some plug-ins can handle those events (but rarely). During the job is running (and actually when not), Slurm can run a `HealthCheckProgram` – a script, which makes quick(!) and harmless(!!) checks of the node. If it fails, e.g., detects important errors in the kernel logs, or a GPU fail, then it may do some actions – usually drain the node. You can specify in which node states it should run and in which interval.

- **Job is preempted** – See the chapter about the preemption.

- **Job ends** – It can happen if the batch script is finished, canceled, or if the job is out of the time limit. The Slurm sends to all job processes on all allocated nodes SIGTERM, then in some time SIGKILL. Then epilogue script is executed and plug-ins hooks, just like for the prologue. And I also recommend using it for additional checks and cleanups.

Note – If prologue script fails (returns nonzero code), Slurm stops the job start, drains the node, and either cancels the job or requeues it. Be careful in the prologue and epilogue scripts.

scontrol

The next important command is `scontrol`. With its help, you can quickly change the state of partitions, nodes, tasks, and much more. Regular users can use it to check full status of a partition of a job and hold/unhold their jobs if needed. The command has many subcommands, Table 15-5 presents the most interesting ones.

Table 15-5. Main scontrol subcommands

Subcommand	Meaning
all	Show the partitions, their nodes, and assignments
cluster NAME	Specify the cluster we are working with, followed by the following subcommand[2]
create OBJECT	Create a Slurm object, see below
delete OBJECT	Delete the Slurm object
show OBJECT	Show Slurm facility
update OBJECT	Modify the Slurm object
hold/release JOBS	Lock/unlock tasks
suspend/release JOBS	Pause running tasks

The main objects that scontrol works with are partition, task, node, and reservation. The delete subcommand works only with reservations and partitions.

Block tasks from running on the nodes (drain the nodes):

```
scontrol update nodename=n[22,25] state=Drain reason='badmem'
```

Show the current running config:

```
scontrol show config
```

Reload all controllers and agents configuration:

```
scontrol reconfigure
```

Drain the node(s) and after the last job finishes reboots the node and set the state to STATE (really useful if you want to apply changes, like new image, kernel version, etc):

```
scontrol reboot asap nextstate=STATE NODE_LIST
```

---

[2] I don't understand why it's not put in an option, but it's far from the only illogical decision of Slurm authors.

Accounting and Statistics

If you have previously configured accounts, you can get statistics on tasks with the `sacct` command, filtering them by start/end time, accounts, logins, or partitions. If the `taskacct_gather` plug-in is enabled, you can get maximum/average CPU, memory, and disk utilization by individual tasks or by groups of tasks with the `sstat` command, filtering them as in `sacct`.

The `sreport` command can be used to get reports on cluster utilization. The following types of statistics are available:

> `cluster` – Total utilization, can be grouped by logins and accounts.
>
> `task` – Stats by task classes; class is set by the interval of number of cores per task, grouped by accounts.
>
> `user` – Utilization by logins.

Here are some examples. Get statistics on tasks for one day: task number, partition, login, number of core-hours, and completion status:

```
# sacct -S 2024-01-01 -E 2024-01-02 \
-o JobID,Partition,User%16,CPUTimeRAW,State%20 -X
 JobID Partition User          CPUTimeRAW State
 ------ --------- ---------- ---------- ------------------
 522783 test      user_12345 7168       COMPLETED
 523455 compute   user_23456 0          CANCELLED by 0
 526258 compute   user_55436 0          CANCELLED by 10107
 527646 compute   user_11231 1624       FAILED
 528244 compute   user_43546 46125352   NODE_FAIL
 528479 compute   user_12345 10526502   COMPLETED
 528480 compute   user_12345 15060654   COMPLETED
```

Another tool for statistics generation is `sreport`. Here is an example for the report for task classes 0–16 cores, 17–1024 cores, and 1024+ cores for the week:

```
sreport job SizesByAccount grouping=0-16,17-1024 \
  start=2024-01-01 end=2024-01-07
--------------------------------------------------------------------
Job Sizes 2018-01-01T00:00:00 - 2018-01-06T23:59:59 (518400 secs)
Time reported in Minutes
--------------------------------------------------------------------
  Cluster  Account 0-4294967295 0-16 cpus >= 17 cpus % of cluster
--------- --------- ---------- -------- ---------- ------------
superhpc  userst500 6678604725  1000612   6677604113 100.00%
```

Total statistics for the cluster for the month – how many resources were spent on tasks, Idle, Reserved, or lost due to downed nodes:

```
sreport cluster utilization Start=2024-11-01 End=2024-12-01 -t percent
--------------------------------------------------------------------------
Cluster Utilization 2024-11-01T00:00:00 - 2024-12-01T00:00:00 Usage
reported in Percentage of Total --------------------------------------------
-------------------------------
Cluster   Allocated  Down     PLND    Dow Idle   Planned   Reported
--------- ---------- -------- -------- -------- --------- ----------
superhpc   85.08%    8.59%    0.00%    2.10%    4.23%     100.00%
```

Statistics on users for the month (top five by resource utilization):

```
sreport user topusage topcount=5 start=2024-01-10 \
  end=2024-02-10
--------------------------------------------------------------
Top 10 Users 2024-01-10T00:00:00 - 2024-02-09T23:59:59
Use reported in TRES Minutes
--------------------------------------------------------------
  Cluster  Login    Proper Name  Account  Used       Energy
--------- -------- ------------ -------- ---------- ---------
superhpc  user_12  UserName12   usert500 43466331   0
superhpc  user_25  UserName25   usert500 35227321   0
superhpc  user_11  UserName11   usert500 35104234   0
superhpc  user_32  UserName32   usert500 30548681   0
superhpc  user_47  UserName47   usert500 27162101   0
```

Troubleshooting

If you have a large cluster, please refer to the recommendation on the page https://slurm.schedmd.com/high_throughput.html. In case of problems, the first place you want to look at is logs of course. By default, there are not so much information, so try to increase the verbosity level of the logs and probably fine-tune DebugFlags parameter to concentrate on something specific. Note that you can temporarily change them on the fly using scontrol setdebug LEVEL and scontrol setdebugflags {+|-}FLAG [{+|-}FLAG ...]. If you add 'nodes=...' with the nodes list, your changes affect only specific nodes.

Another good tool for looking inside your job manager is sdiag. It shows useful statistics, especially RPC stats, so you can detect if your Slurm is dying under request storm.

```
Agent queue size: 0

Remote Procedure Call statistics by message type
REQUEST_PARTITION_INFO (2009) count:325127 ave_time:183 total_time:5978485

Remote Procedure Call statistics by user
root   (       0) count:728986 ave_time:10228  total_time:456422703
user1  (   25002) count:29784  ave_time:13439  total_time:269036
...
```

sacctmgr show stats gives you information about accounts and used resources; sacctmgr show problem displays issues, which Slurm treats as potential problems; and sacctmgr show runawayjobs checks for jobs, which are orphaned somehow and ask for fix if any. scontrol show config shows the current configuration parameters; they may differ from your actual slurm.conf, so it is useful to check for unexpected values.

OK, you detected something odd and want to fix it. Depending on the type of the problem, the solutions may be quite different – sometimes you need to adjust users or accounts limits, sometimes you need to change Slurm scheduler parameters. In the second case, you usually want to change options using SchedulerParameters. There are a lot of them; here are some useful:

CHAPTER 15 SLURM

- **max_rpc_cnt**=N (for large number of jobs) increase max number of slurmd threads, 256 by default
- **defer** – Do not try to schedule each job, do it together with all once in a period of time (for LONG queues)
- **salloc_wait_nodes / sbatch_wait_nodes** – Start the job only when all nodes are ready (prologues and other init procedures are finished).

Advanced Parameters for slurm.conf

Here are some (there are much more, read the latest doc) of parameters in `slurm.conf`, which can help you.

Parameter	Meaning
PropagateResourceLimits	Force SLURM to set specified ulimits for the started jobs, as they are specified on the **submit** node. Possible values are ALL, NONE, CPU, NOFILE, ...
HealthCheckInterval	Interval in seconds between health check script runs, 0 (default) disables it
HealthCheckNodeState	Nodes in which states should run health check script: ALLOC, ANY, CYCLE (run gradually on all nodes), IDLE, NONDRAINED_IDLE, MIXED. You may specify several via comma
PrivateData	Hide some information from regular users – list via comma: accounts, events, jobs, nodes, partitions, reservations, usage, users. See more info below
PrologFlags	Control prologue behavior, list via comma. See more info below
SchedulerParameters	Options for the scheduler
SlurmSchedLogFile	Path to the log file for the schedulers
SlurmSchedLogLevel	1 = scheduler logging is enabled, 0 = disabled

For `PrivateData`, `nodes` and `partitions` hide nodes and partitions state; `reservations` hides the reservations, unless the user can use them; and `accounts`, `jobs`, `usage`, and `users` hide the information, unless the user is a coordinator or an operator. Useful `PrologFlags` (see full list in the docs):

- `Alloc` – Run prologue in the allocation phase. By default, the prologue is executed before the allocation phase and is not executed with salloc. This flag is required by many others.

- `Contain` – Use the ProcTrack plug-in to create a job container on all allocated compute nodes. pam_slurm_adopt then can place processes launched through a direct user login into this container.

- `DeferBatch` – Wait until the prologue completes on all allocated nodes before sending the batch job launch request. May prevent nonsynced MPI jobs start.

- `RunInJob` – Run prologue and epilogue in the extern slurmstepd. Implicitly sets the `Contain` and `Alloc` flag and runs prologue and epilogue in the job's container.

- `Serial` – Run prologue and epilogue on each node sequentially, one by one, instead of default parallel run. This is incompatible with `RunInJob`.

The most useful (in my opinion) `SchedulerParameters` (note that different type of schedulers may take different parameters):

- batch_sched_delay – How many seconds delay the job scheduling (default 3). May be useful if jobs are submitted with a high rate, and we want to collect many jobs before the scheduler starts.

- bf_interval – The number of seconds between backfill iterations. Default: 30, -1 disables the backfill.

- bf_max_job_assoc – The maximum number of jobs per user association to attempt starting with the backfill scheduler. Default: 0 (no limit).

- bf_max_job_part – The maximum number of jobs per partition to attempt starting with the backfill scheduler. Default: 0 (no limit).

CHAPTER 15   SLURM

- bf_max_job_user – The maximum number of jobs per user to attempt starting with the backfill scheduler for all partitions. Default: 0 (no limit).

- bf_max_job_user_part – The maximum number of jobs per user per partition to attempt starting with the backfill scheduler for any single partition. Default: 0 (no limit).

- bf_max_job_start – The maximum number of jobs which can be initiated in a single iteration of the backfill scheduler. Default: 0 (no limit).

- bf_max_job_test – The maximum number of jobs to attempt to backfill. Default: 500.

- bf_max_time – The maximum time in seconds for the backfill scheduler loop. Default: bf_interval value.

- default_queue_depth – The default number of jobs to attempt scheduling after a job completes or other routine actions occur. Default: 100.

- defer – Defer the job scheduling at job submit time, but defer it until a later time when scheduling multiple jobs simultaneously may be possible.

- defer_batch – Like defer, but only will defer scheduling for batch jobs. Interactive allocations from salloc/srun will still attempt to schedule immediately upon submission.

- ignore_prefer_validation – Ignore errors requesting nodes features. May be helpful when you add and remove nodes frequently, but is dangerous otherwise.

- max_rpc_cnt – Defer scheduling jobs, if the number of active controller daemon thread is equal or higher than this. Default: 0 (unlimited).

- max_sched_time – Maximum seconds the scheduler loop can run. If it is set, then other operations will be deferred while scheduling, so ensure that it is lower than MessageTimeout.

- max_switch_wait – Maximum number of seconds that a job can delay execution waiting for the specified desired switch count. Default: 300.

- nohold_on_prolog_fail – By default, if the prologue exits with a nonzero value, the job is requeued in a held state. By specifying this parameter, the job will be requeued but not held.

- pack_serial_at_end – With the select/cons_tres plug-in, put serial jobs at the end of the available nodes rather than using a best fit algorithm. This may reduce resource fragmentation for some workloads.

- salloc_wait_nodes – The salloc command will wait until all allocated nodes are ready for use before the command returns. By default, salloc will return as soon as the resource allocation has been made. The salloc command can use the `--wait-all-nodes` option to override this configuration parameter.

- sbatch_wait_nodes – The sbatch script will wait until all allocated nodes are ready for use before the initiation. By default, the sbatch script will be initiated as soon as the first node in the job allocation is ready. The sbatch command can use the `--wait-all-nodes` option to override this configuration parameter.

- sched_max_job_start – The maximum number of jobs that the main scheduling logic will start in any single execution. Default: 0 (unlimited).

All backfill-related parameters are active only with `SchedulerType=sched/backfill`.

Brief Summary

Slurm is the most actively developed job management system today and most reach of functions (in my personal opinion). It is easy to be integrated with containers, license managers, and much other stuff; the things you are missing often are easy to be added via scripts/plug-ins. Don't try to change the scheduler itself – it is a big pain; the rest is more or less manageable.

Search Keywords

SLURM, Schemd, scheduler, job_submit plugins, LUA

CHAPTER 16

Containers

Today, many applications are available via docker containers – in most cases, they help to avoid dependency hell while recompiling or trying to run a single binary. What is the container? Simply put, it is an isolated set of processes, which don't have any access to other processes and are limited to access full network, full file system, devices, etc. It is similar to a virtual machine, but there is no emulation; all processes are real, and from the "top level," you can see all of them.

In Linux, it is possible thanks to cgroups, namespaces, and chroot technologies. Cgroups allow you to limit sets of processes in use of memory, CPU, network, devices, and some other resources. Namespaces help to isolate PIDs, UIDs, etc., so processes in one namespace don't see others and even can have "virtual" numbers. chroot is a very old kernel trick, which allows to **change root** of the file system for the process to any directory.

Container actually is a combination of those technologies, applied to a set of processes. For example, you want to test a new database, but don't want to install it into your system, as it will conflict with the existing one. If you have a container with this database, it has a file system with all needed files, like binaries, libraries, and even its own libc. When you start this container, this file system is mounted into yours, then a set of cgroups and namespaces is created, and finally, the first container process is started with chroot to mounted file system.

As a result, all processes in the container have access only to other processes in the same container. They have their own set of users and have access only to the file system dedicated to the container as if it was the root file system. From the network perspective, it is a bit more complicated, but the overall idea is the same – you can limit the container to "see" only certain interfaces, usually virtual, which you created especially for this container. But here may be many options. You even can allow this container to use no more than 20% of your memory or only 1 CPU core.

Docker is the most popular container technology today, and in addition to all above, it uses squashfs – "layered" file system. The idea is to have a "base" file system, e.g., a freshly installed Ubuntu, which is a first layer, then you can install some libraries and other software and "save" all changes in a second layer. And you can continue to create new layers as far as you want – all changes will be saved (even file deletions). All layers are stored in the docker repository and/or on your local docker storage. If you install one container, all its layers are cached on your file system, and if you install a second one, which has some same layers (e.g., is based on the same Ubuntu version), only new ones will be loaded. This allows to save space and memory. If you have worked with docker and know about Dockerfile format, you may know that every line in this file creates a new squashfs layer (OK, almost every). When you change the line and rebuild the container, it will be rebuilt only from the changed line, because all previous layers are unchanged.

"OK, but I need to process my data!", a user would say. No problem, in Linux, you can `mount` local directory as a file system into any other directory, using '`--bind`' key. Using this trick, you can make your directory with data or anything else visible in the container. By default, all container systems allow you to specify what you want to mount and at what path inside the container.

How can we use containers in HPC? Unfortunately, docker technology has a lot of limitations, and directly, we almost cannot use it in HPC in 2025. By default, docker requires a special service, running with root privileges, doesn't allow using InfiniBand and GPUs directly, and badly integrates with job managers. There are ways how to overcome those and some other issues, but fortunately, we have many other technologies, which allow using containers and even prebuilt docker containers. Let's talk about the most useful today.

Singularity

This is the project by Sylabs Inc., but it has a mature open source community edition. It uses its own format, but you can easily convert a docker container into singularity. There is an option to run a docker container "directly," but actually singularity will import it, convert, run, and then delete converted one, so it is not recommended.

Also, you can build a singularity container using special "definition file," similar to Dockerfile. Singularity containers were designed especially for HPC and can be easily integrated with any batch system. It allows HPC applications to have transparent access to InfiniBand interfaces and GPU accelerators. To use it with NVIDIA GPUs, you should have `nvidia-container-toolkint` installed.

To run an MPI application in the singularity container, you can use a command like this:

mpirun -n $NP singularity run app.sif /opt/my-mpi-app

Here, NP is the number of processes, app.sif is the singularity container, and /opt/my-mpi-app is the path to the MPI application inside the container. This command line can be used inside the batch file. In case of SLURM, we'd recommend to use srun instead of mpirun.

Read more about singularity here: https://docs.sylabs.io/guides/latest/user-guide.

Apptainer

This technology is a fork of singularity, developed independently by the Linux Foundation. Almost everything, related to the singularity, is applied to apptainers.

> Actually, vice versa, the singularity was a fork, but it is a bit complicated; if you want, you can read some details here: https://apptainer.org/news/community-announcement-20211130/.

CharlieCloud

The open source technology, similar to singularity, but is intended to be lightweight and uncomplicated. It contains several utilities, like ch-image, ch-build, ch-run, and ch-convert, and allows you to deal with docker images, extract the squashfs, build your containers, and run squashfs as a container. It integrates with job management systems via PMIx, so its use is pretty simple.

Pyxis + Enroot

These projects are open source and developed by NVIDIA, so only NVIDIA GPUs will be well managed if you use them. Enroot is a lightweight container implementation; it doesn't require docker or other container engine to be installed. When you run the container using enroot, it extracts the squashfs into the local file system and then runs the application with cgrops/namespaces/chroot set. Pyxis is a complimentary SLURM plug-in, which adds some useful flags to `srun` command and runs the container using enroot transparently. This technology is really easy to use and requires minimum overhead, comparing to the other options.

Caching

If you use containers, please be ready that **each** process before the start will download this container, prepare it (unpack/convert/etc.), and then start. It takes time and also forces the container images to be downloaded many times and often at the same time. This is not efficient, so I recommend to

1. Stimulate your users to load containers into the shared file system and reuse loaded images.

2. Use caching options when available (Charliecloud and Enroot give you some).

3. Use special caching proxy, like docker-registry-proxy project. Regular proxy may be not a good choice, because docker image registries frequently require authorization and also you don't want to cache manifests (at least for a long time).

Brief Summary

Containers are a lightweight option of virtual machines; they are convenient to use if you need to run applications without installing new packages or compiling them from the source code. In HPC world, you should be cautious, because you need low-latency access to devices and ability to run MPI applications.

Search Keywords

Linux Containers, Docker, Open Container Initiative, cgroups, linux kernel namespaces, chroot, singularity, apptainer, charliecloud, enroot, pyxis

CHAPTER 17

Clouds

If you don't have an HPC cluster and cannot build it right now but need to run HPC computations, you can try to get access to an existing one. Another option is build your own HPC cluster in clouds. Today, some cloud providers give you special HPC instances – virtual machines with almost transparent access to high-performance network and accelerators. Please note that the overall performance will still be less than on a "real" hardware, but depending on the provider, it can have a 5-15% performance drop. If it is OK to you, let's take a look to the details.

A very important aspect is price; carefully estimate your expenses, it might turn out that building and managing an on-prem cluster would be even cheaper in the long term! But cloud can be a perfect playground to test technologies and software before production use. Some cloud providers can give you almost raw HPC hardware today, so you can imitate almost real cluster.

Before you buy cloud resources, precisely check which type of the network is used and what resources are included into your instances. In many cases, if you use a high-performance low-latency network, you are limited in number of instances, which can be connected. Make sure they are in one performance subnet (capacity reservation, domain, etc.). Otherwise, the overall performance can be times lower.

Network file system is really important, and you should ensure that you have access to a good one. If it is just an NFS volume, probably it is not what you want. If the cloud provider cannot give you clean performance estimations, you can try to buy cheap instances with this file system and run I/O performance tests, ideally similar to your production I/O. For example, you know that your HPC application saves temporary data every five minutes and size is around the compute node memory. Then you can simulate this pattern and check how long this save takes and how long it loads from the file system.

Some cloud providers allow you to bring up a SLURM-based HPC cluster as an option. In simple cases, it may be really useful. But if there is no such option, or you need some features, not included in this option, you can bring it up by yourself. I recommend to use automation tools like `terraform` for the initial setup. After bringing up the nodes, you need to install all needed software, and this process also should be automated. You can use `Ansible` or other tools. If it is possible to create a custom image and use it on new nodes, this will be the best solution. Some cluster management tools, like BCM, can help you to manage this. Test your solution on cheap instances first!

Check the cloud API to be able to automate any additional actions, like terminating the instance and bringing up a new one, or just power on/off any subset of your instances.

Via cloud API, you might be able to collect useful metrics, like power consumption, network counters, node health, etc. If it is possible, use this ability. If not, try to collect as much as you can directly on the nodes.

All questions, you have to check before building an on-prem cluster, are actual in the cloud, but may be slightly corrected. For example, user management may be integrated with your corp authentication mechanisms, but may be implemented independently. Checking nodes and reporting service tickets may be automated via cloud provider API. Take another look at the chapter "How to Build and Start It?"

Brief Summary

Many HPC applications can be run on HPC clouds today, and in some cases, it may be a cheap solution. Amazon, Oracle, Google, Coreweave, Lambda, and HyperStack are just a few providers I can name off the top of my head.[1] But don't underestimate the management overhead and limited choice of assets in the cloud environment. Check for the network and storage options, price for traffic, price for turned off nodes, and any other possibly hidden factors. Make a test, try to assess the risks and performance first.

Search Keywords

HPC cloud, HPC cloud network, Cloud security, Low-latency cloud network

---

[1] Not an advertisement, they don't pay me :)

CHAPTER 18

Remote User Access

SSH

This is the main method of remote access to supercomputers today. Don't be intimidated by the fact that access will be on the command line and your users are working in graphical environments. They only need to know a few commands to work, and if they use open source projects that require building or developing programs themselves, the command line is no longer scary for them.

To ease the plight of newcomers, I recommend installing the mc (Midnight Commander) file manager package on the access node, the interface of which is very similar to Far Manager or TotalCommander for Windows or other "two-panel" file managers. Our experience shows that beginners rarely have problems in communicating with the command line, because for them, the set of operations is limited to putting a task in the queue and viewing its status. Copying files from or to a cluster is done in a convenient client on a personal computer, and editing is also done.

So, to organize remote access, we need to install **openssh** server (see chapter "Remote Management") and configure it for the mode we need. The "classic" password access will work by default, but I strongly advise against it. Password access can be allowed from a limited set of addresses (from administrator workstations) and only to a limited set of users. This may be necessary to resolve emergency situations.

For regular users, I recommend allowing access only by key. When registering, the user forms a key pair (or uses existing) and sends the public key – this is enough to give access. You need to add this open part to the ~user/.ssh/authorized_keys file (do not replace the contents, and add it exactly!). It was probably already created by you when you created the user account and generated the keys for passwordless access to the nodes. Note that public ssh keys come in two formats: "OpenSSH" and "RFC." They differ slightly in the form of writing, RFC is multiline, and OpenSSH is single line. If you are sent a public key in RFC format, convert it to OpenSSH with the following command:

`ssh-keygen -f -i rfc-key.pub >> ~user/.ssh/authorized_keys`

This command will at the same time immediately add the obtained key to the required file. Now a user only needs to type `ssh -i .ssh/cluster-key cluster` to get to your cluster, if he is running Linux or MacOS and has a private key stored in `.ssh/cluster-key`.

For Windows users, I can recommend the **Putty** suite of programs. It includes the `putty-gen` program, which can generate and convert keys, and the `putty ssh` client itself. To access a cluster, you need to load a `ppk-formatted` key into the program (putty-gen generates it by default) and specify the cluster address. Take a look at the git repository `https://github.com/zhum/hpc-book-matherials;` it has a simple webpage describing basic ssh key creation for Windows users; feel free to use, beautify, and improve it.

In addition to console access, the SSH protocol allows you to organize file transfers. For Linux clients, you can use `scp` command, FISH virtual file system in Midnight Commander, `sshfs`, or remote ssh connections in file managers. For Windows clients, I recommend the **WinSCP** program or the winscp plug-in for FAR. You can also use popular programs like **FileZilla** that support SCP/SFTP, but since they usually do not support key authentication, you need to run the `putty-agent` program beforehand (once) and load an ssh key into it.

FTP and WWW

FTP (File Transfer Protocol) was very popular for file transfer in the early days of the Internet. Nowadays, it is also often used for file distribution, and FTP support is even built into most browsers and supported by many file managers. This protocol allows both downloading and transferring data to a server, which has made it a very popular means of file transfer. A significant disadvantage of this protocol is its very weak security. The only way of authentication for FTP is the transfer of login and password without encryption.

There are several implementations of secure FTP variants, but, alas, they are not standardized and are not supported by all clients. Besides, even with encryption, a password is required for authentication, and the very possibility to enter by password weakens security. It is not so difficult to find a weak password, and it is not always possible to control the strength of user passwords. FTP is a good solution only in one case: for organizing public file storage with anonymous (passwordless) read-only access.

Currently, an excellent alternative to FTP are the **SFTP** and **SCP** protocols, standardized and supported by all SSH server implementations. They allow authentication by key, which virtually eliminates the possibility of tampering. The downside of these protocols is higher CPU time consumption and often slower transfer speeds. This is due to both overhead encryption costs and peculiarities of data transmission over encrypted channels. There is a possibility to apply encryption only at the authentication stage and not to encrypt file transfer, but unfortunately, it is not supported by standard servers and clients.

The second important protocol that can be used to access a supercomputer is **HTTP,** which is the basis for the World Wide Web (WWW). In other words, access through a browser to a web server. Often there is no need for a web server on a supercomputer – all the necessary information can be placed on a separate server that is not part of the supercomputer. This option is much preferable, as any web server becomes vulnerable as soon as it begins to serve dynamic content – cgi-scripts, application servers, etc. Even with static content only, a web server can be vulnerable to attacks through inadvertently included modules.

But sometimes it is necessary to receive or transmit information directly to the supercomputer, e.g., to display the queue status, etc. In this case, you can implement such functionality through an external server, e.g., by receiving data via `ssh` or `rsync`, having previously limited the allowable command line in the server key (see the section about ssh), or configuring the web server in such a way as to exclude the possibility of hacking.

It is advisable to severely restrict it with a `chroot` or, preferably, run it in a virtual machine such as a lightweight LinuxContainer (**LXC**). Do not forget about log analysis and intrusion detection systems (**IDS**): any "unnecessary" services, especially those available from the outside, are a reason to try to break into your system, if only for fun.

X-Window

The main feature of the graphics subsystem in Linux, unlike MS Windows, is that it is not part of the operating system. In Linux, it is possible to work without problems only in terminal mode, without using the graphical interface. This is the mode in which you usually work with a supercomputer. But there are situations when the use of graphical

CHAPTER 18 REMOTE USER ACCESS

programs is necessary. For example, some commercial systems can be configured only through graphical programs or a browser.

Visualization of scientific data is also often preferred on the supercomputer side, as it is much more costly to transfer the data itself for visualization at the user's workstation. This is why I have included a chapter on graphics in Linux to give an idea of how graphics programs work and how to access them remotely. The graphics system in Linux is called the X-Window System (or X-Window, or simply X). It is gradually being replaced by Wayland, but compatibility with X will be maintained for a long time to come.

X-Window implements the basic functions of a graphical environment: drawing and moving windows on the screen, interacting with the mouse and keyboard, but does not define the details of window design – this is handled by **window managers**. Because of this, the appearance of graphical user interfaces in UNIX-like systems can vary greatly, depending on the capabilities and settings of a particular window manager.

A window manager controls the placement and framing of application windows (frame and title bar). It can create a Microsoft Windows or Macintosh-like appearance (e.g., this is how **Kwin** window managers work in KDE, **Metacity** in GNOME), or a completely different style, such as in frame-based window managers like **Ion**.

A window manager can be simple and minimalistic (like **twm**, the basic window manager shipped with X), or it can offer additional functionality close to a full desktop environment (like Enlightenment). Many users use X along with a complete desktop environment that includes a window manager, various applications, and a unified interface style. The most popular desktop environments are GNOME and KDE. The Single UNIX Specification specifies the CDE environment. The freedesktop.org project attempts to provide interoperability between different environments and to develop the components needed for a competitive X-based desktop.

X-Window is built using client/server technology; server is the X server or X process, which "owns" resources such as the screen and input devices, and the clients are graphical applications. The client and server communicate using a specially designed X protocol. At the moment, the 11th version of the protocol is up-to-date, so you can often see the designation **X11**.

X server consists of two main parts: drivers responsible for working with input/output devices (keyboard, mouse, video adapters, monitors, etc.) and a part that provides interaction with applications via X protocol via UNIX sockets or Internet sockets. The ability to communicate over a network allows the X server and client to run graphical applications remotely.

When starting an X server, you can specify the number of the display it will serve. In Linux, multiple X servers can be started to serve different displays. By default, the X server starts on display number :0, after which this number is considered occupied, and an attempt is made to start a server with the same number will fail. Physically, a display can be real hardware (monitor, mouse, keyboard) connected to the server, or it can be virtual. A display in the X sense is not necessarily one monitor and one mouse-keyboard; it can include multiple screens and many input devices.

Most applications that have a graphical interface have a special -display option that specifies which display the program will interact with:

xclock -display :0

If the option is not supported or if you just want to specify a default display, you must use the DISPLAY environment variable:

export DISPLAY=:0

X.Org Foundation's reference implementation, called X.Org Server, is the canonical implementation of X-Window. Modern implementations of X.Org Server are capable of running, automatically detecting hardware parameters and requiring no manual configuration. However, in some cases, this is still necessary, e.g., to specify the use of a particular driver rather than what X.Org considers optimal.

The main X server configuration file is /etc/X11/xorg.conf; many distributions maintain a /etc/X11/xorg.conf.d directory, which may contain multiple files with separate configuration sections. The X server will work with the /etc/X11/xorg.conf file if it exists. The configuration defined in this file has a higher priority than other configurations.

There may be situations when the system will incorrectly detect the parameters of your I/O devices, in which case you need to edit the configuration file. Since this file does not exist by default, you can create it with the Xorg -configure command. This will result in the file xorg.conf.new, which can be edited and copied to /etc/X11/xorg.conf. The structure of this file is described in the chapter "One-Two-Three Instructions," in the standard documentation (man xorg.conf) and on the Internet. If the X server fails to start, more detailed information can be found in the file /var/log/Xorg.0.log. Here 0 is the display number.

CHAPTER 18   REMOTE USER ACCESS

The X server can be started directly from the command line, but this method is very rarely used. Usually it is started as a service at system startup. In addition to the server, at least one client must be started for normal operation. In case of launching from the command line, the `startx` script is usually run, which in addition to the server starts a script that starts a set of clients. When this script (session) terminates, the server also terminates. The session script is typically located in `/etc/X11/Xsession.d` or in `~/.xsession`.

In the case of running X server as a service, its only client is the **screen manager** – an application that allows you to authenticate the user and launch the session of your choice (frequently a desktop environment such as KDE).

The basic Linux screen manager is **xdm**. Gnome and KDE have their own screen managers, **gdm** and **kdm**, and sometimes others, such as **lightdm**, are used. The main function of a screen manager is to allow the user to enter their login and password in graphical mode. Additional functions are selecting the input language, selecting a window manager or a graphical shell, and shutting down the computer without logging in.

The xdm manager configuration files are located in the `/etc/X11/xdm/` directory. After a user successfully logs in, the `/etc/X11/xdm/Xsession` script will run and continue loading the graphics subsystem. Configuration files for gdm are located in the `/etc/gdm/` directory and for kdm (fourth version) in the `/etc/kde4/kdm` directory.

If the workplace is running Windows, you will need to install X server to work with X clients. There are quite a lot of X server implementations for different versions of MS Windows (Exceed, Xwin32, etc.), but almost all of them are commercial products.

However, there is a quality open source and free implementation of the X server. This is the **Xming** package. You can download it from the official site.[1] There are two variants of this software on the site: xming and xming Mesa. The second variant allows you to run applications using OpenGL on a remote terminal. In addition to the X server itself, you can download additional backgrounds for it, including Cyrillic ones, and a program for managing X server startup parameters – `Xlaunch`. After installing the program on your computer, you should make a shortcut for the Xming program on your desktop. The program should be launched with some set of parameters:

```
"C:\Program Files\Xming\Xming.exe" :0 -clipboard \
  -multiwindow -xkblayout us,ru -xkbvariant winkeys \
  -xkboptions grp:ctrl_shift_toggle
```

---

[1] http://www.straightrunning.com/XmingNotes/

Here:

- `:0` – Display number
- `-clipboard` – Allows the use of the system clipboard
- `-multiwindow` – Sets multiwindow mode
- `-xkblayout us,ru` – Sets two keyboard layouts: English and Russian (in case if you need it)
- `-xkboptions grp:ctrl_shift_toggle` – Switch layouts by pressing `Ctrl-Shift`, if you selected two layouts
- `-xkbvariant winkeys` – Allows additional window keyboard keys to be processed

When Xming is first started, it may ask you to unblock ports in the Windows Firewall so that it can receive information over the network. To ensure security, it is recommended that you edit the firewall settings entry for Xming and list only the machines that will be used.

Let's consider an example of a session with a remote system using an X server. First, Xming is started on the local machine. Then use a terminal program (e.g., Putty) to connect to the remote UNIX system. Set the "`Connection/SSH/X11 Forwarding`" option in the Putty session parameters. In this case, Putty will automatically set the `DISPLAY` variable on the remote computer and add an authorization string to the `XAUTHORITY` variable, allowing you to run X applications without any additional steps. Note: The remote computer must have the `xauth` program that manages authentication installed.

If there is no `xauth` command on the remote computer, or if you are using a program for remote access without X connection forwarding, you can edit the `X0.hosts` file, usually located in the `C:\Program Files\Xming\` directory. This file should list the domain names or IP addresses of the computers from which Xming can receive graphical information.

Example file X0.hosts:

```
localhost
cluster.mycompany.org
192.168.32.23
```

A similar function, allowing access via the X protocol, in UNIX systems performs a command:

xhost +computer_name

Authentication via xhost is unreliable and may be turned off by default. It is strongly recommended to avoid it and use xauth if possible.

Alternatives for X11

A serious limitation of the X protocol is its low speed. When running applications with rich graphics, there can be very long delays, leading to almost impossible work, especially on narrow communication channels. An alternative in this case can be protocols that have long been used for Windows systems. The **VNC** protocol is very common; there are many clients for it and several server implementations for Linux. The protocol supports image scaling and compression, which allows you to dramatically increase the speed of transmission at the expense of quality.

The disadvantage of this approach is that it does not support multiuser organization: the server is started on behalf of one of them and then any client connecting to it will have access to the applications and desktop running in the current session. Dynamic session spawning based on username is not available in any of the available servers, as far as I know. Nevertheless, this technology can be used to organize access to dedicated applications – visualization of scientific calculations (if the number of its users is small), administration of specific hardware, etc.

Don't forget to set a password to log in!

For Linux, the best known implementations are **tightvncserver**, its modern fork TigerVNC. They both run as X11 servers, so any X applications can run in their sessions. Images from the server can be sent to clients over the VNC protocol, and there can be multiple clients at the same time. They can be passive, receiving only the image but not being able to enter information, or active – with full access. Similar but more developed technology is the **RDP** (Remote Desktop Protocol), used in the standard delivery of Windows. It supports authorization and simultaneous work of several users, as well as file transfer. The speed of RDP is usually faster than VNC and with higher image quality. Due to the fact that this protocol is closed, there are far fewer Linux implementations of both clients and servers for it. The authors have no successful experience in organizing an RDP server on Linux.

A good alternative is the **x2go** protocol, which is an open source variant of the closed NX protocol developed by NoMachine. x2go clients and servers are available for most distributions from a separate repository, as well as for Windows.

The server doesn't even need to run a separate service – just install the required package. The client accesses the server node via ssh protocol (which solves many authentication problems) and runs the server program there as a user. Thus, the use of x2go is well protected and secure on the server side. In terms of speed, x2go is not inferior to VNC; it also supports compression, scaling, and the ability to transfer the image not the entire desktop but only the windows of one program.

You can also work with the previously mentioned **NX** protocol; it requires a server and a client from `https://nomachine.com/`. There are clients for both Windows and Linux. In the free version, the server allows no more than two users to work simultaneously. An additional plus of NX is the ability to authenticate by password with session saving and possible subsequent reconnection.

Another alternative is the **SPICE** protocol, but it is less widespread. You can learn more about it at `https://www.spice-space.org/`.

Brief Summary

Remote access is the "face" of your computing complex for users (after the official website and registration, of course). It is the one they will use 99% of the time. Try to make the access process comfortable: describe basic procedures, problems on the site, and supplement this information with answers to questions as they come to you from users.

For a supercomputer, as for any server, the principle works: the less access, the better. But at the same time, users should not be clamped in a hedgehog's grip. SSH combined with SCP/SFTP is usually sufficient for normal operation.

Search Keywords

Ssh, putty, shellinabox, secure ftp, xserver, X11, vnc, rdp, nx, spice remote, x2go, IDS, LXC, KVM/QEMU, logcheck, logwatch

CHAPTER 19

Cluster Status Monitoring Systems

SNMP

SNMP (Simple Network Management Protocol) is a protocol designed for management and monitoring. It was created in 1988 and is supported by most network devices. It is a de facto industry standard, and many hardware platforms support it. The goal of this protocol is to give the ability to get monitoring data from (almost) any device and change their settings. At the moment, there are three major versions of the protocol: 1, 2c, and 3.

First version uses "Simple" in the title as a keyword. But because of this simplicity, this version has a lot of problems – short counters, poor security, and no encryption. Version 2c (c = "community") is probably the most common today. It has additional commands, compared to version 1, but still has poor security and no encryption support. The only security feature in both versions is the "community" string with optional password. You can treat "community" as a "login." Third version supports authentication, encryption, and user-based views.

Each network device has its own set of internal variables and commands that are grouped into a tree structure. The names of all these variables are encoded according to this structure (similar to DNS names). Such a name is called an "object identifier" (**OID**). The description of the correspondence of OIDs to their actual purpose and type is stored in the management information base (MIB). There can be a different MIB for each type of device. SNMP supports several types of variables: integers, counters, strings, from more complex types – only tables. As a rule, interface counters of network devices are organized into tables.

OID consists of a sequence of numbers, e.g., `1.3.6.1.2.1.1.1.3`. Such representation is not very convenient for perception, so MIB files usually contain "human-readable" names for OIDs. For the previous example, such a name would be `iso.org.dod.internet.mgmt.mib-2.system.sysUpTime` – the time the device has been running since it was last powered on. Most OID branches are standardized by ITEF, ISO, and IANA, but many are "given" to other organizations. A separate branch is dedicated to manufacturers, where each subbranch is controlled by a dedicated organization, e.g., Cisco, APC, etc.

In SNMP terms, a device supporting SNMP protocol is called an agent (although it essentially acts as a server), and a program communicating with the agent (management or monitoring) is called a manager. As a rule, the agent passively responds to the manager's requests, but the protocol provides "**traps**," notifications, which the agent can send to the manager in special cases. Usually, it is a signal about anomalies in the work, and the set of trap types is hardcoded in the agent. SNMP agent mainly uses UDP protocol and port 161. Notifications are sent to port 162 of the manager. The encrypted version of the protocol (v3 TLS) may use ports 10161 and 10162, respectively,[1] or reuse 161 and 162 ports.

Here is the basic set of commands used in the SNMP protocol:

- `GetRequest` – A request to the agent from the manager to get the value of one or more variables

- `GetNextRequest` – A request to the agent from the manager to get the value of the next variable in the hierarchy

- `SetRequest` – A request to the agent to set the value of one or more variables

- `GetReponse` – A response from the agent to the manager returning the requested values

- `GetBulkRequest` – A request to the agent to get a range of variables

- `Trap` – One-way notification to the manager from the SNMP agent about the event

---

[1] https://www.rfc-editor.org/info/rfc6353

CHAPTER 19 CLUSTER STATUS MONITORING SYSTEMS

When the manager calls the agent, it is necessary to correctly specify not only the OID, but also the protocol version, as well as the community – the name of the group that is allowed to access this variable and, if necessary, the password. Different versions of the SNMP protocol are incompatible, so it is important to specify the exact version of the protocol. Most devices support version 2c.

To install command-line client programs (managers) in most distributions, it is enough to install the net-snmp package or sometimes simply snmp. The most interesting commands for us from this package are snmpget/snmpbulkget and snmpwalk/snmpbulkwalk. With their help, you can read values of specified variables or whole subtrees. If the snmpwalk command is not given the initial OID, it will try to read the entire tree starting from iso.org.dod.internet.mgmt.mib-2 (where almost all branches for network devices start).

The purpose of the snmpset program, I think, is easy to guess: it sets the value of a variable. It can be a sensor threshold, a server name, an email address, etc.

Let's look at an example:

```
$ snmpget -v 2c -c demopublic test.net-snmp.org sysUpTime.0
DISMAN-EVENT-MIB::sysUpTimeInstance = Timeticks: (4935618) 13:42:36.18
```

Here we request the uptime of the test.net-snmp.org server since it was last powered on. Note that by default, it is allowed to omit the prefix "iso.org.dod.internet.mgmt.mib-2.system".

Another example is the description of that MIB element we just received:

```
$ snmptranslate -Td -Ib 'sysUptime'
SNMPv2-MIB::sysUpTime
sysUpTime OBJECT-TYPE
-- FROM SNMPv2-MIB, RFC1213-MIB
SYNTAX TimeTicks
MAX-ACCESS    read-only
STATUS current
DESCRIPTION  "The time (in hundredths of a second) since the
              the network management portion of the system was last
              re-initialized."
::={ iso(1) org(3) dod(6) internet(1) mgmt(2) mib-2(1) system(1) 3 }
```

The `snmptranslate` command outputs the description of the element (description), its access level (max-access), and its full path (last line). This command does not access remote servers; it only translates complex text descriptions of MIBs into a human-friendly format.

The next example is the operation of the `snmpwalk` command. With its help, we can "bypass" a whole tree of values without knowing its composition beforehand. Let's look at the `system` tree on the same test server:

```
$ snmpwalk -v 2c -c demopublic test.net-snmp.org system
SNMPv2-MIB::sysDescr.0 = STRING: test.net-snmp.org
SNMPv2-MIB::sysObjectID.0 = OID: NET-SNMP-MIB::netSnmpAgentOIDs.10
DISMAN-EVENT-MIB::sysUpTimeInstance = Timeticks: (5337593) 14:49:35.93
SNMPv2-MIB::sysContact.0 = STRING: Net-SNMP Coders
SNMPv2-MIB::sysName.0 = STRING: test.net-snmp.org
SNMPv2-MIB::sysLocation.0 = STRING: Undisclosed
SNMPv2-MIB::sysORLastChange.0 = Timeticks: (5) 0:00:00.05
SNMPv2-MIB::sysORID.1 = OID: SNMPv2-MIB::snmpMIB
SNMPv2-MIB::sysORID.2 = OID: SNMP-VIEW-BASED-ACM-MIB::vacmBasicGroup
SNMPv2-MIB::sysORID.3 = OID: SNMP-MPD-MIB::snmpMPDMIBObjects.3.1.1
SNMPv2-MIB::sysORID.4 = OID: SNMP-USER-BASED-SM-MIB::usmMIBCompliance
SNMPv2-MIB::sysORID.5 = OID: SNMP-FRAMEWORK-MIB::snmpFrameworkMIBCompliance
SNMPv2-MIB::sysORDescr.1 = STRING: The MIB module for SNMPv2 entities
SNMPv2-MIB::sysORDescr.2 = STRING: View-based Access Control Model for SNMP.
SNMPv2-MIB::sysORDescr.3 = STRING: The MIB for Message Processing.
SNMPv2-MIB::sysORDescr.4 = STRING: The MIB for Message Processing.
SNMPv2-MIB::sysORDescr.5 = STRING: The SNMP Management Architecture MIB.
SNMPv2-MIB::sysORUpTime.1 = Timeticks: (4) 0:00:00.04
SNMPv2-MIB::sysORUpTime.2 = Timeticks: (4) 0:00:00.04
SNMPv2-MIB::sysORUpTime.3 = Timeticks: (5) 0:00:00.05
SNMPv2-MIB::sysORUpTime.4 = Timeticks: (5) 0:00:00.05
SNMPv2-MIB::sysORUpTime.5 = Timeticks: (5) 0:00:00.05
```

As you can see, the command returned us a set of values along with the names.

Let's see how to configure the SNMP server on the server. With its help, we will be able to remotely receive data about the server operation. Run the `snmpconf` program. The program will ask whether it needs to read existing configuration files and which file to generate. Select `snmpd.conf` (usually item 1).

CHAPTER 19 CLUSTER STATUS MONITORING SYSTEMS

After that, we are taken to the section menu:

```
1: Extending the Agent
2: Monitor Various Aspects of the Running Host
3: Trap Destinations
4: Agent Operating Mode
5: System Information Setup
6: Access Control Setup
```

We are interested in sections 4, 5, and 6. In section 4, you can specify the address (interface) on which the agent will run, as well as the user and group on behalf of which it will run. Section 5 is data about the server, which will be available in the `system` subtree. Section 6 allows you to specify the username (for SNMP v3) and/or `community` name for reading or read-write in a certain subtree (by default – for all values):

```
1: an SNMPv3 read-write user
2: an SNMPv3 read-only user
3: a SNMPv1/SNMPv2c read-only access community name
4: a SNMPv1/SNMPv2c read-write access community name
```

For example, let's set the ability to read all values for the `192.168.0.0` network in a community named public (user input is indicated in bold):

```
Select section: 3

Configuring: rocommunity
Description:
      an SNMPv1/SNMPv2c read-only access community name
      arguments: community [default|hostname|network/bits] [oid]
The community name to add read-only access for: public
The hostname or network address to accept this community name from [RETURN for all]: 192.168.0.0
The OID that this community should be restricted to [RETURN for no-restriction]:
Finished Output: rocommunity public 192.168.0.0
```

After configuration, the program writes the configuration file to the current directory, and it can be copied to /etc/snmp/.

> The **snmpconf** program does not always generate a correct configuration file; be sure to save the original (**cp /etc/snmp/snmpd.conf{,.bak}**) and compare the new file with it if errors occur.

So, our server can now be monitored over the network. Unfortunately, not all its parameters are interesting, and not with the best protection, but most standard monitoring packages will see it and will be able to receive data from it. Monitoring functionality can be extended if desired.

Let's consider another very important service for us – snmptrapd. This program receives notifications (traps) that are sent by other SNMP devices – servers, routers, air conditioners, UPSs, etc.

> To make it work, you need to configure the device to send the necessary notifications to the address of the server where snmptrapd is running!

Now let's edit the snmptrapd configuration file – /etc/snmp/snmptrapd.conf. For minimal configuration, it is enough to add the following line:

```
authCommunity log,execute,net public
```

Restart the snmptrapd server and run the test command:

```
snmptrap -v 2c -c public localhost "" \
NET-SNMP-EXAMPLES-MIB::netSnmpExampleHeartbeatNotification \
netSnmpExampleHeartbeatRate i 123456
```

This command will send a test notification to localhost. If snmptrapd is running, an entry like this will appear in the log (usually /var/log/syslog or /var/log/messages):

```
[UDP: [127.0.0.1]:48680->[127.0.0.1]]:#012iso.3.6.1.2.1.1.1.3.0 = \
Timeticks: (189767908) \
21 days, 23:07:59.08#011iso.3.6.1.6.3.1.1.4.1.0 =\
OID: iso.3.6.1.4.1.8072.2.3.0.1#011iso.3.6.1.4.1.8072.2.3.2.1 =\
INTEGER: 123456
```

CHAPTER 19 CLUSTER STATUS MONITORING SYSTEMS

That is, the message was accepted. If nothing happened but `snmptrapd` is running, it might be using `tcpwrappers`. Then write a line in the `/etc/hosts.allow` file:

snmptrapd: 0.0.0.0.

You can configure `snmptrapd` to only accept messages from certain addresses and communities; the help is well written about this.

Usually, messages sent via notifications are critical or very important, so logging them is useful but not sufficient. We would like to configure some kind of action to be taken when such events occur. And `snmptrapd` helps us with that. Let's open the `/etc/snmp/snmptrapd.conf` file again and add the line:

traphandle NET-SNMP-EXAMPLES-MIB::netSnmpExampleHeartbeatNotification \
/tmp/demo demo-trap

Let's create a /tmp/demo script with the contents:

```
#!/bin/sh
read host
read ip
vars=

while read oid val
do
  if [ "x$vars" = "x" ]
  then
    vars="$oid = $val"
  else
    vars="$vars,\n$oid = $val"
  fi
done
echo -e "trap: $1 $host $ip $vars" > /tmp/demo.log
```

Allow its execution with `chmod a+x /tmp/demo`. Now restart `snmptrapd` and run the `snmptrap` command again to send a test notification. The line like this should appear in the /tmp/demo.log file:

```
trap: demo-trap localhost UDP: [127.0.0.1]:51240→[127.0.0.1],
SNMPv2-SMI::mib-2.1.3.0 = 21:23:11.65,
SNMPv2-SMI::snmpModules.1.1.4.1.0 = NET-SNMP-EXAMPLES-MIB::netSnmpExampleHe
artbeatNotification,
NET-SNMP-EXAMPLES-MIB::netSnmpExampleHeartbeatRate = 123456
```

As you can see, the /tmp/demo script, which we specified in the configuration, is launched when a notification with the specified OID is received and gets all the data about it. Based on this script, you can create your own handler (do not place it in /tmp) and perform necessary actions when critical events occur. Be careful when working with several devices at the same time: running several handlers in parallel may be undesirable. You should also be careful when handling events that arrive at short intervals, e.g., short-term events such as power failure. If possible, outsource notification and SNMP data processing to off-the-shelf, proven monitoring systems.

Ganglia

Ganglia is an open source monitoring system originally developed to work with computing clusters by scientists at the University of Berkeley. Each machine runs the gmond daemon, which collects system information (CPU speed, memory usage, etc.) and sends it to one server (or several, as we will see below).

Ganglia has two network transmission modes – **unicast** and **multicast**. The default mode is multicast. This mode assumes that data is sent to everyone who "subscribes" to the multicast stream. That is, the ganglia agent, which is called gmond, sends a packet of data to a certain multicast address, and all those who are "subscribed" to this address receive it. In the case of unicast mode, the packet is sent to only one subscriber, the server specified in the agent's configuration.

The modern version of Ganglia server is able to process the received data, e.g., compute max or sum, then it stores it, usually in RRD files (Round-Robin Database). It can also pass data up the hierarchy by aggregating it. On a large scale, it is recommended to use aggregation, because otherwise it can affect network performance when gmonds from many nodes start transmitting data at the same time.

CHAPTER 19 CLUSTER STATUS MONITORING SYSTEMS

Install the ganglia package and related packages; they should be available in your Linux distributive by default. If for some reason you can't find them, or if you want to install the latest version, download the source code from http://ganglia.sourceforge.net/ and build with the commands:

```
tar zxvf ganglia*gz
cd ganglia-*/
./configure --with-gmetad
make && make install
```

You may need additional libraries for the build, supplying them if necessary. Now let's install the web interface for ganglia (assuming the web server is already installed and its root directory is /var/www/html):

```
cp -ra web/* /var/www/html/ganglia/
cp gmetad/gmetad.init /etc/rc.d/init.d/gmetad
cp gmond/gmond.init /etc/rc.d/init.d/gmond
mkdir /etc/ganglia
gmond -t | tee /etc/ganglia/gmond.conf
cp gmetad/gmetad.conf /etc/ganglia/
mkdir -p /var/lib/ganglia/rrds
chown nobody:nobody /var/lib/ganglia/rrds
```

By default, ganglia uses multicast packets to communicate with the gmetad server. The IP protocol has a separate subnet for multicast packets. To ensure that this network is properly routed on our server, where the ganglia server will run, add a route:

```
ip r add 239.2.11.71/4 dev eth0
```

Here eth0 is the interface of the network on which the compute nodes reside. Add this setting to the network configuration. Start the server and the ganglia agent and restart the web server (apache on RG-based system in this example, adjust for your system!):

```
systemctl start gmond
systemctl start gmetad
systemctl restart httpd
```

Now you can go to `http://localhost/ganglia`, where you should see a web interface with a single node – our server. Let's add agents to the nodes. To do this, install the gmond package from ganglia on all nodes and run the gmond service on them:

```
systemctl start gmond
```

After some time, all nodes should appear in the web interface.

Ganglia has several predefined metrics, which are collected by gmond, but you can extend this list using C++ modules and python modules or using external tools, which use XDR protocol to mimic gmond.

Ganglia is a handy tool for quickly visualizing the state of cluster nodes and some of its aggregate characteristics. Its limitation is that it has no tools for alerting or any data analysis, just simple aggregations. You can fix it using integration with Nagios, but it requires additional work. Also, as it uses RRD database, carefully plan your data storage for the Ganglia server.

Nagios

The Nagios monitoring system was developed by the company of the same name (`http://www.nagios.org/`) and exists in two variants – core (community) and a set of applications based on core (Nagios XI, Nagios Fusion, etc.). This system has become a default standard in many applications, mainly for monitoring network equipment and network services. It is built on a modular principle – to perform monitoring of a certain type of services. I should note that there is an alternative implementation (a fork), named Icinga (`https://icinga.com/`), which has some additional features, but they lie outside our topic anyway, so I won't make difference between it and Nagios here.

There are numerous plug-ins for Nagios that allow you to monitor almost any type of service – SMTP, HTTP, SNMP, etc., as well as network equipment – Cisco, Brocade, etc.

By default, Nagios is installed in a centralized manner: a server is installed on the master server, and data is collected and transmitted from the other nodes using remote execution via SSH, or local agents, using internal NRPE protocol. Using some techniques, it is possible to build hierarchical monitoring schemes as well as fault-tolerant ones. The basic installation does not include a web or GUI interface, but there are many clients that provide different interface options, but they do not provide configuration capabilities. This is due to the fact that each plug-in is a separate program (or script) and all its configuration consists in correctly specifying the command-line arguments of the startup, which are very different for different plug-ins.

The implementation of plug-ins as separate programs is both a strength and a weakness of Nagios. On the one hand, it gives high flexibility – it is very easy to write your own plug-in. On the other hand, collecting many metrics requires running many separate programs, which creates a high load on the node on which they run. This is why the polling frequency in Nagios is usually a few minutes. This is fine for monitoring services like a database, web server, etc., but it is very inconvenient when monitoring the state of a compute cluster, as it puts an unwanted load on the compute nodes. Besides, there are not so many services in a compute cluster; it is much more important for it to monitor resources; Nagios can do this too, but not as well and conveniently as we would like it to be.

For small clusters, Nagios may be a good choice for tracking the overall health of nodes and infrastructure, such as SNMP hardware, but for clusters of several dozen nodes, it is not recommended or should be limited to a small number of metrics.

Zabbix

Zabbix is a free monitoring system designed to track the state of network services. All information is stored in a database – MySQL, PostgreSQL, SQLite, or Oracle. Zabbix supports several modes of data collection – over the network (for SMTP, HTTP and similar), through an agent installed on the host, and with the help of external programs.

A monitoring complex based on Zabbix can consist of the following components:

- **Server** – Stores configuration data and statistics and is responsible for aggregation and storage of collected data and notification of problems. It can collect information from proxies, agents, and network services.

- **Proxy** – Collects data from other proxies, agents, and network services. The collected data is transmitted to the server. By using proxies, you can build hierarchical configurations and reduce the load on networks and the central server.

- **Agent** – Runs on nodes, collects data on local resource and application usage (CPU, memory, hard disk usage, etc.), ...

- **Web interface** – Usually runs on the same computer as the server and uses a locally installed web server, such as apache or nginx.

Due to the use of data collection hierarchy, Zabbix makes it possible to organize monitoring of up to 1000 nodes. A nice feature is the automatic detection of SNMP devices, which can make it much easier to set up monitoring of network devices and peripherals.

Zabbix supports grouping nodes by attributes and/or manually. Creating synthetic sensors and using scripts allows you to set up very flexible and multistage responses to situations. Unlike Nagios, Zabbix can be configured entirely from the web interface (except for minimal initial setup). Like Nagios, Zabbix is intended solely for monitoring the state of servers and services, so it should be used with caution in large configurations. Collecting data from hundreds of nodes in one local network can completely paralyze its operation or lead to unexpected and irregular performance drops.

The installation of Zabbix usually consists of installing the appropriate packages, preparing and specifying the correct settings for the selected database, and running the necessary components. Zabbix does not support fault tolerance for the central server, so if you need it, you will have to provide it by other means: lightweight monitoring from another server (e.g., `monit`, etc.) or installing another Zabbix server that uses different settings.

Modern Approach

Nowadays, the efficient approach is to use specialized data collectors, time-series database, standalone visualizer, and an analyzing/alerting system. All four components may be chosen judging on performance, storage, and other requirements.

Data collectors – in 2025 really popular is **prometheus**, especially because it is open source and there are a lot of collectors, using the same protocol. They are easily customizable, and you can implement your own relatively easy, based on the existing generic collector code. Another good example is **telegraf** – it includes a lot of metrics out of the box and is extendable. I would also note

collectd – it is modular and includes a lot of ready to use modules. In addition, it supports aggregation modules and store modules, so you can aggregate your data and send it using any protocols or store it in any formats. Action modules are also available, so you can implement a simple alerting system using collect.

Data storage – There are several high-performance time-series databases, one of the most common is **InfluxDB**; it supports many types of requests with aggregations and selections. The next one is **Prometheus TSDB**, which is similar to InfluxDB and works natively with prometheus collectors. **VictoriaMetrics** is highly optimized time-series database; it is much faster than InfluxDB and requires less disk space, but cannot store any string data, only numeric data. I'd like to mention **PostgreSQL** and **MongoDB** time-series extensions, because they have well known by many people query language and decent performance (but I still recommend to use native time-series database).

Data visualization – The leader here today is **Grafana** – it allows getting data from almost any source and visualize it in dozens ways. Because of modular structure, you can create custom databases requests and then filter the data as you want. Next option is **Kibana** – a lot of predefined profiles, visualization methods, and analytics. The drawback is that it highly oriented on the **ElasticSearch** stack, and it is not so easy (but sometimes possible) to integrate it with other software. And, of course, there are commercial solutions like **Splunk** and **DataDog** and commercial options for ElasticSearch and Grafana.

Data processing and alerting – Prometheus has special package called **alertmanager**, Grafana project implemented its own **Grafana Alert**, I mentioned **collectd** processing and action modules and of course commercial options of **ElastiSearch**, **Splunk**, **DataDog**, and companies, who specialized on alerting, like **PagerDuty**.

CHAPTER 19 CLUSTER STATUS MONITORING SYSTEMS

I cannot strongly recommend any of combination of the tools above, but I personally saw really good and scalable results using collectd+victoriametrics+grafana and prometheus (collector and DB)+grafana and telegraf+influxdb+grafana. I should note that in 2025, ElasticSearch is good for analytics, but not so good at security and access protection.

XDMoD

Grafana, data collectors, or ElasticSearch are flexible, but require a lot of work to set up collection and dashboards. Binding collected data to jobs may be really painful, especially if you allow sharing nodes. And here XDMoD[2] (XD Metrics on Demand) can help. It is developed at the University at Buffalo, SUNY, and it ingests data from job management systems, like SLURM, PBS, etc., and provides nice visualizations, which can help to analyze supercomputer resources usage efficiency, plan upgrades, and resources distribution across user groups. All collected metrics are organized in hierarchy, which allows analyzing, e.g., specific user's or user group's efficiency.

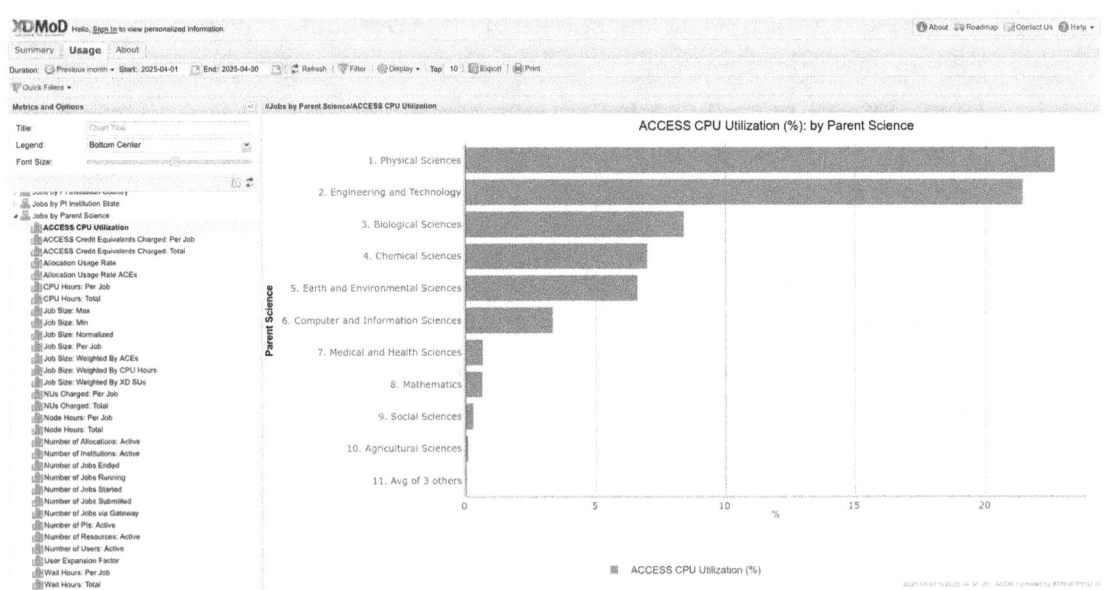

Figure 19-1. XDMoD interface examples

---

[2] https://open.xdmod.org

If you want to see GPU usage, licenses, or energy consumption, they should be enabled in the job manager (TRES/GRES in SLURM). But if you want to see more details, XDMoD has to be extended by SUPReMM module, then you can collect data using prometheus (yes, collection set up is still yours to do). This information automatically applies to your jobs data, and you get the ability to analyze resource usage and individual or overall job efficiency. If you want, you can use Performance Co-Pilot[3] or TACC_Stats[4] instead of prometheus. The installation is well documented and may be done via RPM packages or from source code. It requires MySQL/MariaDB, Apache webserver with PHP, and nodejs installed and some other pretty common packages. XDMoD is open source and is supported by the National Science Foundation under the ACCESS Track 4: Advanced CI Coordination Ecosystem: Monitoring and Measurement Service Program (grant no. 2137603).

Lm_sensors/Hwmon

Yes, I know that this information can be collected by the collectors from the previous subchapter. But I want to show you how to get some low-level information if you haven't installed the collector yet. lm_sensors and hwmon packages collect information from the low-level sensors, like temperature, voltage, and fan speeds. Hwmon is not so common, and I will show you some examples with lm_sensors only.

In the Linux environment, the standard for working with sensors is the `lm_sensors` package, which includes kernel modules for interacting with sensors (most of them are already shipped with the kernel), the `libsensors` library, and a set of basic user utilities for reading data and outputting the read information. This project does not work on creating graphical interfaces for colorful presentation of information, but independent developers have created many utilities and plug-ins based on the `libsensors` library to display information in graphical form.

Unfortunately, for the long history of microprocessor technology development, there are no unified standards for sensors and their connection to electronic devices; on the contrary, their variety is increasing every year. In this regard, the `lm_sensors` package is constantly updated to expand the range of supported devices. Currently, it supports more than 150 different sensors, including sensors:

---

[3] https://pcp.io/
[4] https://github.com/TACC/tacc_stats

CHAPTER 19   CLUSTER STATUS MONITORING SYSTEMS

- On the ISA bus
- Using I2C and SMBus
- Via SPI (Serial Peripheral Interface)
- Integrated into the super-I/O controller
- Integrated into the motherboard's south bridge

as well as

- Temperature sensors integrated into the processor
- Temperature sensors in the memory modules

A special `sensors-detect` script written in perl is used to configure `lm_sensors`. The script sequentially searches through the supported controllers, determining which kernel modules need to be loaded in order to read information from sensors located inside the computer. During operation, `sensors-detect` generates the configuration file `/etc/sysconfig/lm_sensors`, which lists the kernel modules to be loaded.

The `/etc/sensors.conf` file defines the format of data output. In the latest versions of LM-sensors, the `/etc/sensors3.conf` file is used. The file is written during package installation and contains entries for all supported sensors, each of which refers to a certain chip or chip family with the same parameters. The record begins with the keyword `chip`, followed by the names of the associated chips. The names are separated by spaces. They themselves consist of several fields separated by dashes.

The first field is the chip type; the second field is the name of the bus to which the sensor is connected; the third field is the hexadecimal address of the chip. For an LM78 chip with address `0x2d` on the I2C bus, the chip name will look like this: `lm78-i2c-2d`. Any fields other than the controller name can be unspecified by using the * sign. "Any LM78 chip on any bus" can be written as `lm78-*`.

The chip can monitor many sensors. For example, the LM78 chip can control up to seven voltage sensors, one temperature sensor, and three fan sensors. Standardized sensor names are used:

- `in0, in1, in2, ...` – For voltage
- `fan1, fan2, fan3, ...` – For fans
- `temp1, temp2, temp3, ...` – For temperature

CHAPTER 19 CLUSTER STATUS MONITORING SYSTEMS

Each sensor can have several parameters: current value, minimum, maximum, and alarm values. Parameter names are also standardized. For example, for an in0 sensor, the parameter containing the current value is called in0_input; the minimum value is called the in0_min; the maximum value – in0_max; and containing alarm value – in0_alarm. Within the records, four keywords define the format of the output information.

The label operator specifies under which name to output the corresponding sensor:

```
label in3 "+5V"
```

The first field specifies the sensor, and the second field specifies how this sensor will be displayed in the output. The ignore operator specifies that no information should be output from the corresponding sensor. For example, in case the returned value is garbage:

```
ignore fan1
```

The compute statement is used to specify a formula for converting a read sensor reading to an output value. It is commonly used to output voltage data since it is usually taken from voltage dividers:

```
compute in3 ((6.8/10)+1)*@ , @/((6.8/10)+1)
```

The first parameter is the sensor name, and the second is an expression that specifies how the read value should be converted to an output value. "@" indicates the read value. The third parameter is an expression that specifies how the output value should be converted back to the sensor value. In this case, "@" denotes the output value; this formula is used if the data needs to be written to the chip. A comma separates the functions.

The set statement is used to write values to the chip:

```
set in3_min 5 * 0.95
set in3_max 5 * 1.05
```

Not all values can be written to the chip, mainly the minimum and maximum allowable values. To write data to the chip, a command with a special option is used:

```
sensors -s
```

CHAPTER 19 CLUSTER STATUS MONITORING SYSTEMS

The `sensors` command without parameters is used for data output. It outputs the names of detected sensors and the values read from them:

```
host:~->#  sensors
fschds-i2c-5-73
Adapter: SMBus I801 adapter at 1c20
+12V: +12.00 V
+5V: +5.15 V
Vbat: +3.14 V
PSU Fan: 1440 RPM (div = 4)
CPU Fan: 720 RPM (div = 4)
System FAN2: FAULT (div = 4)
System FAN3: 720 RPM (div = 4)
System FAN4: 720 RPM (div = 4)
CPU Temp: +36.0°C (high = +69.0°C)
Super I/O Temp: +38.0°C (high = +52.0°C)
System Temp: +41.0°C (high = +56.0°C)
temp4: +36.0°C (high = +73.0°C)
temp5: +39.0°C (high = +62.0°C)
coretemp-isa-0000
Adapter: ISA adapter
Core 0: +51.0°C (high = +82.0°C, crit = +100.0°C)
Core 1: +51.0°C (high = +82.0°C, crit = +100.0°C)
Core 2: +49.0°C (high = +82.0°C, crit = +100.0°C)
Core 3: +49.0°C (high = +82.0°C, crit = +100.0°C)
```

Modern Linux kernels include support for outputting data from some types of hardware `sensors` directly via the `/sys/class/hwmon` file system. So in many cases, it is possible to obtain information similar to that provided by the `sensors` command simply by reading data from the required file. Note that in any case, you will need to load the required modules and manually recalculate the read values.

IPMI

As it was mentioned in the "Remote Management" chapter, IPMI allows you to read many system sensors, as locally, as remotely. `ipmitool` and similar utilities can read sensors data, but note that often remote sensors reading may overload BMC controllers (depending on the model). I recommend using any metrics collector, like prometheus, and collect local sensors info via local IPMI interface. In addition to sensors, IPMI can store information about system events, which may be useful for hardware issues resolving.

APCUPS

Computing clusters are usually used for solving large resource-intensive tasks. Therefore, it is very important to ensure their reliable uninterrupted operation, and this task cannot be accomplished without the use of a quality uninterruptible power supply system. Such a system includes both physical devices called uninterruptible power supplies (UPS) and software for organizing interaction between the power supply and the protected equipment.

Uninterruptible power supply (**UPS**) is a device that provides power supply to electrical equipment connected to it in case of a short-term loss of voltage in the power grid. The main purpose of a UPS is to maintain equipment operability in the event of a short-term power failure, but the functionality of modern UPS is much broader.

As a rule, the system is designed to provide power to the cluster for at least 10–30 minutes in the event of a power failure. If power is not restored within five minutes, the UPS must ensure that the cluster is shut down correctly. Prepare and test(!) emergency shutdown scripts, taking special care for the proper storage unmount and shutdown.

If your cluster uses APC UPSs, then you can use `apcupsd` service to monitor the UPS equipment and react in case of emergency. The `apcupsd` package is a freely distributed software that allows organizing interaction with most APC UPS models. It consists of several components:

- A daemon that receives information from available uninterruptible power supplies and generates signals for various events
- A program that allows you to read the UPS status information

CHAPTER 19 CLUSTER STATUS MONITORING SYSTEMS

- Programs to adjust the parameters of its operation
- A set of cgi-scripts allowing to use the web interface - to control and manage the UPS

The apcupsd package is included in many Linux distributions, but it is more practical to download the latest version as source code and install it yourself. This allows you to customize the package to your needs at the installation stage. The installation procedure is straightforward and is accomplished by sequential execution of three commands: configure && make && make install. The only command that requires attention is configure, which defines the basic properties of the package. As a rule, it is executed with a set of parameters. In a typical case, the command looks as follows:

```
./configure \
--prefix=/usr \
--sbindir=/sbin \
--enable-threads \
--enable-snmp \
--enable-cgi \
--with-libwrap=/lib64/libwrap.so.0 \
--with-cgi-bin=/usr/apache/cgi-bin
```

After the installation is complete, further configuration is performed by editing the configuration file /etc/apcupsd/apcupsd.conf. Here is an example of the file with brief comments. All variables are commented in English in the real system file. During the installation of the package in the platforms directory, the apcupsd script is configured to run the daemon. This script should be placed in the /etc/init.d directory and is used to automatically start the daemon during the system boot process. On a running system, the daemon is started by the command:

```
systemctl start apcupsd
```

The correctness of the system installation can be checked with the apcaccess command, which gets information about the UPS status from the apcupsd daemon. If everything is configured correctly, the output should look like this:

```
APC : 001,048,1157
DATE : Tue Aug 02 16:01:49 MSD 2011
HOSTNAME : rsufs
```

```
VERSION : 3.14.7 (August 1, 2009) suse
UPSNAME : UPS_3
CABLE : Custom Cable Smart
MODEL : SNMP UPS Driver
UPSMODE : Stand Alone
STARTTIME: Thu Aug 20 14:58:12 MSD 2011
STATUS : ONLINE
LINEV : 226.0 Volts
LOADPCT : 32.0 Percent Load Capacity
BCHARGE : 100.0 Percent.
TIMELEFT : 73.0 Minutes
MBATTCHG : 5 Percent
MINTIMEL : 3 Minutes
MAXTIME : 0 Seconds
MAXLINEV : 227.0 Volts
MINLINEV : 221.0 Volts
OUTPUTV : 218.0 Volts
............[there's a lot more information here]
APCMODEL : Smart-UPS RT 10000
END APC : Tue Aug 02 16:02:47 MSD 2011
```

In addition to the apcupcd daemon and its access command (apcaccess), the package includes a set of scripts that are run depending on the occurrence of a certain event. In normal mode, they simply generate some message that is output to the terminal and sent to the administrator by email. The control functions consist in sending a shutdown command to the protected server when the battery charge falls below a certain critical level.

The scripts are easy to modify to organize flexible management of the whole cluster. The main events captured by apcupsd are switching to battery power and restoring normal power. When these events occur, the onbattery and offbattery scripts located in the SCRIPTDIR directory (/etc/apcupsd) are run, respectively.

In the case of a large configuration, such scripts will certainly not be sufficient. Take care of duplicating UPS monitoring servers, as well as carefully customizing the shutdown procedure for the supercomputer or its parts. Remember that compute nodes should be the first to be shut down – this will significantly relieve the energy load. You

CHAPTER 19   CLUSTER STATUS MONITORING SYSTEMS

should not care about correct task termination – it is not appropriate in this situation, but you should prohibit launching new tasks in advance. Network file systems and monitoring servers themselves should be the last to shut down.

Please note that some shutdown procedures may hang for various reasons and block the general system shutdown process. Such cases should be excluded: shutdown procedures should be run through special wrappers or in the background, etc. Remember that if a supercomputer is powered by several UPSs, it will require more fine-tuned system shutdown procedures. Modern UPSs allow connection of temperature sensors to the control devices, which can be used to organize continuous temperature control in the server room.

The values read from the sensor can be written to a special log file, and if some critical value is exceeded, the cluster can be shut down, as in case of power failure. An example of a script for temperature monitoring is given in the chapter "One-Two-Three Instructions."

APCUPSD UPS Network Monitor Tue Oct 09 16:11:57 MSD 2012									
System	Model	Status	Battery Chg	Utility	UPS Load	UPS Temp	Batt. Run Time	Data
rsusu1	SNMP UPS Driver	ONLINE	100.0 %	230.0 VAC	42.0 %	24.0° C	45.0 min.	All data
rsuib	SNMP UPS Driver	ONLINE	100.0 %	231.0 VAC	43.0 %	25.0° C	71.0 min.	All data
rsufs	SNMP UPS Driver	ONLINE	100.0 %	227.0 VAC	33.0 %	24.0° C	70.0 min.	All data
mmcs	SNMP UPS Driver	ONLINE	100.0 %	221.0 VAC	40.0 %	26.0° C	12.0 min.	All data

***Figure 19-2.** APCUPS web UI*

The `apcupsd` package includes tools for monitoring the UPS status via web interface (see Figure 19-2). During the installation of the package, a set of cgi programs is created, of which the `multimon.cgi` program is the main one. These programs should be placed in the `cgi-bin` directories on all servers controlling the UPS. In the `/etc/apcupsd` directory of the head server, to which the browser will access, a `hosts.conf` file containing the list of servers should be generated. The file has the following form:

```
# Network UPS Tools - hosts.conf
# MONITOR <address> "<host description>"
MONITOR 192.168.5.11 "asile1"
MONITOR 192.168.5.77 "asile2"
MONITOR 192.168.5.99 "storage"
```

If we go to the address http://localhost/cgi-bin/multimon.cgi in the browser, we will see a picture similar to Figure 19-1. Thus, customizing the interaction between the operating system and the UPS will make the cluster system more reliable and user-friendly.

NUT

The apcupsd program is designed only for APC UPSs, although it can work with some other models as well. The purpose of the open source NUT (Network UPS Tools) project is to work with a wide range of UPSs from different manufacturers. The list of supported models is available on the website (http://www.networkupstools.org/). NUT is included in all popular Linux distributions. This package consists of three components: drivers, server, and clients.

Driver – A program that implements all the necessary commands to work with UPS; usually, it is not directly run. Server – A program that runs one or more drivers to monitor the status of UPSs and control them through the network. Clients can connect to a server (or several at the same time) and monitor the status of UPSs or change their mode of operation. One of the most important clients included in the NUT is the monitor. This is a client that reacts to changes in the status of UPSs; it can send an alert about power loss in the network, shut down the equipment when the battery is low, etc.

To install NUT, use the package manager and install the server and monitor. Typically, the directory with the configuration files is located in /etc/nut. All components have their own configuration files:

>ups.conf driver settings

>upsd.conf server settings

>upsd.users access settings

>upsmon.conf monitor settings

Let's start with the driver (ups.conf):

```
[ups1]
   driver = usbhid-ups
   port   = auto
   serial = 1234567890
```

CHAPTER 19 CLUSTER STATUS MONITORING SYSTEMS

The format of the file is simple: in square brackets the name of the UPS, by which we will identify it, and then specify its settings. The only mandatory parameter is **'driver'** – driver name. Various UPSs can be configured in one file. In this example, it is usbhid-ups – UPS connected via USB and using the standard interface. The search for a particular UPS (you can connect several of them) is done by serial number. For different drivers, the set of parameters will be different. For a list of drivers and supported UPS models, see the website or /usr/share/nut/driver.list file.

Server settings (upds.conf) are usually not required, but some settings can be changed if desired:

> **MAXAGE** seconds – Sets the driver response timeout. If it is exceeded, the data from UPS is considered lost (stale).
>
> **LISTEN** interface port – Specifies the interface and port on which the server will respond. Numerous such strings can be specified. The interface is often specified as its IP address, e.g., 172.0.0.1.
>
> **MAXCONN** connections – Sets the number of simultaneous client connections.

It remains to configure access parameters for clients – this is done in the upsd.users file:

```
[admin]
    password =adminpass
    actions = set
    actions = fsd
    instcmds = all
[tester]
    password =tstpass
    instcmds = test.panel.start
    instcmds = test.panel.stop
[monmaster]
    password =123qweasd
    upsmon master
```

CHAPTER 19 CLUSTER STATUS MONITORING SYSTEMS

The format of the file is already familiar to us: section name means the name of the user, and parameters mean his rights. The mandatory parameter is `password` – password, `actions` – allowed actions, `set` – update UPS parameters, and `fsd` – forced shutdown (emulation of "On Battery"+"Low Battery").

`instcmds` allows you to specify a list of commands that can be executed by the user. ALL = any commands. In this example, the tester user can start and stop the UPS panel test procedure (if supported by the driver).

`upsmon` – Predefined set of parameters for the monitor. Here you should specify `master` if our monitor is running on the same server as the server and `slave` if it is running on a different server. Slave servers will be shut down first, and master will be shut down last.

Now we can start the server – usually, its service name is `nut` or `upsd`. Let's check if our configuration works with the command:

```
upsc ups1@localhost
```

The command should output the current state of the UPS, which we configured under the name ups1. Let's configure the monitor on the computer where the server is running (`upsmon.conf`):

```
MONITOR ups1@localhost 1 monmaster 123qweasd master
```

The format of the string is clear from the comment: the keyword `MONITOR`, then the address of the UPS, the conditional power (in this case we write 1), the username from `upsd.users`, the password, and the role of the monitor – `master` or `slave`. It is possible to set more complex configurations, e.g., if the computer is connected to several UPSs, but we will not dwell on it. If you want to react more flexibly to UPS events, e.g., to receive sms about power failure or battery failure, you can configure the following options in the same file:

`NOTIFYCMD` command – When an event occurs, the specified command will be called. The command is passed an environment variable, `NOTIFYTYTYPE` with the name of the event that occurred. Be careful: each event launches its own instance of the command, no waiting for the previous launch to complete.

`NOTIFYFLAG` type flag[+flag][+flag]... – What to do when an event (type) occurs. Types are `ONLINE`, `ONBATT`, `LOWBATT`, `FSD`, `COMMOK`, `COMMBAD`, `SHUTDOWN`, `REPLBATT`, `NOCOMM`, and `NOPARENT`. Flag specifies a list of actions:

- SYSLOG log entry
- WALL alerting with the `wall` command
- EXEC execution of the command we specified in NOTIFYCMD
- IGNORE doing nothing

NOTIFYMSG type message – A message to log if you are not satisfied with the standard ones.

To monitor and visualize the status of UPSs under NUT control, there are many programs, including the "standard" web interface `upsstat`. We will not dwell on its configuration; it is well described in the documentation. Besides the web interface, there are many other clients, including agents for monitoring systems.

Healthchecks

After the node is booted, it makes sense to run checks and decide if it is healthy enough to run users' jobs. Moreover, this is a good idea to do that before each job start. Usually, such checks are called "healthchecks." If you use SLURM job manager, you can enable periodical execution of custom healthcheck script, and it is a good idea to include heltchcheck run in the prologue scripts.

What to check, how to react on issues (drain node, try to fix, alert sysadmins, send emails/notifications, push events into monitoring systems, …), and which tests to run in different cases (full check, prologue, background check) – these are questions you have to answer. Note that prologue time is limited, and it is also included into the job runtime, so you cannot run long tests.

You may implement your own healthcheck script (or a set of scripts), or use one of the opensource solutions. I have good experience using LBNL Node Health Check;[5] it is highly portable, because it is written in bash, has a lot of modules, and simple configuration file. To implement different modes, e.g., full check and prologue check, you can just use different config files. If you miss some functions, you can implement your custom module.

---

[5] https://github.com/mej/nhc

Security Scans

This subchapter should be actually a full chapter and be one of the first ones. In fact, I often can see that only basic security rules are applied, but the rest is just ignored. "The cluster is inside the protected perimeter, we are not exposed to the external world, firewalls will save us" – typical way of thinking, and this is a big mistake.

There are a lot of specialized books and resources about the cybersecurity, so I will just touch the basic rules you can follow:

1. Do regular system software updates. Test them on a small subset of nodes first. Do backups. I recommend doing updates two to four times a year; this supposes to have relatively small updates and short maintenance times.

2. Do daily security scans. You can use opensource solutions like chkrootkit, rkhunter, Nessus, Lynis, and Maltrail. And read the reports!

3. Check remote logins activity, especially who have sudo access.

4. Firewall is still your friend, use it wisely.

5. Monitor unusual activity – this is a hard part; manually, you can just check running processes list and detect new malware, missed by rkhunter. I don't know good opensource automation tools for this, but there are commercial solutions from SentinelOne, Palo Alto Networks, CrowdStrike, and others. You don't have to install them on all nodes, but I recommend protecting all user facing and service nodes.

Brief Summary

Superreliable systems, redundancy, redundant power, and cooling – all of these greatly increase the reliability of your computing complex. But, yes, there's still no guarantee. Moreover, no redundancy will save you if a failure has already occurred and the system is running on standby, and you are not even aware of it. Monitoring is one of the most important components of any computing complex and even more so of a supercomputer. Plan and implement monitoring for as much equipment and services as possible as early as possible – preferably **before the** actual equipment starts working, do not forget about security monitoring too.

If your supercomputer is powered by multiple UPSs, try to provide redundant power to the most critical components: network file systems, monitoring, and management servers. Don't forget to take this into account in the configuration of the monitoring and shutdown systems! Of course, it is best to use complex solutions, but if it takes a long time to implement them and the system is already running, start using at least the basic tools that are available in any Linux distribution.

Search Keywords

Monitoring, SNMP, UPS, lm_sensors, hwmon, security scanner, nodes healthchecks

CHAPTER 20

Backup

Tar

The `tar` (Tape ARchiver) command is one of the oldest commands in UNIX systems and is designed to work with tape drives. The command combines files into a single file to be written to magnetic tape. Although the `tar` command was created to work with tape devices, nowadays it is more often necessary to work with files located on disks; if you use -f option, the archive is stored into specified file. By itself, `tar` is an archiver with very limited capabilities, e.g., it cannot compress files on its own. The Gnu version of the `tar` command on Linux systems can invoke the `gzip`, `bzip2`, or any other archivers to create compressed archives. The use of external archivers is reflected in the names of the archives, which usually have the extensions .tar.gz (.tgz) or .tar.bz2 (.tbz2), depending on which archive was used to compress the files.

When calling `tar`, you must be sure to specify one of the eight modes of operation using one of the key, presented in the Table 20-1.

Table 20-1. *Modes of operation of the tar command*

Key	Meaning
-A, --catenate	Add files to an existing archive
-c, --create	Create a new archive
-d, --diff, --compare	Find the differences between the files in the archive and on disk
--delete	Delete files from the archive (does not work on tapes)
-r, --append	Append files to the end of the archive
-t, --list	List the files in the archive
-u, --update	Add only files that are newer than the existing copy in the archive
-x, --extract, --get	Extract files from the archive

Note that single-letter `tar` options can be specified without the '-' prefix and can also be 'glued' together. If several "glued" options require arguments, you should specify them in the same order as the options, but it is better to avoid such situations and not "glue" such options together.

General view of the `tar` command:

`tar [options] [files]`

To create an archive, the 'c' option is used, frequently in conjunction with 'f', to specify the name of the archive.

`tar cf filename_archive file1 file2`

Here `file1` and `file2` are the names of files that will be added to the archive when it is created. If a directory name is specified, its contents, including subdirectories, will be added to the archive. In the example below, all files with the extension '.c' located in the current directory and the `includes` directory are written to the archive named `project.tar`:

`tar cf project.tar *.c includes`

File compression by archivers is enabled by the options z for the `gzip` archiver and j for the `bzip2` archiver. In GNU-tar, it is also possible to specify your own command for compression with the I key (the specified program must accept the -d key to decompress). This allows to use, e.g., pigz – parallel version of gzip, which can compress (but not decompress) data on many CPU cores. This is what the previous example with compression looks like:

```
tar cvzf project.tar.gz *.c includes  # gzip archive
tar cvjf project.tar.bz2 *.c includes # bzip2 archive
```

The v option outputs a list of processed files. This command will archive all files and folders in the `./folder` directory while preserving its full structure:

`tar cvzf project.tar.gz ./folder`

Files are unpacked using the x option. You can unpack the contents of the `project.tar.gz` file into the current directory with recreation of the entire directory and subdirectory structure from the archive file as follows:

`tar xvzf project.tar.gz`

The 'C' option allows you to specify the directory where the archive will be deployed:

`tar xvzf project.tar.gz -C /path/to/folder`

It is not necessary to use the full path starting from the root directory, you can use a relative path from the current directory. To view the contents of the archive, use the command:

`tar tzf project.tar.gz`

An example of adding files to an archive:

`tar rvf project.tar new_file`

An example of adding directories to an archive:

`tar rvf project.tar new_folder`

You can add files and directories to the archive only if the archive is not compressed by archivers; otherwise, the tar command will generate an error.

The `tar` command is often used to create data backups. Backing up information allows you to avoid complete data loss in case of failures and significantly reduce system recovery time, of course if you store backup on the different physical device, don't you? The `tar` command algorithm is well suited for backup operations; it saves in the archive not just the contents of the file, but also full information about it: who is the owner, access rights to the file, etc.

Moreover, the data structure is fully preserved during copying, i.e., character references and other special file system objects will be correctly restored. This property of the `tar` command is typically used for full copying of file systems, because the standard `cp` command does not always handle special files correctly.

Command to completely copy the `data01` directory to the new `/db01` folder:

`tar cf - data01 | (cd /db01; tar xvf -)`

This example uses the | pipeline. The first `tar cf - data01` command creates an archive and outputs it to the standard output stream, indicated by the "-" sign instead of the archive name; the second | command `(cd /db01; tar xvf -)` goes to the folder where the directory will be located and calls the command to unpack the data received through the standard input stream, indicated by the "-" sign instead of the archive name. Hint – You can use `ssh` or `netcat` to remote host instead of just `cd`.

Using the `tar` command allows you to implement any complex backup schemes. There are two basic schemes: full backup is a long procedure; everyday it will be expensive to use it; the second scheme is making a full copy in days of minimum load, e.g., on weekends, and on weekdays, you can create incremental archives, which will store only the changes that occurred in the system during the day.

Creating an archive with the possibility of incremental archiving:

```
tar --create \
    --file=archive.1.tar \
    --listed-incremental=/var/log/usr.snar \
    /usr
```

In this case, we create an archive of the `/usr` directory. If there is no file specified by the `--listed-incremental` option, it will be created, and metadata about the archived data will be stored in it. If there is no such file, full data archiving will be performed, and only new or modified files will be stored in the archives. To perform full archiving, you should set the `--level=0` option or delete the `/var/log/usr.snar` file:

```
tar --create \
    --file=archive.1.tar \
    --listed-incremental=/var/log/usr.snar \
    --level=0 \
    /usr
```

Please note: compression is not supported when creating incremental archives.

Besides `tar`, there are other classic tools for creating archives – `cpio` and `pax`. `cpio` is not designed to work with tapes and, unlike `tar`, cannot get file lists from the file system by itself – the list of files must be passed to its standard input. Usually `find` is used in conjunction with `cpio` for this purpose. `pax` can be used to make backups on the tape devices, like tar. We will not dwell on `cpio` and `pax` modes and options: they are similar to `tar`. See the documentation for details.

Bacula

Bacula is a backup system that is based on the network principle. It uses several types of server programs, each of which performs a different function. They can run either on different physical servers or on a single server. The types of program servers used in bacula:

- **Storage** server
- Data server (**file server**)
- **Director**

In addition, various client programs can be used to manage and control the system. The purpose of the storage server is to work with archive drives. It receives data for archiving over the network or, conversely, gives the data read from the archives. Data servers supply data to storage servers, they must have direct access to the information to be archived. Finally, the director is the server that gives commands to the rest of the servers and manages the data streams. It also stores information about where and what data has been stored using the database. Officially supported are **sqlite**, **mysql**, and **postgresql**.

For example, you have a disk shelf connected to server `stor1` and a tape library connected to server `stor2`. Your network file system is accessible from the `head` machine `head1`, and you would like to additionally backup local data from servers `srv1`, `srv2`, and `srv3`. In this case, you can install storage servers on `stor1` and `stor2` and data servers on `head1`, `srv1`, `srv2`, and `srv3`. Director can be installed on any server, but it is better if it is the most fault-tolerant server.

Bacula allows you to create very flexible configurations for data archiving; its capabilities are probably the most extensive in its class of programs. The only serious disadvantage of bacula is the need to manually configure all parameters and operations. Once the settings are made, everything will work automatically. To control and manually start archiving or restoring data, you can use the `bconsole` program that comes with bacula, or third-party programs such as `bat` or `web-bacula`. Unfortunately, none of these programs support the ability to edit the configuration.

The bacula configuration is "smeared" across servers – each instance of each type of bacula server has its own configuration file. But this does not mean that the information is duplicated; on the contrary, this approach allows describing the necessary settings only where they are needed. Let's look at the concepts that bacula operates with in the configuration:

CHAPTER 20 BACKUP

- Pool – Pool is a representation of a data store. In our example, a disk shelf and a tape library are two pools.
- Volume – A volume is a single copy of data stored in a pool.
- Device – The device on which pools are stored (usually one device contains one pool).
- FileSet – A set of files describes exactly what we will write to (or read from) the volume.
- Job – Job describes the process of writing or restoring data.

Now let's turn to the files to configure the backup in our example. Let's start with the storage servers (stor1, stor2). By default, their configuration file will be called /etc/bacula/bacula-sd.conf.

All configuration files are internally divided into sections. For a storage server, the main section is Storage. In the file, which is supplied by default, we must be sure to fix the Name parameter – it specifies the name of the server, which does not necessarily have to match the name of the physical server. Storage devices are described in the Device sections, of which there may be several. Example configuration file for stor1 (usually /etc/bacula/bacula-sd.conf):

```
Storage {
  Name = stor1
  SDPort = 9103
  WorkingDirectory = "/var/spool/bacula"
  Pid Directory = "/var/run"
  Maximum Concurrent Jobs = 10
}
Director {
  Name = dir1
  Password = "storage-password"
}
Device {
  Name = DiskArray
  Media Type = MyFiles
  Archive Device = /mnt/backups
  Random Access = Yes;
```

```
  RemovableMedia = no;
  LabelMedia = yes;
}
```

In the `Director` section, we specify the name of the director and the password to connect to it. In the `Device` section, we described the disk shelf connected to `stor1` in the `/mnt/backups` directory. The `Name` parameter specifies the name of the device; the `Media Type` parameter specifies an arbitrary name to be used by bacula when restoring data. For each device describing the file storage (i.e., the directory where the backups will be stored), a unique `Media Type` name must be specified, although this is already obvious. The main parameters of the `Director` section:

- `Archive Device` – The path to the device, in this case a directory. For a `stor2` that uses tape, this will be the path to the tape drive (e.g., `/dev/nst0`).

- `Device Type` – The type of device. For a directory, it is `File`; for a tape drive, it is `Tape`.

- `Random Access` determines whether the device can be accessed by a random address. Write "No" for tape and "Yes" for files.

- `RemovableMedia` indicates whether the device can be removed. For tape, it is "Yes"; for files, it is "No."

- `LabelMedia` instructs bacula to automatically label media.

After configuring the storage servers, you can configure the director. On the physical server where the director is installed, edit the `/etc/bacula/bacula-dir.conf` file:

```
Director {
  Name = my-director
  DIRport = 9101
  QueryFile = "/etc/bacula/query.sql"
  WorkingDirectory = "/var/spool/bacula"
  PidDirectory = "/var/run"
  Maximum Concurrent Jobs = 1
  Password = "my-password"
  Messages = Daemon
}
```

Here Name is the name of the director, and Password is the password for access. The rest of the parameters should be left by default. The Director section is usually followed by the Catalog section, which describes the parameters of the database for storing internal information. Leave this section unchanged, specifying only the necessary name, e.g., "my-catalog".

The next section is Storage; this is where we need to specify our storages:

```
Storage {
  Name = dir-storage1
  Address = stor1.localnet
  SDPort = 9103
  Password = "storage-password"
  Device = DiskArray
  Media Type = MyFiles
}
```

And a similar section is for stor1.

The Name parameter is the unique name used to address the Storage section in the bacula-dir.conf file; the Device, MediaType, and Password parameters are the same as those specified in bacula-sd.conf.

The next section, Pool, describes the media pool:

```
Pool {
  Name = stor1-pool
  Pool Type = Backup
  AutoPrune = yes
  Recycle = yes
  Volume Retention = 1 month
  Maximum Volume Jobs = 1
  Maximum Volumes = 32
  Storage = Dir-Storage1
  Label Format = "stor1-"
}
```

The Name parameter defines the unique name of the pool. The Pool Type parameter defines the type and should be set to Backup for backups. The Maximum Volume Jobs parameter specifies the maximum number of tasks whose data can be placed on the media. For files, it is desirable to set it to 1.

Volume Retention is the time after which the backup data stored on the media will be deleted from the bacula catalog. Too many entries in the bacula catalog can significantly slow down its operation. Maximum Volumes is the maximum number of carriers available in a given pool.

The Recycle parameter indicates that media marked as obsolete should be reused. In this case, the actual overwriting of the media will take place only when there is no free media left, i.e., when there are no blank tapes or the number of files is equal to Maximum Volumes and no new files can be created.

The AutoPrune parameter instructs to remove obsolete records from the catalog automatically after the next task is completed. The Label Format parameter defines the prefix to be used by bacula for labeling media – naming files or labeling tapes. The Storage parameter contains the name of the storage device specified in the Name parameter of the Storage section of the bacula-dir.conf file.

The next section is FileSet. It defines which set of files will be saved (or restored):

```
FileSet {
  Name = "users-set"
  Include {
    Options {
      signature = MD5
      compression= GZIP
      recurse = yes
    }
    File = /home
    File = /etc/passwd
    File = /etc/shadow
    File = /etc/group
  }
  Exclude {
    File = /home/tmp
  }
}
```

The Name parameter defines a unique name for the set. The Include section contains paths to files and/or directories, and Exclude contains paths to files and/or directories to be excluded from the list. The Include section has a possible Options section that defines the reservation parameters. The `Signature` parameter specifies the algorithm for calculating file checksums, the `Compression` parameter specifies the algorithm for compressing files, and the `Recurse` parameter specifies the subdirectories to be included. There can be several `FileSet` sections, such as user data, system settings, installed application packages, etc.

Finally, the client sections, i.e., file servers:

```
Client {
  Name = client-1
  Address = headnode.localnet
  FDPort = 9102
  Catalog = my-catalog
  Password = "my-password"
}
```

Here `Address` specifies the address of the data server, `Catalog` is the catalog name (see it in the `Catalog` section), and `Password` is the password to access the data server. Each data server has its own `Client` section.

Now let's look at the `Schedule` and `Job` sections, which describe the archiving or restoring tasks. All the data relies on the parameters mentioned above.

```
Schedule {
  Name = "Weekly"
  Run = Full sat at 10:00
  Run = Incremental mon-thu at 02:01
}
Job {
  Name = "users-backup"
  Type = Backup
  Client = client1
  FileSet="users-set"
  Schedule = "Weekly"
  Messages = Standard
  Pool = example-pool
  Write Bootstrap = "/var/spool/bacula/%n.bsr"
  Priority = 1
}
```

The Schedule section describes the schedule for starting tasks. You can describe several different schedules for use in different situations. In our example, a task that runs on the "Weekly" schedule should run every night on weekdays at 2:01 AM, making incremental copies, and on Saturday at 10:00 AM, making a full copy.

The Job section describes the actual task. The Type parameter specifies the type of the task; in our case, it is Backup. The Schedule parameter specifies the name of the schedule; it must be described in one of the Schedule sections.

The Write Bootstrap parameter specifies the path to a file to which information will be written that can be used to restore data from a backup without a connection to Bacula Catalog. Instead of %n, the value of the Name parameter will be substituted.

Now let's look at configuring the data server. Its configuration file is usually called /etc/bacula/bacula-fd. For minimal customization, it is sufficient to specify only the Director section, where the password is given, and the FileDaemon section, with the data server settings. In the FileDaemon section, it is necessary to set the Name parameter – the unique name of the data server; it must match the name in the Client section of the Director.

```
Director {
  Name = my-director
  Password = "my-password"
}
FileDaemon {
  Name = client-1
  FDport = 9102
  WorkingDirectory = /var/spool/bacula
  Pid Directory = /var/run
  Maximum Concurrent Jobs = 20
}
```

After starting the corresponding servers on all necessary computers, bacula starts working offline. To perform some manual actions or to monitor the system operation process, it is necessary to launch the client program.

The bacula software includes a console client bconsole. Its configuration file has the same structure as those discussed above. It is typically called /etc/bacula/bconsole.conf. Since it communicates only with the director, the main section of the configuration file is Director:

CHAPTER 20 BACKUP

```
Director {
  Name = my-director
  DIRport = 9101
  Address = headnode.localnet
  Password = "my-password"
}
```

Here Name, Address, and DIRport are the name, address, and port of the director, and Password is the password to access the director. After starting the bconsole client, we are in the command prompt. The list of commands can be obtained by typing help.

Commands, presented in the Table 20-2, are of most interest to us in the initial phase.

Table 20-2. bconsole commands

Command	Meaning
cancel	Cancel the task
disable	Temporarily prevent the task from running
enable	Task startup
exit	Exit
list	View the list of objects in the catalog
messages	View recent messages from the system
quit	Exit
restore	Restore data
reload	Reread the configuration
run	Run the task
status	Show the status of the system (director, storage servers, data servers, or all together)
show	Show detailed information about the task, bullet, etc.

To start the task of archiving user directories, type

```
run job=users-backup
```

Then bacula will start executing the task. If you do not specify a task name, `bconsole` will prompt you to select one from the list. Once started, you will be periodically warned that there are new messages. To view them, use the `messages` command. To see the current state of the system, run the `status` command. If you don't specify an argument to it, you will be asked whether you want to display the status of the director, storage, clients, or all of them together. By issuing this command, you can diagnose problems, if for some reason the tasks terminate with an error. Detailed information about the system configuration can be obtained with the `show` command. Without arguments, it will show nothing and offer no choices. To see a list of available choices, type

```
show help
```

For example, the `show tasks` command will show the most complete information about task descriptions. This can be very useful when searching for configuration errors.

Project website: www.bacula.org.

Rsync and Others

Along with `tar`, the `rsync` program is one of the classic backup tools. The task of `rsync` is to synchronize the contents of two directories, and one of them can be on a remote machine. Synchronization is only one way, i.e., the newer contents of the first directory will be copied to the second, but the newer contents of the second will not be copied to the first. The good thing about `rsync` is that it performs a "smart" comparison of directory contents before copying starts: newer files are detected by update time, and then the contents of larger files are compared side by side using checksums and only the changed parts of the files are copied (this behavior can be overridden). The transport for accessing remote directories is `rsh`, `ssh`, or a proprietary protocol. In the latter case, the `rsyncd` process must be running on the remote machine.

The disadvantages of `rsync` include the absence of the ability to create incremental or differential copies, read data from standard input (for database backups), and the inability to work with removable drives. Nevertheless, for relatively small backup tasks, it remains a great tool.

Let's look at some simple scenarios for using `rsync`.

```
rsync -avz host1:data_dir /backups/host1
```

This command will copy the contents of the `data_dir` directory along with subdirectories on the remote machine `host1` to the local directory /backups/host1/data_dir. To ensure that the `data_dir` directory is not created and only its contents are copied, specify the source as `host1:data_dir/`, i.e., add a slash to the directory name. The key '-a' prescribes saving maximum of meta-information, like permissions, attributes, symbolic links, etc., '-v' - reporting the copying process, and '-z' - compressing the data during transmission.

To explicitly specify that `ssh` is used for remote access, with logging in as a specific user and with a non-standard private key, specify the -e switch:

```
rsync -av -e "ssh -l backuper -i secret_key" \
  host1:/to_backup/ /backups/host1
```

Table 20-3 presents some more useful `rsync` keys.

Table 20-3. Useful rsync keys

Key	Meaning
--delete	Deleting files that are not in the source directory
-b	When overwriting files, back them up by copying them to a separate directory (option --backup-dir) or adding a specific extension to their name (option --suffix)
-u/--update	Do not process files newer than those in the source
-n/--dry-run	Do not perform copying – only show that it will be performed
--ignore-errors	Skip read/write errors
--max-size=N	Skip files larger than N
--exclude=PAT	Skip files and directories with names matching the PAT mask (set in shell style)
--exclude-from=FILE	Similar to --exclude, but read the list of masks from the FILE file
-h/--human-readable	Output file sizes in "human-readable" form, i.e., add MB, GB, etc.
-8/--8-bit-output	Save file names with 8-bit set (for UTF-8 encodings, etc.)
--progress	Copy progress
--daemon	Work in daemon mode (rsyncd)

If you need to perform the same(!) update on many machines at once, you can use the `--write-batch=update` option. In this case, rsync will not perform a copy, but will create two files – `update` and `update.sh`. These files can be copied to the required machines or made available on them via the network FS, and then run the `update.sh` script on each machine, which will perform the required `update`. If `rsyncd` (`rsync --daemon`) is running on the host, you can use the syntax `rsync://host/remote_path` or `host::remote_path` to access it, for example:

`rsync -avz rsync://host1:data_dir /backups/host1`

In this case, `rsync` will not use `ssh/rsh` and additional access control must be taken care of. I recommend to use daemon mode, if possible, because it doesn't require encryption and saves CPU resources. At the same time, it is less secure; therefore, I'd recommend to use chroot and separated secrets file instead of UNIX passwords. See the documentation for more details.

There are several projects, using rsync to make incremental, encrypted, and observable backups. Also, there are some projects, using similar, but more efficient approaches, e.g., **borgbackup**,[1] which implements efficient deduplication and store all backups in a special database. Every backup is a set of internal links to unique file system objects, so there are no incremental or differential backups, and backup database always contains only files, used by one of backups. If you remove a backup, only its unique files are deleted from the database. Borg supports remote backups via sshfs or using its own service and backups encryption.

In the repository `https://github.com/zhum/hpc-book-matherials`, you can find a simple script, which makes managing borg backups a bit easier. Of course, there are many other good projects, open source and paid, you can use if you need more features.

Brief Summary

As you know, all system administrators are divided into "those who don't yet do backups and those who do now" (and there are smart admins, who test backups at least two times a year, because backups may fail silently). Indeed, very often setting up or testing backups remains a task that is done last, and sometimes only after "thunder rumbles." In such a large system as a supercomputer, data backup has a special role – users, as a rule,

---

[1] `https://www.borgbackup.org/`

cannot solve this task on their own, as they have only remote access to the data. And after losing the settings of system software, especially commercial software, it can take weeks or even months to restore the system after a failure.

If data volumes are relatively small, and you don't need to use tape drives, it is possible to organize regular backups of system settings and user data by very simple means. In more complex cases, the task can also be successfully solved by both commercial and free software.

Search Keywords

Backup, gnu-tar, cpio, pax, bacula, archiver

CHAPTER 21

Compilers and Environments, for Parallel Technologies

There are many ready parallel programs and packages which are widely used for calculations. However, progress does not stand still and the need for new programs and packages does not disappear. Often users of supercomputers write compute programs themselves or compile the latest versions of open source packages (which often surpass commercial ones in capabilities) from source texts. This requires compilers and tools to support parallel programming.

At the moment of writing this book, the de facto standard in the HPC world for distributed programs is MPI (Message Passing Interface). This is a standard that describes a set of library procedures for C and Fortran languages. These procedures allow you to organize the launch of several program processes and organize message exchange between them. The standard is approved by a special committee and further supported by various independent implementations.

Why do I need to know this? I am not a programmer but an administrator! – some people may say. But don't hurry, I won't teach you programming with MPI; nevertheless, it is important for an administrator to know how parallel programs are arranged and what "this MPI" does. At least in order to understand the diagnostics being generated.

So, a simple example of a C program using MPI that calculates the number of pi (MPI functions are in bold) is as follows:

```
#include "mpi.h"
#include <stdio.h>
#include <math.h>
#define NINT 1000000
```

CHAPTER 21 COMPILERS AND ENVIRONMENTS, FOR PARALLEL TECHNOLOGIES

```
#define COUNT 100000

double f( double a) {
  return (4.0 / (1.0 + a*a));
}

int main( int argc, char *argv[] )
{
  int done = 0, n, myid, numprocs, i;
  double PI25DT = 3.141592653589793238462643;
  double mypi, pi, h, sum, x;
  double startwtime=0.0, endwtime;
  int namelen;
  char processor_name[MPI_MAX_PROCESSOR_NAME];
  int rep;
  double *mem[1000];

  MPI_Init(&argc,&argv);
  MPI_Comm_size(MPI_COMM_WORLD,&numprocs);
  MPI_Comm_rank(MPI_COMM_WORLD,&myid);
  MPI_Get_processor_name(processor_name,&namelen);
  fprintf(stderr, "Process %d on %s\n",
          myid, processor_name);
  n = 0;
  while (!done) {
    if (myid == 0) {
      if (n==0) n=NINT; else n=0;
      startwtime = MPI_Wtime();
    }
    MPI_Bcast(&n, 1, MPI_INT, 0, MPI_COMM_WORLD);
    if (n == 0)
        done = 1;
    else {
      for(rep=0; rep<COUNT;++rep){
        h = 1.0 / (double) n;
        sum = 0.0;
```

```
      for (i = myid + 1; i <= n; i += numprocs) {
        x = h * ((double)i - 0.5);
        sum += f(x);
      }
      mypi = h * sum;
      MPI_Reduce(&mypi, &pi, 1, MPI_DOUBLE, \
                 MPI_SUM, 0, MPI_COMM_WORLD);
      if (myid == 0) {
        printf("pi is approximately %.16f,"
               " Error is %.16f\n",
               pi, fabs(pi - PI25DT));
        endwtime = MPI_Wtime();
        printf("wall clock time = %f\n",
               endwtime-startwtime);
      }
     }
    }
   }
  MPI_Finalize();
  return 0;
}
```

At the beginning of the program, the MPI_Init procedure is called, to which the main arguments are passed. Only after calling this procedure can other MPI calls be used.

MPI_Comm_size, MPI_Comm_rank, and MPI_Get_processor_name get the number of running processes, their number, and node name, respectively. MPI_Bcast sends information from one process to all others – in the example above, this is a sign of the end of the calculation. MPI_Reduce performs a collective operation on the data of all processes and returns the result – the sum of intermediate results of all processes. Each process is terminated by MPI_Finalize call, after it MPI calls are forbidden.

Besides MPI, popular parallel programming technologies are **OpenMP**, **CUDA**, **OpenCL**, **OpenACC**, and **SHMEM**. **OpenMP** is a standard describing a set of special comments in C and Fortran programs which can help to distribute computations in a program among several threads. Unlike MPI, there is only one process, within which various threads work on shared memory. Since working with shared memory is easier and cheaper, "hybrid" programming is often used (it is often denoted MPI+X, meaning

CUDA, OpenMP, OpenACC, OpenCL under X) – a program is written using both MPI and OpenMP (or similar technology) simultaneously. When running such a task on many compute nodes, usually one MPI process runs on each node, within which the work is distributed using OpenMP, OpenACC, OpenCL, or CUDA, and the processes themselves exchange data via MPI.

CUDA and **OpenCL** technologies allow you to use different accelerators, typically video cards, for computing. CUDA technology was developed by NVIDIA and works only on NVIDIA's graphics cards. It is an extension of the C language, so a special compiler is required to compile CUDA programs. Some CUDA functions are implemented as a library and can be used from ordinary C/C++ and Fortran programs.

OpenCL is an open standard that allows you to work with any gas pedal for which there is an implementation. It is also focused on video cards, but can be applied more widely. Its advantage is the uniformity of code description for both the main processor and the gas pedal. Being universal, it does not provide many optimization possibilities.

OpenACC is also an open standard developed by a group including CAPS, Cray, NVIDIA, and the Portland Group. The first implementation was created by the "Portland Group." The approach of the standard is very similar to OpenMP: code markup is also used with the help of special comments that specify how to execute parallel sections. OpenACC emphasizes using graphic cards, but theoretically, it can be used for any accelerator. As in OpenCL, the same code can run on both CPU and GPU.

OpenSHMEM standard is an attempt to compromise between distributed memory (as in MPI) and shared memory (as in OpenMP). Here memory is explicitly distributed between the processes of a task, but there is a possibility of direct access to "other people's" memory.

Let's take a closer look at compilers and implementations of parallel programming standards. Pay special attention to the last section of this chapter; it is devoted to managing the "zoo" of compilers and other tools.

gcc/gfortran

GNU compilers are one of the greatest creations of open source. Thanks to them, we have such a wide range of open source (and beyond) programs on a wide variety of architectures. The biggest advantages of these tools are that they are available in any Linux distribution and are constantly evolving. As a rule, there are no special subtleties when working with gcc/g++/gfortran. Nevertheless, let's try to highlight the main techniques of working with them. Right away, I will draw your attention to the fact that there is still the **g77** project, an early implementation of Fortran in the GNU project. Today, it is completely replaced by **gfortran**, which supports the language standard more fully.

The simplest variant of compiling a C program from a single file looks like this:

```
gcc myprog.c
```

If the compilation was successful, an executable file a.out will be created. If we want to immediately create an executable with the desired name, we need to add the '-o filename_file_name' key. For large projects consisting of many files, it is often used to compile them into object files first, to assemble (link) them together into an executable by a linker program. This is convenient, because if you change one source file, there is no need to recompile the whole project, just recompile the corresponding object file and link the executable one.

To compile an object file, the '-c' key must be specified. By default (if the -c switch is not specified), the name of the object file will be the same as the original one, but the extension will be changed to '.o'. For convenience, the compiler can work as a linker (more precisely, it calls the linker itself with the necessary parameters). Here is a simplified example of compiling a program from several files with a mathematical library attached:

```
gcc -c *.c
gcc -o myexe *.o -lm
```

First, we compile all '.c' files into object files, then link them in place with the libm library into the myexe executable. The -lzzz switch tells the linker to link a dynamic library named libzzz.so. The -I and -L keys are used to tell the compiler and linker where to find the include files and libraries, respectively.

In order not to compile all the files every time, the make program is usually used, which runs only the necessary commands for compilation on a preprepared Makefile. You can read more about it in the documentation. By default, the compiler does minimal code optimization. To make it perform more serious optimization, various combinations of keys are used. The most common one is the -On key, which sets the "optimization level" equal to n, where n is an integer from 0 to 6.

In fact, each level is simply a combination of other keys specifying different aspects of the optimization. If necessary, you can add or remove the desired optimization with a separate key. By default, level 2 (-O2) is used. In real projects, levels 3 or higher are most often used. To optimize for a specific processor model, specify the -ftune and -farch options. Level 0 (disable optimization) may be required for debugging.

By default, code is generated that should work on any processor of the given architecture, i.e., on the x86 architecture, the code will work even on Pentium-I, but no "advanced" instructions, e.g., AVX, will be generated. All the above options remain valid for the gfortran compiler. Some projects require combining parts of C and Fortran code. In these cases, compiling files into object files and linking them together is used.

Because C and Fortran use slightly different naming conventions for variables and functions in object files, C files are required to be compiled with the -fleading-underscore switch. Combining with C++ requires that all functions to be called in C or Fortran code be in C format. In general, combining code in different languages often leads to compilation difficulties that are difficult to resolve. Added to this is an unpleasant feature of GNU compilers: sometimes the order of keys and even file names changes the behavior of the compiler or linker. Frequently, the place on the command line where a library is specified determines whether it will be accepted by the compiler at all.

Intel and NVIDIA HPC Compilers

Among commercial compilers for the X86/X86-64 platform, I should mention the most popular ones – **Intel Compiler/OneAPI** and **NVIDIA HPC Compilers**. All of them produce noticeably faster programs (on newer processors) than the GNU compilers and are fully compatible in object file format with it, allowing code from different projects to be combined. Note at once that compatibility is lost if nonstandard optimization techniques (e.g., IPO) are used – note this in the documentation. The basic keys of all compilers (including GNU) are the same, the differences mainly concern optimization keys (with -On supported by all of them). When using fine optimization keys, analogs from one compiler may not always be present in another.

Intel Compilers are well integrated with other Intel tools, like IntelMPI, MKL, IntelGDB, Vtune, etc. They have excellent performance even on non-Intel x86-64 processors. NVIDIA HPC Compilers are coupled with CUDA and some other NVIDIA tools, so they are really handy on NVIDIA platforms.

The compilers, I mentioned, in 2025 are free to use, but have paid support option. In the past, good compilers (PGI, Pathscale) had licensed model, and I don't exclude that this can repeat for some special cases in the future. Let me tell you about the license options (it applies not only to the compilers).

The simplest one – for **one person (account) on one fixed computer**. It is usually available from all compiler manufacturers, but in our case, this option is rarely suitable: we need to provide compilation for all our users.

Another type of license is for an **unlimited (or rather large) number of users, but on a fixed computer**. As a rule, this is the most optimal option, but it is not always available from compiler manufacturers.

Another option limits the **number of simultaneous uses of the compiler**, e.g., 3, i.e., three users can compile their programs simultaneously. This variant looks good, but it has one pitfall: in the implementation, I met with the Pathscale compiler, "simultaneity" is counted to the nearest... 15 minutes! 15 minutes! That is, when the compiler is called, it leases a license for 15 minutes, which can be used by this user. They can run the compiler once or 20 times, it doesn't matter, but other users cannot use this license, even if the compiler was called just once.

You should be especially careful when building fault-tolerant schemes: if the license server is installed in this mode on several machines, it usually requires a **quorum**, i.e., at least 50% of the machines must be working. If you use Intel Compiler on one computer, it supports the mode of operation without a license server – just specify the directory with the license file during installation. At startup, the compiler will check the license by itself.

All licenses are "bound" to the MAC address of the network card of the computer with the license server and sometimes additionally to its network name. In some cases, this information is required at the purchase stage, but most often it is required after payment, at the stage of "activation" of the product. I strongly advise you to **always** study the license terms and conditions very carefully. Many obvious concepts may in reality mean things that are not obvious at all.

PMIx

Process Management Interface – Exascale (PMIx)[1] is a standard that allows MPI application to get the information, needed for bootstrapping, like network topology, MPI ranks placement, etc., and start up the app in efficient way. If MPI implementation and job management system have PMIx support, the app is started using job management system agents, takes much less time, and is more controllable.

---

[1] https://pmix.org/

There are old standards PMI-1 and PMI-2, and they can be emulated via PMIx, but it depends on the client and server implementation. Luckily, today, most implementations use PMIx. I recommend to make sure that your job management systems and MPI libraries, used by your applications, have compiled in PMIx support, and it is enabled as default startup method. For example, in SLURM, you can run `srun --mpi=list` and get list of supported MPI startup methods.

mpich

One of the earliest implementations of MPI was created at Aragon Laboratory back in 1992. The first version was based on the Chameleon system, which facilitated portability, and the name originally stood for "MPI over Chameleon." The project's website is http://mpich.org/. This implementation supports a variety of transports, including Blue Gene and Cray network, through so-called drivers, which makes it easy to port it to new systems, but, on the other hand, limits the optimization possibilities. At the end of 2025, the stable branch is MPICH-4, and branches 1 and 2 are frozen.

Many commercial implementations of MPI, such as IntelMPI, HP-MPI, etc., were initially created on the basis of MPICH. In their development, they have gone far away from the initial version, and some developments even returned to the parent project. The MPICH-1 implementation was characterized by the simplicity of launching: a ready executable file can launch an application without additional means. The `mpirun` script only generates a set of necessary keys and runs the ready program with them. At startup, the program launches MPI processes by `ssh` or `rsh` to the nodes and specifying special options to the executable.

At the moment, MPICH is not the best MPI implementation, but pretty good for many applications. It is best to build it from source code, which can be found at mpich.org. If you use non-GNU compilers, specify the `CC=my-compiler` option when building, where `my-compiler` is the name of the compiler, e.g., `icc`. It is also desirable to specify the installation prefix, e.g., `--prefix=/opt/mpich`.

OpenMPI

This implementation was created independently of MPICH, and it is a development of ideas and works of previous implementations – LAM/MPI, FT-MPI, LA-MPI, and PACX-MPI. Its first version was released on November 17, 2005. Project website:

http://www.open-mpi.org/. OpenMPI implementation approaches are very different from MPICH: there is no concept of "driver" here, although many transport environments are supported. The scheme of launching applications here is also different: special daemon programs must be launched on nodes beforehand.

In a standard build, this startup can be done by the `mpirun` program itself, so for the user, the startup process remains simple, but for the administrator, it means that on the nodes it is necessary to install in advance a set of software to run openmpi applications.

OpenMPI is characterized by good performance, and on many applications, it outperforms even commercial implementations. Its disadvantages include very poor documentation; most of the options and settings can be found only on forums and in the updated FAQ of the project. The project is actively developed and supported. Even if you use another MPI implementation, you should keep OpenMPI build as an alternative one. Note that if you build OpenMPI from source (which is recommended), make build variants with different compilers.

Although the `mpicc/mpiCC/mpif77/mpif90` compilation commands included in the OpenMPI distribution support the ability to specify the compiler separately, difficulties may arise during linking if the program is compiled with one compiler and the OpenMPI libraries with another.

OpenMPI is highly customizable via the configuration file, command-line options, and environment variables. For example, by default, OpenMPI uses a library hcoll, which implements collective operations via different transports. Sometimes it works incorrectly, and you want to disable it or give it some hints. Here are some ways how to do that:

```
mpiexec -mca coll_hcoll_enable 0 ... myprog    # disable it
export OMPI_MCA_coll_hcoll_enable=0            # if you use PMIx
  srun --mpi=pmix ... myprog                   # ^^^^^^^^^^^^^^^
-x HCOLL_MAIN_IB=mlx5_0:1                      # force use device
-x HCOLL_ENABLE_NBC=1         # enable non-blocking collectives
-x HCOLL_ENABLE_SHARP=1       # enable SHARP
-x OMPI_MCA_pml=^ucx          # UCX off, if needed (see below)
```

You could note '**MCA**' abbreviation above. This stands for "Modular Component Architecture," and many OpenMPI components are modules in this framework. Main modules are

- **pml** – Point-to-point messaging layer (PML). These components are used to implement MPI point-to-point messaging.

- **btl** – Byte transport layer; these components are exclusively used as the underlying transports for the ob1 PML component.

- **coll** – MPI collective algorithms.

- **io** – MPI I/O.

- **mtl** – MPI matching transport layer (MTL); these components are exclusively used as the underlying transports for the cm PML component.

You can get all available parameters and their current values via `ompi_info -a` command. To change any parameter, you can use these ways (in order of increasing the priority):

- Global config file (usually `/etc/openmpi-mca-params.conf`[2]), format is `key=value`.

- Local config file `$HOME/.openmpi/mca-params.conf`.

- Tuned file – Any file(s), with any mpiexec options inside, you can specify them like `mpiexec --tune file1,file2 ...`, and their content will be interpreted as regular mpiexec options.

- Environment variables, format is `export OMPI_MCA_xxx=value`.

- mpiexec command-line options: `-mca xxx value`.

For example, to force use intranode connection and InfiniBand and forbid using TCP stack, we can export variable `OMPI_MCA_btl=^tcp,self,openib`. The same way you can tune timeouts, communication algorithms parameters, etc.

---

[2] And for PMIx- and PRRTE-related parameters, special file can be used – openpmix-mca-params.conf, or prte-mca-params.conf respectively. For environment variables in this case preixes PMIX_MCA_ and PRRTE_MCA_ are used.

Mvapich/Mvapich2

This implementation was developed at Ohio University based on MPICH-2. The main goal of the project development was to optimize MPICH to work with InfiniBand. Just implementing a driver for mpich was not enough and the developers created their own project, making many changes to the original code. Mvapich is included in the standard package OFED on a par with OpenMPI. At the moment, the implementation with support of MPI-3 standard – Mvapich2 – is being actively developed. The project website is http://mvapich.cse.ohio-state.edu/.

What distinguishes this implementation from MPICH is the way of launching: instead of `mpirun` (which for some strange reason is left in the distribution), you should use `mpirun_rsh` command, and its keys differ from `mpirun` keys from MPICH. At the moment, Mvapich's performance is not superior to OpenMPI on most applications, but the project is actively developing, and perhaps, new implementations will outperform its competitors.

Proprietary MPI: Spectrum MPI and IntelMPI

IBM has its own implementation – Spectrum MPI. It is tuned for use on proprietary IBM hardware, is based on OpenMPI, and supports InfiniBand and GPUDirect RDMA. It is well documented and recommended for use on IBM hardware.

IntelMPI is another good choice; it is developed almost "from scratch," has good InfiniBand support, is well optimized and documented, and is pretty tunable. In 2025, it is free, but has paid support option.

SHMEM Library, OpenSHMEM Standard

The SHMEM programming system (from "shared memory library") was developed by Cray Research in 1999 as a one-way communications interface capable of becoming an effective alternative and complement to MPI and PVM. In fact, SHMEM realizes the simplest variant of PGAS-style programming (Partitioned Global Address Space). Each node has local memory; each node also has access to remote memory: a node can directly access the local memory of any node in the system.

Since remote memory accesses occur through a communication network, their execution time is noticeably longer and their tempo is slower than that of local memory accesses. It is extremely expensive to wait for each single operation to be executed, so it is required that the programmer explicitly allocates accesses to nonlocal memory locations.

Unlike other PGAS languages (e.g., UPC), SHMEM **forces** the programmer to explicitly allocate external accesses using functions, with further grouping of accesses and optimization performed in hardware. Here we can add a comparison with OpenMP's shared memory paradigm, in which the programmer should slice computations into pieces without worrying about memory allocation. This paradigm take into account the difference in memory access price of NUMA systems, especially systems without cache-coherent shared memory. That is why OpenMP support could not be implemented efficiently on systems with distributed memory, although unsuccessful attempts were made (Intel Cluster OpenMP and ScaleMP vSMP).

The PGAS paradigm extends OpenMP's shared memory paradigm in that the programmer needs to distribute not only computations, but also data, and when distributing computations, take into account how the data has been distributed.

Historically, the SHMEM interface has been supported by all MPP systems from Cray, Silicon Graphics, and Quadrics interconnects. All these implementations were essentially proprietary and available only on the equipment of those manufacturers who offered it. Most Russian supercomputers and clusters lacked support for programming with SHMEM. Another problem is the lack of a standard for SHMEM calls. Thus, different implementations from different vendors differed slightly in both call format and functionality. All this had a negative impact both on the portability of existing applications and on the popularity of SHMEM.

Since 2009, a group of members of the SHMEM user community has begun work on standardizing the SHMEM library under the name OpenSHMEM, emphasizing the openness of this initiative. At the time of writing, several references to implementations are available on the community website http://www.openshmem.org, including those in OpenMPI and MVAPICH2-X.

Compilation of programs using SHMEM is done with the oshc/oshfort commands for C and Fortran, respectively. It should be noted that the MPI implementation is used to build and run the GASNET library and the compilers and libraries based on it. Thus, it will be required when building both GASNET and OpenSHMEM. On the other hand, programs can be started using the same commands that MPI programs are started with on the cluster. Although the OpenSHMEM package offers an `oshrun` script, it actually uses `mpirun` in the case of a multiprocessor machine.

At startup, users should control the size of the symmetric heap using the `SHMEM_SYMMETRIC_HEAP_SIZE` environment variable. In the `oshconfig` command help page, users can read about how to control algorithms for performing collective operations such as barrier.

CUDA

The word "CUDA" often refers to several similar but different things: the programming technology offered by NVIDIA, the library and compiler to support this technology, and even the architecture of graphics cards and gas pedals that support this technology. The same is true for the CUDA version: sometimes it may be the revision number of the standard for the programming technology, sometimes it may be the software version, and sometimes it may be the maximum version of the standard supported by the gas pedal. Officially, NVIDIA calls CUDA a "parallel computing platform and programming model."

The main tool for the CUDA programmer is the `nvcc` compiler, which supports the CUDA dialect of the C language. It is used to compile files with the `.cu` extension. Besides direct use of the compiler, it is possible to call CUDA functions from ordinary C or Fortran programs using the `cudart` library; this library is included in the CUDA SDK.

Installation of CUDA SDK is quite simple. Download the RPM package or binary installer from the official website, and make sure the `gcc` compiler is installed on the host. Then install the downloaded package, which will add the official repository entry to the system, perform a repository update (`yum clean expire-cache` or `zypper refresh` or `apt-get update` depending on the distribution), and install the CUDA package: `yum install CUDA` or `zypper install CUDA` or `apt-get install CUDA`.

If a binary installer has been downloaded, just run it, and it will automatically download and install the necessary files. The disadvantage of the binary installer is that it does not install the package into the system, which means that you will need to manually install the binary installer again when upgrading.

Next, it is desirable to specify paths to CUDA files so that they are available to users. It is best to do this by creating a module for environment modules. For CUDA to work, it is necessary to add the path /usr/local/CUDA-VERSION/bin (if the installation was done in /usr/local) to the PATH environment variable and the path /usr/local/CUDA-VERSION/lib64 to the LD_LIBRARY_PATH variable, respectively.

The main CUDA libraries are libcuda and libcudart. The first enables basic GPU operations, like enumeration, read/write GPU memory, check performance, etc. The second one gives access to the CUDA API calls. For more high-level programming, in addition to the CUDA library, you can also install implementations of popular libraries using this technology – cuBLAS, cuFFT, cuRAND, cuSPARSE, and others.

Remember to install the latest version of the NVIDIA driver and CUDA driver on the compute nodes. To diagnose problems, use the nvidia-smi tool included in the driver kit. It allows you to see detailed information about NVIDIA graphics cards and change some parameters of their operation. nvitop and nvtop can be used to quick check and monitor the GPU (and CPU) load.

With nvidia-smi, you can also control some driver and card modes:

- **Enable/disable ECC** (memory error correction – with it, the card works slower but more reliable).

- **Enable/disable persistent mode** – Then the driver always hangs in memory; otherwise at each program launch, at the first call of CUDA function, there is a delay for driver loading.

- Choose **compute mode** – No one counts, or counts any threads but from one process, or counts anyone.

- Check for XID,[3] ECC errors, overheat, and other issues.

Sometimes when installing a new driver, you cannot remove the old driver because it is loaded and not unloaded. In this case, add the kernel module to blacklist, reboot, and then remove it from blacklist. In this case, the module will not be loaded, and you can install the new driver version.

If the driver "hangs," you can try reinitializing it by explicitly unloading and loading it:

rmmod nvidia; modprobe nvidia; deviceQuery

Here deviceQuery is a program from CUDASDK that outputs card information using CUDA. Its call leads to loading the driver. You can use nvidia-smi instead of deviceQuery in this case.

---

[3] XID – eXception ID.

CHAPTER 21 COMPILERS AND ENVIRONMENTS, FOR PARALLEL TECHNOLOGIES

UCX and NCCL

Unified Communication X (UCX) – optimized production-proven communication framework for modern, high-bandwidth, and low-latency networks – supports RoCE, InfiniBand, TCP sockets, shared memory (CMA, knem, xpmem, SysV, mmap), and Cray Gemini/Aries (ugni). It is well-supported by OpenMPI, MPICH, Charm++, NCCL, and many others. If you didn't disable it in your MPI implementation and have problems, you may either disable it or try to tune via specific variables like this (OpenMPI example):

```
mpirun -np 2 -mca pml ucx -x UCX_NET_DEVICES=mlx5_0:1 ./myapp
```

Here we specify to use UCX as PML transport (-mca pml ucx) and pass the UCX-specific variable, forcing it to use specific device (-x UCX_NET_DEVICES=mlx5_0:1). You can get all UCX-specific variables via ucx_info -c command, and if you add '-f' option, you get the documentation about each of them.

NCCL stands for "NVIDIA Collective Communications Library," pronounced "Nickel." It is closed source, but freely available library, implementing a lot of point-to-point and collective operations, like MPI, but intended to be highly optimized to use on GPU and with RDMA. It can be used to scale up an application to use single-GPU, multi-GPUs, many nodes + GPUs. And it works without GPUs, of course, and even together with MPI. The advantage is automatic detection of the network topology, PCI-express configuration, etc.

Via the environment variables, you can tune NCCL-based apps, e.g., in multiinterfaces networks, sometimes you need to specify network parameters explicitly. When you specify interfaces in NCCL, there is a convention:

- If you specify just a string, like 'eth', it means prefix, and it matches to all interfaces, starting with it.

- If you add '=' prefix, it means exact matching, e.g., '=eth1' matches only to one interface, but not to 'eth11'.

- If you add '^' prefix, it means negative prefix, i.e., matches to all, except this prefix.

- '^=' means "except exactly this interface."

You can specify a list of interfaces via comma. Some important environment variables for NCCL, if you need to tune/fix NCCL-based applications:

- **NCCL_DEBUG** – Debug level, INFO is recommended for debugging.
- **NCCL_SOCKET_IFNAME** – List of IP(!) interfaces for communication.
- **NCCL_IB_HCA** – List of RDMA interfaces.
- **NCCL_IB_TIMEOUT** – Timeout in seconds for RDMA communications.
- **NCCL_IB_RETRY_CNT** – Number of RDMA retries.
- **NCCL_IB_SL / NCCL_IB_TC** – IB service level and traffic class, may be important in some IB and RoCE networks.
- **NCCL_TOPO_FILE** – If the PCI topology is detected incorrectly, specify it explicitly.

OpenCL

Open Computing Language – OpenCL – is designed as a standard for programming heterogeneous computing systems. Such systems may include CPUs, GPGPUs, FPGAs, and other devices. All of them must be connected to a host; distributed configurations are not supported in the standard. The basis of the OpenCL programming paradigm is the language of the same name, which is a dialect of C99. Unlike ordinary C, it does not contain pointers to functions, header files, bit fields, recursion is prohibited, memory qualifiers, and some other extensions are added.

The standard defines a set of special procedures for organizing calculations. In this case, calculations can be run on any device available to the system and supported by OpenCL, i.e., the same code can run simultaneously on CPU cores, video cards, and connected FPGA accelerators. This approach greatly facilitates programming in contrast to CUDA, where it is necessary to describe the code for GPGPU and CPU separately. But the price for universality is flexibility and performance (it is more difficult to write efficient code in OpenCL for NVIDIA cards than in CUDA), and optimization possibilities are much less.

Since OpenCL is a set of specifications, independent implementations are made for each type of device. There is an NVIDIA implementation for its own video cards (it is included in the standard driver), AMD implementation for its processors and video cards, and Intel implementation for its processors.

OpenACC

The OpenACC standard is a set of specifications according to which any compiler can implement it. The standard also has a set of implementation recommendations for different gas pedals. Unlike OpenCL, OpenACC supports traditional languages – C, C++, and Fortran. When modifying the program text, only directives-special comments are introduced and the modified program can work without OpenACC, but in sequential mode without gas pedals.

OpenACC directives are very similar to OpenMP directives, and for good reason: the initiators of the new standard were participants and developers of OpenMP standards. As a result, all OpenACC directives are compatible with OpenMP and can be used in the same program, and some OpenACC directives will probably be ported to OpenMP.

From the administrator's point of view, this technology does not require any separate support, except for installation of a compiler supporting OpenACC. Currently, this technology is supported by NVIDIA, GCC (NVIDIA and AMD cards), and Intel (for Xeon Phi processors) compilers.

Environment Modules and LMOD

I already mentioned above that it is very desirable to install several MPI compilers and implementations on a supercomputer at the same time. But how to use them simultaneously? It is very inconvenient to specify full paths to executable files and libraries every time. The problem is mostly solved by adding the necessary paths to environment variables such as PATH, LD_LIBRARY_PATH, and some others. In order to automate adding and removing the necessary paths, the **Environment modules** package,[4] or modules for short, was created.

---

[4] http://modules.sourceforge.net/

CHAPTER 21 COMPILERS AND ENVIRONMENTS, FOR PARALLEL TECHNOLOGIES

For any package or library, it is possible to create a "module" – a file describing what should be added or removed from the required user environment variables when loading or deleting the module. With module, you can easily "switch" between compilers, MPI implementations, and add environments to work with application packages. All commands are implemented through a single command (actually a shell function) – module. It takes as an argument the name of the command and additional arguments, usually a list of modules. Table 21-1 presents the list of the main commands.

Table 21-1. Basic module commands

Command	Meaning
add|load	Add modules to the environment
rm|unload	Uninstall modules from the environment
display|show	Show information about the specified modules
avail	Show list of available modules
switch|swap	Switch the status of the specified modules: if loaded – unload, if not – load
use [-a|--append]	Add a directory with module files
unuse	Delete the directory with module files
update	Try to reload all loaded modules by updating the environment
purge	Unload all modules
list	Show loaded modules
clear	Clear the list of loaded modules, but do not change the environment

For a complete list of commands and options, please refer to the documentation.
Here is an example of a module for OpenMPI:

```
#%Module1.0###############################
proc ModulesHelp { } {
    global version
    puts stderr "\tThis module will set up \
                environment for OpenMPI 4.0.1 \
                (build by Intel compilers)"
    puts stderr "\n\tVersion $version\n"
}
```

```
set base /opt/mpi/openmpi-4.0.1-icc
module-whatis "adds OpenMPI 4.0.1 build by Intel compilers".

prepend-path PATH $base/bin/
prepend-path LD_LIBRARY_PATH $base/lib
prepend-path MANPATH $base/share/man
```

The first line of the module file should be #%Module1.0.

If the version number (1.0) is omitted, the file format is assumed to be compatible with the latest version of Environment Modules.

The module file is a program in the Tcl language. Text output to the standard error stream (stderr) will be shown to the user. It is not worthwhile to output anything to the standard output stream (stdout); it may spoil the whole module system.

It is not necessary to know Tcl to write module files. As you can see, the syntax of the description is simple. The main actions are performed by prepend-path commands (append-path) – they change the contents of variables containing colon path lists, such as PATH, LD_LIBRARY_PATH, and MANPATH. Many other actions are allowed, such as explicitly setting the value of a variable, deleting a variable, loading another module, etc. You can learn more about the syntax in the documentation, e.g., by typing man modulefile.

The original Environment Modules project, also called Tcl modules or Tcl/C modules, stopped development for a while in 2012 with the release of version 3.2.10. The main drawbacks encountered with this version were difficulties in loading a package if another version was already loaded and in tracking dependencies between different modules (e.g., MPI implementations built with different compilers).

To solve these and other problems, an alternative project **Lua Modules**[5] (**LMOD**) was created. As the name implies, this project is designed to use the Lua language for module files. At the same time, it can use files from the original Tcl modules written in Tcl, translating them on the fly. That is, LMOD can be used on a ready-made infrastructure of module files, allowing you to add new functionality to them.

LMOD, in particular, solves the two problems already mentioned. When loading a module for a package for which a module to support another version has already been loaded, the previously loaded module is automatically unloaded (the version change diagnostic is printed). This avoids the situation when two versions of the compiler are available at once, which can create a conflict between their runtime libraries.

---

[5] https://www.tacc.utexas.edu/research-development/tacc-projects/lmod

In addition, LMOD supports on-the-fly change of the list of paths to module files (MODULEPATH variable). This allows you to dynamically generate lists of available modules. For example, when loading a compiler module, the path to the modules directory is added to the MODULEPATH variable for the version of packages built by this particular compiler (and this version of the compiler). When MODULEPATH is changed, not only what new modules are available, but also what modules are no longer visible. Such modules are marked as inactive, i.e., the environment variables are modified as when the module is unloaded, but the module itself remains in the list of loaded modules (with the corresponding marking).

If later, due to changes in the MODULEPATH variable, a module with the same name becomes available, it is automatically loaded. In this way, it is realized as replacement of module versions in case of changes in other modules on which this module depends.

For example, a cluster may have a version of OpenMPI built by two different compilers: gcc and Intel Compiler. We can load the gcc module and the OpenMPI module sequentially. Then, when we unload the gcc module, the OpenMPI module is marked as inactive, i.e., access to OpenMPI is removed from the environment variables. If you then load an Intel compiler module and it has its own OpenMPI module, it will be automatically loaded, and the environment variables will be set for use on the correct build.

LMOD provides module spider command, which provides information about all available modules, selected module, or detailed info about one module version. Here is an example of all modules info:

```
$ module spider
------------------------------------------------------------
The following is a list of the modules currently available:
------------------------------------------------------------
  gcc: gcc/4.8.1, gcc/10.4.0, gcc/15.1.0
    The Gnu Compiler Collection

  lmod: lmod/8.7.60
    Lmod: An Environment Module System

  openmpi: openmpi/4.1.8, openmpi/5.0.7
    Openmpi Version of the Message Passing Interface Library
```

Info about all version of one module can be obtained using module spider MODULENAME command and is pretty similar to the above. Detailed info about exact module version is more interesting:

```
$ module  spider openmpi/5.0.7

-------------------------------------------------------
  openmpi: openmpi/5.0.7
-------------------------------------------------------
    Description:
      Openmpi Version of the Message Passing Interface Library

    You will need to load all module(s) on any one of the lines below
    before the "openmpi/5.0.7" module is available to load.

      gcc/10.4.0
      gcc/15.1.0
```

You can load modules specifying only the module name, or with version (like gcc/15.1.0); in the first case, default version will be taken. In LMOD and latest modules package, you can specify it explicitly; otherwise, the highest version will be selected. In LMOD, versions are sorted as numbers, in modules – as strings (mkl/4.0 is higher than mkl/11.0).

Other nice features of LMOD: saving/restoring a set of modules, hiding modules (e.g., for testing), and flexible dependencies system.

I will not describe the syntax of the modules in Lua. Most of the commands, such as prepend-path, are taken over from the original project, but should be used with Lua syntax in mind. Other commands can be found in LMOD documentation.

At the end of 2017, the original Modules project started to develop quite a bit again. So far, its development goes toward other functionality, which is not very clear how to apply to problems that are solved with LMOD, plus quite a lot of purely technical changes. But it is worth following this project; perhaps, it will have some useful features of its own.

CHAPTER 21   COMPILERS AND ENVIRONMENTS, FOR PARALLEL TECHNOLOGIES

Build Systems

Many HPC packages depend on tons of other packages and libraries. If you need to build a fresh one, it might be a headache. To help admins building and managing HPC software, there are at least two popular packages – EasyBuild and SPACK. Let's take a look, how to use them.

EasyBuild[6] is an open source python package, and you can install it using `pip`. Use python3.6 or higher, and I'd recommend to use venv to install it into a separated namespace:

```
python3 -m venv easybuild
source easybuild/bin/activate
pip3 install easybuild
```

If you use Lmod or EnvironmentModules (and you do, right?), you can install easybuild as a module (after you've done the installation above):

```
eb --install-latest-eb-release --prefix /opt/easybuild
module use /opt/easybuild/modules/all
# How to load module:
module load EasyBuild
```

After loading the module, you are able to use eb command. Simple example – building a new package:

```
eb HPL-2.3-foss-2024a.eb
== Temporary log file in case of crash /tmp/eb-rpdngte7/
easybuild-3761s4k7.log
== found valid index for /home/foo/eb/easybuild/easyconfigs, so using it...
== processing EasyBuild easyconfig /home/foo/eb/easybuild/easyconfigs/h/
HPL/HPL-2.3-foss-2024a.eb
== building and installing HPL/2.3-foss-2024a...
  >> installation prefix: /home/foo/.local/easybuild/software/HPL/2.3-
foss-2024a
== fetching files and verifying checksums...
...
```

---

[6] https://docs.easybuild.io/

Here we use EasyBuild installation in user's foo home and try to build HPL-2.3 package using GCC toolchain. List of directories with configuration files, build descriptions, and default installation path can be found running command eb -show-config. After build, package module and its dependencies are available via modules. EasyBuild has good documentation, and if you want to use it, please check for details, like using optimizations, specific libraries, like CUDA, etc.

Another popular build system is **Spack**.[7] Installation is pretty simple:

```
git clone -c feature.manyFiles=true --depth=2 \
    https://github.com/spack/spack.git
source spack/share/spack/setup-env.sh
```

The last line should be added in your shell profile, if you want to activate Spack in every shell session. After the installation, you can immediately run it, e.g. try to install HPL package:

```
spack install hpl
==> Fetching https://ghcr.io/v2/spack/bootstrap-buildcache-v1/blobs/sha256:
8d2764eefa443c29c7c9120079e3bbe7576bbc496b15843ad18d18892338a5ba
==> Fetching https://ghcr.io/v2/spack/bootstrap-buildcache-v1/blobs/sha256
:a4abec667660307ad5cff0a616d6651e187cc7b1386fd8cd4b6b288a01614076
==> Installing "clingo-bootstrap@=spack~docs+ipo+optimized+python+st
atic_libstdcpp build_system=cmake build_type=Release generator=make
patches:=bebb819,ec99431 arch=linux-centos7-x86_64" from a buildcache
==> Compilers have been configured automatically from PATH inspection
[+] /usr (external glibc-2.39-o6w364jwmtleiolghwv7qzmglqt3zid6)
[+] /usr (external gcc-13.3.0-hl3rnt2aupy5a4k7pzxkqkm3qj6epopq)
==> No binary for compiler-wrapper-1.0-xi6ijcvw2a5xtrfyz4zgtzwscmtmi5t3
found: installing from source
==> Installing compiler-wrapper-1.0-xi6ijcvw2a5xtrfyz4zgtzwscmtmi5t3 [3/44]
...
```

List of available package descriptions can be found running spack list. Be patient, first run may take long. If you want to check which versions and flavors has a package, e.g., hpl, run spack info hpl. All compiled packages can be added into your

---

[7] https://spack.readthedocs.io/en/latest/index.html

environment modules, by command `spack module lmod refresh` (use `tcl`, for tcl modules). This should add your packages as modules, and you should be able to see them via `modules available`. If not, run `module use SPACK_ROOT/spack/share/spack/modules/linux-ubuntu14-x86_64` (check for your path) and add it into default shell profile.

I won't focus on other abilities of EasyBuild and Spack, like support of compilers, libraries, building stacks, etc. Please check their excellent documentation.

Brief Summary

It is not easy to write a parallel program, and the first thing you need is parallel programming technology. There are many such technologies – from manual thread and process management to using libraries with built-in parallel methods. Currently, the most popular are MPI, OpenMP, CUDA, OpenCL, OpenACC, and SHMEM.

MPI and SHMEM are implemented as libraries but require a special way of launching because they support work of parallel processes on several compute nodes. Unlike other technologies, they do not require compiler support. That's why the administrator takes care of installing and configuring them.

OpenMP and OpenACC are implemented as extensions of Fortran, C, and C++ languages in the form of special comments, i.e., a program with OpenMP or OpenACC directives remains a correct program in the source language. CUDA and OpenCL implement C language extensions; a program using them cannot be compiled by a regular compiler.

The efficiency of programs depends on the compiler, so try to install the one that best meets your needs.

Search Keywords

GCC, Gfortran, NVIDIA Compilers, Intel Compilers, MPI, OpenMPI, IntelMPI, MPICH, Mvapich, OpenSHMEM, CUDA, OpenMP, OpenACC, OpenCL, NCCL, UCX, lmod, Environment modules

CHAPTER 22

Parallel Computing Support Libraries

"Libraries? Those are for users, not for sysadmins" – you may say. Correct. But, trust me, even if you don't need to install them (with nonstandard options, e.g., because "they are needed for this latest version of our groundbreaking app!"), you will see the error messages from the user jobs, and the ability to distinguish system issues and userland issues is essential. The bad news is that there are tons of such libraries and frameworks. The good news is that most real apps use the most popular ones.

Here is the shot (really short!) overview of some popular libraries; hope this will help understand how they work, how to build their custom versions, and understand their error messages better. When you have to help users to debug an app, you have to speak to users with common language.

I don't touch here libraries like PyTorch, or TensorFlow, and apps like OpenFOAM, or NAMD. They (and others) are really widely used today, but to cover them, I would need another hundred pages, and, more important, I'm not a big expert on most of them. Probably, I can collaborate with real applied libraries and apps experts and write a book about it, what do you think? Drop me a line if you think it might be useful, and you know someone who can help here.

ScaLAPACK

The most important role in numerical methods belongs to the solution of linear algebra problems. This is reflected in the fact that all manufacturers of high-performance computing systems supply with their systems highly optimized subroutine libraries, including mainly subroutines for solving linear algebra problems. The most common standard libraries in this area are BLAS, LINPACK, and LAPACK, originally developed by Jack Dongarra, Jeremy Du Croz, Sven Hammarling, and other researchers. They are distributed in open source; their optimized variants are included in such libraries as Intel **MKL** (Math Kernel Library) and **ACML** (AMD Core Math Library).

With the emergence of multiprocessor systems with distributed memory, work began on porting the LAPACK library to this platform as the most fully compliant with the architecture of modern processors (subroutines are optimized for efficient use of cache memory). Leading scientific and supercomputer centers of the USA participated in the work on LAPACK library porting. The result of this work was the creation of the ScaLAPACK (Scalable LAPACK) subroutine package. The project was successful, and the package actually became a standard in the software of multiprocessor systems. In this package, the composition and structure of the LAPACK package are almost completely preserved and the references to the top-level subroutines are practically unchanged. The success of this project was based on two fundamentally important decisions:

1. In the LAPACK package, all elementary vector and matrix operations are performed using highly optimized subroutines of the BLAS (Basic Linear Algebra Subprograms) library. By analogy with this, when a parallel version of this library – PBLAS – was developed to implement ScaLAPACK, which eliminated the need to radically rewrite top-level subroutines.

2. All communication operations are performed using subroutines from the specially developed BLACS (Basic Linear Algebra Communication Subprograms) library, so porting the package to different multiprocessor platforms requires setting up only this library.

The general structure of the ScaLAPACK package is shown in Figure 22-1. Here, the package components above the dividing line contain subroutines that are executed in parallel on some set of processors and use vectors and matrices distributed over these processors as arguments. Subroutines from package components below the dividing line are called on a single processor and operate on local data. Each of the package components is an independent library of subroutines that is not part of a library ScaLAPACK, but is necessary for its operation. In cases where optimized proprietary implementations any of these libraries (BLAS, LAPACK) are available on the computer, it is strongly recommended to use these implementations for better performance.

CHAPTER 22 PARALLEL COMPUTING SUPPORT LIBRARIES

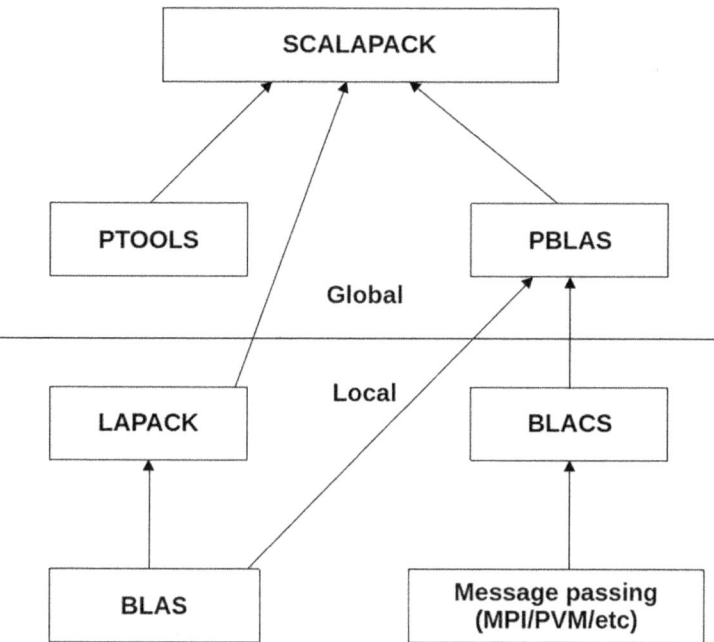

Figure 22-1. ScaLAPACK structure

ScaLAPACK installation begins with the installation of additional software packages. Parallel Basic Linear Algebra Subprograms (PBLAS) implements the second and third level functions of the BLAS library for distributed memory systems. The PTOOLS library is a part of PBLAS. Download the source code of ScaLAPACK http://www.netlib.org/scalapack/. After unpacking the package, edit the SLmake.inc file (only significant lines of the file, which may need to be changed, are shown below):

```
SHELL = /bin/sh
# set the path to the directory where SCALAPACK will be located
# To avoid rebuilding the library on all nodes, we create it
# in a directory that will be available to all nodes in the cluster.
home = /share/download/SCALAPACK
#
# set the string identifier of the platform under which
# A library is being assembled #
#
PLAT = LINUX
#
```

CHAPTER 22   PARALLEL COMPUTING SUPPORT LIBRARIES

```
# BLACS setting. set debug message level 1
# or 0. and the path to the directory where the library is located.
#
BLACSDBGLVL = 0
BLACSdir = /usr/local/lib
#
# MPI setting if used as
# communication library
#
USEMPI = -DUsingMpiBlacs
SMPLIB =
BLACSFINIT = -lblacsF
BLACSCINIT = -lblacsC
BLACSLIB = -lblacs
TESTINGdir = $(home)/TESTING
CBLACSLIB = $(BLACSCINIT) $(BLACSLIB) $(BLACSFINIT)
FBLACSLIB = $(BLACSFINIT) $(BLACSLIB) $(BLACSCINIT)
#
# Catalogs where the corresponding components are located
#
PBLASdir = $(home)/PBLAS
SRCdir = $(home)/SRC
TESTdir = $(home)/TESTING
PBLASTSTdir = $(TESTINGdir)
TOOLSdir = $(home)/TOOLS
REDISTdir = $(home)/REDIST
REDISTTSTdir = $(TESTINGdir)
#
# Customize compilers and their options.
#
F77 = mpif77
CC = mpicc
# Instead of the standard BLAS library, plug in
# a highly optimized goto library
```

```
BLASLIB = -lgoto -lpthread
LAPACKLIB = -llapack
#
PBLIBS = $(SCALAPACKLIB) $(FBLACSLIB) $(LAPACKLIB) \
        $(BLASLIB) $(SMPLIB)
PRLIBS = $(SCALAPACKLIB) $(CBLACSLIB) $(SMPLIB)
RLIBS = $(SCALAPACKLIB) $(FBLACSLIB) $(LAPACKLIB) \
        $(BLASLIB) $(SMPLIB)
LIBS = $(PBLIBS)
```

Note, here we use mpicc and mpif77 as compilers, so they should be available. You can specify regular cc and fortran compilers, but in this case, linking MPI library may become a hard task.

In this example, we used the BLAS implementation from the Goto library. If you use a different variant (MKL, ACML, Atlas, …) you need to substitute the corresponding paths to the library. After editing the SLmake.inc file, run the make command, which will compile and assemble the ScaLAPACK library. The ScaLAPACK library itself consists of 530 subroutines, which are divided into three categories for each of the four data types (real, real with double precision, complex, complex with double precision):

- Driver subroutines, each of which performs the solution of some complete problem, e.g., a system of linear algebraic equations or finding eigenvalues of a real symmetric matrix. There are 14 such subroutines for each data type. These subroutines access computational subroutines.

- Computational subroutines perform separate subtasks, e.g., LU decomposition of a matrix or conversion of a real symmetric matrix to tridiagonal form. The set of computational subroutines significantly overlaps the functional needs and capabilities of driver subroutines.

- Service subroutines perform some internal auxiliary actions.

The names of all driver and computing subroutines coincide with the names of the corresponding subroutines from the LAPACK package, with the only difference that the **P** symbol is added at the beginning of the name to indicate that it is a parallel

CHAPTER 22 PARALLEL COMPUTING SUPPORT LIBRARIES

version. Accordingly, the principle of forming subroutine names has the same scheme as in LAPACK. According to this scheme, the names of the package subprograms are represented in the form **PTXXYYYY,** where

T – Code of the source data type, which can have the following values:

S is a real of single precision.

D is a double-precision real.

C – Complex single precision.

Z is a complex double precision.

XX – Indicates the type of matrix:

DB – Banded general appearance with predominantly diagonal elements.

DT – Tridiagonal of general form with predominant diagonal elements.

GB – General view ribbons.

GE – General view.

GT is tridiagonal of the general form.

HE is Hermite.

PB – Band symmetric or Hermite positively definite.

PO is symmetric or Hermite positively definite.

PT is tridiagonal symmetric or Hermite positively definite.

ST is symmetric tridiagonal.

SY is symmetrical.

TRs are triangular.

TZ – Trapezoidal.

UN – Unitarian.

YYY – Indicates the actions to be performed by this subprogram:

TRF is a factorization of matrices.

TRS – The solution of SLAU after factorization.

CON – Estimation of the matrix conditioning number (after factorization).

SV is the solution of the SLAU.

SVX – SLAU solution with additional studies.

EV and EVX – Computation of eigenvalues and eigenvectors.

GVX is the solution of the generalized eigenvalue problem.

SVD – Singular value calculation.

RFS – Refinement of solution.

LS – Least squares finding.

A complete list of subroutines and their purpose can be found in the ScaLAPACK manual, but you need only to know the basics if you try to debug ScaLAPACK-based apps.

PETSc

The PETSc (pronounced "petsy") library was originally designed for problems that actively use the solution of partial differential equations. The library's Internet address is https://petsc.org/release/. PETSc (Portable, Extensible Toolkit for Scientific Computation) is a set of data structures and procedures that are the building blocks for implementing large-scale application programs for both serial and parallel computers.

This library has in its arsenal not only differential equations, but also many other algorithms used in scientific calculations. PETSc uses the MPI standard, the hybrid MPI+thread model, and the MPI+GPU model (note that not all algorithms can use these models). PETSc includes an extended package of linear and nonlinear equation solvers and time integrators that can be used in applications written in Fortran, C, and C++. The library is organized hierarchically, allowing users to select the levels of abstraction appropriate to their private problem. The library can be used with C, C++, Fortran, and Python.

CHAPTER 22　PARALLEL COMPUTING SUPPORT LIBRARIES

To build the library, download the latest distribution from the website and unzip it. Navigate to the created directory. Run the `./configure` command with the necessary keys. The `--with-cc`, `--with-fc`, and `--with-cxx` keys specify the C, Fortran, and C++ compilers, respectively. I strongly recommend specifying `mpicc`, `mpif90` (`mpifort`), and `mpicxx` (`mpiCC`) as compilers.

If some libraries are not found during compilation, they should be specified with the option `LIBS='...'`. Compiler options for optimization (e.g., explicitly specify processor architecture, etc.) can be specified by variables `COPTFLAGS`, `FOPTFLAGS`, and `CXXOPTFLAGS`, e.g., `FOPTFLAGS='-O5'`. PETSc can use external solvers and packages, such as BLAS/Lapack (required), Hypre, MUMPS, Parmetis, and others. In order to include them, the options `--with`, `--with-PACKAGE-include`, and `-download-PACKAGE` should be used. In the first case, the package must be preinstalled and the option specifies its directory. In the second case, the installer will download the package itself, compile and connect it to PETSc. You can see the full list of external packages with the command `./configure -help`. To utilize the GPU, the CUDA library is used in conjunction with the Cusp package. You will need the CUDA driver version 4.1 or higher installed. If you want to use pthreads, specify the `--with-pthreadclasses` option.

The PETSc library can be built in several ways. Before configuring and installing, set (or set in `configure` and/or `make` commands) the variables PETSC_ARCH and PETSC_DIR, specifying the name of the build profile and the path where the library will be installed.

Example of PETSc build with Intel compiler and Intel MPI and MKL libraries:

```
./configure PETSC_ARCH=linux-intel -with-cc=mpicc \
 --with-fc=mpifort --with-blas-lapack-dir=/opt/intel/mkl
```

After running the `./configure` command, run the `make` command:

```
make PETSC_ARCH=linux-intel all test
sudo make install
```

After installation, users can use PETSc by first setting the PETSC_DIR and PETSC_ARCH environment variables. It is recommended to set them in `/etc/profile` or `/etc/bashrc` or, preferred, use Environment Modules or LMOD.

To diagnose problems, I advise you to use the keys when running PETSc programs:

- `-log_summary` – Provide a performance summary at the end of the program

- `-fp_trap` – Stop on floating-point operation exceptions

- `-trdump` – Perform memory tracing, output a list of unreleased memory areas at the end of the program

- `-trmalloc` – Trace memory

- `-start_in_debugger` [noxterm, gdb, dbx, xxgdb] – Start program in debugger

- `-on_error_attach_debugger` [noxterm, gdb, dbx, xxgdb] – Run debugger when an error is detected

These options should not be used by default, but they can help when diagnosing strange behavior of PETSc programs.

FFT/FFTW

The FFTW (Fastest Fourier Transform in the West) library implements the fast discrete Fourier transform. This transform is often used in many numerical algorithms, especially in frequency analysis. The library is a set of C and Fortran modules for computing the Fastest Fourier Transform (FFTW). FFTW allows you to work with both real and complex numbers, with an arbitrary input data size, i.e., with the data length not necessarily being a multiple of 2^n.

The library also includes parallel FFT processing modules that allow its use on multiprocessor machines with shared and distributed memory. FFTW consists of four different variants of FFT calculation:

- One-dimensional transformation for complex numbers
- Multivariate transformation for complex numbers
- One-dimensional transformation for real numbers
- Multivariate transformation for real numbers

To connect the library, you must specify the `-lttfw` switch to the compiler. In addition, you may have to specify paths to directories, containing include-files and the library itself with the `-I` and `-L` keys. There is a parallel variant of FFTW which uses MPI; to compile with it, you should specify the `-lfftw_mpi` switch in addition to the usual library. You should also use parallel FFTW constructs instead of the usual ones in the program source code. The library can often be found in standard packages, but I don't advise you to install it this way. You can download the source code of the library from the official site http://fftw.org/ and compile it with optimization for your processors.

There are two incompatible versions of FFTW – 2 and 3. Both versions may be needed in different applications, so compile and install them. If you have the MKL or ACML library installed, each includes an optimized version of FFTW and manual installation is not required.

TBB

Intel TBB (Intel Threading Building Blocks) library is a library of C++ templates and functions that allows you to simplify writing parallel programs in terms of threads. It supports various thread implementations – POSIX threads, Windows threads, and Boost threads. The library offers a way of building a program "in blocks," abstracting from threads themselves. Due to this approach, the programmer doesn't have to worry about thread synchronization, thread generation, and thread management.

Most standard parallel constructions and algorithms are implemented in the library in the form of "tasks," which are linked together and generate a graph of dynamically generated threads. In the process, the threads are optimized for efficient cache and CPU usage. On the other hand, this approach practically does not allow adapting a ready-made program – the algorithm must be initially written in terms of TBB task blocks.

TBB library exists in two versions: commercial and free open source. The commercial library provides a wider set of algorithms and technical support. As the name implies, the library implements only thread support; it does not contain distributed block tasks. Therefore, working with MPI and distributed memory is left on the programmer's side. It is necessary to be very careful, because in this case, the work on thread synchronization is hidden from the programmer, and in combination with asynchronous MPI calls, it can lead to hard-to-diagnose errors.

Debuggers and Profilers

You cannot do without debugging in any programming, and even more so when developing a parallel application. Even if you use a third-party package rather than your own development, sometimes you need to find out where and why an error occurs. If it is a program package with open source code, you may launch it under a debugger. The source code is needed to compile the package with the debugging information. Usually, it is enough to add the -g option to the compiler and linker.

Unlike sequential programs, parallel programs are executed on several processes and/or threads and often on different nodes at the same time. In this case, traditional debuggers such as gdb (**GNU debugger**) are of very limited use. Many MPI implementations allow you to run under a debugger, in which case each MPI process is run under a debugger program, and if the process crashes, you can log into the debugger and find out the local cause. Unfortunately, it is impossible to know what is happening in the other MPI processes. In some implementations, it is possible to execute the debugger command simultaneously in all processes, but if there are several hundred processes, the output of this command will be simply unreadable.

There are several debuggers specially oriented to work with parallel programs. One of them is **TotalView**. It was developed by Etnus (later renamed TotalView Technologies), which was bought by RogueWave in 2010. This debugger supports most parallel technologies.

The programmers include MPI, OpenMP, OpenACC, and CUDA. Unlike many other debuggers, TotalView optionally adds the possibility of "reverse" debugging, i.e., recording variable values and execution flow and then playing it back. This allows you not only to see the state of the program at the moment of stopping or crashing, but also to go back some time and thus find the cause of incorrect program behavior.

With TotalView, you can connect to an already running application or initially run the application under a debugger. Work with many queue management systems is supported, as well as remote debugging – you can run the debugger on a supercomputer and control debugging on a remote machine, in a separate application (remote client). In debugging mode, many features are available to make it easier to find errors in a parallel program: memory debugging, simultaneous stopping of all threads and processes of the application, viewing the stack and variables of all processes, and more. Besides TotalView, RogueWave offers other tools allowing you to find not only errors but also "bottlenecks" in a program. For example, the **ThreadSpotter** tool can help you identify inefficient memory utilization, thread conflicts, etc.

Another parallel debugger is **DDT** (Distributed Debugging Tool) developed by Allinea (later it was bought by ARM). Its capabilities are similar to those of TotalView in many respects, in some respects it is better, in some respects it is not. For example, there is no "reverse" debugging feature, but there is an offline debugging feature: the program is launched under the debugger, but without an interactive client. After successful or failed completion, the debugger creates a report file that contains all the data that can help in analysis situations – values of variables, stack, suspected memory leaks, etc.

Besides debuggers, whose main task is to help you find errors, there are two other closely related classes of programs – profilers and tracers. Their task is to collect data about program operation for further use. As a rule, these are data about the operation times of separate subroutines, code sections. For parallel programs, they often add information about when and what synchronization means were executed. This allows you to analyze how efficiently the program worked: how much time was spent on data transfer, how much time was lost waiting for synchronization, and so on. As a rule, the **profiler** collects total data about the resources spent (time, memory size, etc.), while the **tracer** records data about events (subroutine call, message reception, etc.) in a file – a **trace.**

The collected trace can be analyzed, visualized, or used in complex analysis. There are several open standards of trace files, so often a trace collected by one tool can be analyzed in another program. The most common trace file formats are **SLOG**, **CLOG**, **OTF**, and **OTF2**. The MPI standard provides a separate mechanism for profiling – **PMPI,** most implementations support it. This standard allows you to load a library that intercepts all MPI calls and can write information about them into a trace (or do something else). Some parallel debuggers also use this interface to debug correctness of parallel programs.

One of the very first packages for tracing MPI programs – MPE[1] – was created in Argonne Laboratory for MPICH, but currently works with OpenMPI. The package includes a set of libraries for profiling and tracing, as well as the **Jump Shot** SLOG trace visualization package. The package is free and distributed in source code. Figure 22-2 shows an example of visualization of MPI exchanges in Jump Shot. There are several commercial tracers for MPI (and not only), which provide different modes of trace collection, as well as their visualization and analysis. The most popular ones are Intel Trace Collector and Analyzer (ITAC) and Vampir.

---

[1] http://www.mcs.anl.gov/research/projects/perfvis/download/index.htm

CHAPTER 22 PARALLEL COMPUTING SUPPORT LIBRARIES

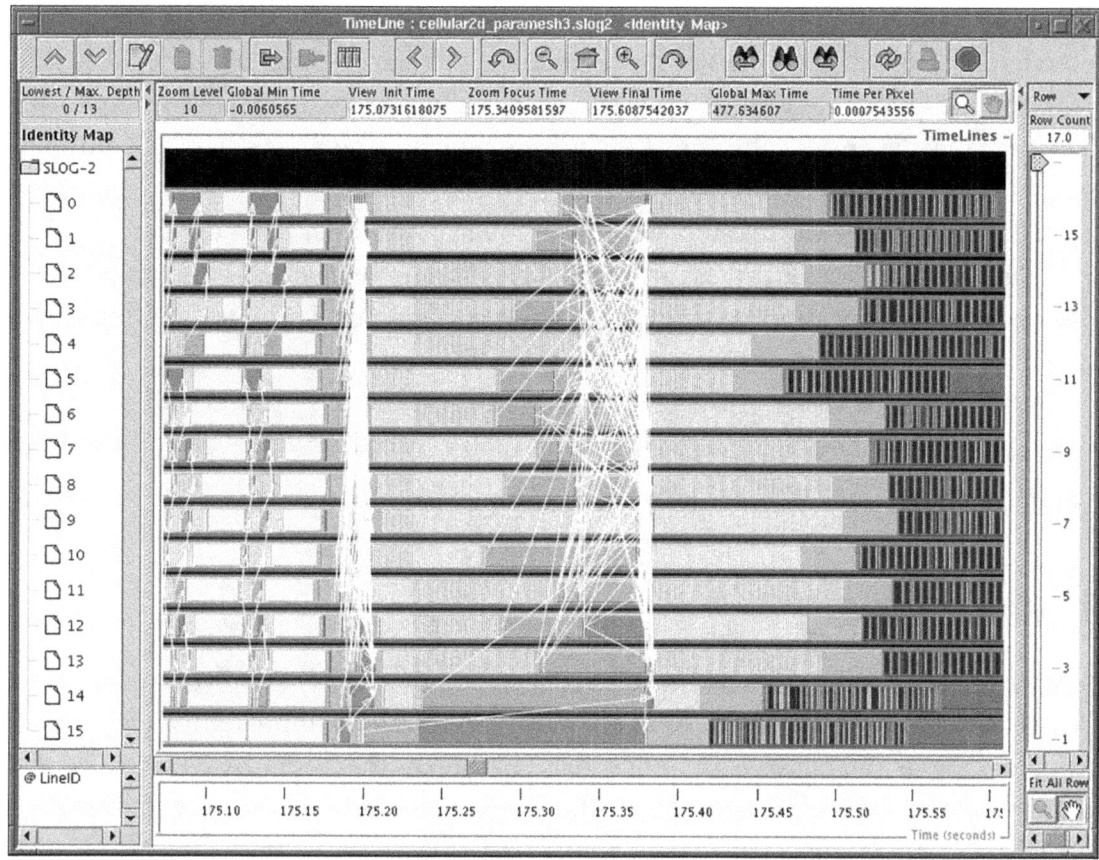

Figure 22-2. Jump Shot interface example

Vampir (http://www.vampir.eu/) is one of the oldest commercial tools for profiling and exploring parallel programs. It can use traces collected by third-party tools; open OTF (Open Trace Format) is used as a standard format. The open library VampirTrace is used to collect traces by means of Vampir itself. This library is widely used for trace collection by third-party programs. Vampir is available for 32- and 64-bit versions of Linux, as well as for Windows and MacOS. A demo version of the product can be downloaded on the website. Vampir supports a variety of options for displaying the collected information and also allows you to automatically search for potential application problems – reduced efficiency, "bottlenecks."

Another popular tools for trace collection and analysis are Intel Advisor, Intel Inspector, and Intel **VTune**, included into **Intel oneAPI HPC Toolkit**. They use its own trace format – **STF**. A trace for ITAC can be collected automatically if the application uses Intel MPI; for this purpose, it is enough to specify an additional key at startup.

CHAPTER 22 PARALLEL COMPUTING SUPPORT LIBRARIES

You can also start an MPI application with a special wrapper program or instrument it beforehand. Depending on the settings, a full trace or a sample trace will be collected; in the latter case, the analysis accuracy will be lower, but the program performance will be close to the real one. VTune and ITAC provide probably the most advanced and deep analysis of the program efficiency.

In the open source world, there is TAU – Tuning and Analysis Utilities,[2] developed in the University of Oregon. This is a powerful toolkit, providing tracing and analyzing collected traces. It has Jump Shot integration and own graphical tools to view and analyze collected data.

For debugging NVIDIA GPU applications, you can use `cuda-gdb` and `cuda-nsight` packages, which should be included into cuda-toolkit by default. cuda-gdb can be used instead of gdb binary in any GUI packages like DDD, VSCode, etc.

Brief Summary

Optimized libraries and debugging tools seem to be unnecessary for a system administrator, but their presence (and active use) significantly improves the efficiency of a supercomputer and increases its efficiency. This means that users are less worried and come to you with problems. It is an important task of an administrator to install and help users to master these tools.

Search Keywords

Scalapack, BLAS, PETSc, parallel debugging, parallel tracer, OTF2, SLOG, MKL, ACML, VTune, oneAPI HPC toolkit, TAU

---

[2] https://www.cs.uoregon.edu/research/tau/home.php

CHAPTER 23

Booting and Init

This chapter is a bit out of the ordinary. It is a bit like Chapter 7, so it will be of no use to experienced administrators. Here I would like to take a closer look at the process of booting the server, both from disk and over the network. Understanding the stages and logic of this process can help a lot in some situations, e.g., with a broken xCAT.

In addition to booting, it also covers the operation of the "main" process in Linux – init, i.e., the first process in the system. So, if you are interested in the details, go ahead! But let's start by describing the procedure of turning on and starting any computer, so that we can understand how init itself is started and what happens before it.

Booting from Hard Disk

The boot procedure automatically starts when the computer is powered up. The process begins by transferring control to the built-in system test program (Power-On Self-Test Procedure – POST). During the test, the hardware is checked, and external devices are numbered and initialized.

There are two[1] mechanisms for booting an operating system, BIOS (Basic Input-Output System) and UEFI (Unified Extensible Firmware Interface). BIOS is a very old system, but still in use. To boot using BIOS, the disk is partitioned using MBR (Master Boot Record). MBR is the first sector of the disk (sector 1, cylinder 0, head 0) with a size of 512 bytes. The MBR contains the disk partition table and the bootloader. The number of **primary** partitions is limited to four; to create more partitions, you must create a special, so-called **extended partition**, in whose space additional partitions are created. The MBR partition size is limited to two terabytes. At boot, BIOS reads the MBR into memory and transfers control to the bootloader.

---

[1] Actually more, but x86/x86-64 systems traditionally use these.

MBR is replaced by GPT – GUID Partition Table, where the possible number of partitions is 128 and the partition size is more than 18 exabytes. Along with GPT, BIOS is replaced by UEFI (Unified Extensible Firmware Interface). For UEFI operation, a special "system" partition is created with the code EF00, formatted in VFAT32, where, in particular, bootloaders, drivers, device firmware, etc., are placed. The size of the system partition can be much larger than 512 bytes, so the situation with bootloaders is much better. The default bootloader is \efi\boot\boot[architecture name].efi, e.g., for x86-64, the file will be called bootx64.efi. In the system menu, you can usually choose an alternative bootloader.

We will consider booting using MBR as an example, since the process is not fundamentally different from UEFI. The first 446 bytes of MBR represent the program code of the bootloader. The 64 bytes located after the bootloader contain the partition table. The table can hold a record of four primary disk partitions (16 bytes each). At the end of the MBR, there are two bytes, and they are called "magic numbers" (0xAA55). This magic number is used to verify the integrity of the MBR.

The purpose of the bootloader is to find and load the main boot program and transfer control to it. Currently, the primary bootloader for Linux operating systems is GRUB (GRand Unified Bootloader).

One of the main advantages of GRUB is that it can understand the file systems used in Linux. GRUB is capable of booting the Linux kernel from file systems such as ext3 and vfat32, unlike previous bootloaders such as LILO, which first had to remember the sector numbers of the kernel disk and read the kernel code from them when booting.

The ability to work with file systems is achieved by introducing another stage at boot, making the two-stage bootloader a three-stage bootloader. Stage 1 (MBR) loads a 1.5-stage loader capable of understanding the file system where the Linux kernel image is stored. Examples are xfs_stage1_5 (for booting from the XFS file system) or e2fs_stage1_5 (for booting from ext2, ext3,ext4 file systems).

After the stage 1.5 bootloader has been run, the stage 2 bootloader can be loaded. After loading stage 2, GRUB offers to make a choice from the available set of kernels, which are listed in a special configuration file /boot/grub/grub.cfg (for old version 1 /boot/grub/menu.lst), or to load a default kernel. It is possible to pass additional parameters to the bootable kernel before starting the boot procedure, or to load a nonstandard kernel and initial system image (initrd). This is very useful if the bootloader is corrupted, and you are booting from an external disk. In this case, you can manually specify boot parameters, and after booting, install the bootloader again.

If the user does not interfere with the boot process, the second stage bootloader loads the default kernel image and `initrd` image into memory. Once the kernel image is in memory, it receives control from the second stage loader. The stage of kernel loading comes. The kernel loading procedure also consists of several stages. In most Linux distributions, the kernel image is compressed. The kernel can be packed using zImage or bzImage, which use the libz or libbz2 library. At the beginning of the compressed kernel image is a program that performs minimal hardware configuration and then unpacks the kernel, placing it in the top memory location.

If the `initrd` RAM disk image is required to start the kernel, the program will also place it into RAM. The program is completed by passing control to the `start_kernel()` function, which performs further actions to prepare and configure the hardware to start the operating system.

`initrd` acts as a temporary root file system in RAM so that the kernel can fully boot without mounting any physical disks. Typically, `initrd` contains the kernel modules it needs to communicate with peripherals. This organization of the boot process allows you to work with a very compact kernel and still support a wide variety of hardware configurations. Once the kernel is booted, the `initrd` root file system is replaced by the real root file system.

In computers without a hard disk, `initrd` is not replaced by another file system or the root file system is mounted using NFS (network file system). After loading the kernel, whose task is to make sure that the computer's devices work, the root file system is mounted, and the `init` process is started. To start it, the kernel looks for the `/sbin/init` executable or the file specified in the kernel's "`init`" parameter at startup. If no such file exists, the kernel tries several standard names and crashes if it finds no candidates for init. As a rule, init has PID = 1.

INIT in SystemV Style

Yes, I know that modern distributions don't use SystemV-style init. You safely can skip it and look into `systemd`. But, some parts of SystemV init are alive even in 2025, so you may spend 15 minutes and know how this legacy works.

A few words about the role of `init` in Linux. It is the only process that is monitored by the kernel – if init terminates, the kernel crashes. The task of init is to configure the system, mount the necessary file systems, and start the initial set of services and programs. Another function of init is to terminate zombie processes if they have no parent (they are automatically "assigned" to init's descendants) by calling the wait system call.

CHAPTER 23 BOOTING AND INIT

The standard init program (SystemV style)[2] reads the configuration file /etc/inittab and starts various processes according to this file. The most important line of the /etc/inittab file is the following line:

id:<number>:initdefault

This entry specifies the startup level of the system at boot time. The startup level determines which scripts the init process will execute. By default, there are six levels in the system:

0. System shutdown

1. Single-user mode

2. Multiplayer mode without network support

3. Multiplayer mode with network support

4. Not being used

5. Multiplayer mode with network support and graphical shell launch

6. Reboot

Different Linux distributions may have their own special system boot levels, but this is very rare.

Linux system is most often booted to either level 3 or level 5. You can change the level by running the following command:

init <Level number>

The init 6 command starts the system reboot, and init 0 turns it off. In addition to the line specifying the default system boot level, there are other lines in the configuration file /etc/inittab. If a line starts with a # sign, it is considered a comment and is not processed by the init command. All other lines consist of four colon-separated fields:

id:runlevels:action:process

---

[2] SystemV is one of the UNIX versions. For a long time, there were two main types of init program configuration files, SystemV-style and BSD-style. Some distributions (e.g., Slackware) use BSD-style init.

where

- `id` – String identifier. It is an arbitrary combination of one to four characters. There cannot be two lines with the same id in the `inittab` file.
- `runlevels` – runlevels at which this string will be used. The levels are specified by numbers or letters without separators, e.g., 35.
- `process` – The process to be run at the specified levels. In other words, this field specifies the name of the program to be called when moving to the specified execution levels.
- `action`.

The `action` field contains a keyword that specifies additional conditions for executing the command specified by the `process` field. Valid values of the `action` field are

- `respawn` – Restart the process if it terminates.
- `once` – Execute the process only once when moving to the specified level.
- `wait` – The process will be started once when going to the specified level and init will wait for this process to complete before proceeding.
- `sysinit` – This keyword indicates the very first actions performed by the `init` process before it moves to any level of execution (the `id` field is ignored). Processes labeled with this word start before processes labeled with `boot` and `bootwait`.
- `boot` – The process will be started at the system boot stage regardless of the execution level.
- `bootwait` – The process will be started at the system boot stage regardless of the execution level, and `init` will wait for it to complete.
- `initdefault` – The line with this word in the action field defines the execution level to which the system switches by default. The `process` field in this line is ignored. If the default execution level is not specified, the `init` process will wait until the user starting the system enters it from the console.

CHAPTER 23   BOOTING AND INIT

- off – Ignore this element. It is convenient to use it for making temporary changes.

- powerwait – Allows the init process to stop the system when power is lost. The use of this word assumes that there is an uninterruptible power supply (UPS) and software that monitors the status of the UPS and informs init that power has failed.

- ctrlaltdel – Allows init to reboot the system when the user presses the <Ctrl>+<Alt>+<Del> key combination on the keyboard. Note that the system administrator can define actions on the <Ctrl>+<Alt>+<Del> key combination, e.g., ignore pressing this combination (which is quite reasonable in a system with many users).

Having determined the boot level number, the system starts executing boot scripts from the /etc/rc.d/rc<number_level>.d directory; if you look through the contents of this directory with the ls command, you will see that there are references with special names like S<number><name> and K<number><name>.

<Number> specifies the sequence number of the script execution on loading. A script reference with the number 15 will be executed before a reference with the number 20.

<name> specifies the name of the script to be executed. The scripts themselves are located in the /etc/init.d directory.

The letter S or K specifies the parameters with which scripts in the /etc/init.d directory will be executed. The scripts in this directory have many options, but the two main ones are start and stop. References starting with S will run scripts with the start option, and those starting with K will be executed with the stop option. Scripts to start services can also be executed at any point in the system. For example, to start the apache web server, just run the following command:

```
/etc/init.d/apache2 start
```

If the web server is already running, the script will give you a message about it.

There are two ways to specify that the server automatically starts at system startup. The first is to run the chkconfig command (for RedHat-like systems) or update-rc.d (for Debian-like systems). Console command:

```
chkconfig apache2 on
```

or

```
update-rc.d apache2 enable
```

By default, apache2 will start at boot levels 3 and 5. The `chkconfig` and `update-rc.d` commands allow you to specify at which boot level the service should start.

In standard UNIX systems, boot scripts were just ordinary scripts that prepared the environment for running daemons (otherwise known as services or services, which we will discuss later in a separate chapter) and took the words `start` or `stop` as command-line arguments.

On Linux systems, `init` scripts are shell scripts, but they often already contain additional information about the procedure for running them, allowing the system to automatically determine when the script should be executed when the system boots. This information is specified in comments in the first lines of the script – the header. Here is an example of such a script header:

```
### BEGIN INIT INFO
# Provides: skeleton
# Required-Start: $remote_fs $syslog
# Required-Stop: $remote_fs $syslog
# Default-Start: 2 3 4 5
# Default-Stop: 0 1 6
# Short-Description: Example initscript
# Description: This file should be used to construct scripts to be
# placed in /etc/init.d.
# Should-Start: $portmap
# Should-Stop: $portmap
# X-Start-Before: nis
# X-Stop-After: nis
# X-Interactive: true
```

Each line is labeled with a # comment icon. The `chkconfig` command analyzes this information when it creates references in the `rcN.d` directories. The `Required-Start` keyword specifies which services must be loaded by the time the script runs. In this example, the remote file system services and the system log must be started.

The `$remote_fs` construct denotes a set of services required to maintain remote file systems. Such services are described in the `/etc/insserv.conf` file.

`Required-Stop` specifies the services that must be stopped before running the script with the `stop` argument.

`Default-Start` specifies the levels for starting the daemon by default; if not specified in the `chkconfig` command arguments, the script will be activated at the appropriate system boot levels when the `daemon enable` command is executed.

The other keywords have the same meanings, specifying when the daemon should be started. The directory structure in which initialization scripts are located can vary significantly from distribution to distribution. The major commercial Linux distributions – SuSE and RedHat – try to follow the directory structure of initialization scripts defined in the UNIX SystemV standard. But since Linux is not always rigidly adhering to the standards, the directory structure can vary.

For example, most Linux distributions have a script called `rc.local`, which historically came from FreeBSD. This script is executed last during the boot process. It can be used to run your own commands, but it is desirable to do it as a separate script. The use of `rc.local` is allowed, but not recommended.

Finishing the topic of system booting, I would like to draw attention to a problem faced by cluster administrators when installing a system on a system installed on a hard disk by cloning. Often a system installed on a hard disk by cloning refuses to boot or mount file systems. This happens because when installing the system, factory disk identifiers are written in the configuration files in the disk partition addresses. This is done to increase the system security, but the system rewritten to another disk will not be able to find the required partitions. Therefore, before the cloning procedure, you should carefully review and correct the configuration files of the bootloader (`/boot/grub/menu.lst` or `/boot/grub/grub.cfg`) and mounter (`/etc/fstab`) on the prototype node by deleting disk identifiers in the partition addresses.

Systemd

Today, the most common init implementation is `systemd`; let's take a look on it.

Besides the standard SystemV-style init, there are several other popular boot managers: `daemontools`, `OpenRC`, `Upstart`, `Initng`, and others. Some of them are just lightweight versions of `init` (for embedded devices, e.g.), and some of them try to solve the problem of parallel loading and service dependencies.

Parallel loading is an important problem of standard init, it starts services only sequentially, and this can take a long time. Attempts to introduce elements of parallelism in standard init by introducing special comments in the start scripts have failed.

Lennart Poettering, working at RedHat, with the participation of developers from Novell, IBM, Intel, and Nokia, has developed a new initialization system for the Linux operating system – systemd. The reason for creating systemd was the desire to make greater use of parallel execution of services at boot time, providing administrators with a number of new features that greatly simplify the process of system maintenance. Currently, systemd is used as init in many distributions, including RedHat/Centos (since version 7), Fedora, Debian, Archlinux, and others.

Standard UNIX and Linux services (daemons) are started via init scripts. Such a script prepares the environment for the daemon and then starts it. Scripts are written in shell, so they are characterized by low speed and are difficult to parse because of the abundance of hard-to-read code. Many tasks arising when working with services are rather hard to solve by means of scripts, e.g., such as organizing parallel execution, correct tracking of processes, and configuration of various parameters of the process execution environment.

There are advantages to using scripts: they are familiar to many administrators, and you can see the progress of starting or stopping a service. Therefore, systemd can also use standard init scripts to start system services, but this is sometimes problematic, so try not to do this.

You can determine which initialization method your distribution uses by looking at the name of the first process. If the process is named systemd, or init is a symbolic reference to /bin/systemd.

The basic concept of systemd is a unit, which is a description of a service, a group of services, just a command to be executed, etc. Units can be related to each other and always have a certain type. The key type is target – analog of runlevel in init, but unlike it, several targets can be activated simultaneously. Essentially, target is a list of dependencies. A normal unit can be stopped or restarted. In the case of a target, restarting is impossible, and it is generally not possible to stop all units included in it. To stop a unit automatically if all the targets it is part of are stopped, you must have the StopWhenUnneeded=yes directive in its description.

If you still need to stop all units from some target, you can use the type following command:

```
systemctl stop -- $(systemctl show \
  -p Wants MYTARGET.target | cut -d= -f2)
```

That is, get the list of required units from the target description, select only the name from the list, and substitute the list into the stop command. There may be other variants.

To force a switch to a target, stopping all units not included in it, type

`systemctl isolate rescue`

Here `rescue` is the name of the target, in this example a single-user mode.

There are various kinds of units in `systemd`, the following are the main ones:

- `service` – Services that can be started and stopped. Services can be classic SysV scripts of daemon initialization.
- `slice` – A group of processes, in a separate `cgroup` space (e.g., user session, cron task, etc.).
- `socket` – Bind points to network or file sockets, allowing to build an association with a certain service (analog of `inetd`).
- `device` – Elements of the device tree that can be handled by udev.
- `mount` – Specify the file systems used, which are found in `/etc/fstab`.
- `automount` – Determines which FS to `mount` when accessing a given directory.
- `target` – Used for logical grouping of units. For example, `multi-user.target` is identical to runlevel 5, `bluetooth.target` causes the bluetooth subsystem to initialize, etc.
- `timer` – Designed to replace cron, runs on a schedule.

Each unit can require other units for its correct operation, conflict with units, define the possibility to run only after or before a certain unit (configuration directives `Requires`, `Conflicts`, `Before`, `After`, `Wants`). Systemd starts each unit in a separate namespace, which allows you to group all processes running within a unit (and if necessary, terminate them forcibly), set uniform restrictions for them, etc.

You can get a list of running services by using the `systemctl` command, which gives the administrator a wide range of options for managing services. Common uses of this command are presented in Table 23-1.

Table 23-1. Some systemctl commands

Command	Meaning
systemctl **stop** name.service	Service stop
systemctl **start** name.service	Service startup
systemctl **restart** name.service	Service restart
systemctl **status** name.service	Service status information
systemctl **enable** name.service	Allow service startup
systemctl **disable** name.service	Prohibit service startup
systemctl **list-units**	List of running services
systemctl **list-units --all**	Status of all running services

Running services, as mentioned above, can be both standard init scripts and systemd units. Files describing the units can be located in /etc/systemd/system (recommended for nonstandard units or standard units modifications), /usr/lib/systemd/system (from the distribution), and /run/systemd/system (created automatically). You can display the list of units and slides in the form of a process tree with the command systemd-cgls.

Chapter "Systemd – A Short Course" will go into more detail about unit files, if you need to create or customize your own service for systemd, look there. There will also be a more complete list of systemctl commands.

Systemd goes beyond service management and includes additional subsystems that you can optionally enable and disable. Table 23-2 presents the types of systemd units, supported at the time of writing.

Table 23-2. Main types of units in systemd

Unit type/function	Description
systemd-tempfiles	Creating and deleting temporary files and directories
systemd-networkd	Network address and route management
timers	Replacing the `crond` service via the `timer` unit type
journal	Replacing `syslog`, `rsyslog` can automatically retrieve data from journal; see chapter "Systemd – A Short Course" for details
Fstab	Mounting file systems is also assigned to systemd, as long as full compatibility with historical `/etc/fstab` is maintained Note separately the `automount` unit type and the `udisks2` subsystem that automatically mounts removable media, it has almost become part of systemd
socket activation	`inetd/xinetd` replacement, implemented in the `socket` unit type
activation by file or directory change	`icron` replacement, implemented in unit type `path`
traffic filtering and counting	In units, you can enable a set of rules to limit the addresses available to the service over the network and traffic accounting
managing some virtual machines	The `systemd-nspawnd` service manages lightweight virtual machines a-la `lxc`
time synchronization	Replacing `ntpd` with `systemd-timesyncd` service
name resolution	Replacing DNS `resolver` with `systemd-resolved` service, use `resolvectl status` to get current settings
user sessions	`logind` – a systemd component, controlling users' sessions

One special type of units – user unit. It describes user session properties and limits. Default files, describing it, are in /usr/lib/systemd/system/user-.slice.d/*.conf, and some useful settings of logind (which controls the sessions) can be found in /etc/systemd/logind.conf. Some interesting parameters in the user-.slice:

- CPUAccounting=yes – Turn on CPU accounting
- CPUQuota=10% – Limit CPU usage by no more 10% CPU (CPU accounting should be on)

- `MemoryAccounting=yes TasksAccounting=yes IOAccounting=yes IPAccounting=yes` – Accounting for memory, processes, I/O, IP addresses
- `MemoryHigh=bytes MemoryMax=bytes` – Set soft and hard mem limits
- `TasksMax=N` – Set processes limit
- `IOReadBandwidthMax=device bytes, IOWriteBandwidthMax=device bytes, IOReadIOPSMax=device IOPS, IOWriteIOPSMax=device IOPS` – Set limits for I/O on a device by bandwidth or IOPs
- `IPAddressAllow=ADDRESS[/PREFIXLENGTH] IPAddressDeny=ADDRESS[/PREFIXLENGTH]` – Limit IP addresses access
- `RestrictNetworkInterfaces=ifaces_list` – Limit access to the network interfaces

In the `logind.conf` file, you can set an option `KillUserProcesses=yes` if you want to kill all processes on session end. Note that it breaks screen/tmux/etc sessions!

If you want to set specific limits to one user, instead of defaults, use `/etc/systemd/system/user-NNN.slice` file (or corresponding directory), where NNN is the numeric user UID.

Network Booting

It is not uncommon for supercomputer nodes to be diskless, and even if there are disks on the nodes, they do not have their own copy of the OS. In this case, network booting is required to start the nodes. To boot over the network on a node, you need a network card whose BIOS supports PXE booting (most cards can do this), as well as the option to boot over the network in the node's BIOS/UEFI. DHCP and TFTP services must be running on the server.

The boot process is similar to booting from a local disk:

- The BIOS/UEFI of the node is started at power up.
- Control is transferred to the BIOS of the network card.
- The BIOS of the network card sends a BOOTP request.

- The DHCP server sends boot parameters (TFTP server address, etc.).

- The BIOS of the network card loads the bootloader via TFTP protocol and transfers control to it.

- Loader loads the kernel and `initrd` image over the network and passes control to the kernel.

We will look at DHCP and TFTP configuration in more detail later.

Typically, a parameter is passed to the kernel at boot to indicate that the root file system is located on a network drive. Linux so far only supports NFS as a network root. It is theoretically possible to use other options (e.g., Lustre), but this would require a lot of manual work to optimize the `initrd` image. The best option is to use read-only NFS for the root system.

When booting a large number of nodes, you should be careful and boot them one by one with an interval of at least one to two seconds. This is due to several factors. Firstly, it is dangerous for the infrastructure equipment to increase power consumption sharply; it may end up with an emergency shutdown. Secondly, if a one-rank network and one DHCP/TFTP server are used, then at mass startup the network will be flooded by broadcast requests. The servers may not be able to cope with the flow of UDP packets, since UDP is a protocol without reliable data transmission, some nodes will simply fail to boot. For such a "DDOS-attack,"[3] it is usually enough to have five to ten nodes booting at the same time.

When mounting a network root, there is a problem with directories that should be writable – `/tmp`, `/var`, possibly some others if specific software is installed. To avoid this, you can apply a **tmpfs** file system that uses RAM. For the `/tmp` directory, this is solved simply by writing to `/etc/fstab`. For `/var`, it is a bit more complicated, as it must include a system of subdirectories and the contents of some of them do not change (e.g., `/var/lib`). One solution is to use `/var` on NFS and replace the directories in which the files should change with symbolic links to directories located on tmpfs or directly mount them as tmpfs. Be careful using tmpfs, as it takes up RAM. Just in case, set a hard limit on its size with the option `size=xxxMb` or `size=yyy%`, where xxx is the size in megabytes and yyy is the percentage of total memory. This parameter is specified in the `options` field in the `/etc/fstab` file.

---

[3] A distributed denial of service attack.

I recommend setting up remote logging so that node logs are not written to /var/log on the node, but to the server. Check the documentation for rsyslog or the version of syslog you have installed to configure remote logging.

So, to make network booting work, install DHCP and TFTP servers, install and configure the network bootloader, prepare images for booting, and configure nodes for network booting. Let's see how to do all this!

DHCP

Dynamic Host Configuration Protocol is a protocol used for initial configuration of computers. It allows you to get data about IP addresses, boot parameters, and some other parameters. I will focus only on the ones we are interested in for computing cluster operation: IP addresses, routing settings, and DNS server. Currently, there are many implementations of the DHCP server, but in most cases, Linux uses the ISC implementation, so this is what we are going to look at.

First, install the dhcp-server from the OS package manager (usually the package is called dhcp-server). After that, make sure that the server starts automatically in the init scripts. The DHCP server configuration specifies the parameters of the server itself, the address ranges that will be "handed out" by the server, and the parameters that will be passed along with the address. These parameters are known as options and have fixed numbers and names. A list of them can be found on the Internet, e.g., at this address: https://www.iana.org/assignments/bootp-dhcp-parameters/bootp-dhcp-parameters.xhtml.

We will be interested in the following options:

- routers – List of IP addresses used for the default route
- ntp-servers – List of NTP servers addresses
- domain-name-servers – List of DNS servers addresses

In addition, the parameters passed to clients are important: next-server and filename. These are, respectively, the address of the TFTP server from which the file will be downloaded and the name of the file. The configuration is typically located in the /etc/dhcp/dhcpd.conf file, and usually, there are already some commented examples there. Unlike "office" solutions, where the workstation does not care what IP address it gets, in a cluster, it is highly desirable that each node has a fixed address. Otherwise, diagnosing hardware problems can become very difficult.

CHAPTER 23 BOOTING AND INIT

First, we need a list of MAC addresses of all nodes. This is not an easy task, as it is not very convenient to load each node and write out its address. There are several ways to solve it:

- If the nodes themselves have the MAC address written on them, you can collect them manually.

- If your Ethernet switch has SNMP support, you can enable all nodes and collect MAC address statistics by port.

- Or use the same dhcp server!

Let's consider the last option, because the server keeps records of all requests. By default, requests are logged via syslog to the /var/log/syslog or /var/log/messages file. If this does not happen for some reason, check if logging is enabled in your DHCP server, or run it in debug mode and redirect the output to a file.

Beforehand, we need to create a "normal" configuration file, such as this one:

```
subnet 192.168.123.0 netmask 255.255.255.0 {
  range 192.168.123.10 192.168.123.100;
}
```

Here we specify that in the 192.168.123.0/24 network, a range of addresses with the last octet from 10 to 100 is allocated for distribution to clients. Make sure that the addresses do not conflict with the addresses on the main network! Now start the DHCP server with the dhcpd eth0 command, where eth0 is the compute node network interface (don't confuse it with an external interface). To make the DHCP server start correctly from the init script, specify this interface in the /etc/sysconfig/dhcpd file (for RH-like systems) with the line "DHCPDARGS=ethX" or in the /etc/default/dhcp3 file (for Debian-like systems) with the line "INTERFACES=ethX". Check if everything worked: click on the power button on the first node and wait for loading to start. A message like this should appear in the log:

```
dhcpd: DHDISCOVER 00:01:02:03:04:05 via eth0
```

That is, the MAC address of our server is 00:01:02:03:04:05. It remains to turn on all nodes in turn (do it with an interval of 5–10 seconds, no less) and get the list of addresses in the required order by command:

```
grep DHDISCOVER /var/log/syslog | awk '{print $3}' > macs.txt
```

Make sure that you get the same number of addresses as nodes. If there is a discrepancy, check which node did not make it to the download.

Now let's generate a new configuration file for dhcpd. Let's make a script:

```bash
#!/usr/bin/env bash
n=10
for mac in $(cat macs.txt); do
  n0=$(printf "%02d" "$n")
  echo <<END
  host node-$n0 {
    fixed-address 192.168.123.$n;
    hardware ethernet $mac
    option host-name node-$n0;
  }
END
  n=$((n+1))
done
```

In this script, we assume that node names will be of the form node-NN. If this is not the case, modify the script as you need. It is also assumed that addresses are issued sequentially from 192.168.123.10.

The script generates a record of the form for each node:

```
host node-10 {
  fixed-address 192.168.123.10;
  hardware ethernet 01:02:03:04:05:06
  option host-name node-10;
}
```

Here we specify that MAC address 01:02:03:04:05:06 will be given the IP address 192.168.123.10 and assigned the name 'node-10'. Let's run the script and redirect the output to the dhcpd.conf.new file. Edit the resulting file by adding to the beginning of the line:

```
max-lease-time 1200;
default-lease-time 600;
ddns-update-style none; ddns-updates off;
```

```
subnet 192.168.123.0 netmask 255.255.255.0 {
      range 192.168.123.150 192.168.123.200;
      allow unknown-clients;
      allow bootp;
      filename "pxelinux.0";
      next-server 192.168.123.222;
      option routers 192.168.123.222;
      option ntp-servers 192.168.123.222;
      option domain-name-servers 192.168.123.222;
```

Add one line '}' at the end to close the subnet definition block. In this example, we have specified the address range that is "served" by this DHCP server (subnet). The range from which addresses will be issued (from 150 to 200) – there is no MAC address binding for them (range), specified DNS-, NTP-servers, and default route (domain-name-servers, ntp-servers, routers), as well as the file name for TFTP upload and TFTP server addresses. Global options at the beginning of the file specify the lifetime of the issued address (max-lease-time) in seconds, the recommended address update time (default-lease-time), and disable DNS server notifications about address issuance (ddns-*).

Now you can save the old /etc/dhcp/dhcpd.conf file somewhere (don't delete it!), rename our new one to /etc/dhcp/dhcpd.conf, and restart dhcpd, making sure it is configured for the correct interface. If you don't want to stay in the machine room for a long time, you can try to "pull" the MAC address records of the enabled nodes from the Ethernet router. To do this, use the snmpwalk command. If it is not found, install the net-snmp-utils or snmp package. Run the following command:

```
snmpwalk -c public -v2c swaddr iso.org.dod.internet.mgmt.mib-2.dot1dBridge.
dot1dTp.dot1dTpFdbTable.dot1dTpFdbEntry.1
```

Here swaddr is the address of the switch. The result should be a list of strings of the form:

```
17.4.3.1.1.1.0.0.12.7.172.8 = Hex: 00 00 00 0C 07 AC 08
17.4.3.1.1.1.0.1.2.27.80.145 = Hex: 00 01 01 02 1B 50 91
```

where each line is a representation of one cell in the switch's arp-cache. To understand which port each cell corresponds to, run the following command:

```
snmpwalk -c public -v2c swaddr iso.org.dod.internet.mgmt.mib-2.dot1dBridge.
dot1dTp.dot1dTpFdbTable.dot1dTpFdbEntry.2
```

As a result, we get a list of the form

```
17.4.3.1.2.0.0.12.7.172.8 = 13
17.4.3.1.2.0.1.2.27.80.145 = 14
```

Here we see the same cell numbers, but their values are not MAC addresses, but port numbers. There can be multiple addresses on one port, but in the case of compute nodes, this should not usually be the case. I leave writing a script that builds a correspondence of port number to MAC address and generates configuration for DHCP server as an exercise.

Please note that UEFI and legacy BIOS require different bootloaders (see PXE below), and if you have a mix, then you need to provide correct "filename" option for each. The DHCP client sends information about the architecture, including UEFI support,[4] and you can include block like this in your subnet definition (codes are taken from RFC4578):

```
class "uefi-x86-64" {
  match if substring(option vendor-class-identifier, 0, 20) = "PXEClient:Arch:00009";
  filename "ipxe.efi";
}
class "legacy" {
  match if substring(option vendor-class-identifier, 0, 20) = "PXEClient:Arch:00000";
  filename "pxelinux.0";
}
```

TFTP, PXE, and NFS-Root

TFTP (Trivial File Transfer Protocol) was developed as a simple variant of FTP specifically for implementation in hardware. It is actively used for downloading data to routers, network cards, PBXs, etc. Unlike FTP, there is no authentication, the set of commands is extremely simplified (there are only two commands on the client side), and the transfer is performed in blocks.

---

[4] http://tools.ietf.org/html/rfc4578

To set up a tftp server, it is enough to install the standard package from the distribution and configure it to distribute a separate directory (usually /tftproot or /srv/tftproot). In network booting, an OS bootloader is passed to the network card via the TFTP protocol. This is regulated by the standard **PXE** (Preboot eXecution Environment, pronounced "pixie") environment. Typically, a file from the syslinux package is used as the bootloader. Install this package and copy the file /usr/share/syslinux/pxelinux.0 to the root directory of the TFTP server.

Besides the bootloader itself, the kernel and initrd image to be booted and the directory with the bootloader configurations should be copied to this directory. If all nodes are loaded the same way, you can use one configuration file for all of them. All configuration files are located in the pxelinux.cfg directory, you need to create it yourself. Make sure it is read-only for everyone. The default configuration file is named default.

An example of such a file:

```
default linux
timeout 30

label linux
kernel vmlinux
append initrd=myinitrd splash=silent ip=dhcp root=/dev/nfs \
  nfsroot=192.168.123.1:/noderoot,rsize=8192,wsize=8192,\
  retrans=10,soft,intr

label single
kernel vmlinux
append initrd=myinitrd single ip=dhcp root=/dev/nfs \
  nfsroot=192.168.123.1:/noderoot,rsize=8192,wsize=8192,\
  retrans=10,soft,intr
```

Here the long lines are moved for ease of reading, but in a real file, everything should be on one line. At the beginning, we specify the default linux boot option, with a timeout of three seconds (timeout 30). Then we describe the boot options themselves. In this case, there are two of them – linux and single. The label directive marks a new variant and its name. The kernel directive specifies the name of the kernel file on the TFTP server, and the append directive specifies the kernel parameters.

In the kernel parameters, we specify:

- `initrd` – Name of the file with the `initrd` image on the TFTP server.
- `ip` – IP address of the host; in this case, it is obtained via `dhcp`.
- `root` is the path to the root file system; here it is NFS.
- `nfsroot` – Mount parameters of the final NFS partition.

Note that network booting can also be successfully used for initial installation of the OS on local compute nodes. In this case, you should use the files from the distribution intended for network installation as the kernel and `initrd`. Most likely, you will need to perform a "reference" installation on a node and use the resulting file with its description for network installation (e.g., `kickstart.cfg`, `autoinst.xml`). For more details, see the instructions for network installation of the OS.

Now, after turning on the host and passing control to the BIOS of the network card, we should see DHCP address acquisition, `pxelinux` booting, and a small menu with a list of boot options (in our case `linux` and `single`). After three seconds, the default option should boot.

The root file system on NFS has a lot of peculiarities, and simply taking a copy of the file system from a local disk will not work. If this is really necessary, you will need to add lines to `/etc/fstsb` to mount some directories in `tmpfs`, such as `/var/run`, `/var/cache`, `/var/lock`, `/tmp`, etc. It is best to use ready-made solutions from your OS distribution that generate `initrd` with the right parameters and perform the necessary preparation. For RedHat, it is `dracut-network`; for Debian/Ubuntu, it is `nfsbooted`.

Brief Summary

Booting compute nodes over the network is a good idea, but requires a lot of preparation. If you don't want to do this preparation yourself, use xCAT (see Chapter 19), but you need to know how it works.

Search Keywords

systemd, SystemV, linux init, UEFI, DHCP, Bootp, PXE, ARP, network broadcast, syslinux, pxelinux, kickstart, autoyast

CHAPTER 24

Node Setup and Software Installation

Network and Hardware Drivers

Most network drivers are included in the Linux kernel. However, some types of network cards may require separate installation of drivers from the manufacturer. In this case, pay special attention to the list of officially supported operating systems and warranty terms. Also pay attention to how the network equipment is managed: some switch models require installation of special programs that do not work with all OS versions, or installation of browser plug-ins that may also not work with all OSes. For example, at the time of writing, there is no Oracle Java plug-in for 64-bit Linux variants, and the open source version of the IcedTea plug-in does not work with all products.

There is support for the InfiniBand stack directly in the Linux kernel, but in most cases, it is not worth using it, as the performance of applications may be lower than expected. For efficient operation of HPC applications, it is better to use the **OFED** package, which is developed and supported by the InfiniBand consortium, or take a ready-made package from the card manufacturer. This package includes drivers for most card models as well as a full stack of libraries (`mad`, `verbs`, `ibutils`), network diagnostic programs, `simple subnet manager`, and MPI implementations with IB support (`openmpi` and `mvapich`). MPI implementations in OFED are compiled with predefined settings, so I recommend compiling them separately, specifying exactly the settings you need.

Note that OFED is extremely demanding on the version of the Linux kernel and libc. Usually you can download ready-made packages for some distributions from the official website, but the best way is to download and run the installer, which will compile the packages for the target system and install them. If you upgrade OFED, make sure to make backup copies of its packages, because before starting the build, the installer deletes all OFED packages it found, and if the build fails, you will get a system without InfiniBand.

If the build is successful, all packages will be saved in a separate directory in the installer. Note: Not all of them will be actually installed; some of them are mutually exclusive. Manufacturers of IB-equipment can provide their own implementations of IB-stack. In this case, it is worth using these packages first, because OFED may not support such equipment fully.

Pay special attention to RAID support. If any important data is located on hardware RAID, take care of regular backups and maintenance. No RAID will save you in case of failure of the main board, as well as in case of failure of several disks in case of power failure (even with UPS it happens). A very good solution is hardware mirroring. It is reasonable to add RAID-0 (stripe) to it to speed up operation, but it is better to implement it at the level of Linux itself: there will probably be no loss in speed, almost no load on the system, but the protection against failures will be much higher.

Configuring the Control and Compute Nodes

In the simplest case, a computing cluster consists of a control computer and an array of compute nodes. Of course, when building large cluster systems, the set of nodes will be much larger. Let's consider a simple variant and the actions that need to be performed to install and configure the software.

A small compute cluster software installation is typically performed in the following sequence:

- Installation of the control server
- Installation for the network file system, if used
- Installation of the compute node
- Installation of communication software (OFED)
- Installation of the second compute node
- Creation of a minicluster of a control computer and two compute nodes
- Installation of compilers and test packages

- Testing of communication equipment
- Installing a task management system
- Task completion testing
- Cloning compute nodes or creating an image for network booting and connecting all nodes to the cluster

The main idea of this approach is that before proceeding to the stage of cloning compute nodes, the cluster should be at maximum readiness and its functionality should be fully tested. In the course of testing, the main attention should be paid to checking whether the technical parameters of the cluster, such as communication network bandwidth and performance of compute nodes, correspond to the parameters declared by computer hardware manufacturers.

Testing a minicluster does not guarantee the subsequent failure-free operation of the full cluster, as it does not fully identify such issues as response time to network requests when their intensity increases and reliability of network services. But nevertheless, it allows you to detect most of the problems at an early stage and not to clone failed solutions. If a local copy of the OS is required on each node, it is sufficient to clone the image of the first node on the hard disks of the others. This can be done by physically connecting the disks to the reference node (note: both disks and controller must support hot swap, otherwise the connection should be made only when the node is powered off) or by performing a network installation of the OS on them and adding the changes that were made on the reference after the installation.

Installation and Configuration of the Login Node

The login node by its functional purpose is a link between the user and the array of compute nodes. On the one hand, it provides user interaction with the cluster, and on the other hand, it serves various requests from compute nodes. Therefore, the login server must have at least two network interfaces – external and internal. Note that internal services should generally not be accessible from the outside. I strongly recommend that you configure a firewall on the external interface.

In case of small clusters, often the login node has a role of the management (control) node too. I always recommend having a separated control node if possible, because you won't lose control in case of incorrect user's doings.

If the cluster uses a high-speed network, it is worth connecting the control node to it, as this typically makes it easier to manage the network and collect statistics. In addition, some communication software packages require the appropriate hardware to be installed.

If the control server acts as a storage of user data and exports them to compute nodes, it should have a sufficiently powerful disk subsystem capable of storing a large amount of data and providing high-speed access to them. For large cluster systems, I advise using a dedicated file server or a group of distributed file system servers for the data storage.

NFS Server Configuration

This procedure can be easily performed by usual admin routine and consists of the following steps:

1. The `nfs-server` package install, enable its autostart by `systemctl enable --now nfs-server` or via `chkconfig` or `update-rc.d` command (name of the package and service may differ).

2. Open the corresponding RPC services in the firewall if it is enabled on the internal network interface.

3. Edit `/etc/exports` file and specify the exported directories and lists of nodes that are allowed to mount, with client permissions parameters.

4. Run `exportfs -av` command for force nfs server config reload.

Configuring the Communication Software

Currently, the most common communication network on computing clusters is the InfiniBand network, for which the **OFED** (OpenFabrics Enterprise Distributions) package has become the de facto standard software. The package is freely distributed in the form of source code and therefore can be easily interfaced with various GNU/Linux OS implementations. It includes

- InfiniBand network card drivers
- InfiniBand network management utilities

- Various MPI implementations (MVAPICH, OpenMPI, ...)
- IP protocol support over InfiniBand network
- IB network performance tests

The OFED package is often included in GNU/Linux distributions, but the OFED developers do not recommend using software from distributions, but rather perform a full installation by downloading the latest stable version from the project's website http://www.openfabrics.org/downloads.

The installation procedure starts with deploying the distribution kit:

tar xzvf OFED-<version>.tgz

It is recommended to unpack the package into a network file system, which will simplify the installation of the package on the compute nodes. Installation on the host computer or, if it does not have an InfiniBand network card, on the first compute node is performed in interactive mode. To do this, go to the directory with the unpacked distribution kit and run the install.pl script without parameters. At the beginning of the procedure, you are offered to answer a number of questions that define the installation parameters. They are mainly related to the selection of components of the software to be installed. Before starting the installation, you should carefully study the list of basic OS components that must be present in the system and install them if necessary.

Lists for different GNU/Linux OS implementations are given in the installation instructions. The installation process compiles the source code of the modules, assembles them into packages, and installs the packages on the system. All stages are executed in automatic mode. It should be noted that before starting the installation, previous versions are searched for and completely removed from the system, so I do not recommend doing this on a working system. Each of the MPI implementations is built by all available in the system by compilers. By default, all created versions are placed in the /usr/mpi directory.

Separately, a configuration file is created for the IPoIB (IP over IB) subsystem, which allows the high-speed network to be used by application software packages oriented to TCP/IP protocols as a communication medium. This fact somewhat complicates the launching of these packages through the task management systems, because the task management systems generate the names of the nodes connected to the Ethernet network, and the communications should be performed over the InfiniBand network.

In this case, it is necessary to replace the generated node names with names associated with InfiniBand interfaces. For InfiniBand interfaces to work correctly, the following lines must be added to the /etc/security/limits.conf file.

```
* soft memlock unlimited
* hard memlock unlimited
```

The complete installation of the communication software on the control node will not be possible if it does not have an InfiniBand card. In this case, the installation must be performed on one of the nodes and the necessary files must be copied to the control node.

Typically, the installation process creates packages that are then installed via the in-house package management system, so you can simply install the desired set of packages on the management node.

Installing Compilers and Libraries

As a rule, installation of compilers is not very difficult. It is important that the libraries that are needed during the operation of programs compiled by them are available on compute nodes. For this purpose, it is best to install the compiler in a directory on the network file system.

In order to make the libraries available to the dynamic linker, you need either to write the paths to them in the LD_LIBRARY_PATH environment variable (which is conveniently done via environment modules), or explicitly specify these paths in the /etc/ld.so.conf file and run the ldconfig command. In the latter case, do not forget to update this file when you update the compiler version: the path to the libraries may change. And of course, don't forget to update the information on the nodes – run ldconfig on all nodes of the cluster.

Customizing the Job Management System

This stage was described above, we will not dwell on it in detail. After installing, configuring, and testing the task management system, you can start deploying the rest of the compute nodes. As soon as the cluster is ready to run tasks, there is a great temptation (or pressure from users and not only) to put it to work right away.

If possible, I advise against doing this until the monitoring and backup systems are set up. Otherwise, there will be catastrophically little time to set them up, which can lead to very dire consequences.

Installation and Configuration of the Cluster Compute Node

The main purpose of a compute node with maximum efficiency is to execute user tasks received by it. These can be both independent programs and parallel program processes. Due to the different functional purpose of a compute node compared to a control computer, its architecture may differ significantly.

The compute node does not need a powerful disk subsystem; moreover, its complete absence is acceptable. However, in this case, the load on the network infrastructure, which is already very busy, increases and the size of memory, available for user jobs, is decreased. NFS file system may become a bottleneck, especially for programs generating many temporary files during the computations; even parallel file system performance may degrade in such cases. I strongly recommend having at least local /tmp directory and suggest your users to use it as a scratch space. Here also, enroot and others will unpack the container file systems by default.

The main purpose of the disk subsystem in a compute node is to store temporary files. It can be used for the local version of the OS as well. If you decide to install the operating system locally, create a separate partition at least of 50-100 GB for it.

Be sure to create a swap partition and a partition for the /tmp directory. The swap partition does not need to be large – its purpose is to provide a small reserve for RAM. If a large amount of swap is required, the task will spend more time waiting for memory pages than running. Allow all remaining space for the /tmp partition. If you have two local disks, I recommend that you create a swap partition on each and merge the partitions for /tmp into a logical RAID-1.

A more careful approach is required when configuring the network subsystem. It must provide, firstly, high-speed communication between nodes for data exchange between processes of a parallel program; secondly, interaction with control and service nodes. The first task is solved by using specialized high-speed communication equipment, e.g., InfiniBand. To solve the second task, standard Ethernet networks are used as a rule. However, the load on this network can also be quite significant, so it is quite common practice to use two or more networks. In this case, it is possible to separate different services on different networks, e.g., to allocate a separate network for servicing NFS, which accounts for most of the network traffic.

You can load the OS directly into the RAM disk, but it will reduce the memory, available to the user jobs. If you want to install the OS on a computer node, it can be done in two ways – on a local disk or as an NFS-root image. In the first case, the installation can be performed from a USB drive, having previously written the installer image to it or using virtual drive via IPMI if it is supported. Please note that in this case, the path to the drive will be specified in the node repositories configuration, so you should remove it from the settings after the installation. By the way, to simplify OS updates, you may want to create a local update repository available on the internal network and specify it in the node settings, but this is a topic beyond the scope of this book.

If there are many nodes, I recommend performing a network installation. For some distributions, it is possible to perform remote installation of a compute node in text (via ssh) or graphical (via VNC) mode directly from the management node. Almost all distributions support automated installation. In this case, a file with the installation description is created, and the installer follows it to perform all actions in automatic mode.

For example, for RedHat-like systems, this is done using the `kickstart` system. When installing to a host in manual mode, a file `/root/anaconda-ks.cfg` is created, which represents all the settings specified during installation: disk partitioning, network settings, package list, etc. This file can be edited and placed on a flash drive or NFS server if necessary. When writing to a flash drive, the file name should be `ks.cfg`. For automatic installation over the network, you must specify the path to the `kickstart` in the DHCP server settings:

```
filename "/opt/ks.cfg";
next-server server.cluster.myorg;
```

The `filename` is the path to the `kickstart` config file on the NFS server, and the `next-server` specifies the name or address of the NFS server. If the `filename` returned by the BOOTP/DHCP server ends with a slash ("/"), it is treated as a directory. In this case, the client system connects that directory over NFS and looks for a file named `<ip-addr>-kickstart`. For example, a client with the address `10.0.0.2` will search the file named `10.0.0.2-kickstart`. This is how you can install multiple servers with different

CHAPTER 24 NODE SETUP AND SOFTWARE INSTALLATION

installation parameters. If you do not specify a directory or file name, the client system will first try to mount the /kickstart directory located on the NFS server and then try to find the kickstart config file as described above.

To reduce system overhead on a compute node, you try to minimize the number of services running on the compute node. Many services that are installed by default are not required on the compute node, such as mail server, print server, etc. Note that some of them do not run all the time, but run on a cron schedule, e.g., updating the man page cache or the locate database. Mounting a network file system solves the problem of availability of programs and user data on compute nodes. Besides, this mechanism can be conveniently used to ensure availability of specialized application packages on compute nodes.

The NFS client can be configured using a system utility, but really you just need to add a line to the /etc/fstab file:

```
myserver:/export /export nfs defaults 0 0
```

The first field contains the name of the NFS server and the exported directory; the second field contains the name of the directory to which the network file system will be mounted; the third field contains the file system type; the fourth field contains the mount options; the value 0 in the fifth field prohibits automatic backup of the file system; the same value in the last field prohibits checking the file system with the fsck command.

The next step is to install proprietary compilers. In normal operating mode, they are not used on compute nodes but will be required when configuring the node for installing communication software. In the future, only runtime libraries will be used. It is advisable not to rewrite the compilers from the control computer, but to perform a full installation again so that their presence is fixed in the system, and they participate in the installation of communication software, or to use a compiler available over the network via NFS.

The installation and configuration of the communications software is described above, although it is not mandatory for the control computer and may not always be done in full volume. For compute nodes, this procedure is one of the most important ones.

The configuration of the computer node is completed by installing the client part of the task management system. Next, you should prepare the second compute node for work. You can clone the hard disk of the node to the disks of the others, e.g., using the Clonezilla program, and write the finished image to an NFS partition or flash drive and

CHAPTER 24 NODE SETUP AND SOFTWARE INSTALLATION

specify it during cloning. If the disks are identical and their number is small, you can connect them to the node one by one and perform a full disk cloning with the following command:

dd if=/dev/sda of=/dev/sdb

Here /dev/sda is the name of the disk with the prepared system, and /dev/sdb is the disk to be fabricated. This procedure may fail, and the system prepared by the cloning method will not boot if the prototype system is not adjusted beforehand. The point is that many systems associate device names with factory identification numbers in the bootloader and mount configuration files. For example, in SUSE OS in GRUB bootloader configuration file /boot/grub/grub.cfg, you can see an entry of this kind:

root=/dev/disk/by-id/ata-WDC_07TMA0_WD-WCAPW5389339-part1

It will not be correct on another computer with a different disk number. Therefore, before cloning, such entries should be replaced with anonymized device names, e.g., root=/dev/sda1. The /boot/grub/grub.cfg and /etc/fstab files should be edited in this way. After that, you will get a prototype OS that can be moved to other disks.

Another problem can arise if the OS binds network interfaces to MAC addresses. Usually, these are specified in /etc/udev/rules.d/70-persistent-net.rules or similar. If this is the case, you will need to mount the new file system and correct the MAC address after cloning. There may be other nuances – pay attention to the first boot from the cloned disk.

A safer and faster option in this respect is to install the operating system on an NFS-root. To do this, you need to prepare a minimal image of the system ready for network booting and allow its mounting via NFS in read-write mode. After that, DHCP and TFTP servers are prepared, pxelinux is configured, and the initrd image is prepared. Once the node is booted, packages can be installed and configured. Do not put the node name in any configuration files. After installation, the node is shut down and the NFS server changes the NFS-root access mode to read only. If you need to update the software (except OFED), you can do so in the chroot environment on the node where the NFS server is installed. Remember to set up passwordless ssh login for the root user during the initial installation. This will help if the network partition with user home directories is not mounted.

Final testing of the cluster requires the following:

- Configure the ability to run remote commands without password for the superuser
- Register a regular user on the cluster
- Set it up to run remote commands without password
- Customize the user's environment for any of the installed MPI versions
- Prepare a running script for the corresponding test program from the OFED package
- Check if the program is started for execution

If the whole chain – launching the program, executing it, writing the result to the working directory – goes correctly, you can start connecting the remaining nodes to the cluster.

Brief Summary

Be sure to plan your cluster deployment; make sure you understand all the steps, if you are unclear or have doubts: practice on a minicluster. In Linux, it is usually not difficult to configure networks initially; most drivers come with the kernel. InfiniBand is usually best used with the OFED package. Test all hardware and software components on the minicluster. Be careful with systems controlled via Java applets or proprietary programs.

Search Keywords

Linux network driver, ofed, ulimit, NFS, diskless

CHAPTER 25

Out-of-the-Box Stacks and Deployment Systems

As we have seen, it is not easy to install the software of an entire cluster. And it still needs to be updated, new software installed, etc. Linux "cluster distributions" were created to simplify this task. Unfortunately, they only solve the problem of cluster deployment to a limited extent. It is not always possible to install additional software, commercial, or even open source tools in them. I don't recommend using them if your cluster will not work with a limited set of tasks, but with a growing set of tasks or if users will compile their own or open source packages. But if the set of tasks is small, and they can successfully work with the stacks under consideration, using them can save you a lot of time and effort. Let's take a look at some of them.

ROCKS

This project was developed by the National Partnership for Advanced compute Infrastructure and San Diego Supercomputer Center in 2000. The distribution is based on the RedHat distribution, but currently uses CentOS. A modified version of the RedHat anaconda auto-installer is used for automatic installation. The distribution is divided into so-called **Roll CDs** with software suites, e.g., for Java, Lustre, Ganglia, etc. It is possible to create Roll CDs yourself. All information about the cluster configuration is stored in a MySQL database, and you can update the installed software using new Roll CD images.

For typical tasks and small configurations, this distribution may be a good choice. However, if you plan to use nonstandard or not-so-standard hardware, network topology, or applications, it can take a lot of time and effort to optimize and configure ROCKS.

Let's imagine the simplest installation of ROCKS on a cluster. We will need two Roll CDs: Base and HPC. Turn on the head machine and boot from the Base Roll CD. At the beginning of the boot, you need to specify 'frontend' mode instead of 'compute', which is the default. When the installer asks "**Do you have a roll CD/DVD?**", answer "Yes" and the CD drive should open and the HPC Roll CD should be inserted. After the installer recognizes the CD and reports it, it will ask "**Do you have a roll CD/DVD?**" again, this time you should answer "No." Then insert the Base Roll CD into the CD drive and continue with the installation.

The installation process will ask general questions as well as questions regarding the network settings of the cluster. Consider in advance what network settings will be used on your system. The hard disk of the head machine can be partitioned manually, but it is better to rely on the '**Autopartition**' option. Be careful when specifying network card settings: the installer will decide which of them will be for the internal network and which will be for the external network, and this choice will not necessarily be the same as yours. For the internal network, select manual mode (unselect "**configure using DHCP**"). We will not dwell on all the questions asked by the installer, as most of them are standard for all distributions. After answering all the questions, the installer will format the hard disk and start unpacking the packages. During the unpacking process, it will require additional Roll CDs, in our case the HPC Roll CD. After installation, the system will automatically reboot and be ready for use.

Now you need to install and configure the compute nodes. Assume that the nodes are diskless, or you do not want to remove the operating system installed on them (e.g., if the nodes are used as workstations in a computer lab). Make sure that the nodes are capable of booting over the network (PXE protocol). To start the installation, turn on the host machine and log in as root. From the command line, run the insert-ethers program, select '**compute**', and click 'OK'. After that, turn on the first compute node in network boot mode (e.g., by selecting this option in BIOS). While the node is booting, the insert-ethers program will display information about its MAC address and start installing the node.

Since the node is diskless, the installation is reduced to downloading the image of the compute node over the network and writing the data about the node in the base of the head machine. Turn on the other compute nodes in the same way. After all the nodes of the cluster are installed, exit the insert-ethers program by pressing "F1." After the compute nodes are installed, the cluster is ready to work. To get started, I recommend creating a regular (nonprivileged) user with the command useradd USERNAME on the root machine. Then log out of the root console and log in as the newly created user.

You can compile programs using the mpicc or mpif77 compilers. Before running an MPI program for the first time, execute the following commands:

```
ssh-agent $SHELL
ssh-add
```

To run the MPI program myexe in manual mode, create a machines file with a list of compute nodes on which to run the task, one node per line. After that, run the task with the command like this (mpich example):

```
/opt/mpich/gnu/bin/mpirun -nolocal -np 2 \
  -machinefile machines ./myexe
```

By default, ROCKS uses the Grid Engine task management system. Therefore, to start tasks, you must first create a startup script.

An example script can be found on the ROCKS website. To run it via Grid Engine, use the following command:

```
qsub sge-run-script.sh
```

For more information, visit http://www.rocksclusters.org/.

Parallel Knoppix/PelicanHPC

This is a distribution that is usually not installed on the host machine and nodes, but runs in LiveCD mode. It is not usually used for permanently running clusters, but is used for a quick temporary transformation into a classroom or workstation computing cluster. The distribution is based on Debian. Please note that it is not in active development, so it may be outdated.

You can install the head machine image for permanent operation and load nodes as needed. Cluster monitoring and management capabilities are practically absent in this distribution. Since the purpose of the distribution is to run one or more tasks after hours, management is typically not needed. Changes in images are made as in most LiveCD distributions, so adding packages, updates, and configuration changes are done manually.

Here is an example of a PelicanHPC session. Boot from the LiveCD/LiveUSB. From the menu that appears, select "**Start Debian Live**." The next screen is "Pelican Setup," where you will be prompted to set the location of the /home directory. The default suggestion is to place it on a virtual disk in RAM. If you need to save the state of home directory between reboots, you can specify mount command keys to mount a preformatted(!) partition. If you are booting for the first time, it is better not to change anything, but just press "**Enter**" and after booting examine the /home/user/pelican_config file, which describes different home directory mount configurations.

The next setup screen is a prompt to copy the initial settings for users to the /home directory. If you booted with the default settings, select "Yes"; if you are using persistent storage for /home, you should only copy these data on the first boot. The next step is to set a password for the user user. Delete the phrase "PleaseChangeMe!" and enter a new password. After that, the download will continue and soon a login prompt (login:) will appear. Enter the name 'user' and the password you just entered. If you are more comfortable working in a graphical environment, type 'startx' and the Xfce graphical environment will be loaded.

To start forming your cluster, type the pelican_setup command. The program will prompt you to select the network interface that corresponds to the cluster network. Be careful, as there will be a DHCP server on this network, which can disrupt your regular network if you specify the wrong interface.

The next screen of the program prompts you to start the required services. If you are ready and are sure you have selected the correct interface, click "Yes." After the services start, a screen will appear inviting you to start the compute nodes. Select "Yes" and begin powering on or rebooting the compute nodes. Make sure the nodes are booting over the network. Once booted, the compute node screen should display "**This is a PelicanHPC compute node.**" and the standard prompt.

After all compute nodes have been loaded, the pelican_setup program should display the number of nodes. If all went well, click "Yes." On the next screen, the program will provide brief information about the newly created compute cluster. Click "OK" and a simple cluster performance test will be run, and the program will finish.

The /home/user/tmp/bhosts file contains a list of the nodes in your cluster and some other parameters. If you need to add or remove compute nodes, run the pelican_restart_hpc command, which automates these tasks. If you need additional packages, you can deliver them with the apt-get command. Keep in mind that the downloaded system is Debian-based, so only deb packages will do. If you wish, you can create your own PelicanHPC image with the required packages (see the documentation for details). By default, PelicanHPC includes parallel versions of Linpack and Octave, as well as OpenMPI.

Project website – https://sourceforge.net/projects/pelicanhpc/

Brief Summary

To solve simple typical tasks, a "real" supercomputer is not always required; a BeoWulf class cluster is quite sufficient, i.e., assembled from improvised materials, or you can simply use the computers of an idle classroom or office at night. A ready-made stack that does not require much time for installation (or no installation at all) will be useful for this purpose. It should be remembered that the flexibility of this solution is much lower than installing all the necessary components yourself.

The deployment system can help with the initial installation and configuration of the OS – after spending a day on it, you can install the entire cluster in an hour, and if necessary, expand it or change its configuration to do everything in half an hour. The solutions we have considered are by no means the only ones, but they are probably the most popular at the moment.

Search Keywords

HPC, LiveCD, LiveUSB, beowulf, rocks, knoppix, pelicanhpc

CHAPTER 26

Cluster Management Systems – xCAT and Others

As your cluster contains a lot of nodes, it is reasonable to have a system, which tracks all their names, addresses, OSes, and other attributes and helps you to update them and keep consistent. There are several solutions; the most popular open source (at the date of writing this book) is **xCAT**. We will talk about it and show how to use such systems, then will mention some alternatives.

xCAT – Extreme Cloud Administration Toolkit (http://xcat.org). This toolkit was developed by IBM and has been fully open source since 2007 and is being actively developed. It is not a distribution, unlike ROCKS and PelicanHPC, but a cluster deployment and management system.

xCAT can

- Create OS images for downloading over a network or installing on a hard disk
- Automatically perform image installation
- Manage nodes via IPMI, ILO, and other protocols
- Maintain information about hosts in the internal database and in TFTP, DHCP, DNS, and hosts databases

Please note that not all OS and even OS versions are supported. You can have problems using fresh images and/or kernel; make sure that all your drivers and system software, especially proprietary, are compatible!

Installation and Initial Setup

You can install xCAT by cloning the git repository and compiling the required packages (most of them are perl modules) or by installing the required packages from the repository. Repositories for RedHat-compatible, SuSE, and Debian-compatible distributions are supported. Let's consider the RedHat repository option.

Install the xCAT management server on the selected node (management or dedicated service node). Download the xCAT-core.repo file from the download section of http://xcat.org/ and place it in the /etc/yum.repos directory. Now run the command and respond affirmatively to all prompts. After installation, the /opt/xcat directory should appear, where all the necessary programs are located.

Now you can either re-login or run the command source /etc/profile.d/xcat.sh, and we are ready to work with xCAT.

---

xCAT changes NFS, DHCP, apache, and TFTP settings without preserving the original settings. Save your settings, if any, before executing xCAT commands.

Architecture and Commands

xCAT stores data about all objects in a specialized database. The tabdump, tabedit, and tabrestore commands are used to view, modify, or replace data in it, respectively. To maintain data integrity with complex objects, the commands lsdef, mkdef, rmdef, and chdef are often used to view, create, delete, and modify data, respectively.

Based on data from the xCAT database, it creates configuration files for NFS, TFTP, DNS, and DHCP. Be careful, old configuration files will be overwritten! Updates do not occur automatically, but only by the corresponding command.

When a node listed in the xCAT database is powered on, it attempts to perform a network boot (except in certain cases) and the DHCP server offers it a special bootloader via TFTP, which in turn performs the download or installation of the desired image. If the network is divided into several segments, a subordinate xCAT server with its own DHCP and TFTP servers can be installed in each segment. The xCAT includes many service commands, including those for node power management via IPMI and mass execution of commands, similar to pdsh.

First, let's run the `tabdump site` command. Here `site` is the name of the table that is responsible for the settings of our cluster as a whole. Here is an example of such output (some lines were removed):

```
1  #key,value,comments,disable
2  "domain", "mycluster",,
3  "installdir","/install",,
4  "ipmiretries", "3", "3",,
5  "ipmitimeout", "2", "2",,
6  "master", "10.0.5.1",,
7  "forwarders", "8.8.8.8,4.4.4.4",,
8  "nameservers", "10.0.5.1",,
9  "SNsyncfiledir","/var/xcat/syncfiles",,
10 "nodesyncfiledir","/var/xcat/node/syncfiles",,
11 "tftpdir","/tftpboot",,
12 "xcatconfdir","/etc/xcat",,
13 "timezone","Europe/London",,
```

The structure is quite simple: the first line contains a list of fields, of which the first two – key and value – are the most interesting. Line 2 specifies the common domain name; lines 3, 9, 10, 11, and 12 are directories with key files; lines 4 and 5 specify IPMI parameters; line 6 is the address of the xCAT head server; and lines 7 and 8 are addresses of external and internal DNS servers. Line 13 specifies the time zone; most likely, it will need to be changed to the one you need.

The same information can be obtained with the command `lsdef -t site -l`, but the presentation will be more concise:

```
Object name: clustersite
  domain=mycluster
  forwarders=8.8.8.8,4.4.4.4
  installdir=/install
  ipmiretries=3
  ipmitimeout=2
  master=10.0.5.1
  ...
```

You can change data in tables with the `tabedit` command – the editor defined by the EDITOR variable will open, and you can edit one or more rows of the table. If you need to change just one key, or do it in a script, the `chtab` command will come in handy. Here is an example of its use:

```
chtab key=tftpdir site.value=/tftpboot
```

Since some descriptions can affect multiple tables, there is a `chdef` command. Here is an example of its use:

```
chdef -t node -o node01 groups="all,compute"
```

Here we change the object of type "node," named node01, and specify that it is now a member of the "all" and "compute" groups. This change will affect both the node and group descriptions.

For some objects, such as nodes, there are specialized commands and the previous action can be performed like this:

```
nodech node01 groups="all,compute"
```

The `lsdef` command has a `-z` switch, which can be used to save the current object description, which can be edited and then loaded back with the `mkdef -z` command:

```
lsdef -z node01 > /tmp/n01.stanza
vi /tmp/n01.stanza
cat /tmp/n01.stanza |mkdef -z
```

What objects does xCAT support? Here is a partial list:

- site (cluster(s))
- node
- group (group of nodes)
- network (subnetwork)
- osdistro (OS distribution)
- osimage (OS image)
- route (routing description)

Besides these types, there are `auditlog`, `boottarget`, `eventlog`, `firmware`, `kit`, `kitcomponent`, `kitrepo`, `monitoring`, `notification`, `osdistroupdate`, `policy`, `rack`, and `zone`.

Alas, not all of them have clear descriptions. For example, you can specify `racks`, `firmware`, or `switches`, but there seems to be no tools to use or manage them (I'd be happy to be wrong).

The description of one object can be distributed over several tables – tables are the repository of all data in xCAT. There are already many more table types than object types, and some of them can store data from different object types to link these objects together.

For example, a `node` description affects at least the tables `domain`, `hosts`, `hwinv`, `hypervisor`(for container nodes), `ipmi`, `litetree`, `mac`, `nodegroup`, `nodelist`, `nodetype`, `postscripts`, ...

The list of all tables can be obtained with the `tabdump` command. If you add the `-d` parameter, you will get the same list with explanations in English.

By default, xCAT commands can only be executed by a superuser, which is inconvenient. xCAT supports permission sharing and remote management, i.e., you can install the xCAT server on the service node and execute commands on the management node. This requires installing the xCAT package on the management node and creating access certificates. It is important that the usernames on the remote server and on the xCAT server match and that the user details on the xCAT server are in `/etc/passwd`. In the example, the username would be `xadmin`.

On the xCAT server, let's perform certificate generation:

`/opt/xcat/share/xcat/scripts/setup-local-client.sh xadmin`

The following files will appear in the `~xadmin/.xcat` directory: `ca.pem`, `client-cert.pem`, `client-cred.pem`, `client-key.pem`, and `client-req.pem`. If we plan to perform remote management, we will copy them to the same directory on the remote server. Also, the environment variable `XCATHOST=<xCAT-server>:3001` must be set on the remote server.

Now let's allow the `xadmin` user to execute commands. To do this, edit the `policy` table with the `tabedit policy` command:

```
#priority,name,host,commands,noderange,parameters,time,rule,comments
"1","root",,,,,,,"allow",
"2","xadmin","*","nodels",,,,,"allow",
```

Here we have allowed the xadmin user to execute the nodels command from any remote servers. If we specify nothing instead of nodels, then any command will be allowed. You can specify more complex restrictions, like this:

```
mkdef -t policy -o 7 name=xadmin commands=rpower \
  parameters=stat noderange=h02-h05 rule=allow
```

Here we allow the rpower stat command to be executed only for nodes h02..h05. That is, you cannot execute rpower on h02 or rpower stat h01.

Note the key in this table is the execution priority. This is a numeric parameter, but it can be dotted, such as 6.1 or 7.012. Viewing policies is sorted in ascending order; the first matching rule is triggered.

Node Management

Let's add the first node to our cluster. Nodes in xCAT are of three types – statefull (OS is installed on the hard disk), stateless (OS is loaded over the network and runs in RAM), and statelite (OS is loaded via NFS in read only and stores some files in RAM). The most convenient variants are statefull (for service nodes) and statelite (for compute nodes).

First, we need to get the necessary packages and files to create the images. To do this, we will need an iso-image of the selected distribution. xCAT supports Redhat, Ubuntu, SLES, CentOS, and Windows, but not all versions, be careful. Other distributions are not officially supported. Example for RHEL 7.6:

```
copycds RHEL-7.6-20181010.0-Server-x86_64-dvd1.iso
```

Let's create images to bootstrap the node:

```
genimage
```

By default, the install, netboot, and statelite images will be created. The image name, if not explicitly specified during generation, will be rhel76-x86_64-statelite-compute.

Let's add descriptions for the nodes in the "compute" group:

```
chtab node=compute \
  noderes.netboot=pxe \
  noderes.tftpserver=10.0.0.0.102 \
```

```
  noderes.nfsserver=10.0.0.1 \
  noderes.installnic=eth0 noderes.primarynic=eth0
chtab node=compute \
  nodetype.os=rhel76 \
  nodetype.arch=x86_64 nodetype.profile=compute \
  nodetype.nodetype=osi
chtab key=system \
  passwd.username=root \
  passwd.password=cluster
chtab netname=main_vlan \
  networks.dynamicrange="10.0.0.200-10.0.0.254"
```

Now any node added to the compute group will get the specified parameters. Let's add a description of the node:

```
mkdef -t node node1 groups=all,compute arch=x86_64 \
  bmc=node1ipmi bmcusername=ADMIN bmcpassword=admin \
  mac=xx:xx:xx:xx:xx:xx mgt=ipmi netboot=pxe \
  provmethod=rhel76-x86_64-statelite-compute
```

To avoid writing the node's IP address every time, you can use the template mechanism. Let's execute the command:

```
chtab node=compute hosts.ip='|\D+(\d+)|10.0.0.(10+$1)|'.
```

With this rule, we set the IP address for each node in the compute group as 10.0.0.X, where X is obtained by adding 10 to the node number. So node node15 will get the address 10.0.0.25.

Let's check the obtained parameters for the node:

```
lsdef node1
Object name: node1
  arch=x86_64
  bmc=10.1.1.3
  bmcpassword=admin
  bmcusername=ADMIN
  groups=all,compute
  mac=00:10:30:30:40:03
```

```
mgt=ipmi
netboot=pxe
postbootscripts=otherpkgs
postscripts=syslog,remoteshell,syncfiles
provmethod=rhel76-x86_64-statelite-compute
```

Let's look at the characteristics of the image:

```
lsdef -t osimage rhel76-x86_64-statelite-compute
Object name: rhel76-x86_64-statelite-compute
  imagetype=linux
  osarch=x86_64
  osname=Linux
  osvers=rhel76
  otherpkgdir=/install/post/otherpkgs/rhel76/x86_64
  authorization=755
  pkgdir=/install/rhel76/x86_64
  pkglist=/opt/xcat/share/xcat/netboot/centos/compute.rhel7.pkglist
  profile=compute
  provmethod=statelite
  rootimgdir=/install/netboot/rhel76/x86_64/compute
```

Note the pkglist parameter - this file specifies the list of packages for the image. This list is rather sparse and can be expanded if you need additional packages. It is best to create a new profile, e.g., by copying compute.rhel7.pkglist to myprofile.rhel7.pkglist. The template should be copied in the same way.

If you want to add packages that are not included in the distribution (or not copied from disk with the copycds command), you should copy them to the /install/post/otherpkgs directory and list their names in the file

/install/custom/install/centos/compute.rhel7.otherpkgs.pkglist

To change other image parameters, such as disk partitioning, if any, we will use a template. The default image creation template is located in the file /opt/xcat/share/xcat/install/centos/compute.rhel7.tmpl (or similar file corresponding to the distribution). Copy it to the /install/custom/install/centos directory and edit it. In the same way, you can create a new template, e.g., for a service node. The file name must match the template, e.g., for the service template, the name would be service.rhel7.tmpl. Now you can regenerate the image, but it is highly desirable to delete the old one with the command

rm -Rf /install/netboot/rhel76/x86_64/compute/

For the statelite version of the image after (re)generation, execute the command

liteimg rhel76-x86_64-statelite-compute

This command modifies the image for statelite mode. It cannot be used for stateless mode.

As it was mentioned earlier, in the statelite mode, the image is loaded by the root on NFS in read-only mode. For normal operation, some files and directories must be writable; this problem is solved by mounting these directories and files in tmpfs, i.e., they are located in memory. Their list is set in the litefile table. By default, it is empty, but I recommend adding at least these files and directories (with the tabedit litefile command):

```
#image,file,options,comments,disable
"ALL","/etc/adjtime",,,
"ALL","/etc/inittab",,,
"ALL","/etc/ntp.conf",,,
"ALL","/etc/ntp.conf.predhclient",,,
"ALL","/etc/resolv.conf",,,
"ALL","/etc/resolv.conf.predhclient",,,
"ALL","/etc/ssh/",,,
"ALL","/etc/sysconfig/",,,
"ALL","/etc/sysconfig/network-scripts/",,,
"ALL","/etc/udev/",,,
"ALL","/opt/xcat/",,,,
"ALL","/root/.ssh/",,,
"ALL","/tmp/",,,
"ALL","/var/",,,
"ALL","/xcatpost/",,,
```

Here "ALL" is a special name for all images. If you want to specify a specific image, specify its name in the first column. After updating the `litefile` table, `liteimg` must be run again. Note that it is highly undesirable to do this when nodes using this image are enabled.

If desired, you can save the state of files and directories between node reboots; in this case, they should be listed in the `statelite` table, but it is desirable to use a separate network storage for this purpose. Read about the specifics of this method in the official documentation.

If after generating the image you want to modify it by adding some files or something else, you can do it with the postscript located in the `/opt/xcat/share/xcat/install/centos/compute.rhel7.postscript`. The following arguments are passed to this script: directory with the finished image, OS version, architecture, profile name, and working directory (where `genimage` is launched from).

It is not uncommon for some actions to be performed after the node has been booted. In this case, you can also execute one or more scripts. Sets of these scripts are listed in the `postscripts` table. The scripts themselves should be located in the `/install/postscripts` directory.

For example, let's create the script `/install/postscripts/mypost` and specify its execution for node1:

```
chdef node1 -p postbootscripts=mypost
```

Pay attention to the file, which is used to generate the actual script that will be executed after the image is generated, or the node is booted: `/opt/xcat/share/xcat/mypostscript/mypostscript.tmpl`. Instead of the line, the contents of the desired scripts will be inserted. By the contents of this file, you can judge what environment your scripts will have when executed. The script generated from this template will be placed in `/tftpboot/mypostscripts/mypostscript.<node name>`. If the script is not automatically generated, run the command `nodeset <node_name> osimage=<image_name>`.

Loading and Controlling

Having prepared the image, we are ready to upload it to the nodes. But first, we need to update the information about it for DHCP, DNS, and TFTP services. Let's execute the commands:

CHAPTER 26 CLUSTER MANAGEMENT SYSTEMS – XCAT AND OTHERS

```
makenamed.conf
makehosts compute
makedns compute
makedhcp compute
systemctl restart dhcpd
systemct restart bind
nodeset compute osimage=rhel76-x86_64-statelite-compute
```

Run the command rpower node1 boot, and if the IPMI settings on this node match the ones we specified in the configuration, it will reboot into the new image.

The rpower command controls node power over IPMI, its first argument is a list of nodes and/or groups, and its second argument is an action on them. Table 26-1 presents some examples of using 'power' command.

Table 26-1. Examples of how the rpower command works

Command	Meaning
rpower compute stat	Output the status of nodes in the compute group
rpower node1 off	Shut down node1
rpower node1 cycle	Turn the unit off and on
rpower node[1-100] on	Enable nodes node1… node100
rpower node1 reset	"Press" the reset button on the node

The psh and pscp commands are similar to pdsh and pdscp, respectively, but have fewer parameters and settings. You can execute the command on all nodes in the compute group with the command:

```
psh compute uname -n
```

Copy the file to all nodes – with the command

```
pscp /tmp/myfile all:/tmp
```

In addition to the features discussed here, xCAT supports other features such as node identification by switch port (instead of MAC address), multiple head servers, hierarchy of subordinate servers, and more. We will not dwell on these features here; you can read about them in the project documentation.

CHAPTER 26 CLUSTER MANAGEMENT SYSTEMS – XCAT AND OTHERS

xCAT is really good tool for your nodes management, but it has some flaws too. In my opinion, the most critical are

- Limited support of the Linux distributions; you usually cannot add the latest version, because the image creation fails.

- You cannot use already installed image snapshot as a base for the image.

- DNS and DHCP management is limited to managed nodes; you cannot add custom zones, sections, options, etc.

- No verification for the images, installed to the local disk.

- No statistics, history, etc.

Be aware, test before use, and plan wisely.

Canonical MaaS

MaaS stands for "Metal-as-a-Service" and is widely used. For example, xCAT can be considered as a MaaS platform. Canonical company has a product with the same name, and it is designed, how you can guess, to automate the process of installing operating systems on cluster computing nodes and collecting information about the hardware of cluster nodes. Later, we use "MAAS" for canonical MAAS product.

MAAS provides the following functions:

- Storing images of Ubuntu, CentOS 7, CentOS 8, Oracle Linux, Windows, and VMware ESXi operating systems

- Deploying stored OS images to computing nodes

- Collecting information about the hardware of computing nodes

- DNS, DHCP, TFTP, PXE, and NTP server functions

- Computing node power management functions via the IPMI protocol

- Network address space management functions

Also, it has native integration with Ansible, Chef, Puppet, SALT, and Juju, REST API, CLI and Python bindings, which makes it really easy to build custom workflows. Support for KVM and LXD makes possible to provision virtual machines.

MAAS server hardware requirements depend on the number of nodes; minimum requirements are the following:

- It is recommended to use SSD drives in RAID-1.
- Disk space over 120 GB.
- Dual-core processor with a frequency of each core over 2 GHz, enabled virtualization option.
- 2 GB of RAM.
- Network adapter operating at 1 Gb/s.

To install MAAS, you need to add it to the repository with the command (adjust the version to the actual one):

```
sudo apt-add-repository ppa:maas/3.2
sudo apt update
```

Then install MAAS packages:

```
sudo apt-get -y install maas
sudo apt install maas-region-controller
```

After installation, you can log in to the web UI: http://<MAAS_IP>:5240/MAAS. First, you have to make an initial setup:

- Download the image(s) you want to use for your nodes in the "Images" tab.
- In the DNS tab, add a domain.
- Create the required subnet and enable DHCP MAAS in the "Subnets" tab. DHCP is configured in the "vlan type → Configure DHCP" section.

Now we're ready to add a new node! For a physical node, we need to get its BMC IP address and administrator credentials first, and of course, BMC should be enabled to operate via LAN. Node boot should be set as network, and we need to copy its MAC address.

Go to the MAAS "Machine" tab, click "Add Hardware → Machine," specify name, domain, arch, kernel version, zone, pool, IPMI as "Power type," LAN_2_0(ipmi2.0) as a "Power driver" and "Automatic" for "power boot type." Put copied MAC address, BMC address, and credentials, and click "Save Machine." You'll see your new machine in the list with "New" status. In the "Actions" menu, select "Commission" and the initial provisioning (commissioning) should start. MAAS supports many power drivers, not only IPMI – Redfish, Intel AMT, HP iLO, etc.

After the initial provisioning, in the "Network" tab inside the machine information, we can see all the network cards found and can assign an IP address in our subnet. You can make a bond connection, selecting several interfaces and then clicking "Create bond."

The next step is the OS installation – in the action menu, select "Deploy" and wait for "Deployed" status of the node. After the node OS is installed, the IP address cannot be changed.

To simplify the overall process, you can set default values for the new nodes in the global "Settings" tab: default image, kernel and kernel parameters, NTP server, etc. MAAS can act as a proxy for deployed distributions; this is convenient and does not require the creation of local repositories. It is not recommended to use public repositories for clusters, since the nodes have drivers installed (Mellanox, NVIDIA), which may stop working after updating through public repositories and will require reinstalling these drivers. If you need to install packages from public repositories, you have to test on a node that is not involved in the calculations.

By default, MAAS is taking role of DNS and NTP server in the cluster, but you can specify additional ones. MAAS supports LDAP authentication via FreeIPA, so you can configure it too. For virtual machines, use KVM tab – it supports KVM and LXD VMs. For large installations, MAAS has HA support; you can deploy "rack controllers" in addition to the region controller and distribute the load.

MAAS supports custom images, but it requires Ubuntu Pro license, and I'm not sure if you can use any custom distributions. More information on `https://maas.io/`.

Foreman

Another management tool is Foreman (`https://www.theforeman.org/`) – open source solution for provisioning and managing servers. It supports virtual machines (KVM, Vmware, some others), docker, and clouds (OpenStack, Amazon EC2, Microsoft Azure, Google CE). Foreman supports many popular OS, but you have to download the installation media first. The overall procedure for the initial installation image preparation is a bit complicated, but is more flexible, than in MAAS, and you can add any custom installation medias and adapt the installation process for your needs. Foreman has an API, so you can build your automation, and it has command-line tools and web UI.

Postinstall management is provided via Puppet, Ansible, or Salt; installed hosts state is monitored via Puppet (by default) and indicates only the basic states, but it can be enhanced. The project is actively developed and is highly extensible via plug-ins.

The Foreman server itself is not scalable, but the project includes so called "smart-proxies," which allows you to use it in the large-scale installations. I don't have experience with Foreman, but it is actively used in many large installations.

NVIDIA Base Command Manager

This product is proprietary and doesn't have a "community edition" (at 2025), but it has a free license for the cluster of 16 nodes and 16 GPUs or less. Formerly it had title **Bright Cluster Manager**, and you might hear about it before. This solution is HPC-oriented and provides compute node provisioning, storage setup, network switches control, monitoring, OS consistency control, and many more. IB and CUDA support is available out of the box, Slurm setup and control are included by default, and other job management systems are available.

In addition, there is support for Kubernetes and CEPH, if it is needed for any tasks. Baremetal clusters can be combined with cloud nodes; fully cloud clusters are also supported. Available providers are Amazon EC2, Microsoft Azure, and Oracle Cloud, but new ones are added gradually. One of the most interesting features is seamless Slurm integration – new nodes are automatically added into the Slurm configuration and become available just after provisioning and are removed if you delete the node in the configuration. Base Command Manager supports integration with external LDAP, DHCP, and DNS servers, which makes it easy to integrate into existing infrastructure. Command-line interface makes automated control simple, but you can use web UI. My experience using BCM is very positive, but note that it requires commercial license.

CHAPTER 26   CLUSTER MANAGEMENT SYSTEMS – XCAT AND OTHERS

Brief Summary

xCAT is a very powerful open source tool for deploying and maintaining clusters. It does not include elements such as account synchronization and task management, but does an excellent task of managing OS images and booting nodes. It has a lot of caveats, so maybe take a look at alternatives. Choose wisely – switching from one system to another is very difficult.

Foreman and MAAS are good open source alternatives, but they are less oriented on HPC; you will need to spend some time to make them convenient for managing HPC cluster. In contrast, BCM is HPC-oriented, but is available only with a commercial license.

Search Keywords

xCAT, DHCP, pxe, tftp, Canonical MAAS, Foreman Manager, Base Command Manager

CHAPTER 27

Communicating with Users

One of the most important "components" of any supercomputer is its customers, or users. Without them, it is of no use to anyone. Therefore, like any system administrator, a supercomputer administrator must communicate with users and help them solve problems that arise during operation.

Correspondence

Email is one of the most popular ways of communicating in IT environments, including administrators with users, especially when users are mostly remote. There are several options for organizing user support via email. We will consider the most convenient one, from our point of view; in your work, you can adapt this set of techniques to your own needs.

First, create an address for user addresses. Do not specify a personal or work address! Set up a virtual address (alias) on your mail server and forward emails from it to multiple addresses. This will help you over time or immediately connect to support assistants and easily separate user requests from other correspondence. You can create a separate mailbox, but in our opinion, it is inconvenient, even if everyone will use IMAP and store mails on the server.

For most mail servers on Linux, to configure an alias address, all you need to do is write a line similar to this one in the `/etc/aliases` file:

```
cluster-support: foo, bar, expert@supermail.org
```

Then you usually need to run the `newaliases` command, after which all mail sent to the "virtual" address `cluster-support@your.server` will be forwarded to `foo@your.server`, `bar@your.server`, and `expert@supermail.org`. In your email client, be sure to create a **support** folder where all emails addressed to support will go – this is done by simply creating a filter. For example, in your Thunderbird mail client, go to the "Tools/Message Filters" menu and create a filter by the "to whom/copy" field. Add here emails sent from the `cluster-support` address.

It is better to create another folder, e.g., **support_done**, and put into it the emails that are finished (problem solved, question answered, etc.). This allows you to keep "in view" all user issues in the process of solution and conveniently store the history. Set up a profile in your email program to be able to reply from the `cluster-support` address and reply only from that address. Be sure to set up your profile to set the headers "return address (`reply-to`)" and "blind carbon copy (`bcc`)" to "`cluster-support@your.server`". This way, your helpers will immediately see your replies, and you will see their replies to users.

In addition to individual communication, it is often necessary to notify all users about something: software updates, preventive maintenance, etc. You can use address groups in your mail client for this purpose, but then you and your assistants will have to manually add each new address to such a group. It is enough to forget to do it once and the user will be offended.

To automate such operations, you can use **mailing managers** such as **mailman**, **majordomo,** and others. If your registration process is somehow automated, supplement it by calling a program that adds a new user's email to the mailing list (usually manager programs allow this). After that, only the operations of changing the address on request or deleting the address when a user is deleted will remain manual.

Don't forget to set moderated mode in the mailing list manager: there will definitely be situations when a user will reply not to the address specified as the return address (**reply-to**), but to the mailing list and his reply should not go to everyone. If the manager supports the possibility to limit the reception of mails to a set of addresses, then specify only the address `cluster-support`. Don't forget to confirm sending a mail to the mailing list when moderating mode is enabled!

If you have an internal chat or messenger, like Slack, Rocket.Chat, Microsoft Teams, Telegram, etc., where you can create a dedicated channel for the cluster support, it is a wonderful idea to do that. But the problem here is that the requests in the chat/messenger are not tracked, it is hard to keep up with a long-term problem or refer to old solutions. I highly recommend to force users to create tickets, or add any automation (bots, etc.) into the channels, which help to create such tickets. The same is about the emails – try to automate transform questions via emails into the tickets and track them.

Observe the culture of communication in email correspondence with users. Remove unnecessary quotations of the question (address, etc.), leaving only the key ones, and write your answer underneath them. If there are several questions in the letter, answer each one separately under the corresponding quotation.

If you are asked a question that comes first in the documentation, you should not write "read the docs, it's written for you!"; it's much better to write "pay attention to point 1.1 of frequent questions in our documentation (`http://your.server/docs/faq.html#p1.1`)." Don't be lazy to create templates for typical emails – alerts, answers to common questions.

Accounting for Requests from Users

Various software systems have already been created to facilitate communication with users, as well as to keep track of requests, problems, etc. Unfortunately, most of them are focused on a rather narrow range of tasks and do not involve close integration with third-party systems, especially such as a supercomputer. Nevertheless, they perfectly fulfill the tasks of processing and accounting of requests. Classic examples from the open source world in this area are **RT**, **OTRS**, **Track,** and **OpenProject**. All these systems are actively developed and supported.

The main object in such systems is a ticket. It is created by a user (the administrator is also a user), and its processing can be subject to strict rules. A ticket has a status, a creator, and a party responsible for the decision. Notes or correspondence can usually be attached to it, which allows tracking the history of problems solving. As applied to a supercomputer, a request can be a user's request for technical support, records about equipment failures and its transfer to service, records about installed software, and even users' requests for access to the supercomputer.

Such systems are often well integrated with email, both for sending information messages and for receiving applications. Often they can be well integrated with web forms. The main problems that arise when using such systems are

- Complexity of authorization of users, as they are not tied to the users of the supercomputer

- Complexity of linking actions in the system to actions on the supercomputer and vice versa

The solution to these difficulties always depends on many nuances specific to a particular supercomputer. And if we take into account that the configuration of such systems itself requires serious qualification, their implementation becomes a very difficult task. In addition to storing information about requests from users, such systems can also store internal data: event logs, requests to technical support (not yours, but those of hardware and software manufacturers), preventive maintenance plans, etc.

Nevertheless, the use of such systems, even in their simplest form, can make accounting tasks much easier. I do not advise you to use bug accounting systems in programs like **Bugzilla**, **Redmine**, etc., as their adaptation to our tasks is much more difficult and often simply impossible, despite the apparent similarity of the problems being solved.

Actualization

This part applies only to those supercomputers whose resources are not only given to internal users (employees of your organization).

Let's say you've already built a great system for account management, set up registration, alerts, etc. But think about what to do in three or four years when the number of accounts is in the dozens or even hundreds? I'm not talking about active users; I'm talking about accounts, many of which will be dead souls. How can you tell the difference between an account that has not been used for a long time and one that is no longer needed? And if it takes up 5% of the disk and the question arises, "Can I delete all this data?"

A solution is to introduce "draconian rules" and delete all accounts that have not been logged in, e.g., for more than a year. But it is better not to do this, because sooner or later you will delete the data of an important experiment or an important employee, and you will be guilty despite the rules. And in general, this policy is not very friendly to users.

I recommend that you follow the re-registration procedure. This consists of regularly, e.g., once a year, asking users to confirm that their account is up-to-date. It is a good practice to ask for a report on the activity for the specified period. A "report" is a general term; it can be, e.g., a web form with a survey on several topics.

Users who have not re-registered within a given period of time are blocked.

The duration of the re-registration period should be at least two to three weeks, as people may be on business trips, vacations, and writing a report may take a considerable amount of time, if it is supposed to describe the work or its results. Unregistered reports should not be deleted until at least the next re-registration. If disk space is important to you, send the data of such users to the archive.

Users who have not re-registered should be able to re-register later. The form of re-registration can be very different – choose the most convenient for your infrastructure. It can be email distribution with subsequent automated processing of letters (if the number of users is not very large), but it is more convenient to use filling out a web form with entering the results into the database, log, etc.; the web form can be a part of your IT infrastructure or a separate cgi-script. It does not matter much.

If you develop a web-based re-registration form yourself, don't forget about handling duplicate data (someone will probably submit the form by mistake two or three times), saving the submission date, notifying the administrator, and, of course, notifying the submitter that the data has been accepted. It is a good idea to give the submitter a message number that they can refer to if there are any problems.

Education

Provide as much as possible information to your users, if it may help them to solve their issues and answer their question before they ask you. This is related not only to day-to-day cluster usage, like cluster limits, partitioning, and priorities structure, but also links to the best practices, FAQs and docs of software vendors, and other useful materials. I may recommend very good series "The Art of HPC"[1] by Victor Eijkhout from TACC (Texas Advances Computing Center). It touches many parallel programming aspects, HPC applied packages usage, basic SLURM knowledge, and many other aspects.

---

[1] https://theartofhpc.com/

CHAPTER 27 COMMUNICATING WITH USERS

Brief Summary

Communication with users is an integral part of an administrator's work. Try to organize it as transparently as possible for users and conveniently for yourself. Keep a history of correspondence; make a list of problems and solutions. Use automation tools for routine processes to communicate; they will save you a lot of time.

Compile help notes on basic actions, such as gaining access, working with login and file transfer programs, how to contact tech support, and solving typical problems.

Search Keywords

Mailman, majordomo, mail alias, RT, OTRS, Trac, helpdesk, openproject

CHAPTER 28

One-Two-Three Instructions

What? I promised you that this book is not about guides "you have to do it that way," how come? Keep calm, here you can find kind of "guides," but you don't have to follow them. But you can use them as a good start point.

This is a very "harmful" chapter and is inserted more for reference than for actual use. Here are brief instructions on how to install or configure various components of a supercomputer. Depending on real-world conditions, they may simply not work, as I have given the simplest and most typical options. The purpose of this chapter is to remind you of the basic steps, give you examples of configurations, etc. That is why there are no explanations, and all steps are described in the style of "do one, do two, do three!" Please do not use it as a guide to action.

Now that you've been warned, let's get started.

NTP

1. Install the `ntp` package.

2. On the server, fix /etc/ntpd.conf.
   Example:

   ```
   server 1.us.pool.ntp.org
   server 2.centos.pool.ntp.org
   interface listen eth0 # internal interface
   ```

CHAPTER 28   ONE-TWO-THREE INSTRUCTIONS

3. On the nodes, in /etc/ntpd.conf, write only the line server server.cluster.myorg.

4. Put the ntpd service in autoload on nodes and servers.

Configuring the NFS Server

1. Install the nfs-server package or similar and portmap if needed.

2. Start the portmap and nfsd services, and include them in the services that start at startup.

3. To export the /home directory to clients on the 10.0.0.0/8 network, write the following line in the /etc/exports file:

   /home 10.0.0.0/8(rw,no_subtree_check)

4. Run the exportfs -ra command.

Configuring the NFS Client

1. Install the nfs package or similar.

2. To mount the /home directory from server 10.0.0.1, add a line to /etc/fstab:

   10.0.0.1:/home /home nfs rw,noatime,nodiratime 0 0

3. Create a /home directory (if necessary).

4. Run the mount /home command.

Installing Lustre (No HA)

1. Install the lustre package or similar.

2. On all servers and clients, create proper lnet configuration in lustre.conf file (in /etc/modprobe.d), e.g.,

   options lnet networks="o2ib0(ib0),tcp0(eth2)"

CHAPTER 28 ONE-TWO-THREE INSTRUCTIONS

3. Load lustre module on all servers and clients.

4. On the MDS server, create MGS and MDT volumes:

   ```
   mkfs.lustre --mdt --mgs --fsname=large-fs /dev/sdX
   mount -t lustre /dev/sdX /mnt/mdt
   ```

5. On all OSS, execute (create as many OSTs as you need)

   ```
   mkfs.lustre --ost --fsname=large-fs --index=0 \
     --mgsnode=mds.your.org@tcp0 /dev/sdZ
   mount -t lustre /dev/sdZ /mnt/ost0
   ```

6. After the OSS is initialized, mount the file system on the clients with the command (use you MGS address ad mgsnode):

   ```
   mount -t lustre mgsnode:/large-fs /mnt/lustre/
   ```

NIS+ Server Installation

1. Install the required packages and their dependencies from the packages (nis or ypserv).

2. On the server, in /etc/sysconfig/network (for RH), add a line:

   NISDOMAIN="MYCLUSTER"

3. For Debian-like systems, write in /etc/default/nis:

   NISSERVER=master

4. In the /etc/defaultdomain file, also write the domain name: MYCLUSTER.

5. In the /etc/ypserv.securenets file, enter the internal network settings and remove access from everywhere:

   ```
   255.255.255.0 192.168.123.0    # format: MASK SUBNET
   host 192.168.111.222           # individual host
   ```

403

6. Create the NIS server database with the command /usr/lib/yp/ypinit -m. When asked for a list of NIS servers, enter the name of our server.

7. Start the NIS+ service:

   systemctl start rpcbind ypserv yppasswdd ypxfrd
   # or
   service nis start
   service portmap restart
   # or
   service ypserv
   service yppasswdd start
   service portmap restart

8. Enable autostart of the service:

   systemctl enable rpcbind ypserv yppasswdd ypxfrd
   or
   update-rc.d nis enable
   or
   chkconfig ypserv on
   chkconfig yppasswdd on
   chkconfig ypxfrd on

9. Update the NIS database:

   cd /var/yp; make

Installing the NIS+ Client

1. Install the required packages and their dependencies from the packages (nis or ypserv).

2. In the /etc/yp.conf file, add the line:

   domain MYCLUSTER my-nis-server-ip-address

3. In the /etc/nsswitch.conf file, change the lines:

```
passwd:   compat nis
group:    compat nis
shadow:   compat nis
hosts:    files dns nis
```

Installing OpenLDAP (Using RH As an Example)

Let's install the packages on the server:

```
# yum install openldap-servers openldap-clients nss_ldap
```

Generate a hash of the administrator password – the program will request the password twice and output its hash to the console:

```
# slappasswd
>>> {SSHA}ABCDEF1234567890.
```

Copy this line and open the LDAP server configuration file /etc/openldap/slapd.conf for editing. Before opening it, make a backup copy.

Find and correct the lines in this file:

```
database bdb
suffix "dc=ldap,dc=server,dc=org"
rootdn "cn=Manager,dc=ldap,dc=server,dc=org"
rootpw {SSHA}ABCDEF1234567890
```

Here `database` is the type of database, and `suffix` is the path to the subtree of directories where your information will be located. Instead of `ldap.server.org`, you can use any other address; it does not have to match the DNS name of the server.

`rootdn` – Path to the administrator record. In this example, his name is `Manager`. And the last entry is the password hash we generated earlier.

Now let's specify in this file the circuits that we will need for our work:

```
include /etc/openldap/schema/core.schema
include /etc/openldap/schema/cosine.schema
include /etc/openldap/schema/inetorgperson.schema
include /etc/openldap/schema/nis.schema
```

CHAPTER 28   ONE-TWO-THREE INSTRUCTIONS

```
include /etc/openldap/schema/redhat/autofs.schema
include /etc/openldap/schema/openldap.schema
include /etc/openldap/schema/misc.schema
```

Save file. Copy the sample database configuration to the "live" database:

```
cp /etc/openldap/DB_CONFIG.example /var/lib/ldap/DB_CONFIG
chown ldap:ldap /var/lib/ldap/DB_CONFIG
chmod 600 /var/lib/ldap/DB_CONFIG
```

Add lines to the LDAP configuration file /etc/openldap/ldap.conf:

```
BASE    dc=ldap, dc=server, dc=org
URI     ldaps://ldap.server.ru:636/
```

Now the LDAP server is ready to work. You can check it using the `systemctl start sldapd` command. If everything started, go on; if not, look for errors and descriptions of their solutions, maybe there were changes in the `openldap` configuration. Now we need to add data about the administrator (in our case, it is Manager) to the `openldap` database itself. To do this, let's create a `ldif` file that describes this information. In your favorite editor, create a file, e.g., with the name /etc/openldap/ldap-init.ldif, and fill it with this content:

```
dn: dc=ldap,dc=server,dc=org
objectclass: dcObject
objectclass: organization
o: Servidor LDAP ldap
dc: ldap
dn: cn=Manager,dc=ldap,dc=server,dc=org
objectclass: organizationalRole
cn: Manager
```

Here instead of `ldap.servser.org` and `Manager`, we specify our own values. Save the file. Enter these data into the database:

```
# /usr/bin/ldapadd -a -x \
  -D 'cn=Manager,dc=ldap,dc=server,dc=org' \
  -W -f ldap-init.ldif
> Enter LDAP Password:
```

```
adding a new entry "dc=ldap,dc=server,dc=org"
adding new entry "cn=Manager,dc=ldap,dc=server,dc=org"
```

The program will prompt for the password we entered earlier in the `slappasswd` command, and then add two entries to the database – the root branch and the Manager user.

Let's check the contents of these records in the database:

```
# ldapsearch -h 127.0.0.1 -x -b "dc=ldap,dc=server,dc=org"
# ldap.server.org
dn: dc=ldap,dc=server,dc=org
objectClass: dcObject
objectClass: organization
o: Servidor LDAP ldap
dc: ldap
# Manager, ldap.server.org
dn: cn=Manager,dc=ldap,dc=server,dc=org
objectClass: organizationalRole
cn: Manager
# search result
search: 2
result: 0 Success
# numResponses: 3
# numEntries: 2
```

The server returned two records, and their contents match what we entered earlier.

Let's migrate user information from `passwd` to LDAP. Usually the `openldap` package includes migration tools. Edit the file /usr/share/migrationtools/migrate_common.ph, specifying our LDAP root:

```
# Default DNS domain
$DEFAULT_MAIL_DOMAIN = "ldap.server.org";
# Default base
$DEFAULT_BASE = "dc=ldap,dc=server,dc=org";
```

CHAPTER 28   ONE-TWO-THREE INSTRUCTIONS

Let's convert `passwd` to `ldiff` format and enter data from the resulting file into the database:

```
/usr/share/migrationtools/migrate_passwd.pl \
  /etc/passwd people.ldif
ldapadd -x -W -D "cn=Manager,dc=ldap,dc=server,dc=org" \
  -f people.ldif
```

We will do the same with the groups:

```
/usr/share/migrationtools/migrate_group.pl \
  /etc/group group.ldif
ldapadd -x -W -D "cn=Manager,dc=ldap,dc=server,dc=org" \
  -f group.ldif
```

Our server is ready to work. Now we need to configure clients. On the clients, we need to configure authentication with PAM. Install the `openldap-clients` and `nss_ldap` packages and edit the `/etc/openldap/ldap.conf` file:

```
base dc=ldap,dc=server,dc=org
rootbinddn cn=Manager,dc=ldap,dc=server,dc=org
port 389
scope sub
pam_filter objectclass=posixAccount
pam_login_attribute uid
nss_base_passwd ldap,dc=server,dc=org?sub?bjectClass=posixAccount
nss_base_shadow ldap,dc=server,dc=org?sub?bjectClass=posixAccount
nss_base_group ldap,dc=server,dc=org?sub?bjectClass=posixGroup
ssl no
pam_password SSHA
```

In the `ssl` line, disable encryption. In the future, of course, it is desirable to enable it, for which it is necessary to generate certificates and correct settings. In the last line, specify the password hashing method – it must match the one given (or explicitly specified by us) by the `slappaswd` program.

After that, it is necessary to give our password to the PAM module. For this purpose, our password is saved in a file in text form so that it is readable only by the superuser. Execute the commands:

```
vi /etc/ldap.secret
chmod 600 /etc/ldap.secret
chown root:root /etc/ldap.secret
```

The first command is to create and edit a password file. Edit the /etc/nsswitch.conf file by changing the following lines:

```
passwd: files ldap
shadow: files ldap
group: files ldap
```

Finally, make changes to the PAM authentication procedure. To do this, add (not replace!) lines to /etc/pam.d/system-auth:

```
auth sufficient /lib/security/pam_ldap.so use_first_pass
account sufficient /lib/security/pam_ldap.so
password sufficient /lib/security/pam_ldap.so use_authtok
session optional /lib/security/pam_ldap.so
```

PAM authentication will now include authentication via LDAP. It is strongly recommended that you do not delete entries for traditional (unix) authentication, as you will not be able to log in as root or dedicated admin user to the host in case of boot or network problems.

Customizing Xorg

In most cases, Xorg server does autodetection of everything pretty well. But sometimes you need to override something or give Xorg some hints. The /etc/X11/xorg.conf file is divided into sections using the keywords section and end section. Let's look at the most important sections. The ServerFlags section specifies the options with which the X server is started. In most distributions, the options for starting the server are set by window managers and are outside the xorg.conf file.

In this example, the AllowMouseOpenFail option tells the server to start even if the mouse is not present. The ZapWarning option causes the X server to sound a long beep when the user presses the Ctrl-Alt-Backspace key combination, rather than terminating (as it did before). Only pressing Ctrl-Alt-Backspace again will terminate the X server.

```
Section "ServerFlags"
  Option "AllowMouseOpenFail" "on"
  Option "ZapWarning" "on"
EndSection
```

The `Files` section sets the paths to files that are necessary for the X server to function properly. For example, the paths to the X server fonts are specified here. Fonts can be located not only on the local computer, but also on a remote computer where XFS (X Font Server) is installed:

```
Section "Files"
  FontPath "/usr/share/fonts/misc:unscaled"
  FontPath "/usr/share/fonts/local"
  .....
EndSection
```

The `Modules` section lists the modules that will be loaded by the X server at startup:

```
Section "Module"
  Load "dri"
  Load "glx"
  ....
EndSection
```

There can be several `InputDevice` sections; they are distinguished by a unique identifier (`Identifier`). For each input device connected to the computer, an `InputDevice` section is created in the file. If a mouse and keyboard are connected, the `xorg.conf` file will have at least two sections: one to describe the keyboard and one to describe the mouse:

```
Section "InputDevice"
  Driver "kbd"
  Identifier "Keyboard[0]"
  Option "XkbLayout" "us,ru"
  Option "XkbOptions" "grp:ctrl_shift_toggle,grp_led:scroll"
EndSection
Section "InputDevice"
Driver "mouse"
```

```
    Identifier "Mouse[1]"
    Option "Buttons" "9"
    Option "Device" "/dev/input/mice"
    Option "Protocol" "explorerps/2"
    Option "ZAxisMapping" "4 5"
EndSection
```

Let's take a closer look at the options of the `InputDevice` section for the keyboard. The `Driver` parameter specifies the keyboard driver for graphical mode only; consoles and terminals are controlled by the terminal driver built into the kernel. The `XkbLayout` parameter specifies keyboard layouts. `XkbOptions` sets the keys for switching between layouts, in this case `Ctrl+Shift`, and that the `Scroll` indicator on the keyboard will light up when the Russian layout is enabled.

The second `InputDevice` section describes the mouse. The `Option "ZAxisMapping"` parameter `"4 5"` is responsible for scrolling the mouse wheel. If the numbers 4 and 5 are swapped, the scrolling will work in the opposite direction. The `Device`, `Monitor`, and `Screen` sections describe the output devices. The `Device` section contains information about the video card and its drivers, the `Monitor` section describes the physical characteristics of the monitor, and the `Screen` section describes the screen characteristics (resolution, etc.). At least one such section should be present in the configuration file, and if there are several devices (when several monitors are connected), then a corresponding section should be created for each device:

```
Section "Device"
  Identifier "Intel Video Controller"
  Driver "i810"
EndSection

Section "Monitor"
  Identifier "Universal Monitor"
  Option "DPMS"
  HorizSync 28-64
  VertRefresh 43-60
EndSection
Section "Screen"
  Identifier "Default Screen"
  Device "Intel Video Controller"
```

```
  Monitor "Universal Monitor"
  DefaultDepth 24
  SubSection "Display"
  Depth 16
  Modes "1280x1024" "1024x768" "800x600"
  EndSubSection
  SubSection "Display"
  Depth 24
  Modes "1280x1024" "1024x768" "800x600"
  EndSubSection
EndSection
```

There may also be several `ServerLayout` sections. They describe combinations of I/O devices for the X server. If multiple monitors or keyboards are connected, one section will specify one keyboard and another will specify another:

```
Section "ServerLayout"
  Identifier "Default Layout"
  Screen "Default Screen"
  InputDevice "Generic Keyboard"
  InputDevice "Configured Mouse"
EndSection
```

APCUPSD

Below is an example `apcupsd.conf` configuration file with comments under each line:

```
# apcupsd.conf v1.1 ##
# for apcupsd release 3.14.7 (August 1, 2009) - suse
# ========== Basic Configuration Parameters ============
UPSNAME Smart-UPS RT 10000
# Device name.
UPSCABLE smart
# Possible values:
# simple, smart, ether, usb.
UPSTYPE snmp
DEVICE 195.208.252.115:161:APC:private
```

CHAPTER 28 ONE-TWO-THREE INSTRUCTIONS

```
#POLLTIME 60
# Time interval for device polling. Default is 60 sec.
LOCKFILE /var/lock
# Directory for storing the process ID of the daemon.
SCRIPTDIR /etc/apcupsd
# The directory where the daemon's configuration and command files
are stored.
PWRFAILDIR /etc/apcupsd
# Directory where the flag file is created on power failure.
NOLOGINDIR /etc
# The directory where the nologin file for blocking is created
# of log-ins.
#
# == Parameters used in case of power failure ==
ONBATTERYDELAY 6
# The time (in seconds) after which the system starts to
# react to a power failure.
# Note. Three parameters: BATTERYLEVEL, MINUTES
# and TIMEOUT - work in conjunction.
# The one that trips first will shut down the system.
BATTERYLEVEL 5
# The remaining battery charge (in percent) at which the battery will be
# shutting down the server.
MINUTES 3
# Remaining battery life (in minutes) at which
# will shut down the server.
TIMEOUT 0
# Battery runtime (in seconds) allowed for the UPS.
# If set to 0, # this timer is disabled.
ANNOY 300
# Time (in seconds) between alarm and shutdown.
ANNOYDELAY 60
# Delay after power failure before users
# sends a notification to exit
# out of the system.
```

CHAPTER 28   ONE-TWO-THREE INSTRUCTIONS

```
NOLOGON disable
# A condition that determines at what point users
# it is forbidden to connect to the server during a power failure.
# Possible values: disable, timeout, percent, minutes, always.
KILLDELAY 0
# The time interval between shutting down the UPS and issuing the shutdown command.
# If the value is 0, the UPS shutdown command will not be issued
# is served.
#
# ==== Configuration parameters for NIS ====
NETSERVER on
# Variable enables or disables NIS startup.
NISIP 0.0.0.0
# IP address that the NIS server will listen to.
# Address 0.0.0.0 means handling all requests on the network.
NISPORT 3551
# The port number (3551 is the default value) on which to send
# data exchange with UPS.
EVENTSFILE /var/log/apcupsd.events
# A file in which all events are logged.
EVENTSFILEMAX 10
# Maximum log file size (in kilobytes).
# Older records are deleted if the specified value is exceeded.
# ===Configuration parameters for shared UPSs=====
#
UPSCLASS standalone
# UPSCLASS [ standalone | shareslave | sharemaster ]
UPSMODE disable
# UPSMODE [ disable | share ]
#
# ===== Configuration parameters for log files.
#
STATTIME 0
# Time interval between UPS status records.
# A value of 0 will block recording.
```

```
STATFILE /var/log/apcupsd.status
# STATUS file name (if STATTIME is not equal to 0).
LOGSTATS off
# LOGSTATS [ on | off ]
# Setting the variable to on produces a very large
# output volume.
DATATIME 0
# Time interval between log file entries.
# A value of 0 will block recording.
#FACILITY DAEMON
# FACILITY defines the service in the syslog file.
# Parameters for writing to non-volatile storage
# UPS memory.
# Parameters are only used by the apctest program for
# of modifications to settings in the UPS EEPROM.
UPSNAME UPS_3
# UPS Name. Maximum 8 characters.
BATTDATE 02/04/08
# Date of installation of new batteries.
#SENSITIVITY M
# SENSITIVITY H M L (default = H)
# Voltage measurement sensitivity.
WAKEUP 60
# WAKEUP 000 060 180 300 (default = 0)
# Delayed UPS turn-on when voltage is restored.
SLEEP 180
# SLEEP 020 180 300 600 (default = 20)
# Standby time before the UPS shuts down.
LOTRANSFER 208
# Minimum voltage to switch to batteries.
HITRANSFER 253
# Maximum voltage to switch to batteries.
#RETURNCHARGE 15
# RETURNCHARGE 00 15 50 90 (default = 15)
# Percentage of battery charge to be ready for operation.
#BEEPSTATE T
```

CHAPTER 28   ONE-TWO-THREE INSTRUCTIONS

```
# BEEPSTATE O T L N (default = 0)
# Alarm Delay.
# O = zero delay, T = + 30 seconds, L = low level,
# N = never.
LOWBATT 2
# LOWBATT 02 05 07 10 (default = 02)
# Low level alarm delay
# of battery charge (in minutes).
OUTPUTVOLTS 230
# UPS output voltage during battery operation.
# Depends on the UPS model.
SELFTEST 336
# SELFTEST 336 168 ON OFF (default = 336)
# Interval (in hours) between UPS self-tests
# (336 = 2 weeks, 168 = 1 week, ON=on power up).
```

Table 28-1 lists the possible UPSTYPE and DEVICE values.

Table 28-1. *UPSTYPE and DEVICE values*

UPSTYPE	DEVICE	Meaning
apcsmart	/dev/tty**	Connection via computer COM port.
usb	-	In most cases, the daemon will find the USB connected UPS itself.
net	hostname:port	Connection type is used when UPS is not directly connected to a computer, but communicates through the daemon on the computer to which the UPS is connected.
dumb	/dev/tty**	Connection for older unmanaged UPSs.
pcnet	ipaddr:username: passphrase	PowerChute Network Shutdown protocol – a replacement for SNMP protocol for network communication with the uninterruptible power supply.
snmp	hostname:port: vendor:community	Communication between the computer and the uninterruptible power supply is carried out via SNMP protocol. The UPS must support SNMP capability and SNMP protocol operation must be enabled on the device.

Example of onbattery script:

```
#!/bin/sh
SYSADMIN=root
APCUPSD_MAIL="/usr/bin/mail"
HOSTNAME=$(hostname)
MSG="$HOSTNAME Power Failure !!!"
#Sending a mail message when switching to batteries
(
   echo "Subject: $MSG"
   echo " " " "
   echo "$MSG"
   echo " " " "
   /sbin/apcaccess status
) | $APCUPSD_MAIL -s "$MSG" $SYSADMIN
# Run the script that shuts down the cluster
```
nohup /etc/apcupsd/haltall &
```
exit 0
```

In bold is the added line that runs a special shutdown script. This script takes quite a long time to execute, and power may be restored during its execution. In this case, the apcupsd daemon will run the offbattery script, which can be used to interrupt the shutdown procedure. The offbattery script has been amended for this purpose:

```
#!/bin/sh
SYSADMIN=root
APCUPSD_MAIL="/usr/bin/mail"
HOSTNAME=$(hostname)
MSG="$HOSTNAME Power has returned"
(
   echo "Subject: $MSG"
   echo " " " "
   echo "$MSG"
   echo " " " "
   /sbin/apcaccess status
) | $APCUPSD_MAIL -s "$MSG" $SYSADMIN
```

CHAPTER 28   ONE-TWO-THREE INSTRUCTIONS

```
echo "::: Interrupt Shutdown process...$(date):::" | \
  wall -a
echo "::: Interrupt Shutdown process...$(date)::::" >> \
  /etc/apcupsd/halt.log 2>&1
#Stop the haltall script.
pkill -9 haltall
exit 0
```

The haltall script implements the controlled staged cluster shutdown algorithm, which should ensure the longest possible uptime of nodes busy with task execution. In real life, this script can be much larger, as it controls shutdown of, e.g., several clusters and workstations.

Below is a fragment related to one of the real clusters. Immediately after a power failure, the onbattery script is started, which runs the haltall script. The script outputs to the log file the information about that the shutdown process has started and the start time. The process then goes into standby mode for 30 minutes in case power is restored, and the shutdown process is interrupted. Next, all nodes are scanned to see if they are loaded and a poweroff command is sent to those that are not loaded.

The tlwait function is then started and waits for the battery charge to drop to a level sufficient for only five minutes of battery life. When this state is reached, the task queue is stopped and a list of currently running tasks is generated. The user jobs are stopped; after a one-minute pause, the procedure of shutting down all nodes is started, and after next minute – shutting down the server itself. Such an algorithm allows keeping busy nodes in a workable state for as long as possible.

Script for shutting down a cluster (PBS version):

```
#!/bin/sh
#
CLUSTERNAME=MYCLUSTER
OUT=/etc/apcupsd/halt.log
TPRED=7200
# Function to print the expected battery life.
tlprint()
{
  t=$(/sbin/apcaccess | \
    awk '$1 == "TIMELEFT" {printf "%.0f\n", $3 }')
```

```
    echo "TIMELEFT = $t" >> $OUT 2>&1
}
# Standby function until the time reserve is reduced to
# of a given number of minutes.
tlwait()
{
  while [ $t -gt $1 ]
  do
    sleep 60
    t=$(/sbin/apcaccess | \
        awk ' $1 == "TIMELEFT" {printf "%.0f\n", $3 }')
    echo "TIMELF=$t SECONDS=$SECONDS" >> $OUT 2>&1
    if [ $SECONDS -gt $TPRED ]; then
      break
    fi
  done
}

echo ":::: Starting Shutdown process: $(date) ::::" | wall
echo " " >> $OUT 2>&1
echo ":::: Starting Shutdown process: $(date) ::::" >> $OUT 2>&1

tlprint
sleep 1800
tlprint

# Turn off free nodes
echo "Shutdown free nodes ... $(date) " >> $OUT 2>&1
for host in $(cat /etc/nodes) ; do
  ping $host -i 1 -c 1 > /dev/null 2>&1
  if [ $? -eq 0 ]; then
    avg=$(ssh $host /usr/local/cluster/ndload)
    if [ $avg -lt 10 ]; then
      echo "Send poweroff to $host" >> $OUT 2>&1
      ssh $host /sbin/poweroff
      sleep 1
```

```
      fi
    else
      echo "$host not answered!" >> $OUT 2>&1
    fi
done
tlprint
tlwait 5

echo "Stop running task... $(date) " >> $OUT 2>&1
qstop $CLUSTERNAME
LIST=$(qstat -a|grep $CLUSTERNAME | grep " R " || \
       awk -F. '/^[0-9]*\./ {print $1}')
qdel $LIST

sleep 60

# Turn off all nodes
echo "Shutdown all nodes" >> $OUT 2>&1
tlprint
for host in $(cat /etc/nodes) ; do
  ping $host -i 1 -c 1 > /dev/null 2>&1
  if [ $? -eq 0 ]; then
    echo "Make poweroff to $host" >> $OUT 2>&1
    ssh $host /sbin/poweroff
  else
    echo "$host not answered!" >> $OUT 2>&1
  fi
done
tlprint
echo ":::  End Shutdown process: $(date) :::" >> $OUT 2>&1

sleep 60
echo ":::  Shutdown host-computer $(date) :::" >> $OUT 2>&1
/sbin/poweroff
```

upstemp temperature monitoring script:

```sh
#!/bin/sh

echo >> /usr/local/cluster/upstemp.txt
HOST=$(hostname)
TMAXW=25.0
TMAXSH=30.0

while :
do
  TEMP=$(/usr/local/cluster/ambtemp.sh)
  echo "$(date '+%F/%T') temp = $TEMP" >> \
    /usr/local/cluster/upstemp.txt
if [ $(echo "$TEMP > $TMAXW"| bc) -eq 1 ]; then
  mail root << EOT
Temperature UPS $HOST = $TEMP
EOT
  write root << EOT
WARNING! Temperature UPS $HOST = $TEMP
EOT
fi

if [ $(echo "$TEMP > $TMAXSH"| bc) -eq 1 ]; then
  /usr/local/cluster/haltall
fi
sleep 600
done &
```

The temperature is polled every ten minutes. If the temperature exceeds 25 (TMAXW) degrees, notifications will be sent to the administrator at the terminal and by email. It is possible to organize a mailing to several addresses or to issue an alert to all terminals.

If the temperature situation continues to worsen, the haltall script – cluster shutdown – is launched when the temperature exceeds 30 (TMAXSH) degrees. The difference between it and the previously discussed haltall script is that the shutdown of all equipment is immediate. The ambtemp.sh script, which reads the temperature from the sensor, communicates with the UPS, like the apcupsd daemon, via snmp protocol.

CHAPTER 28   ONE-TWO-THREE INSTRUCTIONS

The ambtemp.sh script:

```
#!/bin/bash
# SNMP command that retrieves the internal temperature of the UPS.
inttempcmd=".1.3.6.1.4.1.318.1.1.1.2.2.2.0"
# SNMP command that receives data from an external sensor.
ambtempcmd="1.3.6.1.4.1.318.1.1.10.2.3.2.1.4.0"
# Function that sends a request to the UPS
function sendcmd(){
  host=$1
  cmd=$2
  res=$(snmpget -c public -v 2c $host $cmd | awk -F: '{print $4}')
  echo $res
}
tempamb=$(sendcmd ups_3 $ambtempcmd)
# print the temperature obtained.
echo $tempamb
```

Note once again that these scripts are given as an example – in a real configuration, you will need to take into account many nuances: storage servers, job management system (here I used Torque), equipment connection schemes, load distribution on the UPS, etc.

xCAT

To install xCAT, let's download the files for the repositories and install the packages:

```
cd /etc/yum.repos.d/
wget https://xcat.org/files/xcat/repos/yum/2.12/xcat-core/xCAT-core.repo
wget https://xcat.org/files/xcat/repos/yum/xcat-dep/rh6/x86_64/xCAT-dep.repo
yum install -y xCAT
```

CHAPTER 28 ONE-TWO-THREE INSTRUCTIONS

Let's set the domain name for our cluster:

```
chdef -t site -o clustersite domain=mycluster
```

Change the cluster parameters if necessary:

```
tabedit site
```

Let's fix the list and settings of networks:

```
tabedit networks
```

Let's copy the distribution files:

```
copycds CentOS-7.6-x86_64-bin-DVD1.iso
```

Let's create a description of the nodes:

```
mkdef -t node node node[1-100] groups=all,compute \
  arch=x86_64 \
  mgt=ipmi \
  netboot=pxe
```

Let's set the rule of forming IP address by node name:

```
chtab node=compute hosts.ip='|\D+(\d+)|10.0.0.(10+$1)|'
```

If we have a list of MAC addresses, let's match them with IP addresses:

```
chdef -t node node1 mac=xx:xx:xx:xx:xx:xx
```

Let's create a boot image:

```
genimage
```

Set the nodes in the compute group to have an image to load:

```
chdef compute provmethod=centos7.6-x86_64-statelite-compute
```

Prescribe a set of files and directories stored in memory:

```
tabedit litefile
#image,file,options,comments,disable
"ALL","/etc/adjtime",,,
"ALL","/etc/inittab",,,
```

CHAPTER 28　ONE-TWO-THREE INSTRUCTIONS

```
"ALL","/etc/ntp.conf",,
"ALL","/etc/ntp.conf.predhclient",,,
"ALL","/etc/resolv.conf",,,
"ALL","/etc/resolv.conf.predhclient",,,
"ALL","/etc/ssh/",,,
"ALL","/etc/sysconfig/",,,
"ALL","/etc/sysconfig/network-scripts/",,,
"ALL","/etc/udev/",,,
"ALL","/opt/xcat/",,,
"ALL","/root/.ssh/",,,
"ALL","/tmp/",,,
"ALL","/var/",,,
"ALL","/xcatpost/",,,
```

Add keys and users from /etc/passwd to the image:

```
cd /opt/xcat/share/xcat/netboot/add-on/statelite
./add_ssh /install/netboot/centos7.6/x86_64/compute/rootimg/
./add_passwd /install/netboot/centos7.6/x86_64/compute/rootimg/
```

Update the statelite image and service configurations:

```
liteimg centos7.6-x86_64-statelite-compute
makehosts
makedhcp compute
systemctl restart dhcpd
makenamed.conf
makedns compute
```

Update the tftp configuration:

```
nodeset compute osimage=centos7.6-x86_64-statelite-compute
```

Overloading the nodes:

```
rpower node[1-100] boot
```

Brief Summary

Use these instructions with care; they may be (really may be) outdated. Use them only as a plan of work.

Search Keywords

apt, yum, dnf, NTP server, NFS server, Lustre, NIS server, OpenLDAP server, Xorg config, APCUPSd, xCAT

CHAPTER 29

Shell Scripts – Basics and Common Mistakes

This chapter is not intended to be a tutorial on shell programming but to cover some basic concepts that are useful for beginners to know about and some common mistakes that are often encountered. I strongly recommend that you study the Advanced Bash Scripting Guide and use this chapter as a quick reference only. Here we treat bash syntax as the most common syntax. Most of the constructs will work in shells other than csh/tcsh. I deliberately do not include all shell expressions and do not show all the features of the described constructs, but only the main ones. I highly advise you to learn advanced bash syntax, as it helps you to understand not yours scripts and write efficient bash code.

In a script, the '#' character is a comment character; the rest of the line after it is not processed by shell. Scripts actively use special characters that are processed by shell (e.g., $, !, etc.). In order to cancel their special action, 'escaping' is usually used – inserting a backslash '\' before the character.

If a script starts with the characters '#!' (shebang) and the script file is marked as executable, it can be run directly by the operating system. In this case, the OS will run the command that is written after these two characters and pass the path to the script as the last argument. Note that there can be no other characters before or between them. This means, in particular, that if the script text was prepared in a text editor in UTF-8 mode, it may add a BOM (Byte Order Mark) character to the beginning of the file. It is not displayed, but the OS will not be able to determine that this file should be run as a script.

A script consists of a sequence of commands; each command is a call to a program, possibly with arguments, or a call to a built-in shell command. Since a command can have multiple arguments, there are special delimiter characters to help you understand where one command ends and the next begins. These delimiters are

- Line feed (UNIX-style '\n' ONLY)
- End of file

CHAPTER 29 SHELL SCRIPTS – BASICS AND COMMON MISTAKES

- Semicolon (;) or double semicolon (;;) in the `case` construction
- Ampersand (&)
- Pipe (|)
- I/O redirection (<, >, &>, >&, >>, <<)
- Logical commands (&&, ||, !)

For example, you can write the condition like this:

```
if mytest; then echo OK; else echo Fail; fi
```

or you could do this:

```
if mytest
then
  echo OK
else
  echo Fail
fi
```

or even like this:

```
if mytest; then
  echo OK
else echo Fail; fi
```

All operators that check conditions take a **command** as an argument, execute it, and check the return code. If the return code is 0, the result is interpreted as logical `true`; if not, it is interpreted as `false`. This applies to the `if`, `elif`, `while`, and `until` commands. The built-in shell command can act as a command. Unlike "usual" languages like C, you cannot substitute the value of a variable. If you write $myvar instead of a command, the interpreter will get the value of the variable and use it as the name of the command. To check the value of a variable, use the built-in `test` command. There is "syntactic sugar" for the `test` command in the form of the '`[`' program, i.e., the following lines are completely equivalent:

```
test "$myvar" = "ok"
[ "$myvar" = "ok" ]
```

That is why there must be a space before and after a square bracket and a line feed, semicolon, or other command delimiter after a closing square bracket. By the way, the closing square bracket is mandatory – the `test` program checks for its presence. Pay attention to quotation marks; they are very important in shells. For example, the strings

```
myvar='1 > 3'
if [ $myvar = '1 > 3' ]; then ...
```

equivalents

```
myvar='1 > 3'
if [ 1 > 3 = '1 > 3' ]; then ...
```

It is clear that the `test` command will generate an error on such a set of arguments. In this case, the value of `myvar` was substituted "as is" – with spaces. To avoid such problems, you should enclose the variable in quotes in the argument of the `test` command: "$myvar". Try to avoid tests where the variable can be empty, as it will cause an error. For example:

```
v=''
if [ $v = '' ];then ....
```

It's better to write it like this:

```
v=''
if [ "x$v" = 'x' ];then ....
```

Shell separates script text, input argument values, and variable substitution results into separate words separated by spaces, tabs, or line feeds. If a variable must contain text with spaces, you can either escape the spaces or enclose the text in quotation marks.

Quotation marks in the shell are of three types: single, double, and inverse. Text in single quotes is processed "as is," without changes. If you need to insert a single quote in this text, it must be escaped. Double quotes allow you to interpret the text internally, i.e., to substitute variable values. In the example above, we used double quotes to get the value of the variable v.

In addition to variable values, double-quoted variables reveal history by the '!' character (unless explicitly disallowed), backquotes, and their alternate entry. Backquotes interpret the string inside as a command with arguments, execute it, and return the output of the command as a string.

CHAPTER 29   SHELL SCRIPTS – BASICS AND COMMON MISTAKES

Interestingly, within double quotes, nested double quotes are grouped together, meaning such a string would work fine:

`base="`basename "$file" .bak`"`

You can use the $(...) construction instead of backquotes, and I recommend using it. For built-in variables $@ and $* that represent script (or function) arguments, enclosing them in double quotes will list the arguments as if they were each enclosed in quotes.

For example, by calling this script

`for i in "$@"; do echo "$i"; done`

with arguments 'abc 123' 'qwe', we get

```
abc 123
qwe
```

If you remove the quotation marks around $@, the result is this:

```
abc
123
qwe
```

Quotation marks should be put everywhere, except where they are definitely not needed (e.g., when a variable contains a prepared command line). Without quotation marks, even a simple command like

`echo $var`

may produce unexpected results if `var` contains a word that matches the command key, such as '-n'.

Shell supports the '&&' and '||' 'conditional' constructs. They can be used both in 'if' conditions and instead of them. The `com1 && com2` construct will execute `com1`, and if it returns 0 (i.e., true, completed successfully), then `com2` will be executed and its result returned. If `com1` terminated with a code other than 0, `com2` will not be executed. That's why this construction is often used for "light" implementation of conditions. The same is the case with `com1 || com2`, but in this case, `com2` will be executed only if the completion code of `com1` is not equal to 0.

CHAPTER 29   SHELL SCRIPTS – BASICS AND COMMON MISTAKES

It is not uncommon to see lines of this kind in scripts:

```
[ "x$inp" = '' ] && { echo "Empty input. Exiting"; exit 1}
# or
grep "$search" testfile || echo "Nothing found."
```

instead of

```
if [ "x$inp" = '' ]; then
  echo "Empty input. Exiting"
  exit 1
fi
# or
if ! grep "$search" testfile; then
  echo "Nothing found."
fi
```

Remember, it's wrong to write that way:

```
if [ "$x" = one || "$x" = two ]; then ...
```

The || and && constructs combine different commands, and the -o and -a options are used within the test command arguments for similar purposes.

The right options are

```
if [ "$x" = one ] || [ "$x" = two ]; then …   # 2 'test' runs
if [ "$x" = one -o "$x" = two ]; then …       # 1 'test' run
```

You can invert the logical result of a command execution with an exclamation point:

```
if ! my_test; then echo my_test failed; fi
```

If you are familiar with programming in C, Java, or a similar language, you have noticed an unfamiliar comparison operator – an equal sign instead of the usual double equal sign. This is not the only surprise: the usual comparison signs =, !=, >, and < work with strings only (and the value of any variable is a string). To compare numbers, use keys -eq, -ne, -gt, and -lt of the test command, respectively.

For example:

```
if [ $count -gt 10 ]; then ...
```

CHAPTER 29 SHELL SCRIPTS – BASICS AND COMMON MISTAKES

Any command can use I/O redirection.

```
mycommand < ./infile
mycommand > ./outfile
mycommand 2> ./errfile
mycommand &> ./fulloutput
mycommand | grep failed
mycommand |& grep error        # like &>, but for pipe
```

In the first line, standard command input is redirected from the `./infile` file (by default, input is taken from the terminal); in the second line, output is redirected to `./outfile`; in the third line, the error stream is redirected to the `./errfile` file. In the fourth line, we use the pipeline – the output of a command is redirected to the standard input of another command, in this case `grep`. Multiple redirects can be used at the same time. The '&>' is used to redirect the output and error stream to the same file at the same time.

We have already used the control constructs in the shell more than once. Let's briefly list them:

```
if COND then ... [elif COND then] [else ...] fi
while COND do ... done
until COND do ... done
for VAR in LIST; do ... done
case WORD in PAT[|PAT...]) … ;; [PAT[|PAT]) … ;;;] esac
select VAR in LIST; do ... done
```

The square brackets contain optional elements. We are already familiar with the `if` operator. As you can see, it allows you to use one or more branches with additional `elif` conditions:

```
if mytest_one; then
  echo "test one passed"
elif mytest_two; then
  echo "test one failed, test two passed"
else
  echo "both tests failed"
fi
```

The classic `while` loop – its body is executed as long as the `COND` condition is true. The `until` loop is made for convenience – its body is executed while the condition is false, i.e., it is fully equivalent to the `while ! COND; do ....` The `for` loop is very popular when processing files. At each of its iterations, the `VAR` variable is assigned a value from the `LIST` list. For example, this is how to extract all zip files in the current directory into the corresponding subdirectories:

```
for i in *.zip; do
  base=$(basename "${i}" .zip)
  mkdir "$base"
  pushd "$base"; unzip "../$i"; popd
done
```

We use `basename` program to get the archive name without the extension, then create the directory, save the current dir path in a special stack by `pushd` command, and go into the new directory, unzip the content there, and return into our directory using `popd`, which takes the path from the stack. One more important detail: the variable name can be enclosed in curly brackets to avoid misinterpretations.

The `case` branching command is only slightly similar to its C counterpart. It gets a string and compares it with templates in each branch. Templates are similar to file name templates: metacharacters * and ? and lists in square brackets are allowed. Multiple templates can be listed via pipe sign. One or more templates are followed by a closing parenthesis, followed by a block of commands that will be executed if the string falls under the template. The block ends with two semicolons. Example:

```
case "$input" in
  y*|Y|YES)
    echo "ok, let's go."
    ;;
  n*|N|NO)
    echo "program canceled."
    exit 1
    ;;
  *)
    echo "Bad answer. Try again."
    retry=1
    ;;
esac
```

The `select` operator is introduced to facilitate exactly one, but often used operation – user selection from the offered options. Example:

```
PS3='Select action: ' # prompt
echo
select action in "reboot" "on" "off"
do
  echo "Executing $action."
  break # without 'break' you will get an infinite loop.
done
```

The prompt from the $PS3 variable will be displayed, followed by the list passed to the `select` command, with a number before each item. The user enters a number, and `action` will get either the value of the corresponding item in the list or an empty string if an invalid number is entered.

You can get user input in another way – by using the `read VAR` command. When this command is executed, the user will be prompted, and after pressing the Enter key, everything he has entered will be written to the VAR variable. If the script input is directed and is read from a file or from the output of another program, one line will be read.

Another useful operator in bash is `getopts`; it allows you to process command-line options in a really convenient way. The syntax is `getopts "abc:d:" arg [...]`, where `"abc:d:"` are options description and `arg` is the variable name and optional list of strings; if it is specified, it is used instead of `"$@"`. Options description is a string; each letter is a possible option (only one-letter options are allowed); if it is followed by ':' then this option requires additional argument. If ':' is specified in the string beginning, the "quiet mode" is activated – the messages about bad options won't be printed. Quiet mode can be activated also by setting OPTERR variable into 0. `getopts` gets one option per call and saves the current index in the options array in the OPTIND variable (you can change it if it is needed, e.g., set it into 1 to reset the index), if the option is successfully processed, it returns 0, puts its value into the `arg` variable, if there was an argument, puts it into the OPTARG variable. If the option was not found or the argument was required but not found, then `arg` will be set into '?', and the OPTARG will be unset. In quiet mode, if the argument was not found, `arg` is set into ':' and OPTARG into the option value.

Here is an example:

```
while getopts ":ht:" arg; do
  case $arg in
```

```
    h)
      echo "Usage: myscript [-h][-t dir]"
      ;;
    t)
      targetdir=$OPTARG
      ;;
    :)
      echo "$OPTARG requires an argument!"
      exit 1
      ;;
    *)
      echo "Oops! Bad option $OPTARG!"
      exit 1
    esac
done
```

Commands can be grouped using parentheses or curly brackets. Commands in curly brackets are executed sequentially, and the result of the operation is the result of the last command. The command block in parentheses is executed in the same way, but in a separate shell instance (called subshell). This is important to remember, because if you change the value of a variable in such a block, it will not change in the main shell:

```
myvar=10
(echo subshell; myvar=20)
echo $myvar
true && { echo shell; myvar=30; }
echo $myvar
```

The result will be this:

```
subshell
10
shell
30
```

CHAPTER 29 SHELL SCRIPTS – BASICS AND COMMON MISTAKES

Subshell is convenient to use to execute parts of a script in the background or in a separate directory (in this case, you don't need to return to the current directory).

Another useful feature of shells is functions. Although bash has the `function` keyword, it is better not to use it, but define a function like this:

```
myfunc () {
   ....
}
```

You should not write anything inside the parentheses! All arguments passed to the function will be available in the body via position variables $1, $2, etc., or via variables $@ and $*. Local variables can be defined in the function body; for this purpose, the declaration must be preceded by the keyword `local`.

You can exit a function by executing either the last command in its body or the `return` command. A function is called in the same way as a normal command; no brackets for arguments and no commas between them are needed:

```
myfunc arg1 arg2 arg3
```

The shell has exception and signal handling. It is done with the `trap` command. The first argument of the trap command is the handler command or the '-' sign, followed by the names of the signals to be handled. If the second argument is '-', the handlers of the specified signals will be reset. You can pass a function name as a handler:

```
myhandler () {
   echo "Auch"
}
trap myhandler SIGINT SIGTERM
sleep 60
echo I was not interrupted
```

This script will run for a minute and print how many times it was attempted to be interrupted by pressing `Ctrl-C` or sending a `SIGTERM` signal. The special "signals" are RETURN, ERR, EXIT, and DEBUG. It is better to read about them in the documentation.

Not-a-Mistake

Here are some command lines, I often can see, but which have more handy and practical shortcuts:

Often used	May be better
sudo su	sudo -s / sudo –i
cat file | grep	grep file # in scripts
grep 'abc' file | awk '{print $2}'	awk '/abc/ {print $2}'
exit	Ctrl-D
echo "$var" | wc -c	"${#var}"
echo "$var" | sed 's/^.*abc//'	"${var#*abc}"
if ["x$var" = "x"]; ...	if [${var:-none} = none]; ...
sort | uniq	sort -u # exception: sort | uniq -c
if ["x$VAR" = "x"]; then VAR=abc; fi	${VAR:-abc} (default value)${VAR:=abc} (assign value)

Brief Summary

Bash scripts are powerful tools you can use almost everywhere. They are relatively slow, and it is useful to know how you can optimize them.

Search Keywords

BASH scripting manual, Advanced BASH Scripting Guide

CHAPTER 30

Systemd – A Short Course

Units

There was a brief introduction to `systemd` in the chapter "Booting and init." The basic concept for `systemd` is **unit** – it can be a description of a service, an action, or a rule. As a rule, a unit is a file with a standard structure in the style of ini-file, i.e., the file is divided into sections, and the name of the section is given in square brackets. Within a section, each line has the form "key = value."

All processes, defined in units, are running inside Linux control groups; each group is called "slice," and inside the slice, you can specify various control group limits; we'll stop at this later. Units can belong to system or to user, but here we'll talk only about system ones.

If you have changed or created a new unit, its description file should be copied to `/etc/systemd/system`. Generally, units are stored in the `/lib/systemd/system/` directory (or sometimes in one of many others, refer to the man page), but if you copy the file there, it may be overwritten when the package is updated, so the `/etc/systemd/system` directory was created to prevent such situations. Descriptions from this directory have higher priority, so you can override defaults.

Moreover, you can override not the full unit definition, but just selected parts. And I recommend using this approach, instead of replacing system unit, even in /etc folder. In this case, future updates will be applied gently, if they don't interfere with your changes.

To do that, for service `servicename`, you have to create a directory titled `/etc/systemd/system/servicename.d` and then put there file(s) with `.conf` extension. This applies not only for service units, but for all unit types. In those files, you can specify only sections you want to modify and only keys/values you want to add, update, or delete. To delete the value, usually you just need to specify an empty value. Note that some keys can be specified multiple times, e.g., ExecStart. If you specify such key, it will be just added, if you want to replace the current value, specify an **empty** value first, the key(s) and value(s) you want to set.

After updating the unit descriptions, you should force `systemd` to reread them with the `systemctl daemon-reload` command.

Here is an example unit describing a service:

```
[Unit]
Description=MDM Display Manager
Documentation=man:mdm(1)
Conflicts=getty@tty7.service
After=system-user-sessions.service

[Service]
ExecStart=/usr/sbin/mdm --nodaemon
ExecReload=/usr/sbin/mdm-restart
ExecStop=/usr/sbin/mdm-stop
Restart=always
RestartSec=1s
TimeoutStopSec=5s

[Install]
WantedBy=graphical.target
Alias=display-manager.service
```

The first section, `Unit`, describes the dependencies; it also contains a description and optionally a link to documentation. Dependencies are managed by the following options:

`Requires=srv1, ...` – If our unit starts, the units listed here start and continue only if all of them have started successfully.

`Requisite=srv1, ...` – If at least one of the specified units is not started, the start of this unit automatically fails.

`Wants=srv1, ...` – Before starting this unit, the units listed here are started, but their start status is not checked.

`BindsTo=srv1, ...` – Similar to `Requires`, but in addition, if one of the specified units stops, this also stops.

PartOf=srv1 – All actions (start, restart, stop) on the specified unit will be performed on this unit as well.

Conflicts=srv1, ... – Starting this unit will cause the specified ones to stop and vice versa.

Before=, After= ... – Specifies the launch order relative to other units, if they are launched simultaneously or by dependency.

PropagatesReloadTo= ... – When restarting this unit, the specified ones will be restarted.

ReloadPropagatedFrom= ... – When one of the specified units is restarted, this unit is restarted.

StopWhenUnneeded=true/false – Stop this unit if it is no longer needed for any other unit. The default is false, i.e., if the unit was started by dependency and the "parent" unit is stopped, this continues to work.

You can also specify other options here, but it is better to read about them in the documentation.

The next section is Service; it describes the life cycle of our service and everything related to it. For the different types of units, this section will be omitted and replaced by a relevant one, e.g., for timer unit, section [Timer] will be used. The most necessary options are in this section:

Type=... – Variant of service startup. Possible values:

- simple starts the program specified in the ExecStart option and monitors this process. Its completion means that the service is terminated.

- forking is similar to simple, but expect the program to call fork and create a new process group (a standard "daemonizing" mechanism in UNIX-like systems). It is recommended to specify the PIDFile parameter if the program creates a PID file.

- oneshot is similar to simple, but the program is expected to terminate shortly, only then running units by dependencies.

- dbus is similar to simple, but expect the program to register the name in D-BUS. The name is specified in the BusName= parameter.

- notify is similar to simple, but expect the program to call sd_notify and send a notification. Only after the notification, the units by dependencies will be started.

- idle is similar to `simple`, but program start is delayed until other active tasks are started. This is done only so that the output of this unit is not mixed with others and is at the very end.

`RemainAfterExit=true/false` – If `true`, then after the program specified in `StartExec` is terminated, the service is considered to continue running (convenient in combination with `Type=oneshot`).

`ExecStart=prog` – Start string. For `oneshot` type, you can specify any number of such options, for all others – only one. One or more prefixes can be specified before the start string:

- "@" – The second word in the string will be passed as `argv[0]` to the running process. In other words, it will be shown in the list of processes as specified by the second word in the string.
- "-" – Ignore the return code (a nonzero return code is also considered a successful completion).
- "+" – Run the process with full permissions; `User=`, `Group=`, `CapabilityBoundingSet=`, etc., options are ignored.
- "!" – Similar to "+", but only `User=`, `Group=`, and `SupplementaryGroups=` are ignored.
- "!!" – Similar to "!", but does not work on systems without `AmbientCapabilities=` support and may be used if they are required.

Multiple prefixes can be specified, but only one of "+", "!", and "!!" can be used. The same prefixes work in other options where startup strings are specified: `ExecStartPre=`, `ExecStartPost=`, `ExecReload=`, `ExecStop=`, and `ExecStopPost=`.

`ExecStartPre=`, `ExecStartPost=` – Execute the command before/after `StartExec=`.

`ExecReload=` – Execute the command if necessary to reread the unit's configuration.

`ExecStop=` – Execute command to stop the unit. Often needed for `forking` or `oneshot` types, when `systemd` does not know the PID of the service.

`ExecStopPost=` – Execute the command after stopping the unit.

`RestartSec=` – Time to wait before restarting the unit. It can be set as a number in seconds or as a string like "1min 15sec"; default is 100 ms.

Restart= – In which cases, the service will be automatically restarted:

- **no** – Never
- **on-success** – Upon successful completion or completion by a standard signal (TERM, PIPE, INT, HUP)
- **on-failure** – When terminated with a nonzero code, by abnormal signal or by timeout
- **on-abnormal** – When terminated by timeout or abnormal signal
- **on-watchdog** – On timeout
- **on-abort** – On an abnormal signal
- **always** – In any of the above cases

TimeoutStartSec=/TimeoutStopSec= – Waiting time for confirmation of unit start/stop for dbus/inotify types. For other types, when stopping the unit, the TERM signal is sent first, and if the process has not finished after the specified time, the KILL signal is sent.

WorkingDirectory= – The directory to which the transition will be made before launching all commands.

User=, Group=, SupplementaryGroups= – Username, group, and the list of supplementary groups with which the unit will be launched.

LimitCPU=, LimitFSIZE=, LimitDATA=, LimitSTACK=, LimitCORE=, LimitRSS=, LimitNOFILE=, LimitAS=, LimitNPROC=, LimitMEMLOCK=, LimitLOCKS=, LimitSIGPENDING=, LimitMSGQUEUE=, LimitNICE=, LimitRTPRIO=, LimitRTTIME= – Limits (see ulimits).

Umask= – File and directory creation mask

Nice= – Specify the level of "politeness," nice

Environment= – Specify environment variables in the following format: "VAR1=word1 word2" VAR2=word3 "VAR3=$word 5 6". The list is separated by a space, values are specified in double quotes, and the '$' sign has no special meaning.

EnvironmentFile= – Full path to the file with environment variables in the format "VAR="word1 word2"", one variable per line. Lines starting with '#', ';', without '=' or empty lines are ignored. If there is a '-' sign before the file name, the file may be absent; otherwise, an error will be generated, and the unit will not start.

CHAPTER 30 SYSTEMD – A SHORT COURSE

StandardInput= – Where to redirect standard input from, possible values:

- null (default) to /dev/null.
- tty to the console specified in TTYPath=.
- tty-force is similar to tty, but first disconnect the occupying process, if any, from the terminal.
- tty-fail is similar to tty, but if the terminal is occupied by another process, complete the startup crash.
- data to the thread connected to the running process specified in StandardInputText=/StandardInputData=.
- file:path into a file system object (file, FIFO, socket, device).
- socket (only for socket-activated units) to the active socket.

StandardOutput=/StandardError – Where to redirect the output/error stream. Possible values:

- inherit to the same place as standard input.
- null to /dev/null.
- tty to the console specified in TTYPath=.
- tty-force – As tty, but if the terminal was used by a running process, detach it first.
- tty-fail – As tty, but if the terminal was used by a running process, then fail.
- journal to a journal that can be accessed via journalctl.
- syslog to log and syslog to log.
- kmsg to the kernel log buffer (you can then see this output in dmesg).
- journal+console, syslog+console and kmsg+console – Similar to the above three options and additionally to the system console.
- file:path into a file system object (file, FIFO, socket, device).
- socket (only for socket-activated units) to the active socket.

Environment variables are set for all running processes (they can be changed via the Environment and EnvironmentFile options):

- $PATH is forcibly reset to /usr/local/sbin:/usr/local/bin:/usr/sbin:/usr/bin:/sbin:/bin.

- $LANG is the locale from locale.conf or kernel.

- $USER, $LOGNAME – Username.

- $HOME is the home directory.

- $SHELL – Login shell.

- $INVOCATION_ID is a string with a hexadecimal representation of a 128-bit number unique to each unit run.

- $XDG_RUNTIME_DIR is the directory to save the state.

- $XDG_SESSION_ID, $XDG_SEAT, $XDG_VTNR – Session, login, and virtual terminal identifiers.

- $MAINPID – PID of the head process, if known, is passed to processes started via ExecReload= etc.

- $TERM – Terminal type (only for units connected to the terminal).

- $SERVICE_RESULT for service type only, passed to processes started via ExecStop= and ExecStopPost=, the value reflects the service termination status:

    - **success** – The service was completed successfully.

    - **protocol** – The service did not perform the necessary steps at startup.

    - **timeout** – One of the startup steps has timed out.

    - **exit-code** – The service has terminated with a nonzero status; the start code is passed to $EXIT_CODE.

    - **signal** – The service was terminated by sending a signal without saving the core file.

    - **core-dump** – The service was terminated abnormally by sending a signal with saving the core file.

- **watchdog** – The watchdog for the service has been activated, and the timeout time has passed.

- **start-limit-hit** – The service start time limit was set, and the service failed to meet the limit.

- **resources** – The service has exhausted the resource limit.

- $EXIT_CODE for service type only – Service termination status ("exited," "killed," or "dumped").

- $EXIT_STATUS for service type only – The return code of the service process or the name of the signal by which it was terminated.

This data should be enough to implement almost any service description similar to the SystemV start script. I will not write here how to start the service by timer, file system change, socket connection, etc., and leave it as an exercise. Hint – There is nothing complicated; in addition to the service description, you will need a description of .timer, .path, etc., and their binding together.

As I said before, systemd uses "**slices**" to run everything. There is a possibility to run several instances of the same service or several user sessions in different slices. This is done by creating a unit template with a name ending in '@'. For example, the file getty@.service:

```
[Unit]
Description=Serial Getty on %I
BindTo=dev-%i.device
After=dev-%i.device systemd-user-sessions.service

[Service]
ExecStart=-/sbin/agetty -s %I 115200,38400,9600
Restart=always
RestartSec=0
```

You can see that in some lines, the parameters %I and %i are used; the instance name will be passed through them when creating an instance from the template. The difference between them is that in %I will be the real name, and in %i – an adapted name, in which the characters '/' will be replaced by '-', and special characters (including '-') – by their hex code in the format '\xAB'. Therefore, the second option is convenient when forming file names, e.g., in the bind-to parameter.

CHAPTER 30 SYSTEMD – A SHORT COURSE

You can start an instance of such a template as follows: `systemctl start getty@-dev-ttyUSB0.service`. In this case, our service will start the service with the command

`/sbin/agetty -s /dev/ttyUSB0 115200,38400,9600`

User sessions are slices too. They are controlled by `logind` service. Using logind settings and user slices you can control user limits, sometimes in a more flexible way than we considered in the chapter "Users – Quotas and Access Rights."

Here is an example you can use to set limits for all users' sessions by default - file `/etc/systemd/system/user-.slice.d/10-defaults.conf`:

```
[Slice]
TasksAccounting=yes
CPUAccounting=yes
TasksMax=1250
CPUQuota=100%
MemoryMax=160G
```

Here two first lines turn on the accounting for the number of tasks and resources, and later – set exact limits. Note that CPU quota 100% means "one full cpu core." Note that the corresponding "Accounting" should be enabled to make quotas work.

If you need to change such limits for the exact user (but not for group), you can create file like `/etc/systemd/system/user-UID.slice.d/10-defaults.conf`; it will override the default settings. You should specify the UID, not the username.

All these limits can be used for **any service/slice** in the system! Here are some useful limits, you can use:

Option	Meaning
CPUAccounting=yes MemoryAccounting=yes TasksAccounting=yes IOAccounting=yes IPAccounting=yes	Turn on CPU, memory, processes, IO, network accounting
CPUQuota=10%	Limit service or user session more than 10% of one CPU
MemoryHigh=bytes MemoryMax=bytes	Soft and hard memory limits (see `ulimit`)

(*continued*)

CHAPTER 30 SYSTEMD – A SHORT COURSE

Option	Meaning
TasksMax=N	Max number of processes (see `ulimit`)
IOReadBandwidthMax=device bytes, IOWriteBandwidthMax=device bytes, IOReadIOPSMax=device IOPS, IOWriteIOPSMax=device IOPS	Limit read or write bandwidth/IOPs on the specified device
IPAddressAllow=ADDRESS[/PREFIXLEN] IPAddressDeny=ADDRESS[/PREFIXLEN]	Limit access to/from specified IP address ranges
RestrictNetworkInterfaces=LIST	Limit access to specified network interfaces
DeviceAllow=DEV	Limit access to devices
Slice=NAME	Put this service into a slice with specified name. By default, for services – `system.slice`

More info in man `systemd.resource-control`. Logind service has its own config file – `/etc/systemd/logind.conf`. Here are some useful options you can tune in its [Login] section:

Option	Meaning
KillUserProcesses=yes	Kill all user processes on the session end. Breaks screen/tmux/nohup/etc
SessionsMax=N	How many sessions can a user have at one time. Default 8192
RemoveIPC=yes|no	Free any allocated IPC resources (shared memory, semaphores, etc.) after the session ends. Default – yes
RuntimeDirectorySize=N	Limit the size of the `$XDG_RUNTIME_DIR`

systemctl Commands

In addition to the `systemctl` commands discussed in the chapter "Booting and init," note the following:

  `list-sockets [PATTERN...]` – List of socket units. Example output:

```
LISTEN UNIT ACTIVATES
[::]:22 sshd.socket sshd.service
```

You can see that port 22 is listening to the description of the socket unit in `sshd.socket`, and it starts the `sshd.service` unit.

`list-timers [PATTERN...]` – Similar to the previous one, but timer units are listed.

`try-restart units` – If the listed units are running, restart them; if not, do nothing.

`cat unit` – Display the text of the unit description file on the screen.

`show unit` – Show all internal properties of the unit.

`set-property unit key1=value1 ...` – Change the unit property on the fly, if possible. Useful for changing limits if they are set for a unit.

`list-dependencies unit` – List of unit dependencies with sub dependencies.

`reset-failed unit` – Reset the failure counter. If a service has failed to start several times in a row, `systemd` gives it a `failed` status. After that, even an attempt to execute `systemctl start srv` will fail, `systemd` will generate an error and will not even try to start `srv`. With this command, you can reset the `failed` status and try to start the service again.

`mask/unmask unit` – Similar to `disable/enable`, but in the disabled state, the unit cannot be started even manually.

`set-default target` – Specify this target by default, i.e., it will be loaded after reboot.

`daemon-reload` – Reread unit description files.

`rescue/emergency/halt/poweroff/reboot` – Similar to running `systemctl isolate X.target`, where X is the specified mode, but in addition, a message is sent to all users with the `wall` command.

Journald

The `systemd-journald` service is optional, but it is usually enabled by default. It can run in parallel with the regular **syslog** server, and messages will appear in both. Events are stored in a special database, which allows you to quickly find the necessary data. You can view logs with the `journalctl` command. Its useful keys are

- `-a` – Show all fields completely, even if they contain problematic characters (control characters, etc.).

- `-f` – Go to the end of the list and show new lines as they appear.

- `-n NNN` – Output NNN lines of logs (10 by default); if "**all**" is specified instead of a number, then output all.

CHAPTER 30   SYSTEMD – A SHORT COURSE

- `-e` – Go to the end of the list; default assumes the key '-n1000'.
- `-x` – Add auxiliary information (return codes, etc.).
- `-u unit` – Show information only for the specified unit; you can specify a mask, e.g., "***tty***".
- `--disk-usage` – How much space the binary logs take up.
- `--sync` – Flush the data from memory to local files.
- `--vacuum-size=NNNN` – Delete old events from the log until the log size is less than the specified size (the number is assigned to 'K', 'M', and 'G' for kilo-, mega-, and gigabytes, respectively).
- `--vacuum-time=NNNN` – Remove events from the log older than the specified value; the suffix "`s`", "`min`", "`h`", "`days`", "`months`", "`weeks`", or "`years`" is specified to the value.
- `--no-pager` – Do not use an external program to display information; the default is `less`.
- `--since` / `--until` – From what moment/to what time to show logs (time format YYYYY-MM-DD HH:MM:SS; some fields can be omitted, also acceptable are the words `today`, `yesterday`, and `tomorrow`, to which you can add relative time, e.g., "yesterday-10:00:00").
- `-b` – Show logs since the last time the server was turned on; you can add relative time to it as in the previous option.
- `-p prio` – Limit output to events with priority not higher than specified. The priority is specified by number or name in syslog format: **emerg (0), alert (1), crit (2), err (3), warning (4), notice (5), info (6),** and **debug (7)**.

You can select the output option with the `-o` key. We will not dwell on the possible variants in detail; I will note only `short-iso`, `verbose`, and `json` variants, which may be useful for further processing in some script. If you need to clean your journal records for some reason, use a command like `journalctl --sync --vacuum-time=5s`. Note that without `--sync`, only records written to the disk will be cleaned.

Network Config, Time Sync, and Hostname Resolving

`systemd-networkd` service can be used to control and automatically configure your network interfaces. When a new network device link appears, this service checks the rules from the config files, and it finds a match, applies them. Files should have `.network` extension and by default are located in `/usr/lib/systemd/network` directory. In the `/etc/systemd/network`, you can place files to override defaults.

The file has two main sections: `[Match]`, which defines if the configuration should be applied to the link, and `[Network]`, defining the interface configuration. The first matched file will be applied, and the rest will be ignored, so the file name is important. It has really many options and cases of application. I don't describe them here, and if you see that some interfaces in your systems are managed by `networkd` (or want to use it), please read the official documentation.

To replace ntp client service in the systemd ecosystem, there is a `systemd-timesyncd` service. The main section of the service definition is `[Time]`, and the main key there is "NTP" – space-separated list of remote ntp servers. Note that some NTP servers can be obtained by `networkd` from DHCP server; in this case, they are added to this list.

`systemd-resolved` is a service, implementing the hostname DNS resolving. To enable it, add '**resolve**' to the list of options in '**hosts:**' line in `/etc/nsswitch.conf` file. Also if `127.0.0.53` or `127.0.0.54` are used as a DNS server (e.g., in `/etc/resolve.conf`), then also local resolved service will be used. Configuration file is `resolved.conf`, located in well-known places. The most important options:

Option	Meaning
DNS=LIST	A space-separated list of IPv4 and/or IPv6 addresses of DNS servers
Domains=LIST	A space-separated list of domain prefixes, used in search
Cache=yes|no|no-negative	Controls whether the DNS responses should be cached or not. `no-negative` means caching only positive results

This service can be controlled by `resolvectl` command. `resolvectl status` shows current settings, including the actual list of remote DNS servers. `resolvectl query` works like `dig` command – resolves the given hostname. Other useful subcommands are `statistics`, `reset-statistics`, `flush-caches`, `show-cache`, and `monitor`.

CHAPTER 30   SYSTEMD – A SHORT COURSE

Analyzing

systemd-analyze allows you to analyze some issues in services loading and overall system boot process. systemd-analyze blame shows you the sequence of all services, started in the current session with times, taken for start. The list is sorted by times, so it is easy to check which services are slow to start. Another option is systemd-analyze critical-chain, showing only the longest chain of dependent units:

```
$ systemd-analyze critical-chain
The time after the unit is active or started is printed after the "@"
character.
The time the unit takes to start is printed after the "+" character.

graphical.target @4min 4.109s
└─watchdog.service @4min 3.616s +492ms
  └─multi-user.target @4min 3.552s
    └─remote-fs.target @1min 48.526s
      └─remote-fs-pre.target @1min 48.526s
        └─open-iscsi.service @1min 48.101s +407ms
          └─iscsid.service @1min 34.602s +13.496s
            └─network-online.target @53.979s
              └─iptables-openvpn.service @26.857s +26.862s
                └─basic.target @26.853s
                  └─paths.target @26.853s
                    └─acpid.path @26.853s
                      └─sysinit.target @26.301s
                        └─sys-fs-fuse-connections.mount @53.921s +51.085s
                          └─systemd-modules-load.service @9.274s +2.112s
                            └─systemd-journald.socket @8.536s
                              └─system.slice @8.230s
                                └─-.slice @8.230s
```

If you use systemd timers and want to use complicated time expressions, you can check them using systemd-analyze calendar, like this:

```
systemd-analyze calendar --iterations=2 '*-2-29 0:0:0'
  Original form: *-2-29 0:0:0
Normalized form: *-02-29 00:00:00
```

```
    Next elapse: Tue 2028-02-29 00:00:00 PST
       (in UTC): Tue 2028-02-29 08:00:00 UTC
       From now: 2 years 9 months left
 Iteration #2: Sun 2032-02-29 00:00:00 PST
       (in UTC): Sun 2032-02-29 08:00:00 UTC
       From now: 6 years 9 months left
```

`systemd-analyze cat-config` works line systemctl cat, but for configs, not for units. For example, if you put additional info into `/etc/systemd/logind.conf.d/50-override.conf`, `systemd-analyze cat-config systemd/logind.conf` shows you full config with changes.

When you modify or create a systemd unit, a good idea is to check if you didn't make any types, or other mistakes; in this case, `systemd-analyze verify path-to-file` can help. It will check the syntax, dependencies, and if all referenced files and services exist in the system. If your file name is not in systemd format, you can specify alias for this unit: `systemd-analyze verify ./myfile:alias.service`. For other useful commands, see the documentation.

Brief Summary

Systemd today is the central system for managing services and many other aspects of the OS; even if you don't use it, you have to know about its abilities and how it can spoil (or help) your life. For example, if you don't see a cronjob, but something is running as a cronjob, it may be a systemd timer.

Search Keywords

systemd, journald, logind, systemd-resolved, systemd unit, systemd service, systemd slice, systemd timer, systemd socket

Conclusion

We have looked at the various components that make up a modern computer system. Some of them have been analyzed in more detail; some of them have only been touched upon. Surely some information has become outdated since the publication of this book. I really believe that the information on the subject should be constantly updated; therefore, I ask **you** to write me about what you would like to know in detail and what information is missing in the book. Please write at `supercomputerbook@gmail.com`, using the word "**superbook**" in the subject line. Check and contribute to `https://github.com/zhum/hpc-book-matherials` git repo; it helps all of us.

As I mentioned before, supercomputers and cluster systems are a very vast and dynamic area, so you have to constantly keep up with changes and study new technologies. But it is also very important to remember why and for whom all these technologies are realized. Do not forget about users behind the "hardware" and programs: without them, all this loses its meaning. It is easy to lose the trust of users, but it is very difficult to regain it.

Of course, not everything depends on you: sometimes equipment fails, software issues arise, etc., but it is very important that your users take these events as calmly as possible. To do this, try not to consider support as a secondary task and keep users informed about the events of the computer complex. Try not to infringe on the rights of some in favor of others without good reason, and if there are any, warn them about it in advance. Love your users, even though it may not always be easy.

It is especially difficult to communicate with those who do not know how to work with a supercomputer (or even with Linux in general). But you need to take care of them too! Place information for beginners on your site, and create a section with solutions to common problems (FAQ). Hold regular meetings and seminars with your users; this will help you maintaining good relationships, and get more support from users resolving common issues. These are not just "general wishes" – your relationship with your users will largely determine your mode of operation. It is up to you to determine how often, or infrequently, they will contact you, whether they will be willing to communicate with you about solving certain issues. It is a good idea to organize trainings in the use of

CONCLUSION

application packages and system software. For this purpose, you can involve both users and outside specialists. It is also useful to get support from management. Remember: By increasing the level of user training, you increase the efficiency of using the system and reduce the amount of unnecessary work.

I hope that this book is useful and interesting for you. I would like to continue communicating and learning. If you think the material in this book should have been organized differently, please let us know – your opinion is very important to us.

Best of luck with your supercomputers!

Index

A

Access control lists (ACLs), 182
Account management
    classic approach, 167–169
    LDAP protocol, 171–172
    NIS distribute information, 170–172
    schemes, 171
    synchronization, 167
ACLs, *see* Access control lists (ACLs)
ACML, *see* AMD Core Math Library (ACML)
AMD Core Math Library (ACML), 326
apcupsd package
    components, 275
    configuration file, 276
    installation procedure, 276
    SCRIPTDIR directory, 277
    short-term loss, 275
    shutdown procedures, 278
    system installation, 276, 277
    web UI, 278
APCUPSD
    ambtemp.sh script, 422
    configuration file, 412–416
    offbattery script, 417
    onbattery script, 417
    scripting process, 418–420
    tlwait function, 418
    upstemp temperature, 421
    UPSTYPE and DEVICE values, 416
Asymmetric encryption, 140

B

Bacula backup system
    bconsole commands, 296
    Catalog section, 294
    Client section, 295
    client programs, 289
    client sections, 294
    configuration file, 289, 295
    Device sections, 290
    Director section, 291
    FileSet, 293
    Pool parameter, 292
    program servers, 289
    Schedule sections, 295
    show command, 297
    storages, 292
    storage servers, 291
Bash Scripting Guide, 427
Basic Input-Output System (BOIS), 339
BOIS, *see* Basic Input-Output System (BOIS)
Booting process
    dynamic host configuration protocol, 353–357
    network booting, 351–353
    TFTP/PXE/NFS-root, 357–359
Booting services, 339
    extended partition, 339
    hard disk, 339–341
    init (*see* SystemV Style (init))
    initial system image (initrd), 340, 341
    magic number, 340
    primary partitions, 339

INDEX

C

CIFS, see Common Internet file system (CIFS)
Clouds
 HPC instances, 245
 low-latency network, 245
 network file system, 245
Cluster management systems, see xCAT (Extreme Cloud Administration Toolkit)
Clusters
 clouds, 245
 cloud technologies, 9
 commands, 104–105
 compute/service nodes, 28
 concepts, 10
 differences, 10
 high availability, 9
 historical perspective, 10
 pdsh commands, 151–153
 performance, 9
 productivity, 9
 remote management, 153–155
Common Internet file system (CIFS), 38
Communication, 395
 actualization, 398–399
 correspondence, 395–397
 education, 399
 mailman/majordomo, 396
 processing/accounting requests, 397–398
 RT/OTRS/Track/OpenProject, 397
Compute infrastructure, 16
Compute nodes, 15
Compute Unified Device Architecture (CUDA), 313–314
conman (console manager), 164

Containers
 apptainers, 243
 caching, 244
 cgroups/namespaces/chroot technologies, 241
 CharlieCloud, 243
 Enroot, 243
 meaning, 241
 Pyxis, 244
 singularity, 242
 squashfs, 241
C programming
 gcc/gfortran, 305–307
 MPI program, 301–304
CUDA, see Compute Unified Device Architecture (CUDA)

D

DAS, see Direct attached storage (DAS)
DDT, see Distributed Debugging Tool (DDT)
Debugging process, 334
 jump shot interface, 337
 MPI programs, 336
 parallel programs, 335
 profilers/tracers, 336
 remote client, 335
 sequential programs, 335
 ThreadSpotter tool, 335
 TotalView, 335
 Vampir, 337
 VTune and ITAC, 338
DHCP, see Dynamic Host Configuration Protocol (DHCP)
Direct attached storage (DAS), 37
Directed route addressing, 48
Direct Memory Access (DMA), 42

INDEX

Distributed Debugging Tool (DDT), 335
DMA, *see* Direct Memory Access (DMA)
Documentation, 21–22
Dynamic Host Configuration Protocol (DHCP), 353–357

E

Email correspondence, 397
Encryption, 126

F

FairShare, 220–223
Fastest Fourier Transform (FFT), 333
Fastest Fourier Transform in the West (FFTW), 333–334
FFT, *see* Fastest Fourier Transform (FFT)
FFTW, *see* Fastest Fourier Transform in the West (FFTW)
File Transfer Protocol (FTP), 248–249
FTP, *see* File Transfer Protocol (FTP)

G

GCC, *see* GNU compiler collection (GCC)
General Parallel File System (GPFS), 136–137
Global Routing Header (GRH), 47
GNU compiler collection (GCC), 304–306
GPFS, *see* General Parallel File System (GPFS)
GRand Unified Bootloader (GRUB), 340
GRH, *see* Global Routing Header (GRH)
GRUB, *see* GRand Unified Bootloader (GRUB)
GUIDs (globally unique ID), 47

H

Hardware
  components, 27
  compute node, 27–29
  DMA technology, 42
  HyperThreading, 42
  InfiniBand, 43
  infrastructure, 15
  login node, 29
  NUMA technology, 40, 41
  processor/kernel, 39
  service nodes, 27, 29–31
    access/control nodes, 30
    compilation, 29
    license services, 30
    network file system, 30
    pre-/postprocessing nodes, 30
    roles, 29
    storage, 30
    visualization nodes, 30
  storage systems, 37–40
  symmetric system, 40
Hardware/network drivers
  libraries, 361
  OFED package, 361
  types of, 361
HCA, *see* Host Channel Adapter (HCA)
High-Performance Computing (HPC), 9
Host Channel Adapter (HCA), 46
HPC, *see* High-Performance Computing (HPC)
HPC applications, *see* Clouds

I, J

IBM storage scale, 136–137
IDS, *see* Intrusion detection systems (IDS)
iKVM (KVM-over-IP), 164–165

459

INDEX

InfiniBand network technology, 45
    addressing method, 48
    administrators, 45
    data transmission, 45
    hardware, 43
    HCA/TCA, 46
    identification, 47–49
    IPoIB interfaces, 51–52
    LIDs (local ID), 47
    network commands, 95
    OFED technology, 45
    performance of, 46
    ports, 46
    reverse path, 49
    RoCE and SlingShot, 59
    subnet manager (SM), 49–50
    SystemImage GUID, 47
    utilities, 51
        bit error rate, 55
        capability mask, 53
        connected/datagram modes, 58
        ibstat command, 51, 52
        ibstatus command, 53
        mlxlink command, 54
        physical state, 52
        saquery command, 58
        smpquery utility, 57
        state data, 52
Intelligent Platform Management Interface (IPMI), 159–164
    channel configuration, 163
    ipmitool package, 159
    main subcommands, 161
    management controller, 159
    MC network settings, 160
    monitoring systems, 275
    power supply, 161

Intel Trace Collector and Analyzer (ITAC), 336
Intrusion detection systems (IDS), 249
IPMI, *see* Intelligent Platform Management Interface (IPMI)
ITAC, *see* Intel Trace Collector and Analyzer (ITAC)

K

Keyboard+Video+Mouse (KVM), 164–165
Knoppix, 375
Kubernetes, 187
KVM, *see* Keyboard+Video+Mouse (KVM)

L

LAG, *see* Links aggregation groups (LAG)
LDAP, *see* Lightweight Directory Access Protocol (LDAP)
Libraries, 325
    debugger program, 335–339
    FFT/FFTW processing modules, 333–334
    overview, 325
    PETSc library, 331–333
    ScaLAPACK, 326–332
    TBB library, 334
Lightweight Directory Access Protocol (LDAP), 171–172
    configuration file, 406–410
Links aggregation groups (LAG), 100
Linux
    containers, 241
    soft/hard quotas, 176
    supercomputer (*see* Supercomputer)
    SystemV Style (init), 342
    UNIX (*see* UNIX/Linux)

INDEX

LinuxContainer (LXC), 249
LiveCD/LiveUSB, 376
LMC (LID Mask Control), 48
lm_sensors and hwmon
        packages, 271–274
LNDs, *see* Lustre Network Drivers (LNDs)
Lua Modules (LMOD), 319–323
Lustre file system
    advantage, 126
    architecture, 126, 127
    clients, 127
    components, 126–128
    data duplication/redundancy, 132
    initialization, 130
    lnetctl command, 129
    network interface, 128
    redundancy, 132
    scalability, 126
    services/clients/servers, 129–132
    soft and hard quotas, 134–135
    striping/PFL, 133–134
Lustre Network Drivers (LNDs), 128
Lustre (No HA)
    installation, 402
LXC, *see* LinuxContainer (LXC)

M

MaaS, *see* Metal-as-a-Service (MaaS)
Management Client (MGC), 128
Management server (MGS), 126
Master Boot Record (MBR), 339
Matching transport layer (MTL), 310
Math Kernel Library (MKL), 326
MBR, *see* Master Boot Record (MBR)
MDC, *see* Metadata Client (MDC)
MDS, *see* Metadata servers (MDS)
MDT, *see* Metadata target (MDT)

Message Passing Interface (MPI), 301
Metadata Client (MDC), 128
Metadata servers (MDS), 127
Metadata target (MDT), 127
Metal-as-a-Service (MaaS), 390–392
MGC, *see* Management Client (MGC)
MGS, *see* Management server (MGS)
MKL, *see* Math Kernel Library (MKL)
Monitoring systems
    apcupsd service, 275–279
    data collectors, 268
    efficient approach, 268–270
    Ganglia server, 266–268
    healthchecks, 282
    IPMI interface, 275
    lm_sensors/hwmon packages, 271–274
    Nagios, 266–267
    NUT project, 279–282
    processing and alerting, 269
    security rules, 283
    SNMP (*see* Simple Network
        Management Protocol (SNMP))
    standardized sensor, 272
    visualization methods, 269
    XDMoD (XD Metrics on
        Demand), 270–271
    Zabbix, 268–269
MPI, *see* Message Passing Interface (MPI)
mpirun script, 308
MTL, *see* Matching transport layer (MTL)

N

Nagios monitoring system, 266–267
NAS, *see* Network attached storage (NAS)
NCCI, *see* NVIDIA Collective
    Communications Library (NCCI)
Network attached storage (NAS), 37

461

INDEX

Network file system (NFS)
    configuration, 402
    data access, 119
    different rules, 123
    distributed proprietary, 137, 138
    exports file, 124
    exports options, 124
    features, 125
    GPFS/IBM storage scale, 136–137
    implementation, 122
    Lustre (*see* Lustre file system)
    modern versions, 123
    mount options, 125
    NFS implementation, 122–126
    NFS server (nfsd), 123
    NTP server, 119–122
    PanFS, 135–136
    peculiarities, 122
    recommendations, 119
    RPC protocol, 122
    scratch directories, 122
    server implementation, 123
Network information service (NIS+)
    client installation, 404
    server installation, 403–404
Network information system
    (NIS), 169–171
Networking technologies
    commands
        active interfaces, 102
        column values, 101
        router (gw), 102
        interface aliases, 104
        IPoIB (IP over InfiniBand), 95
        physical devices, 97
        ping command, 93, 94
        route command, 101
        spanning tree protocol, 100
        static routing table, 98
        statistics, 103
        traceroute command, 95, 96
        virtual networks (vlans), 101
        VLAN implementation, 99
    compute nodes, 27
    equipment, 31
        characteristics, 32
        compute nodes, 31
        Dragonfly/Dragonfly+, 35
        2d torus, 35
        external network, 31
        fat tree, 34
        hypercube, 34
        InfiniBand, 33
        latency/throughput, 32
        multidimensional torus, 35
        requirements, 31
        throughput/latency, 31
        topology, 33, 34
    file system, 27
    infrastructure maintenance, 27
Network time protocol (NTP), 119–122
    installation, 401
Network UPS Tools (NUT)
    project, 279–282
NFS, *see* Network file system (NFS)
NIS, *see* Network Information
    System (NIS)
Node management, 384–388
Nonuniform memory access
    (NUMA), 40, 41
NUMA, *see* Nonuniform memory
    access (NUMA)
NVIDIA, *see* Compute Unified Device
    Architecture (CUDA)
NVIDIA Collective Communications
    Library (NCCI), 315–316

O

Object Storage Client (OSC), 128
Object storage servers (OSS), 127
Object storage target (OST), 127
OFED, *see* OpenFabrics Enterprise Distributions (OFED)
OpenACC standards, 317
OpenACC technologies, 304
OpenCL, *see* Open Computing Language (OpenCL)
OpenCL technologies, 304
Open Computing Language (OpenCL), 316
OpenFabrics Enterprise Distributions (OFED), 45, 364
OpenLDAP, 405–409
OpenMPI implementation approaches, 309
OpenPBS, *see* Torque system
OpenSHMEM technologies, 304
OSC, *see* Object Storage Client (OSC)
OSS, *see* Object storage servers (OSS)
OST, *see* Object storage target (OST)

P

PAM, *see* Pluggable authentication modules (PAM)
PanFS file system, 135–136
Parallel Basic Linear Algebra Subprograms (PBLAS), 327
Parallel data processing
　acceleration time, 7
　elements, 6
　execution process, 6
　full-fledged processors, 7
　hardware/software level, 8
　independent, 5
　libraries, 8
　multithreading technology, 5
　parallelism, 5
　parallel program, 7
　pipelining, 6
　system administrators, 8
　variants, 8
　vectorization, 6
Parallel technologies
　build systems, 322–324
　CUDA version, 313–314
　environment modules, 317–321
　gcc/gfortran, 304–306
　IntelMPI, 311
　Intel/OneAPI/NVIDIA HPC compilers, 306–307
　libraries (*see* Libraries)
　mpich, 308
　MPI program, 301
　Mvapich/Mvapich2, 311
　OpenACC, 317
　OpenCL, 317
　OpenMPI, 309–311
　PMIx, 307
　programs and packages, 301
　SHMEM programming system, 311–313
　Spectrum MPI, 311
　UCX/NCCI, 315–316
PBLAS, *see* Parallel Basic Linear Algebra Subprograms (PBLAS)
PelicanHPC session, 376–378
PETSc, *see* Portable, Extensible Toolkit for Scientific Computation (PETSc)
PFL, *see* Progressive File Layouts (PFL)

INDEX

Planning options
    benchmarks/tests, 17
    capacity planning, 18
    characteristics, 17
    checklist, 19, 20
    cooling and place, 18
    data and storage, 19
    memory modules, 18
    network aspects, 19
    power, 18
    steps, 20
    technical support, 17
    upgrading, 17
Pluggable authentication modules (PAM), 111–114
    auth/account identifies, 112
    configuration file, 112
    debug module, 114
    flag/action, 112
    list notation, 113
    modules, 112
    password/session, 112
    values, 112, 113
Portable Batch System (PBS), *see* OpenPBS
Portable, Extensible Toolkit for Scientific Computation (PETSc), 331–333
POST, *see* Power-On Self-Test Procedure (POST)
Power-On Self-Test Procedure (POST), 339
Preboot eXecution Environment (PXE), 358–360
Process Management Interface–Exascale (PMIx), 307
Progressive File Layouts (PFL), 133–134
PXE, *see* Preboot eXecution Environment (PXE)

Q

QoS, *see* Quality of service (QoS)
Quality of service (QoS), 217–219
Quotas and limits, 175–179
    command format, 177
    edquota command, 177
    file systems, 175, 178, 179
    restriction systems, 184
    setquota sets, 176
    ulimit tool, 179–181
    user access, 182–184

R

RAID (redundant array of independent disks), 37
RDMA, *see* Remote Direct Memory Access (RDMA)
RDP, *see* Remote Desktop Protocol (RDP)
Remote Desktop Protocol (RDP), 254
Remote Direct Memory Access (RDMA), 42
Remote management
    cluster shell, 153–155
    conman, 164
    iKVM (KVM-over-IP), 164–165
    IPMI management controller, 159–164
    IPMI remote access, 139
    nodes, 139
    pdsh program, 152–154
    SSH (*see* ssh and Parallel ssh)
    tmux and GNU screen, 155–159
    See also User access
Remote Procedure Call (RPC), 122
Reservation, 224–225
Resource management systems
    access problem, 187
    agents, 186

batch systems, 185
components, 185
external service, 186
operation, 186
optimal mode, 185
partitions, 186
queues, 185
scheduler, 186
RoCE (RDMA over Converged Ethernet), 43
ROCKS installation, 373–375
RPC, *see* Remote Procedure Call (RPC)
rsync program, 297–299

S

SAN, *see* Storage area network (SAN)
ScaLAPACK (Scalable LAPACK), 326
    computational/service subroutines, 329
    data types, 329
    driver subroutines, 329
    fundamentals, 326
    multiprocessor systems, 326
    numerical methods, 325
    package subprograms, 330–332
    SLmake.inc file, 327, 329
    standard libraries, 325
    structure, 326, 327
Security systems, 15
Server message block (SMB), 38
shell programming
    bash syntax, 427
    built-in shell command, 427
    case command, 433
    concepts, 427
    conditions, 428
    control constructs, 432
    elif conditions, 432
    function keyword, 436
    OPTARG, 434
    parentheses/curly brackets, 435
    quotation marks, 430
    return command, 436
    scripts, 431
    select operator, 434
    shortcuts, 437
    single/double/inverse, 429
    subdirectories, 433
    test command, 428, 429, 431
SHMEM programming system, 311–313
Simple Linux Utility for Resource Management, *see* Slurm
Simple Network Management Protocol (SNMP), 257
    agent, 258
    command-line, 259
    commands, 258
    community, 257, 261
    description, 259
    human-readable, 258
    management/monitoring, 257
    object identifier (OID), 257
    snmpconf program, 278
    snmpset program, 259
    snmptranslate command, 260
    snmptrapd, 262, 263
    snmpwalk command, 260
    system tree, 260
    tcpwrappers, 263
    /tmp/demo script, 263
    /tmp/demo.log file, 263
Singularity container, 243
Slurm
    accounting
        options, 209

INDEX

Slurm (*cont.*)
    parameters/limits, 208–210
    set up, 209–210
    statistics, 233–235
  backfill algorithm, 216–217
  commands, 207, 225–230
  configuration file, 210–212
  control nodes, 206
  FairShare, 220
  functions/structures, 205
  generic resources, 214–216
  installation, 206
  job life cycle, 230–231
  levels, 222
  limit definition, 218
  modules, 205
  network topology, 223
  nodes, 214–215
  partitions, 212–214
  preemption, 217–218
  priorities, 219-222
  PrologFlags, 237
  prologue scripts, 206
  quality of service, 217–219
  reservation, 224–225
  sacctmgr command, 219
  sbatch/srun primary keys, 226
  SchedulerParameters, 237
  scontrol subcommands, 232–234
  sinfo primary keys, 229
  parameters/slurm.conf, 236–239
  slurmctld, 205
  squeue formats, 228
  trackable resources, 215–216
  troubleshooting, 235–236
SM, *see* Subnet management (SM)
SMB, *see* Server message block (SMB)
SMP, *see* Subnet management packets (SMP); Symmetric multiprocessor systems (SMP)
Software, 17
Software installation
  communication network, 364
  compilers/libraries, 366
  compute node
    cloning method, 370
    DHCP server settings, 368
    disk subsystem, 367
    high-speed communication, 367
    installation/configuration, 367
    kickstart config file, 368, 369
    proprietary compilers, 369
    remote installation, 368
    swap partition, 367
    testing, 371
  compute nodes, 362–363
  login node, 363–364
  network drivers, 361
  nfs-server package, 364
  task management system, 366
Spanning tree protocol (STP), 100
ssh and Parallel ssh
  agent, 143
  asymmetric encryption, 140
  client configuration, 146–150
  environment variables, 142
  file transfer, 143
  host-based authentication, 150
  host section, 150
  man-in-the-middle attack, 140, 141
  openssh server, 142
  port forwarding, 142
  private key, 140
  secure shell, 139
  secure versions, 141

INDEX

server configuration options, 144–146
symmetric encryption, 140, 141
X forward connection, 143
Stack software
    component, 61
    control system, 63
    job management system, 62–64
    mpirun/mpiexec command, 63
    operation, 63
    startup process, 63
    user session, 62
Storage area network (SAN), 36, 37
Storage systems
    block devices, 39
    categorization, 37
    direct attached storage, 37
    external storage systems, 36
    local hard disks, 36
    NFS, SMB and CIFS, 39
    RAID arrays, 38
STP, *see* Spanning tree protocol (STP)
Subnet management (SM), 49–50
Subnet management packets
    (SMP), 48, 57
Supercomputer
    administrator, 1
    anatomy, 16–18
    book information, 1
    centralized management, 13–14
    cluster, 9–11
    concepts, 25
    configuration files, 3, 4
    cooling requirements, 11
    disk arrays, 12
    documentation, 21–22
    flexible and extensible tools, 14
    hardware, 2
    hardware/software solutions, 13

    maintenance, 23
    parallel data processing, 5–9
    responsibilities, 24–25
    stack software, 61
    standard servers, 11
    SysAdmin, 22–24
    system monitor, 2
    utilization, 12
    virus, 12
Supercomputers
    communication, 455
    computer system, 455
Sweeping, 50
Symmetric encryption, 140, 141
Symmetric multiprocessor systems
    (SMP), 40
Synchronization, 167
systemd
    analyzing session, 452–453
    dependencies, 440
    environment variables, 445–446
    journald service, 449–450
    Logind service, 448
    logind settings, 447
    network configuration, 451
    output/error stream, 444–445
    prefixes, 442
    restart service, 443
    service, 439
    service option, 441
    service/slice, 447
    slice, 439
    socket, 444
    standard input, 444
    string, 442
    systemctl commands, 448–449
    systemd-resolved, 451
    systemd unit, 453

INDEX

systemd (*cont.*)
    timer unit, 441
    unit descriptions, 439, 440
SystemV Style (init)
    chkconfig and update-rc.d
        commands, 345
    commands, 342
    process fields, 343
    rc.local, 346
    script reference, 344, 345
    start/stop commands, 345
    startup level, 342
    systemd, 346–351
        advantages, 347
        boot managers, 346
        command, 347
        concepts, 347
        logind.conf file, 351
        parallel loading, 347
        parameters, 350
        single-user mode, 348
        systemctl commands, 349
        units, 348
        unit types, 350
    zombie processes, 341

T

tar (Tape ARchiver)
    command, 285–288
Target Channel Adapter (TCA), 46
TAU, *see* Tuning and Analysis
    Utilities (TAU)
TCA, *see* Target Channel Adapter (TCA)
Terascale Open-Source Resource and
    QUEueue Manager, *see*
    Torque system

TFTP, *see* Trivial File Transfer
    Protocol (TFTP)
Threading Building Blocks (TBB)
    library, 334
tightvncserver, 254
tmux and GNU screen
    configuration file, 157
    features, 159
    keys, 156–157, 159
    options, 156
    terminals, 155
Topology, 223
Torque system
    attribute values, 191
    components, 189
    compute nodes, 196–197
    configuration file, 191–196
    control commands, 203, 204
    events, 198
    FIFO strategies, 199
    functional tasks, 190
    log file, 195
    multithreaded program, 201
    property, 191
    qmgr command, 192, 193
    qsub command, 201–204
    queue operation, 193
    routing queue, 192
    scheduler selection, 198–200
    server interaction, 194
    services communication, 190
    sorting, 199
    time interval, 195
    torque scheduler, 199
Trivial File Transfer Protocol
    (TFTP), 357–359
Tuning and Analysis Utilities (TAU), 338

U

UCX, *see* Unified Communication X (UCX)
udev subsystem
    assignments, 110
    device file, 108
    major and minor numbers, 108
    names/meaning, 109
    rule variables, 110
    special variables, 111
    /sys file system, 108
UFM, *see* Uniform Fabric Manager (UFM)
ulimit tool, 179–181
Unified Communication X (UCX), 315–316
Unified Extensible Firmware Interface (UEFI), 339, 340
Uniform Fabric Manager (UFM), 50
Uninterruptible power supplies (UPS), 275
UNIX/Linux
    access rights, 71–75
    ancient systems, 65
    attributes, 73
    cluster commands, 104–105
    commands
        catalogs, 82
        directory tree, 81
        files, 83–90
        keyboard commands, 86
        vi keyboard, 89
    concepts, 66
    control access/ACLs, 182
    file extensions, 79
    file naming conventions, 78
    file system, 72
    historical background, 66
    load average, 67
    manuals, 77
    network commands, 93–104
    operating systems, 66
    packages, 90–93
    unique identifier (PID), 67
    process, 67–71
    repositories, 91
    service, 75–76
    shell wildcards, 78
    signals/actions, 69
    sorting options/commands, 68
    standard services/ports, 76
    systemd, 347–352
    tar command, 285
    templates, 80–81
    working techniques
        command-line options, 117
        PAM modules, 111–114
        shell tricks, 114–117
        sysctl command, 107–108
        udev subsystem, 108–111
    X-Window system, 254–256
UPS, *see* Uninterruptible power supplies (UPS)
User access
    FTP variants, 248
    NX protocol, 255
    OpenSSH, 248
    openssh server, 247
    public key, 247
    SFTP and SCP protocols, 249
    SPICE protocol, 255
    SSH, 247–248
    X11 protocol, 254–255
    X-Window, 249–254

INDEX

V

VDURA storage management software, 135
Vectorization, 6
Virtual Local Area Network (VLAN), 99
VLAN, *see* Virtual Local Area Network (VLAN)

W

World Wide Web (WWW), 249–250
WWW, *see* World Wide Web (WWW)

X, Y

xCAT (Extreme Cloud Administration Toolkit)
　architecture/commands, 380–384
　certificate generation, 383
　chtab command, 382
　cluster deployment, 379
　configuration file, 422–424
　description, 383
　Foreman server, 393–394
　installation/initial setup, 380
　loading/controlling, 388–390
　lsdef command, 382
　MAAS platform, 390–392
　node management, 384–388
　NVIDIA base command manager, 393
　rpower command, 389
XDMoD (XD Metrics on Demand), 270–271
Xorg server, 409–412
X-Window system
　client/server technology, 250
　configuration file, 251
　drivers, 250
　graphical interface, 249
　screen manager, 252
　visualization, 250
　window manager controls, 250
　xauth command, 253
　xdm manager, 252
　Xming package, 252, 253

Z

Zabbix, 268–269
Zabbix monitoring system, 267–268

GPSR Compliance

The European Union's (EU) General Product Safety Regulation (GPSR) is a set of rules that requires consumer products to be safe and our obligations to ensure this.

If you have any concerns about our products, you can contact us on

ProductSafety@springernature.com

In case Publisher is established outside the EU, the EU authorized representative is:

Springer Nature Customer Service Center GmbH
Europaplatz 3
69115 Heidelberg, Germany

www.ingramcontent.com/pod-product-compliance
Lightning Source LLC
LaVergne TN
LVHW080309260326
834688LV00038B/1027